Negative Hermeneutics and the Question of Practice

Also Available from Bloomsbury

Ethics, Aesthetics and the Historical Dimension of Language, Hans-Georg Gadamer
Hermeneutics After Ricoeur, John Arthos
The Art of Gerhard Richter: Hermeneutics, Images, Meaning, Christian Lotz
Hans-Herbert Kögler's Critical Hermeneutics, ed. Mertel and Dunaj
The Ontology of Improvisation in Music and Philosophical Hermeneutics, Sam McAuliffe

Negative Hermeneutics and the Question of Practice

Nicholas Davey

BLOOMSBURY ACADEMIC
LONDON · NEW YORK · OXFORD · NEW DELHI · SYDNEY

BLOOMSBURY ACADEMIC
Bloomsbury Publishing Plc, 50 Bedford Square, London, WC1B 3DP, UK
Bloomsbury Publishing Inc, 1385 Broadway, New York, NY 10018, USA
Bloomsbury Publishing Ireland, 29 Earlsfort Terrace, Dublin 2, D02 AY28, Ireland

BLOOMSBURY, BLOOMSBURY ACADEMIC and the Diana logo
are trademarks of Bloomsbury Publishing Plc

First published in Great Britain 2024
This paperback edition published 2025

Copyright © Nicholas Davey, 2024

Nicholas Davey has asserted his right under the Copyright, Designs and
Patents Act, 1988, to be identified as Author of this work.

For legal purposes the Acknowledgements on p. x constitute
an extension of this copyright page.

Cover image: Body of water during sunset (© Panos Teleoniatis / Unsplash)

All rights reserved. No part of this publication may be: i) reproduced or
transmitted in any form, electronic or mechanical, including photocopying,
recording or by means of any information storage or retrieval system without
prior permission in writing from the publishers; or ii) used or reproduced in any
way for the training, development or operation of artificial intelligence (AI)
technologies, including generative AI technologies. The rights holders expressly
reserve this publication from the text and data mining exception as per
Article 4(3) of the Digital Single Market Directive (EU) 2019/790.

Bloomsbury Publishing Inc does not have any control over, or responsibility for,
any third-party websites referred to or in this book. All internet addresses given
in this book were correct at the time of going to press. The author and publisher
regret any inconvenience caused if addresses have changed or sites have
ceased to exist, but can accept no responsibility for any such changes.

A catalogue record for this book is available from the British Library.

A catalog record for this book is available from the Library of Congress.

ISBN: HB: 978-1-3503-4765-6
PB: 978-1-3503-4764-9
ePDF: 978-1-3503-4766-3
eBook: 978-1-3503-4767-0

Typeset by Deanta Global Publishing Services, Chennai, India

For product safety related questions contact productsafety@bloomsbury.com.

To find out more about our authors and books visit www.bloomsbury.com
and sign up for our newsletters.

Dr Gisela Schmidt (Heidelberg).
In Memorium

Contents

Acknowledgements x
Hermeneutical *Regulae*: Guidelines xi

Introduction: A trajectory of argument 1

1 Enabling configurations 7
　　1. Introduction 7
　　2. Orientating remarks 7
　　3. Nihilism and negativity 10

2 Negative receptions 17
　　1. Falling-into-question 17
　　2. Expectations of completion 21
　　3. Differential spaces and perspectival multiplication 25
　　4. Negative receptions 26
　　5. Distanciation, theory and alienation 28
　　6. Nihilism and theory 35
　　7. The humanities in question 39
　　8. Humanities, hermeneutics and transformative questions 43
　　9. Negative hermeneutics and the accentuation of the positive 59

3 The way of the negative 63
　　1. Negation's optimism 63
　　2. The negativity of experience 69
　　3. Liminal spaces 76
　　4. The fore-conception of completeness 78
　　5. Completeness and meaning 79
　　6. Completeness and envisioning identity 81
　　7. Formal completeness and aesthetic completeness 81
　　8. Truthfulness and completeness 85
　　9. Images and coming to completion 95
　　10. The *Vorgriff* and practice 100

4	Towards a poetics of practice	113
	1. *Sprachlichkeit* and practice	113
	2. The forgotten question of practice	114
	3. Practical steps	117
	4. Practice: A historical problematic	122
	5. Cassim and *praxis*	126
	6. *Praxis*, ontology and the way of understanding	131
	7. Practice and *Dasein*	135
	8. MacIntyre, tradition and practice	136
	9. Hadot, Sloterdijk and anthropologies of practice	144
	10. Practice and re-earthing of theory	155
	11. Platonism and worldly estrangement	156
	12. Theoria: Participating from a distance	161
	13. Differential spaces	164
	14. A poetics of hermeneutic practice	170
5	The provocations of practice	179
	1. Introduction	179
	2. Negative moments: Practice and the instabilities of understanding	182
	3. Practice and repetition	184
	4. Practice and speculative movement	188
	5. The negativity of provocative expectations	190
	6. Regulative completeness and hermeneutic displacement	193
	7. Integration and completeness	196
	8. The positivity of negative outcomes	199
	9. The confidence of practice	202
	10. The provoked self	206
	11. The way of hermeneutical practice	209
	12. Negative hermeneutics and the redemption of the negativity	211
	13. Vectoring the immeasurable	217
	14. Recursion and repetition	222
	15. The returns of aesthetic completeness	224
	16. The dialectic of word and concept	232
	17. Hermeneutical openness as *praxis*	239
	18. Seeing understandingly	241
	19. Hermeneutical *praxis*	249
	20. The transcendental conditions of hermeneutical praxis	258

| 21. A post-metaphysical philosophy of practice | 269 |
| 22. Summative thoughts | 279 |

| Bibliography | 285 |
| Index | 292 |

Acknowledgements

This volume is the outcome of a long-term project on the nature of hermeneutical understanding. Its key arguments were trialled in recent conferences and publications. Adapted sections of the following appear within the main text and are cited appropriately. 'Hermeneutics and the Question of the Human', in *International Yearbook for Hermeneutics*, Mohr Siebeck, 15, 2016, pp. 130–43; 'The Turning Word: Relational Hermeneutics and Aspects of Buddhist Thought', in Paul Fairfield and Saulius Ceniusas, *Relational Hermeneutics, Essays in Comparative Politics*, London, Bloomsbury, 2018, pp. 177–92; 'The Impossible Future of Hermeneutics', *Journal of the British Society for Phenomenology*, Routledge, 2017, vol. 48, no. 3, pp. 209–21; 'Dialogue, Dialectic and Conversation', in *The Gadamerian Mind*, ed. Theodor George and G. J. van der Heiden, London, Routledge, 2020; and 'On the Other Side of Writing', in *Language and Linguistically in Gadamer's Hermeneutics*, ed. Lawrence K. Schmidt, Lanham, Lexington Books, 2000, pp. 108–10.

I offer my thanks to Dr Ian Heywood (University of Lancaster), Prof. Gaetano Chiurazzi (University of Turin), Prof. Peter Rickman (City University, London) and Prof. Gordon Leff (University of York). I am much indebted to Dr Dorothea Franck (Bern) for her insights and formative conversations, to Linda Bolsakova (Riga) for her many discussions about practice and to Professor Babette Babich (Fordham University, New York) who many years ago introduced me to members of Gadamer's International Hermeneutics Seminar, Heidelberg.

Hermeneutical *Regulae*: Guidelines

The following remarks outline the main body argument in this study of hermeneutics, negativity and the question of practice:

1. Negative hermeneutics does not concern a method of hermeneutics but the articulation of the hermeneutical. The hermeneutical is not discipline specific. It involves the reflective *experience* of either an ambiguous body of meaning unexpectedly achieving a discernible pattern of sense or of established expectancies of meaning falling into question.
2. An experience is hermeneutical in that it entails a specific mode of self-reflection. The orientation of the practitioner is implicated in what has been brought into question.
3. Hermeneutical experience is an effect of practical engagements and their expectations.
4. Negative hermeneutics does not concern the loss of meaning per se but transitions in and between fields of meaningfulness.
5. Hermeneutic truth lies in what it does. It has an integrative function across bodies of experience.
6. Better argument and the confidence it inspires derive from the creativity and intellectual mobility that uncertainties of definition allow.
7. Practices denote ontogenetic processes that produce the forms which come to symbolize and represent them.
8. There is no such thing as hermeneutics, only hermeneutical experiences.
9. It would be better to talk of hermeneutically conceived being rather than of a hermeneutics of Being.
10. To think hermeneutically is to think about what is at stake in the ways we think about a subject matter.
11. Hermeneutical thinking involves is the constant interplay between foreground and background issues.
12. Hermeneutical practice can be described as a consequentialism of unintended effects.
13. Hermeneutical experience involves a conscious *experience of movement*, that is, of being moved from one level of understanding to another.

14. The values and meanings attached to a set of signs and symbols in one practice can have a destabilizing effect on the meanings given to the same symbols in another practice. An emergence of meaning in one horizon can prompt an emergency of meaning in another.
15. Precisely because of its location in language-being, the forward impetus of a practice's anticipation of completion will prove to be the instrument of its deconstruction.
16. Because they are situated in *Sprachlichkeit*, practices always transcend their particular boundaries. They are not closed monadic systems but have porous boundaries susceptible to influences from contiguous practices.
17. Practice demands the courage and preparedness to risk the consequentialism of unknown effects.
18. Hermeneutic reflection is an experience of cognitive movement such that I come to think of an artwork and myself differently.
19. Plainly, there are analytic reading techniques but their application does not render them hermeneutical. Hermeneutical understanding occurs when engagement with a text forces a radical reorientation of the reader's sense of being in the world.
20. In hermeneutical practice, where one begins is not as important as that one begins. Only by beginning does one meet with what has already started. Practices hermeneutically conceived are always eccentric: they stand outside themselves, rooted in an interrelational mode of being that impels them beyond their own centre.
21. The repetitions of practice are not orientated towards the production of the same but towards generating the different and unexpected.
22. The truth of the *Vorgriff der Vollkommenheit* lies not in the arrival of an anticipated meaning but in the bringing-into-structure that expectation facilitates. As a regulative principle, the *Vorgriff* is the transcendental condition of objects being thought of as hermeneutical, that is, as objects whose structures *anticipate* the possibility of a completable meaning.
23. Because of its grounding in *Sprachsontologie*, philosophical hermeneutics conspires to perpetuate the circumstances that render any stability of meaning problematic. Negative hermeneutics induces such instability. Living in the productive endowment of that uncertainty reflects the productive worth of such negativity.
24. Epistemological negativities tend to inhibit practical engagement and depress the movement of understanding whereas negative capability,

considered ontologically, encourages deeper practical involvement and accelerates the movement of understanding.
25. The epistemological prejudice is a principle of deficit. Facticity viewed from an epistemological perspective always appears to lack something, to resist conceptual capture, and to be always falling away from the truth.
26. Being resides in the actualization of its possibilities but is never reduced to its actions or exhausted by them.
27. A dialectic of loss and hope is integral to our linguistic experience of being in the world. Hermeneutical being is a *passio*.
28. Complete hermeneutic understanding is rendered impossible by the *Vorgriff der Vollendung* but consequential hermeneutical insights are not possible without it.
29. Aesthetic representations of completeness are not of anything in the world but make a place for something that were if not represented would have no place in the world. Representations of completeness are representations of the possibility of things being other than they are. Art's importance resides not in closing the differential space between the actual and the possible but in keeping it open. The artwork creates a space in which determinations of meaning other than those given in actuality can emerge.
30. Philosophical hermeneutics does not offer a theory of practice but a hermeneutical approach to practice. It seeks a reflective participatory awareness of what is in play within humanities' practices.
31. Hermeneutical practice cannot be taught. Only the preconditions of its emergence can be established.
32. The finitude and contingency of existence can no longer be viewed as an epistemological negative but valued for providing the ontological grounds for maintaining understanding's movement and expansion.
33. *Mimesis*, becoming more, non-identical repetition, and recursive looping all stress the interactive framework of hermeneutical practice.
34. Recognizing a subject matter as 'indefinable' does not place it beyond thought but brings its possibilities to the forefront of reflection.
35. The speculative is relational by definition and ties the interpretive act not just to the spoken but to the unspoken horizons of meaning upon which the spoken depends.
36. For an explanation to be valid, one must presuppose an established frame of reference whereas performance brings about its own criteria of validity.

37. Negativity establishes the anticipation of completeness as the formal condition of cumulative learning within hermeneutics and the humanities. Such understanding is never final but expands through the accumulation of its non-identical repetitions.
38. If language is the medium of understanding and language-being maintains itself in the movement of constant anticipations, the *Vorgriff der Vollendung* emerges as the ontological form of understanding itself.
39. By opening a differential space between how we experience the world and think of its subject matters, the anticipation of completion establishes the space within which the movement of hermeneutical reflection becomes possible.
40. Hermeneutic participation with a text is not a matter of reconstruction but one of thinking with the movement of its terms and anticipating their potential meaningfulness.
41. The question is not whether hermeneutic completion is realizable but what the pursuit of the unrealizable within language-being gives rise to, that is, its performative capacity to generate adjunctive and aleatoric effects.
42. Though the edges of a word's finite meaning delimit and define its distinctive sense, its porous edges leave it open to other fields of meaning. The porous edges of linguistic meaning enable movement between practices. This provokes the disclosure of further hidden alignments of meaning within the totality of language-being.
43. A practice's pursuit of completion in language-being provokes unexpected alignments of meaning.
44. Productive and negative changes in how a hermeneutic agency understands its world are part of its ontological narrative. The non-identical repetitions of practice ground the continuity of an agent's narrative.
45. The worlds at play within the ongoing stream of our understanding are caught in the act, as it were, by the differences between recursive readings. These render discernible the shifting narrative structures of a subject agent's being (*Dasein*).
46. To honour the complexities of experience, disciplinary frontiers must be crossed. Intense and complex experience demands multiple registers of interpretation.
47. Negative hermeneutics trusts in language-being as that which carries and sustains us, is more than us and which draws expectations of a more complete self towards us.

48. Negative hermeneutics bids us live with confidence and reasonable expectation within uncertainty.
49. The paradox of negative experience is that it brings us to both see and to dwell more fully in the world of our possibilities.
50. Humanities practices entail engaging inspiring uncertainties with confidence.
51. Negative hermeneutics replaces the ontological priority of an unknowable noumenal world with an all-surrounding language-being which simultaneously sustains and transcends the subjectivity of individual linguistic consciousness.
52. Precisely because it enables practice, dialogical exchange both roots individual subjectivity in what transcends it and establishes the conditions whereby it can expand the limitations of its understanding. 'Becoming more' involves the possibilities of language-being breaking into subjective awareness via the accidental and aleatoric collision of ideas and concepts.
53. By means of tradition and its practices, language-being not only shapes our sense of existence but also guides us towards harbours of meaningfulness. Though nothing is certain about such practices, their ability to sustain existence is manifest. Language-being bids us face the uncertainties of practice with confidence.
54. Whilst the negative perceptions of hermeneutics and the humanities indicate the nihilistic consequences of disappointed metaphysical beliefs, the ability of the humanities to create other ways of inhabiting the uncertain is key to overcoming the nihilistic estrangement from actuality that undermines belief in the cognitive worth of hermeneutic practices.
55. Negative hermeneutics has a therapeutic capability. It emphasizes the priority of practice in exploring possible cures to that philosophical sickness which is inclined to see actuality as a problem when it is not. It seeks to displace the demand for epistemological certainty with the practical confidence acquired from taking creative and transformative risks.
56. Whereas the epistemological perspective problematizes actuality, the principle of ontological surplus recognizes that within finite existence there is always more to know. The finitude and contingency of existence is no longer viewed as an epistemological negative but as the ontological ground for maintaining understanding's movement and expansion.
57. As Wittgenstein noted, scepticism cannot be refuted but only displaced. In its appeal to the confidence-building powers of practical action, negative

hermeneutics displaces the nihilism implicit in the epistemological demand for certainty. Practical action has never required certainty. It requires confidence and trust in the uncertainties of tradition and its possibilities.

58. Abandoning the quest for certainty in favour of the likely and the probable is not to abandon critical rigour. Negative hermeneutics is a vigilant hermeneutics. It never accepts the completeness of the given and risks seeing otherwise. The accomplished practitioner who 'sees understandingly' knows that just as no work can realize all of its possibilities, none can complete them. Something always remains undone and to be done. Criticism keeps such portals open.

59. The vitality of a tradition and its sustaining practices depend on the continual reasking of its grounding questions. Negative hermeneutics recognizes that permanent critique is at the heart of a practice. The differential space which drives a practice generates a permanent tension between the shortcomings of a practice's achievements and the goals it yet aspires to.

60. Though, ontologically speaking, a tradition maintains itself through the perpetual review of its core concerns, the sceptic will bemoan the fact that there is no end to such a process. For negative hermeneutics, such scepticism misses the point. By inhibiting practical action, scepticism frustrates the emergence of new collateral forms of insight which are the consequential effect of the serendipitous collision of different vectors of understanding within language-being. Of course, there can be no end point to critique other than maintaining the vitality of practice itself.

61. Continuous critique is not idealistic nonsense. It is an ever-present way of checking for the presence and limits of our prejudices. Negative hermeneutics is not a hermeneutics of complacency. It knows not only that there can be no end to asking about the meaning of educational and social justice but also that costs of failing to repose such questions will be counted in human suffering. Negative hermeneutics is by definition an unsettled practice.

62. Limit situations expose the finite nature of hermeneutical understanding. Wittgenstein recognizes the paradox: 'for in order to be able to set a limit to thought, we should be able to find both sides of the limit thinkable.'[1]

---

1 Ludwig Wittgenstein, *Tractatus Logico-Philosophicus* (London: Routledge, Kegan, Paul, 1961), Preface, 3.

63. As the postulation of a limit on the other side of language can only be proposed in language, the idea of a metaphysical infinity beyond language is simply nonsense. However, Wittgenstein's truncation of the metaphysical does not dissolve the question of the infinite. To the contrary, the language ontology of negative hermeneutics shows that the question of the infinite lies *within* language and not beyond it.
64. That which 'limits' a practice and renders its understanding finite is not the proximity of an infinite intelligence on the other side of language but the proximity of an infinite number of perspectives within language-being itself.
65. The dialectical movements within negative hermeneutics turn the negativity of experience into an ecstatic affirmation of the infinite possibilities for understanding within language-being. Negative experience entails an experience affirmation and not just one of denial.[2]
66. Precisely because negative hermeneutics reveals what limits a given perspective epistemologically, it also discloses how that perspective can extend its limits by becoming more than itself, that is, by revealing the nexus of other perspectives it belongs to.
67. By revealing its ground in language-being, negative hermeneutics may limit a practice epistemologically but it extends its limits ontologically.
68. The renunciation of certitude in favour of hermeneutic perspectivism renders the pursuit of impossible completion worthwhile. That pursuit multiplies possibilities for extending and transforming a practice's perspective by provoking unexpected moments of summative understanding within language-being.
69. Negative hermeneutics implacably opposes that nihilistic scepticism which prefers in life's practices the certainty of nothing to the probable and likely something.

---

2 Theodor Adorno, *Hegel Three Studies* (Cambridge, MA: MIT Press, 1993), Introduction, xvii.

Introduction
A trajectory of argument

According to Friedrich Schleiermacher, we must begin with something positive but continually orient ourselves towards the negative.[1] This book proposes a new hermeneutics of practice. It shows how Gadamer's 'dialectics of experience' points beyond itself towards 'a negative hermeneutics' in which negativity is both a central driver of creative and reflective practice and fundamental to the growth of understanding and learning across the arts and humanities.

Schleiermacher's remark about the negative announces a key theme in this study: considered as a reflective practice, the positivity of philosophical hermeneutics is driven by a negative dialectic that probes the limits of our understanding. The maxim that understanding presupposes misunderstanding establishes a pattern of hermeneutical engagement which guides these reflections on practice, hermeneutics and the humanities.[2] Misunderstanding, Schleiermacher writes, is 'the consequence of one's hastiness and prejudice', its roots lying in a 'mistake which lies deeper'.[3] For Gadamer this implies that misunderstanding is ubiquitous and follows automatically from the fact that all understanding is limited in both scope and finitude.[4] In the life-world, we simply proceed with practical tasks rather than reflect upon their grounding presuppositions. Initially, this renders us forgetful of the perspectives and prejudices which curtail understanding. The emergent awareness that what we thought we understood we actually misunderstood implies a passage of hermeneutical experience.

Previous understandings do not know themselves as misunderstandings as such. They become disclosed as misunderstandings only when the scope of what was previously 'understood' is revealed by subsequent experience to

---

1 Friedrich Schleiermacher, *Hermeneutics and Criticism* (Cambridge: Cambridge University Press, 1998), 22.
2 Ibid., 23.
3 Ibid.
4 Hans-Georg Gadamer, *Truth and Method* (London: Sheed and Ward, 1985). This text will be referred to throughout this chapter with the abbreviation ™.

be inadequate, insufficient or incomplete. This for Gadamer is the negativity of experience: new experience 'negates' the adequacy of what was previously 'understood' and reveals the latter as a misunderstanding.[5] The passage of hermeneutical experience suggests a corrective process which allows us to see the limits of what we thought we understood or, in other words, the extent of our misunderstanding. The axiom that new understanding is enabled by the scope of previous 'misunderstanding' underpins this reflection on hermeneutics, the humanities and the role of negativity within their operational practices. Our central focus concerns those 'deeper mistakes' that perpetuate the 'misunderstanding' that hermeneutics, aesthetics and the humanities lack substantive cognitive content and worth.

To explore these 'deeper mistakes' this chapter adopts a Nietzschean hermeneutical tactic: if a belief proves false, what are the circumstances that prompted belief in its truth? The arguments of Feyerabend, Karl Popper and Gödel have long established that robust scientific certainty is procedurally limited. If so, the epistemologically based distinction between the *Naturwissenschaft* and the *Geisteswissenschaft* is no longer tenable. Why then is it that 'the arts' continue to be denigrated for their lack of formal foundation and procedural certainty? If the latter claims are indeed misunderstandings, what perspectives, values or 'deeper mistakes' convince us, as Nietzsche puts it, that they 'should count as true'?[6] In a similar therapeutic-hermeneutic manner, Wittgenstein asks what it is about our 'way of life' that disposes us so negatively towards both the uncertainty and lack of formal grounding that characterize operations in the arts and humanities? Why are such features so persistently misunderstood as negativities rather than as the basis for extending and transformative understanding? This is the key question that this study attempts to navigate. It will argue that the overt negativities and formal limitations of understanding within hermeneutics and the humanities should not be regarded negatively but as instrumental to its expansion.

To realize that what was understood was a misunderstanding is to discover that one has already embarked upon a hermeneutical journey. To discern what was previously understood as a misunderstanding is to have passed beyond the limits that circumscribed that understanding. This study in negative hermeneutics attempts to chart the philosophical presuppositions of such a journey. It endeavours to appropriate the negativities that drive and disrupt hermeneutic

---

5 TM 354.
6 Friedrich Nietzsche, *The Will to Power* (London: Weidenfeld and Nicolson, 1968), Sec. 552. This volume will be referred to in the text with the abbreviation WP.

and creative practice as fundamental to the expansion of understanding and learning. Hermeneutic reflection emerges as a *via negativa* which by disclosing more of the limits of our previous and present understandings also reveals paradoxically more of the ignorance we did not know were subject to.

Within philosophical hermeneutics the passage from misunderstanding to understanding is facilitated by the dialectic of negative experience. The passage takes place within and is facilitated by language-being in which misunderstanding and understanding moderate each other as cognitive processes with different degrees of reflective awareness. Within language-being all understandings are necessarily finite, circumscribed by the perspectival limitations that define their scope. To a degree, misunderstanding entails pre-reflective understandings that are blind to the prejudices that distort them. Conversely, though reflective understandings are more aware of their constraining limits, they are by no means transparent. They retain opaque and yet to be realized possibilities for understanding within them.

Misunderstanding and understanding are not binary opposites but different modes of awareness which both entail and moderate each other. The emergence of new understanding does not simply displace previous misunderstanding but rather sets the conditions under which it too will be surpassed. The interaction between the two modes of awareness is continuous, a process whereby aspects of the indeterminate possibilities for understanding and creativity within language-being are realized. Their emergence sets the terms of their own transcendence. Though any new understanding can transcend its previous limitations, in relation to language-being it will remain both limited and finite. In other words, it will always remain vulnerable to the challenge of negative experience. Yet this negativity is precisely the driver of extended learning and creativity. In the context of language-being, the negativity of experience is never negative.

Formative experiences (*Bildung*) are a consequence of our becoming (*Werden*). They are indicative of participation in social and cultural practices which both shape and transcend our immediate engagements in the world. Arising from the transmitted inheritances of tradition and convention, such practices are animated by historically established norms of excellence and expectation. In the wider context of language-being, the struggle of practices to achieve excellence is rendered unstable. *Each practice strives to overcome its limitations and to become 'more'. Given that the possibilities for meaning within language-being are indeterminate, hermeneutic practice reveals itself as a quest to complete the incompletable.* The movement from misunderstanding to understanding is clearly driven by a fundamental antinomy between the indeterminacy of language-being and the determinacy of each practice. The infinite extent of language-being renders the understanding of all practices finite, circumscribing them by both what they have overlooked and have yet to understand. Yet the fact that the negativity of experience brings practices to confront their limits does not disrupt the impetus to understanding but enhances it. The revelation of yet more to understand only emphasizes that the struggle of practices to complete their aspiration to completeness is like the impetus to understanding itself, that is, infinitely extendable. Only by pursuing the impossible (the attainment of completion) does a practice attain the possible (the attainment of a complete understanding). *The negativities of hermeneutical experience entail an affirmative Ja-sagen, a 'saying-yes' to the complexities of experience and the opportunities for growth they offer.*[7] To deny them denies the 'always more' to be understood. This book explores the negativities underwriting hermeneutical experience and learning to the end of offering a dialectical hermeneutics of practice.

This study is a dialectical endeavour which responds to recent deconstructive critiques of the epistemological foundations of hermeneutics and the humanities. It argues that the negativity of experience central to human existence is a fundamental driver of that creativity in hermeneutical and artistic practices necessary for transforming our understanding of the negative. To undermine faith in the contingent foundations of hermeneutics and humanities practices is to deplete the capacity of these disciplines to offer a transformative response to the unavoidable challenge of negativity. *This study offers not so much a negative hermeneutics as a hermeneutics of negativity.*

Our reflections commence with a discussion of the critical arguments that deconstruction and post-structuralism direct at the methodological foundations of hermeneutics and the humanities. The task of this study is, however, not to refute these criticisms but to recognize in their limits the possibility for their transcendence. Rather than rejecting hermeneutics and the humanities on the grounds of their procedural weakness, we shall approach their limitations as portals to a transformed understanding of their practices. As this discussion is itself enabled by hermeneutical and creative disciplines, we cannot stand beyond them. Only by working through their limitations can transform our understanding of their cognitive potential. In short, this dialectical endeavour pursues its own passage from misunderstanding to understanding. It passes from a recognition of how the limits which govern hermeneutics and the

---

7 See Friedrich Nietzsche, *The Gay Science* (New York: Vintage, 1974), Sec. 276.

humanities have been misunderstood to the realization that these limitations drive the possibility of continuous transformative understanding.

The epistemological validity, cultural legitimacy and social relevance of hermeneutics and the humanities have been subject to intense sceptical attack both from within and without the academy. This chapter seeks to restore faith in the cognitive content and social worth of hermeneutical thinking in the arts and humanities by offering a different understanding of the transformative effects of their collective practices. Hermeneutical thought demonstrates that the productive worth of the humanities lies in the transformative power of its disciplines to change the creative response repertoires of practitioner and audience alike. The cultural, material and spiritual well-being of society depends upon managing those accidents of understanding which both enable new insight and derive learning from the unpredictable and the unexpected. To develop this possibility, a hermeneutics of practice is required. This will demand rethinking the epistemological and ontological foundations of the humanities in terms of a negative hermeneutics of practice.

The theme of practice is central to this chapter. Practice holds both knowing and being in play. For negative hermeneutics there is no systematic starting point outside itself to review the conceptual interactions already underway within it. Participation and knowing involvement are key to opening the entailments of hermeneutical practices. *Where one begins is not as important as that one begins. By beginning, one meets with what has already started.* This study attempts to draw out and chart the key epistemological and ontological interactions at work within a hermeneutics of practice: it is the negative aspects of these interactions which drive understanding. If philosophical hermeneutics is not a method of interpretation, what sort of practice is it? If it is a practice of interpretation, what is 'hermeneutical' about that practice? What renders practice 'hermeneutical'? How does practice engender movement within understanding? As we shall see the 'negativity of experience' and its ontological grounding in language-being is key to answering these questions.

The incommensurability between the act of knowing and the place of that act in being is key to the instability and unsettled character of hermeneutical practices. Throughout this chapter we formalize this relation as *the principle of hermeneutic surplus*. Within Gadamer's language ontology (language-being), individual language acts (interpretation) not only take place within but also reflect and are shaped by what transcends them. As a particular expression of language-being, an individual linguistic act is always more than itself, that is, x is always equal to $x+$. This establishes a differential space critical to the movement of hermeneutic understanding. Grounded in x+, a specific act of interpretation is always in excess of itself. Even though all instances of x are, ontologically speaking, more than themselves, no single x can capture the totality of x+. On the other hand, the being of x+ maintains itself in the totality of the expressive acts it sustains. The incommensurability between the act of interpretive knowing and its grounding in language-being opens a differential space in which the dialectical oscillation between part and whole is continuous: the more I wish to understand a particular interpretative act, the more I have to understand the language-being that informs it. I can only understand more of what the totality of language-being might entail by understanding more of the particular expressive acts it informs. Practice sustains the differential space within which the recursive and anticipatory movements of understanding become possible. It is this dialectical framework which shapes our study of negative hermeneutics and its relation to practice.

1

Enabling configurations

1. Introduction

Hermeneutical reflection concerns the dynamic passage of understanding. Irrespective of whether their subject matters are aesthetic, literary or musical, such passages entail experiences of movement. These involve not just the passing from misunderstanding to understanding but also the emergence of new ways of thinking that disclose the inadequacies of present outlooks. This movement is enabled by the interplay of a distinctive set of conceptual configurations and intellectual manoeuvres which characterize negative hermeneutics and its relation to practice. How are the philosophical circumstances which drive the movement of hermeneutics and practice to be understood? Before we can engage in the complexities of the interaction between hermeneutics and practice, the conceptual stratagems underlying our approach need to be introduced. This will introduce some of the key enabling conceptual configurations operating within our broad argument.

2. Orientating remarks

Critique involves negation. And yet, negation has a positive turn. It anticipates thinking differently about what falls into question. There is no doubt that hermeneutics and the humanities have fallen into serious question. Their epistemological validity and educational legitimacy are the object of frequent sceptical attack. *This chapter seeks to restore faith in the cognitive content and social worth of hermeneutical thinking.* The principal claim is that the productive worth of the humanities lies in the transformative power of its disciplines to change the creative response repertoires of its practitioners. The humanities transform rather than manufacture. Their social value lies in the critical dispositions their practices generate. To make this case, philosophical hermeneutics and specifically its relation to the question of practice needs to be rethought. This has positive implications for reconsidering the ontological and epistemological basis of the humanities.

We will argue that philosophical hermeneutics is a negative hermeneutics and that its future philosophical development, specifically with regard to practices within the humanities, demands articulating its entailments.[1] We suggest that reflective practice in the humanities is driven by those negative moments in which limitations of judgement are revealed and acted on in practices of individual and social transformation.

Philosophical hermeneutics knows there is no systematic starting point: it joins debates already underway. It implies a relational mode of thought in which ontological engagement in cultural practices is primary whilst epistemological awareness of what is at play within them is secondary. Participation is key to drawing out what is entailed in this play.[2] How do the tactics of repetition, recursion and anticipation within the humanities deepen understanding? If they do, how does the poetics of hermeneutical engagement work? If hermeneutics is a practice of interpretation, what is hermeneutical about it? Negative hermeneutics concerns the 'hermeneutical' rather than hermeneutics per se: it endeavours to articulate those moments of realization which reveal

---

[1] I offered an undeveloped version of this thesis in an earlier volume. A relevant passage states the following: 'The tactical arguments underpinning the skepticism with which philosophical hermeneutics regards the ambitions of method, reveal philosophical hermeneutics as a *negative* hermeneutics. Like the arguments of negative theology, the skeptical contentions of philosophical hermeneutics cause the formal languages of philosophical methodology to ring hollow. In its negative mode, philosophical hermeneutics demystifies the universal claims of method by particularising them as expressions of a specific historical *Weltanschauung*. Yet a discernible signature of philosophical hermeneutics is that its *via negativa* effects a shift from a perspective of doubt regarding universal claims to meaning toward an ecstatic, almost untheorizable, awareness of the inexhaustible possibilities for understanding' (see Nicholas Davey, *Unquiet Understanding* (Albany: State University Press of New York, 2006), 27). The purpose of the present volume is to draw out the positive consequences of this negative position specifically with regard to the understanding of hermeneutical practices within the arts and humanities.

[2] The notion of *Sache* is complex. Although it can be translated as 'thing', that is, the 'thing that concerns' us, such usage can be misleading as it tends to denote an object as the focus of response. The term, however, also refers to an idea or concept that makes a claim upon us. The difference is dialectical. Considered as an embodied object, the physical manifestation can only be one determination of the many possible determinations of the *Sache* as idea. The concept is in a sense ahead of its embodiment and can serve as a critical reminder that the physical instantiation of a *Sache* is only one possible realization of its grounding concept. The institutions of democracy are thus always subject to criticism from their conceptual ground. As important is the fact that the full determinations of an idea can never be anticipated. However, unseen tensions and developments in its embodied deployments can bring to light hitherto unexpected determinations of the idea. This emphasizes why practice is so central to hermeneutics. Interpretive engagement with a subject matter not only draws out unseen determinations of its meaning but in so doing extends its effective being.

my judgements to be limited. This is why philosophical hermeneutics remains a philosophy of experience. Negative experiences are not exclusive to the arts. Once the practice turn is taken, science emerges as no more or less hermeneutical than the humanities.

If the arts and sciences are not different in kind but only in mode of operation, then methodical activity, rigour and analysis are no longer the prerequisite of the sciences alone whilst creative intuition and ingenuity cease to be exclusive to the humanities. If both modes of practice are subject to failures of expectation and judgement, both can exemplify to mutual advantage the virtuous disciplines of confronting negativity and seeking out creative responses to its challenge. To engage with this, *hermeneutics should enable reflection on what is at play within a practice whether poetic or philosophical.*

To engage with what is at play within a practice entails a degree of recursive looping. Such looping is a way of coping with the historical limitations placed on hermeneutics. Like participatory epistemology, it holds all knowing to be relational and finite. If finite, no understanding of a subject matter can be definitive: there will always be more to be said. If understanding is beyond closure, there can be no foreclosure on what disciplines can be brought to bear on a subject matter. Openness drives stratagems of return seeking out what may have been overlooked. Recursive looping is a feature of participatory epistemology: only by altering one's finite perspective within a whole can that whole be better though never completely understood. Recursive looping is central to the formation of non-identical patterns of repetition and therefore to the building of knowledge within the humanities. Clearly, the condition of achieving recursive insights is participation in the practices that enable them.

Like other practices, hermeneutics cannot be conceptually totalized. *Relational ontology and participatory epistemology imply that the being of knowing exceeds the knowing of being.* The practitioner cannot step outside a practice and survey the totality of relations of which it is a part: we *are* always more than we *know* ourselves to be. Negative hermeneutics cannot accordingly be theorized as a formal practice. It knows that which is not present is not necessarily absent. What exceeds the practitioner's knowing (the totality of its underpinning cultural and linguistic relationships) is still implicit within knowing. A practice is the effect of what transcends it, and what transcends it is the condition of that practice being able to know more of the implicit, intensive and extensive relations that constitute its being. Negative hermeneutics does not deny the possibility of a completer knowledge only the possibility of final completeness. Practice is more important to philosophical hermeneutics than its literature suggests.³ If the possibility of completer understanding entails making explicit the already implicit in a practice's involvements, the condition of its attainment is clearly participation.

3. Nihilism and negativity

Disillusionment with the intellectual worth of hermeneutics and the humanities indicates that an adequate philosophical response to nihilism has yet to be found. Nihilism's challenge provides a welcome opportunity for hermeneutics and the humanities to rethink their orientation. As will become apparent, nihilism per se is not the problem but those cultural pre-understandings which dispose us towards seeing it as a difficulty rather than as an opportunity. Nihilism is not so much to be refuted as understood differently. Placing hermeneutics within a context of relational ontology and participatory epistemology is of strategic importance: it displaces the inverted neo-platonic foundationalism which renders nihilism problematic. The problem with nihilism is not that it is anti-metaphysical but that its anti-metaphysical posture is metaphysically grounded.

Nihilism's epistemological violence is extensive. It mobilizes a seemingly irrefutable scepticism towards universal truth claims, essence and meaning. Questions of identity and definition have, of course, always dogged the humanities. *The condition of being in question and being rendered strange by questions is almost constitutive of the humanities in their modernist iteration.* The problem is the corrosive scepticism engendered by deconstruction and post-structuralism's adherence to an inverted foundationalism, that is, because of the absence of what they suppose *has* to be present in order to render a hermeneutic claim meaningful, they erroneously conclude that none can be meaningful. However, for philosophical hermeneutics and its participatory epistemology, meaning and truth have never depended on external legitimization but upon those negotiable precepts within given practices which have rendered the world meaningful. The corrosive scepticism of deconstruction can only be overcome once its inverted foundationalism is displaced. Claims to truth and meaning no longer depend on external legitimization but upon participatory dialogue and negotiation. Negative hermeneutics shares a good deal with nihilism.

---

3   Two notable exceptions to this are Matthew Foster, *Gadamer and Practical Philosophy, The Hermeneutics of Moral Confidence* (Atlanta: Scholars Press, The American Academy of Religion, 1991), No 64; and Paola Cesar Duque Estrada, *Gadamer's Rehabilitation of Practical Philosophy*, an unpublished manuscript with Edinburgh University Press, 2017.

Both challenge the existence of metaphysical truths and atemporal essences. Indeed, metaphysical nihilism establishes the enabling conditions of negative hermeneutics. Whilst metaphysical nihilism laments the negation of those things which supposedly give existence its meaning, negative hermeneutics celebrates it. Freed of its inverted foundationalism, the negations of nihilism establish that questions of truth and meaning are not issues of arbitrary convention but subject matters of ever-open exchange and debate.[4] An issue for this study is exactly how engagement in the practices of hermeneutics and the humanities can displace nihilism's tacit foundationalism? *Uncertainty will need to be revalued as an inspiration to rather than as an inhibitor of practical activity.* This study will argue that understanding the productive dynamics of practice in hermeneutics and the humanities is central to the possibility of displacing nihilistic scepticism.

Once doctrines of foundation are renounced, the business of recalibrating the humanities becomes inseparable from reflecting upon the nature and workings of language. In their efforts to rethink old problems in new ways, Nietzsche, Heidegger and Gadamer deploy variants of the *philological tactic*. Far from antiquarian, the purpose of recursing earlier meanings of philosophical concepts is to reveal the limitations of contemporary usages and to consider what they omit or occlude and what possibilities they have not as yet foreclosed. The tactic of creative retrieval is central to coming to thinking differently about the humanities. The philological tactic is of utility not because it retrieves gold-standard meanings but because it opens different ways of thinking about a question.

Seeking certainty of definition for the humanities forces reflection into an epistemological *cul-de-sac*. Such searches are reductive quests for an ever-narrower if not elusive conception. Renouncing their feasibility, relational ontology defends a non-essentialist approach to key subject matters: no one form of life can monopolize their meaning. Recognizing them as 'indefinables' or as 'immeasurables' does not place them beyond reflection but brings the inherent possibilities of what they might yet mean to the forefront of reflection. Immeasurables demand multiple forms of cognition; the uncertainty of meaning within the key concepts of the humanities keeps them open. It expresses the conviction that there is always more to them, and that this 'more'

---

4 Nietzsche's distinction between active and passive nihilism is useful here. He speaks of 'the possibilities of the most fundamental nihilism' which does 'not mean that it must halt at negation' but 'wants rather to cross over to the opposite – to a Dionysian affirmation of the word as it is'; see *The Will to Power* (London: Weidenfeld and Nicolson, 1998), Sec. 1041. See also Sec. 26–56. From henceforth the text will be referred to as WP.

is always compelling and possibly wonderful: (for) *all that is, is not yet all that could be.*[5] Precisely because they are not reducible to a single set of determinate propositions, their content is best mapped from a variety of philosophical and cultural perspectives. The negativity of an underlying Cartesian prejudice in favour of certainty is exposed and, with it, the way to a positive revaluation of the cognitive content of both hermeneutics and the humanities is opened.

A discussion of practice is of strategic importance: it is in the expedition of practices within the humanities that subject matters are received, modified and transmitted. Practice also transforms a practitioner's self-understanding. Key to this is Gadamer's compelling approach to practical application in the humanities. This is not to do with a Cartesian consciousness applying a pre-established theory to experience. Phenomenologically speaking, application acquires the sense of a sudden intuition of relevance, a moment when a passage of argument or configuration of images 'speaks' to me. *It is not that I learn to apply an 'argument' but, rather, I have come to understand that it applies to me.* What are the mechanisms within humanities practices that enable such application? An understanding of their workings must surely underpin any educational defence of the humanities.

Wolfgang Iser's accounts of literary transmission offer platforms of response to many of the questions philosophical hermeneutics leaves open. They provide a practicable approach to a defining question within the humanities: what is the nature of subjectivity? We would simply not be drawn to art and literature unless they illuminated (spoke to) our individual concerns. Gadamer claims that the task of hermeneutics is to 'discover in all that is subjective the substantiality that determines it'.[6] Insistence on the phenomenological primacy of the experience of meaning in art or literature does not lead to 'a merely subjective hermeneutic': the totality of meanings present in experience always transcends the meaning apprehended in intention. Iser insists on a participatory framework of interaction between the subjective and objective dimensions of meaning in art. This interaction suggests that engagement in the humanities is worthy of the most robust promotion as participation in its practices generates serendipitously new configurations of thought and insight of profound significance for the renewal and rejuvenation of cultural and social well-being.

Negative hermeneutics provides the philosophical underpinning of the endeavour to rethink the humanities in terms of an ontology of practice: negative

---

5 Rowan Williams, *Faith in the Public Square* (London: Bloomsbury, 2012), 72.
6 TM 302.

hermeneutics is not the negation of the hermeneutical but its very apotheosis. Participatory hermeneutics presupposes a negative hermeneutics. Participatory epistemology is incommensurable with the possibility of a single systematic hermeneutic method but this does not exclude epistemic movement within and between practices: transformational understanding relies on this possibility.

The leading concepts of the humanities are always, logically speaking, incomplete. Custom, convention, social inertia and convenience conspire to overlook alternative ranges of meaning. Given that such subject matters cannot be surveyed from afar, negative hermeneutics insists that we can achieve a fuller understanding of their possibilities precisely because we are circumscribed by their possibilities. *Negative hermeneutics is not about denial but challenging contemporary intellectual perspectives to become more.*

Negative hermeneutics is, in Kantian terms, a regulative idea.[7] It circumscribes the limits of what hermeneutical thought may legitimately engage with. It is nihilistic insofar as it is an anti-Platonic philosophy of nothingness that repudiates classical accounts of Being, essence and truth. Negative hermeneutics frees hermeneutical engagement from its illusory metaphysical anchors. By repudiating the notion that subject matters are reflections of unchanging essences to which our knowing must be every more finely attuned, negative hermeneutics enables participatory knowing to become historically accumulative and to see the proliferation of perspectives as a strengthening of rather than as a dissipating of the being of a subject matter. The anti-metaphysical stance of negative hermeneutics establishes the conditions within finite being whereby knowledge of subject matters can accumulate and develop. In Catherine Keller's phrase, negative hermeneutics 'performs its negations for the sake of the most positive relations possible'.[8] This *via negativa* has the 'negative capability' to transform a 'hermeneutics of suspicion' concerning universal claims to truth and meaning into a positive affirmation of the inexhaustible possibilities for understanding. The negation of an interpretation's claim to being the whole of a given subject matter serves as a *via negativa*: it speculatively invokes that infinite horizon of understanding which cannot itself be stated but which does not exist beyond statements. The negative capability attached to an interpretation seemingly limits its claim but at the same time points beyond it to other possibilities. In other words, negative capability assumes the possibility of transcendence.

---

7 See Immanuel Kant, *Critique of Reason* (London: Macmillan St Martin's Press, 1970), A 179 and B 222, 210.
8 Catherine Keller, *Cloud of the Impossible; Negative Theology and Planetary Entanglement* (New York: Columbia University Press, 2015).

Interpretation's impetus towards completeness is negentropic. It refuses any attempt by religion or ideology to foreclose the understandings of practice. The principled defence of openness guarantees possibilities for further understanding. Against any completeness claim, the negentropic is productively destabilizing. Whatever an interpretation claims, it cannot be all that is the case. Prior ontological involvement in practice is emphasized. Only by arriving at a sense of its contingent limits can an awareness of what those limits make possible be expanded. Negative hermeneutics relies on 'the shadow'd source' of possibilities which is always in excess of its knowing.[9] As Gadamer puts it, 'In the end, all practice suggests what points beyond it.'[10]

Transcendence implies moving in and between practices but not a moving beyond them in any supernaturalist sense. Hermeneutical transcendence does not entail metaphysical transcendence. *Negative hermeneutics requires the possibility of language-based transcendence to justify the notion of understanding as entailing movement between horizons. It is language-being that enables transcendence and it is language-being within which transcendence occurs.*

The incommensurable space between a subject matter and its articulations drives negative hermeneutics. On the one hand, a subject matter is always in excess of its interpretations, always having the capacity to mean more, whilst on the other hand, an interpretation of a subject matter is never exhaustive, always leaving something else to be said. Negative hermeneutics sustains this incommensurability. By negating any particular claim to a completeness of interpretation, it opens other finite possibilities which allow the subject matter to become more. Gadamer's account of the logical spaces within language points to the generative capacity of such incommensurability. For Gadamer, the human word is always incomplete: it contains endless undetermined possibilities for meaning. These implicit potential meanings constitute 'the advance work of language' which 'thought turns to for its own instruction.'[11] Precisely because language and its potential determinations are always ahead of us, negative hermeneutics is never merely negative.

Questioning a subject matter exposes the incommensurability between how that subject matter is presently understood and the undetermined possibilities for future understanding it presently contains. The 'negative capacity' of such questioning allows that subject matter to become more. Negative capacity opens

---

9 The phrase "shadow'd source" comes from Charles Anthony Silvestri's text to Eric Whitacre's choral piece "Her Sacred Spirit Soars," London, Boosey and Hawkes, 2002.
10 Hans-Georg Gadamer, *In Praise of Theory* (New Haven: Yale University Press, 1998), 36.
11 TM 429.

the differential space within which the movement of hermeneutic reflection establishes itself. Hermeneutic consciousness comes to itself and traces its transitions within the differential spaces of incommensurability, a space which negative hermeneutics vigilantly strives to keep open. The negative capacity of negative hermeneutics lies in its prowess for being questionable, a questing that by keeping the differential spaces of language and thought open makes the movement of hermeneutic reflection possible.

Negative hermeneutics sets the limits and scope of our debate. Whilst it questions intelligible access to essential truths and meaning which transcend the contingencies of existence, it also celebrates the infinite capacity for further development of the accumulated finite 'truths' (*Bildung*) within existence and its established practices. In short, negative hermeneutics and the question of practices in the humanities are two sides of the same coin. Practices in so far as they strive to extend themselves and increase the cultural effectiveness of their subject matters always strive to negate and surpass how they have been previously understood. Negative hermeneutics fuels the desire for such an increase, always insisting that no matter how well a practice has been articulated, it can always be articulated both further and differently. It is driven by a dialectic of optimistic scepticism, by a hunger to see and learn more. Difference and non-identical repetition give negative hermeneutics the capacity to unsettle practices and maintain the impetuous movement of understanding. Negative hermeneutics gives structure and impetus to understanding's disquiet and renders that disquiet hermeneutical. In short, negative capability overcomes nihilism. Having introduced the enabling conceptual configurations which will shape our examination of hermeneutical practices and their dynamics, we pass to Chapter 2.

2

Negative receptions

Things Fall part.

W. B. Yeats, *The Second Coming*, 1919

1. Falling-into-question

Questions invite the uncertain. Yet falling-into-question is far from negative. New understanding can be promoted by journeying into the unease initiated by a question. This study opens with a critical summary of the negativities governing recent perceptions of hermeneutics and the humanities. To pose a question presupposes the presence of something questionable.[1] Our argument is not a simple defence of hermeneutics and the humanities and the way of knowing they present. We must concede that there is much that limits the credibility of these disciplines. Gadamer argues, 'To ask a question means to bring into the open. The openness of what is in question consists in the fact that the answer is not settled.'[2] Bringing-into-question can be a positive stratagem: it is 'to open the ground of possibility', to become open to different ways of thinking about a subject matter and to find ourselves opened by such possibilities.[3] The relation between bringing-into-question and bringing-new-modes-of-understanding into being underpins this reflection on hermeneutics and the humanities. That hermeneutics and humanities have fallen into question offers an invitation to think of their limitations in new ways. Responding to that invitation initiates the negative hermeneutics at the heart of this reflection. What is it about hermeneutics and the humanities that have brought them into social

---

1 TM 326.
2 Ibid.
3 Ibid.

and cultural disrepute?[4] Within universities, the teaching of hermeneutics has declined. Whereas hermeneutical reflection should be the driver of creativity in any discipline, its procedures are regarded as ancillary. Of the disciplines that have vociferously resisted the commodification and bureaucratization of higher education, hermeneutics and the humanities now find themselves judged as expensive marginalia. What has prompted such scepticism?

General uncertainty about the social significance of hermeneutics and the humanities is a response to several factors.

1. There is confusion about how hermeneutics to be defined? Without a doubt the proliferation of modes of hermeneutic understanding has caused confusion. Wilhelm Dilthey's pivotal transformation of hermeneutics from a disparate set of regional philological and theological concerns into a general hermeneutics of historical understanding is now plainly in question. Recent work on feminist hermeneutics, hermeneutical aesthetics and the hermeneutics of information jostles for attention with developments in legal, theological and medical hermeneutics. All make claims on how the meaning of understanding and interpretation can be stretched. They also ask what is the proper object of hermeneutics? Is it a musical composition or what happens to us in the practice of music? Is hermeneutics a general descriptor for a whole variety of reflective procedures that seek deeper engagement with their subject matters?
2. What is the aim of hermeneutic study? Pervasive cultural scepticism uncovers what George Steiner called the well-kept secret of hermeneutics: anything can be said about anything.[5] This encourages disengagement from hermeneutics and the humanities. This is, as we shall argue, is a disastrous response. This study argues that the target of hermeneutic interpretation is not as consequential as the collateral understanding the process of interpretation can serendipitously achieve.
3. Does not the historical finitude of all understanding imply that it is impossible to get to the bottom of knowledge claims in hermeneutical disciplines? Without some notion of an objective-correlative, is not all

---

4 Gianni Vattimo is to the point about the issue: 'it is no exaggeration to say that hermeneutics is now the expression of a mode of intellectual life and activity that has been progressively marginalised within contemporary academic hierarchies, and in being so marginalised, politically as well as intellectually, is thereby pushed together with many other similarly marginalised groups'; how is this marginalization to be understood? Gianni Vattimo, 'The Future of Hermeneutics', in *The Routledge Companion to Hermeneutics*, ed. Jeff Malpas and Hans-Helmuth Gander (London: Routledge, 2016), 721–8.
5 George Steiner, *After Babel* (Oxford: Oxford University Press, 1975), 319.

interpretation undecidable? What, then, is the worth of what Ricoeur identified as 'the conflict of interpretations'? Do Nietzsche's words apply, 'if everything is false, anything goes?' Hermeneutics and the humanities appear to render existence even more confusing.
4. If nihilism is correct and we have lost access to substantive truth and meaning what is the point of engaging in hermeneutic and creative practice? Is education reduced to technical training solely for pecuniary advantage?

As these questions suggest, there is considerable uncertainty about the nature and future direction of hermeneutics. Yet bringing a subject matter into question can be a positive stratagem. It is 'to open the ground of possibility', to become open to different ways of thinking about a subject matter and to find our sense of self opened by such possibilities.[6] The relation between bringing-into-question and bringing-new-modes-of-understanding into being underpins this reflection on hermeneutics and the humanities. Not only is a question implicitly guided by the unexpressed semantic horizons from which it springs, but it often seeks a better grasp of what is entailed in those horizons. Hermeneutics is a participatory adventure that opens towards the unexpected. It is not about fixing meaning but discerning the movement of understanding and its experiences. Negative hermeneutics recognizes that the question of what hermeneutics is will always remain open and that it is that openness which invites further creative involvement. Gadamer's citation of Symmachus is appropriate: 'we cannot arrive at such a great secret by one path alone.'[7]

The negativity which shades popular perceptions of both the humanities and hermeneutics represents a misunderstanding. Is it not the case that hermeneutics and the humanities have always been in question? Has a sense of what limits these disciplines not always been a driver of their development? Perhaps uncertainty about hermeneutics and its legitimacy could be overcome if we ceased asking what hermeneutics essentially is and asked instead what it does? A hermeneutics of practice is accordingly at the core of our reflection. Theoretical uncertainty will always be present but hermeneutics is not a theoretical object to be defined. It is a practice to be engaged with. The question is not how hermeneutics is to be conceptualized but what it means to engage in a hermeneutical practice? Theoretical scepticism should be displaced by the quiet confidence of doing.

---

6 Ibid.
7 Hans-Georg Gadamer, *Praise of Theory, Speeches and Essays* (New Haven and London: Yale University Press, 1998), 49.

Before we pass to the next section of our argument, two points will be briefly discussed as they have bearing on developing the centrality of practice in our argument. The first concerns issues relating to the grounding of hermeneutics, and the second addresses the difficult relation between hermeneutics and deconstruction.

1. A clear methodological starting point for hermeneutical activity is untenable. To seek a methodological grounding for hermeneutics is to step beyond its operations and to ground it in something else. Hermeneutic theory has no metaphysical ground that legitimates its activities. In Heideggerian terms, it always starts in the middle. This strengthens the importance of practice for our argument. If it is not possible to step outside practice, then, as with language-being itself, the only way of extending knowledge of its possibilities is to reflect upon its actions from within. Hermeneutical reflection is not something apart from a practice but integral to how we understand its unfolding. To approach a practice hermeneutically is not to theorize it but to engage with its history and anticipations more fully. To be involved with a practice hermeneutically is to participate in a way of life and what is at play within it. Practice becomes a means of world-disclosure. This is why maintaining confidence in hermeneutic practice is critical to our overall argument.

2. Hermeneutics has not always responded well to the challenge of deconstruction. That there is no final arbiter to resolving questions of meaning gives an ironic form to Derrida's critique of hermeneutics: a responsible hermeneutics must be an 'irresponsible hermeneutics'.[8] Underlying any definitive statement of meaning is a penumbra of peripheral meanings of infinite extent. Deconstruction aims, responsibly enough, to release the creative ambiguities in dominant semantic frameworks. To this end anything goes for there is no end to the chain of linguistic relations underlying an assertion of meaning. This, it can be objected, is empty abstraction. A proliferation of possible meanings may offer a range of alternatives to established ones but none will make sense unless they relate to a prior set of linguistic commitments which can be recognized subsequently as being illuminated or changed. Multiplying possibilities per se achieves little. The question is what new insight

---

8 Derrida Jacques, *Of Grammatology*, trans. Gayatri Spivak (Baltimore: Johns Hopkins University Press, 1997) and *Writing and Difference*, trans. Alan Bass (Chicago: University of Chicago, 1978).

transforms understanding of the difficulties we face. In other words, deconstruction only makes sense in relation to pre-established linguistic and cultural practices. It is these that deconstruction 'supplements'. Outside the practical contexts which limit and give sense to the deconstructive stratagem, deconstruction undermines the meaningfulness of the play it is meant to enhance. This will become apparent in our discussion of 'the living word' and 'summative completeness'. However, let us return to our main concerns.

It is evident that hermeneutics and the humanities are negatively perceived. Why are these negativities perceived as negative, as being detrimental to rather than as enhancing of hermeneutic practices? What misunderstanding or deep mistake informs these perceptions? As we shall argue, it is not their negativity that is questionable but the evaluation of that negativity. To understand what happens in hermeneutic engagement we need to ask how participation in interpretive processes alters the participant and how participation alters what is participated in. This dialectic is central to our discussion of practice. It emphasizes the transformative nature of dialogical engagement and that the formative notion of education demands practical engagement. What is transformative about hermeneutical practice? There is something bold in Peter Sloterdijk's claim that 'we must suspend virtually everything that has been said about humans as working beings in order to translate it into the language of practising'.[9] What are the effects of engaging in a hermeneutical practice? Clarity on these points will illuminate how humanities' practices operate.

2. Expectations of completion

A practice turn within hermeneutics facilitates the question, 'What drives understanding? What keeps hermeneutic understanding in motion?' Gadamer's reasoning suggests that it is a hermeneutical drive for completion. A paradox within hermeneutic philosophy is that whilst it knows understanding to be finite and barred from formal completion, it presents understanding as striving for ever greater completeness. What does completer mean in this context? Gadamer's reconstruction of the aesthetic is key to answering this question.

---

9   Peter Sloterdijk, *You Must Change Your Life, On Anthropotechnics* (London: Polity, 2014), 4.

Images may be likened to 'signs' of understanding. They bring a manifold of different experiences into a singular form, so much so that a particular image lights up much that was initially unseen and unspoken. In this field of argument, two Gadamerian terms are crucial: the 'anticipation of completion' (*Vorgriff der Vollkommenheit*) and the 'coming to fruition' or 'fulfilment' (*Vollzug*). Both are counterpointed by notions of totality, the speculative and the aesthetic.

The speculative totality of meaning is, ontologically speaking, synonymous with the language-being that circumscribes all existence. This, metaphysically speaking, is a nihilistic conception involving the repudiation of any intelligible supersensible realm beyond the everyday. For negative hermeneutics there is nothing beyond actuality. Negative hermeneutics is the ontological complement to a speculative totality. It circumscribes that totality with a 'nothingness,' with an indeterminacy through which no thought can pass. Furthermore, Gadamer speaks of 'a totality of meaning' that words bring into play, each pointing 'to an infinity of meaning to be explicated and laid out'.[10] Though it marks the limit of linguistic intelligibility,[11] that totality is capable of generating infinite variations of meaning.[12] Language's speculative completeness – the totality of its possible configurations of meaning – is the basis of the hermeneutical axiom x always equals x+.[13] Though the notion of a speculative totality of meaning formally limits any interpretive claim to complete meaning, it does not express an imperfection but an infinite capacity for perfectibility.

The totality of possible configurations of meaning, on the one hand, and the infinite expressions of meaning, on the other, are ontologically speaking mutually dependent modes of *Sprachlichkeit*. Their incommensurability operates as a (dis) functional relation. The negative dialectic at the core of Gadamer's thinking presupposes that a 'hermeneutic sublime' (an infinity of possible meaning) will always disrupt the perceived 'aesthetic completeness' of a particular expression of meaning. However, if the expansion of hermeneutic understanding requires uncovering the as-yet-unrealized determinations of meaning from within an

---

10 TM 458.
11 'The speculative structure of language' emerges 'as the coming into language of a totality of meaning' (TM 474). Such a totality marks the regulative limit of intelligible being. 'Being that can be understood is language' for language (immersion in speculative structures) 'is the being that all things have' (ibid.).
12 Gadamer deploys the notion of speculative totality in a double context. It refers (1) to the infinite totality of meaning entailed in the universal horizon of *all* linguisticality and (2) to the totality of meaning that is contained within singular linguistic or cultural horizons. Both function as a speculative limit to what can be expressed within horizons.
13 See Nicholas Davey, *Unfinished Worlds, Hermeneutics, Aesthetics, Gadamer* (Edinburgh: Edinburgh University Press, 2013), 118.

anticipated totality, how are they to be drawn out? As we shall see, analysing the dynamics of hermeneutic practice suggests an answer.

An image's claim to 'aesthetic completeness' rests on its ability to render as one a multiplicity of features. Images are exemplars of sense-giving structures so much so that having become acquainted with their efficacy, we seek them out to make sense of complex patterns of relations. *It is the quest for aesthetic completeness that drives understanding's disquiet. Practices are forms of 'sense-making'.* They represent different ways of organizing the indeterminacies of experience. *However, it is not what the practice pursues that matters but rather that something is pursued. The generative effects of the pursuit are formatively more important than the pursued.* The pursuit of interpretation's end – aesthetic completeness – is but a means to inducing a key effect, that is, achieving that transformation of understanding which, we contend, is the primary if indirect end of hermeneutic practice.

Even though it knows all understanding to be finite and barred from formal completion, the hermeneutic quest for completeness is neither futile nor paradoxical. Though the quest for aesthetic completeness can never achieve a final understanding, it can achieve a transformative understanding of aspects of the speculative totality within which it operates. Practice is a way of drawing out of what is entailed within that totality. This suggests that hermeneutical understanding is not a body of knowledge but more an acquired knowingness. It is an *undergoing*, an experience of transition, a process of coming to know the unexpected entailments within one's concerns and involvements, entailments brought to light precisely as a consequence (the effect) of engaging in a hermeneutic practice.

Wittgenstein indicates that the intelligibility of a practice depends not just upon grasping any internal articulation of its ambitions but also upon appreciating its place in a wider life-world of concerns. Though the pursuit of a practice may be singular, its effects rarely are. Humans live within multiple domestic, professional and cultural horizons. Though each is different in orientation, all share (to a degree) a commonality of concerns: 'what is a truthful, a courageous, or an appropriate response to a subject-matter?' Horizons inevitably embrace agonizing ambiguities, conflicts of interpretation, unresolved and unsettling questions. These common concerns or subject matters function as placeholders across different horizons of understanding such that the emergence of new insight in one might unexpectedly resolve difficulties in another. The effect of understanding in an individual practice transcends its initial boundaries, impacting on those of others. Though the quest for aesthetic completeness within one discipline may fail, it may achieve transformative effects in another.

This argument underpins our philosophical reflection on the interdisciplinary value of the humanities. In terms of the achievement of transformative effects, it is not what a practice aims at (aesthetic completeness) that is of primary importance but, rather, what that quest brings into play and keeps in play across related horizons. The argument demonstrates the relational nature of hermeneutical thought and that it is practice's pursuit of completeness that is the primary driver of understanding's emergence. A point of importance should be noted here.

Without doubt hermeneutics has fallen into critical dispute. The Nietzschean maxim 'There is no truth, only interpretation' continues to haunt the discipline. And yet what is perceived to be the problem in hermeneutics is not necessarily what is problematic. Wittgenstein noted how the solution to a problem can lie in coming to see that what was thought to be the problem is not the problem at all.[14] In this connection, the relations discussed earlier – the indeterminacy of linguistic meaning and the incompleteness of interpretation – instantiate a differential space at the heart of hermeneutical thinking, namely the space between x and x+. Yet this incommensurable space poses a problem for hermeneutics only if it is presented epistemologically. The methodological disrepute of hermeneutics suggests that it remains victim to that epistemological prejudice which mistakes forms of knowing for the objects known. Manifold interpretations of a subject matter may ideally suggest a final or end interpretation but this is not to say that such an 'intelligible' truth exists. Nihilism and postmodern thought reject this epistemological bias: hermeneutics can never get to the bottom of things. If there were a truth which rendered all conditional relationships complete, 'it must lie outside the world'.[15] In other words, the traditional hermeneutic quest for a final truth rests on an epistemological fallacy. *To seek the final truth underlying a body of interpretation is to want to eliminate the incommensurable space upon which knowledge and self-awareness depend.* Understanding depends on open movement and not finality. Whereas the negative perception of hermeneutics sees the incommensurable space of its operations as a fatal flaw, negative hermeneutics regards this instability as a core driver of reflective and creative practice.[16]

---

14 Ludwig Wittgenstein, "The Solution of the Problem of Life is Seen in the Vanishing of the Problem", in *Tractatus Logico-Philosophicus*, ed. Ludwig Wittgenstein(London: Routledge and Kegan Paul, 1961), Sec. 6.521.
15 Ibid., 6.41.
16 As we shall argue later, the German for 'experience' (*Erfahrung*) has connotations which are much closer to the English notion of an 'experienced' sailor or cook. It implies a lot more than having gone through a technical training. The term suggests the evolution of a reflective mode of practised being, undergoing repetitions of performance from which arise memory, expectation and inference.

3. Differential spaces and perspectival multiplication

The issue is, then, whether the differential space between a subject matter and its interpretations is appraised negatively as a space of entrapment which finite understanding cannot escape or positively as an enabling space in which the possibilities for interpretation and understanding are unlimited. The consequence of the negative epistemological evaluation is scepticism: any sense for the world can only lie outside the world. This is why negative hermeneutics is adamant in its repudiation of intelligible Being. The affirmation of such a world as the 'true' but unattainable renders the differential spaces of actuality as spaces of containment, imprisoning us in an infinitude of incomplete understanding. If, however, the differential spaces between a subject matter and its interpretation are appraised ontologically, they become spaces of enablement: the sense of the world lies *within* the shifting totality of linguistic relationships which ground our language-being. Whereas the epistemological perspective excludes us from ever knowing the truth of that totality, the ontological perspective grounds us in the continuous unfolding of its possibilities.

The differential spaces between a concept and its determinations are spaces of the 'in-between'. This is why practice plays such an important role in this chapter. *Practice is ontologically speaking the embodiment of the in-between, always between how it has come to understand itself and how it will come to understand itself.* Language-being embraces the totality of its past and future determinations of meaning, and these impel it towards new articulations of itself. Differential spaces impel practices towards the as-yet-unthought-out possibilities they hold. Negative hermeneutics turns differential spaces into places of ontological possibility, that is, into places of more knowing. Though no knowing can grasp the infinite, all finite knowing can be infinitely extended.

By denying the epistemological perspective, negative hermeneutics denies the primacy of theory and celebrates the particularities of practice. It is impossible to predict the unrealized possibilities of meaning that a practice may contain. Only by engaging with it can its possibilities be drawn out. Participation is vital for such unfolding. Negative hermeneutics sets the anti-metaphysical framework in which the continuing movement and life of understanding can be affirmed. It negates the metaphysical appeal to completeness and infinite understanding not just to rid us of the needless prejudice that our actual knowledge is second rate but rather to affirm and celebrate the infinite possibilities for understanding afforded by the finitude of understanding itself. *Negative hermeneutics is fundamentally an enabling posture.* Its principled resistance to fixity and closure maintains a stalwart openness towards the ever-present possibility of realigning the elements of meaning within a given concern (*Sache*) into new and informative configurations.

Negative hermeneutics is not concerned with making positive counter-assertions with regard to what is held to be negative about the humanities but with dismantling negative attitudes towards the negative. If meaning is relational, the meaning of a question changes when the relations governing its understanding change. The meaning of a subject matter or question depends not just on its grammatical structure but also on how it relates to the unexpressed horizons of semantic meaning which give that subject field sense and direction in the first place. No such speculative totality can be expressed as a whole but if one's place within it alters, so one's understanding of the particulars it sustains changes. This has direct relevance to our discussion of the way hermeneutics and the humanities are negatively perceived. They are negatively perceived because their failure to achieve decisive closure in the form of a definitive truth-claim or a completeness of understanding is regarded as an insurmountable flaw. Why are such features judged as flaws rather than as providing incentives to understanding more? We will return to this question throughout this study.

Negative hermeneutics endeavours to negate those dispositions which lead to the incompleteness and finitude of understanding being judged as shortcomings. It does not seek to refute the claim that no interpretation can be decisive or final. To the contrary, it affirms the positivity of such limitations. It proclaims the possibilities for the infinite extension of understanding that follows from an acceptance of its finite dimensions. Negative hermeneutics seeks to make explicit what implicitly informs our perceptions and, in so doing, to affirm the negativity that shapes human understanding. Turning from the negative perceptions of hermeneutics, we shall consider the negativity that underpins contemporary views of the humanities.

4. Negative receptions

If hermeneutics finds itself in question, even more so do the humanities. Cultural and economic uncertainty has created a climate of opinion that doubts the social and economic legitimacy of these disciplines. Our concern is with the misunderstandings that fuel this negative reception and with achieving a critique that can evaluate such negativity differently.

Vattimo laments that the 'most suitable activities for humanity are no longer those that involve the creation of works of art or of thought' but those that 'seek the technological, scientific and organisation of the world'. Technology and managerial thinking erode precisely those 'free' spaces which Gadamer defends as places of spontaneous and creative irruption. Contemporary political disquiet concerning hermeneutics and the humanities as well as general unease about the professionalization of academia display the afterlife of inappropriate sets of underlying assumptions. The mode of thought which fuels such negative dispositions concerns such prejudices as 'poetry obfuscates, and science liberates'.[17] Gadamer's *riposte* is admirably terse: 'does not the experience of art contain a claim to truth which is certainly different from that of science, but just as certain and not inferior to it'.[18] We will later explore what Gadamer means by this. Furthermore, uncertainty is now no longer a feature of the arts alone: 'for most practical intents and purposes, the condition of uncertainty has shifted from the realm of epistemology to that of ontology'.[19] Probability and likelihood have replaced certainty. Contemporary hermeneutics must dismantle the methodological dichotomy between the arts and the sciences that, historically speaking, it is in part responsible for and because of which, paradoxically enough, it finds itself judged as methodologically wanting. What is needed is a revaluation of those systems of thought which perpetuate norms of certainty and predictability above all else. Subject-centred epistemologies need to be replaced with frameworks of thought that allow the hermeneutic agent to be integrated into their environment as a participant rather than distanced from it as an estranged epistemological sovereign.

Though we live in a social climate preoccupied with the manageable, technological regimes appear to achieve the opposite of what was intended. Gadamer notes how we are riddled with uncertainty and foreboding.[20] Nietzsche's question returns: What happens when science – the guarantor of predictability and control – bites its own tail? In his notebooks, Nietzsche outlines an answer.

> It is a measure of the degree of strength of will to what extent one can do without meaning in things, to what extent one can endure to live in a meaningless world because one organises a small portion of it oneself.[21]
>
> To introduce a meaning – this task still remains to be done.[22]

---

17 Peter Atkins cited by Mary Midgley, *Science and Poetry* (London: Routledge, 2001), 21.
18 TM 97 (insert ND).
19 Zygmunt Bauman and Rein Raud, *Practices of Selfhood* (London: Polity, 2015), p. ix.
20 Hans-Georg Gadamer, *On Education, Poetry and History, Applied Hermeneutics* (Albany: State University of New York Press, 1992), 165–80.
21 WP 585A.
22 WP 605.

In this context, the notion of the humanities as sense-making practices assumes a cultural poignancy the significance of which emerges once the misunderstandings denigrating these disciplines as subjective indulgences are dismantled. The arts and humanities are not the problem but its answer. Paradigms of reflections which offer escape from enclosing models of certainty and control need to be developed. Practices able to negotiate the uncertain, able to develop creative responses to the unexpected and able to develop confidence to voyage into the unknown need to be nurtured rather than removed from the curriculum. Once the underlying prejudice in favour of certainty and control is displaced by those favouring the uncertain and the unpredictable, the grounds for preferring the sciences to the humanities as epistemologically superior disappear. The problem is not with hermeneutics and the humanities but with those ways of thinking that would have us believe that they are problematic.

5. Distanciation, theory and alienation

Developing a photographic image reveals something we are all intimately familiar with, that is, those moments of concentration in which we hope and wait for something to be disclosed.[23] Both the poetic and the photographic image address us because they reveal our deep familiarity with the ontological structures of the life-world. When such familiarity is broken, art no longer speaks directly and becomes problematized as an aestheticized autonomous object severed from the life-world. How does this estrangement (aesthetic alienation) come about?

> The consciousness of art – the aesthetic consciousness is always secondary to *the immediate truth-claim* that proceeds from the work of art itself. To this extent, when we judge a work of art on the basis of its aesthetic quality, something that is really much more intimate and familiar to us is alienated. This alienation into aesthetic judgement always takes place when we have withdrawn ourselves and are no longer open to *the immediate claim of that which grasps us*.[24]

In *Truth and Method*, Gadamer observes that a theoretical stance towards art involves dealing with something that no longer speaks to us directly but has

---

23 See Lee Miller's photograph 'Women's Auxiliary Air Force (WAAF) darkroom assistant processing a negative in the darkroom at RAF Waddington, Lincolnshire, May 1943', in *Lee Miller: A Woman's War*, ed. Hilary Roberts and Antony Penrose (London: Thames and Hudson, 2015), 109.
24 Hans-Georg Gadamer, *Philosophical Hermeneutics* (Berkeley: University of California, 2008), 7, (emphasis added ND).

become alien.[25] The artwork ceases to be indicative of a world we participate in but of an object that assists or resists our purposes.[26] The breaking of such initial intimacy is the precondition of aesthetic estrangement emerging.

Current questioning of the social legitimacy of the humanities indicates not that Gadamer is wrong about aesthetic alienation but that he underestimates the extent of its consequences. The issue of alienation and its epistemological underpinnings prompts estrangement from the humanities, influences the commodification of higher education and warps learning with the prioritization of economic values. Three of Heidegger's strategic differentiations influence Gadamer's account of aesthetic alienation: (1) the ontological and the ontic, (2) the ready to hand and the present to hand and (3) the apophantic and the epiphanic in language. These three differentiations betray something of a 'way of life' that is estranged from the uncertainties of actuality.

1. *The ontological and the ontic.* Heidegger's ontological enquiry is a reflection on the question of Being from the perspective of existence rather than metaphysics. As 'the is-ness of all beings', Being *manifests* itself. The ontological is both antecedent to and exceeds whatever consciousness might grasp of it. *Dasein* suggests a way of life inextricably caught up with and shaped by the prior presence of Being. Gadamer refers to this as 'the totality of our involvements' within which our individual being is immersed. By contrast, the 'ontic' is secondary to the ontological and concerns the distinguishing features of the things within this world, their properties and attributes. However, the immediate truth-claim of art (its emerging out of and its subsequent revelation of the totality of our worldly involvements) has the status of an ontological disclosure. The 'secondary' derivative world of aesthetic properties prises details out of the primary life-world, simplifies them and makes them seem primary when, ontologically speaking, they are secondary. What prompts the shift from the openness of ontological awareness to the blinkeredness of ontic consciousness? We shall consider this question later.
2. *The 'ready to hand' and the 'present to hand'.* Heidegger's distinction between instinctively reaching out for a tool on one's work top and having to feel one's way along the walls of an unilluminated cave is of the same order as that which Wittgenstein makes between walking through a town known to one like the back of one's hand and entering a foreign

---

25 TM 14.
26 TM 84.

city where a map is needed. For Gadamer, to view a work of art as an aesthetic object is to treat it as a phenomenon that is only 'present to hand': it stands before us as an alien object to be deciphered. To approach objects as 'aesthetic phenomena' is to have lost or to have suppressed one's primary acquaintance with them as objects which speak to and of one's life-world. A landscape will no longer convey envelopment and belonging but real-estate opportunities. To view landscape as a development zone is, as John Muir understood,[27] to have become subject to that alienation in which an artwork or landscape is no longer perceived as a life-world to be participated in but as an object to be decoded or utilized. Reducing an artwork to a collection of aesthetic properties betrays the fact that an epistemological estrangement from the life-world has taken place.

3. *Apophantic and apophatic language.* Heidegger's distinction between apophantic and apophatic language distinguishes between language with the ontological empowerment to bring something to mind and language which is propositional asserting the nature of a subject solely in terms of its predicates. Apophantic language is clearly ontic. Gadamer distinguishes similarly between 'speculative language' and the 'language of statements'. *Whereas in propositional language the individual subject or institution speaks and states what is the case, in speculative language that which arises in and through the utterance speaks.* Propositional language pares away the contextual involvements of the thing identified, reducing it to its (alleged) intrinsic properties. Why do we no longer hear or see the language of things and accept propositional language as the only legitimate way of speaking of actuality. It is our cultural fixation with the conscious and with the statement that estranges us from the uncertain and unclear and prompts our sense of the speculative in language to decay. In consequence, we lose access to and cease to trust the implicit understandings which shape our being.

Heidegger's argument that 'all interpretation is grounded on understanding' guides our argument.[28] The ontological primacy Heidegger gives to 'understanding' mirrors that which Gadamer gives to 'language-being'. Linguistic consciousness is ontologically speaking a derivative form of and hence secondary to language-being in which all possible determinations of

---

27 John Muir, 1838–1914. See, *Environmental Thinkers*, ed. Joy A. Palmer Cooper and David E. Cooper (London: Routledge, 2017), 130–4.
28 Martin Heidegger, *Being and Time*, trans. John Macquarrie (London: Blackwell, 1960), Part V, Sec. 33.

thought are housed. The hermeneutic axiom that x equals x+ clearly reflects Heidegger's ontological prioritization of understanding over interpretation. *Understanding 'houses' the 'always more to said'.* When established interpretations break down we look to language-being for alternatives. The importance of practice is stressed once again: we have no access to the potentials for further thought and meaningfulness other than through practices being grounded in both what enables and transcends them. The possibility for achieving new transformative insight rests upon the ontological priority of understanding over interpretation or, in Gadamer's terms, upon the fact that language-being transcends linguistic consciousness. This philosophic rationale drives Gadamer's defence hermeneutics and the humanities. Precisely because the practice of hermeneutical and creative interpretation gives ontological access to what lies beyond it (i.e. the unending possibilities for transformed understanding within language-being), the denigration of such practices as groundless threatens to estrange and alienate a community from the very stock of ideas which in times of challenge can provide new ways of thinking and seeing. This is why a philosophical defence of hermeneutics and the humanities practices is of strategic importance. Upholding these practices maintains access to the streams of possible meaning that sustain them. In relation to language-being, practices per se are not as important as what they enable.

Practice enables, crucially, the drawing out of what understanding in Heidegger's sense holds. It makes manifest what cannot otherwise be given as a pregiven epistemological object. Practice is able to disclose the elements at play within its processes which cannot be revealed in any other way. A participatory epistemology consequently gives greater emphasis to practical engagement and thereby betrays its open nature. To participate in the life-world of understanding is to participate in a situation. Gadamer remarks,

> The very idea of a situation means that we are not standing outside it, and hence we are unable to have an objective knowledge of it. We always find ourselves within a situation and throwing light on it is never entirely finished. [29]

Participatory epistemology clarifies the conditions which enable our life-world to speak to us with immediacy: as modes of *Dasein* we are *already* intimately acquainted with its voices and receptive to its nuances. It is attunement to such understanding that the diminishment of the humanities threatens. However, the fact of aesthetic alienation and the estrangement of theory from actual

---

29 TM 301.

experience betrays for Gadamer that the covenant between ourselves and the life-world has already been broken. We no longer hear a child's lullaby but only a series of note progressions. The artwork as a portal through which our life-world reveals itself, is recognized and shared, is subverted. Aesthetic alienation stifles the voice of the artwork and turns it into an object of theory. Only its formal 'objective' properties are regarded as discursively significant; association with cultural significance is regarded as subjective and, hence, marginal. This suggests how alienation from the life-world arises. For theoretical consciousness to obtain its hold, it must distil the complexities of the experiential world into forms facilitating its manipulation. No longer does an artwork address or reflect its life-world but is reduced to being either a pleasing or displeasing object in the spectator's gaze. Kant's aesthetic disinterestedness exhibits estrangement from the life-world par excellence. We no longer attend to what the artwork says but analyse its aesthetic properties; theory subverts lived experience.

The contemporary privileging of theory over the life-world culminates in the criticism that the humanities have 'sold out' to theory. Questions of dialogical application are displaced by demands for theoretical justification. George Steiner sensed how fixations with methodological legitimacy haunt the humanities. 'In the American climate . . . the prestige of the pure and applied sciences is paramount; it entails the primacy of theory and the theoretical. The humanities (have) long aspired to such distinction.' Why, then, the adulatory reception of theory? 'Deconstruction and post-structuralism seemed to validate resort to the theoretical, to an idiom comparable to that of the sciences.'[30] Not only does this push the primacy of the first-person voice in poetry and philosophy to one side, but it also leads, as Tony Judt suggests, to 'the self-conscious grasping of humanists for the security of theory and methodology'.[31] Bauman worries that the esoteric jargon of modern theory in the humanities manifests a chronic lack of certainty (confidence) about their formal status and an overt eagerness to earn 'scientific credentials through the emulation of the natural-scientific incomprehensibility to a lay reader/listener'.[32] These remarks betray a deeper alienation. Later on we shall argue that we have lost confidence in personal intuition and judgement and prefer to defer to theory. We fear taking responsibility for individual judgement. This is why maintaining confidence in practice is so central to our debate.

If hermeneutics and the humanities are negatively perceived as a consequence of the participatory epistemologies of the life-world being displaced by subject–

---

30 George Steiner, 'War and Peace', *TLS*, 25 March 2011.
31 Tony Judt, *The Memory Chalet* (London: William Heineman, 2010), 202.
32 Bauman and Raud, *Practices of Selfhood*, 23.

object epistemologies, the challenge is to develop a more participatory way of thinking. Although Gadamer perpetuates a strict opposition between the arts and the sciences, the life-world does not go away. In *Being and Time*, Heidegger emphasizes that the apophantic language characteristic of subject–object epistemologies does not belong to a different language world compared to that of the poetic. To the contrary, it is a derivative form of the disclosive forms of language that reveal our 'fore-having'.[33] Indeed, much of Gadamer's argument about estrangement might be said to derive from the following passage:

> The entity which is held in our fore-having (a hand tool or pen) is proximally ready to hand as equipment. If this entity becomes the 'object' of an assertion, then as soon as we begin this assertion, there is already a change-over in the fore-having. Something (that was) ready to hand with which we have to do or perform something, turns into something about which about which the assertion that points it out is made.[34]
>
> Only now are we given any access to properties or the like.[35]

Heidegger argues, however, that there is no straightforward demarcation between the kind of interpretation which is still wholly wrapped in a concernful understanding (i.e. the understanding that structures *Dasein*) and the extreme opposite case of a theoretical assertion about something present-at-hand (the world of phenomena). 'There are many intermediate gradations, assertions about the happenings in the environment', on the one hand, and 'fixing the facts of the case', on the other.[36] Heidegger and Gadamer recognize the necessity of science and technology standing back from aspects of the life-world in order to resolve its problems. To a degree, distanciation is necessary in order to confront the life-world's threatening aspects whether famine or disease. Neither Gadamer nor Heidegger has difficulty with scientific thinking so long as it springs from the demands of 'concernful understanding' to address disturbances in the life-world. Problems arise, however, when the designations made to intervene in and assist the life-world become valued as entities in their own right and start to obscure the world they sprang from in the first place. It is possible to describe the Indian monsoon as a 'tropical disturbance' associated with temperature drops, a low pressure and prolonged rain. These designations are appropriate to meteorological studies: determining the passage of the 'disturbance' has implications for agriculture and road management. However, the term monsoon

33 Heidegger, *Being and Time*, Part 5, Sec. 32.
34 Ibid (insertions by ND).
35 Ibid.
36 Ibid.

also carries enormous significance in Indian culture marking the season of fertility and regrowth. A monsoon *raga* has an intensely sad and longing mood – roads are flooded, lovers are separated and yet joined in their yearning. Though the term's meteorological designations may have been 'concernfully' developed to manage storm seasons, the pragmatically designated world of pressure charts can displace the term's cultural nuances. The world of foreknowledge attached to the terms is pushed back and dwindles as its 'enviromentality' (its ability to speak of longing and separation) is lost. This displacement potentially sows the seeds for a cultural tragedy: the simplifications of the designated world are mistaken for actuality itself! Actuality then becomes subject to the criticism that it is neither as ordered nor as predictable as the systems of designation used to chart it. As Nietzsche suspected in the case of metaphysics, these designations are then taken as a template for an intelligible world of being beyond actuality. The projection of a simplified world of designations as an independent reality has the consequence of devaluing the life-world of *Dasein* as secondary and apparent. The issue here is not with scientific and technological reasoning per se but with those underlying interests which propagate the fiction that only such reasoning serves as criteria for the truth and the real. Once such fictions become persuasive, the world of designations counts as the true world, *Dasein* falls into the background and the ontologically primary becomes epistemologically secondary. Science and technology lose their connection with the concerns of the life-world upon which their basic orientation depends. *The irony is that the very values used to pragmatically orient ourselves to the world only serve to alienate ourselves from it.* To succumb to the mistake of assuming that only scientific and technological reasoning can serve as criteria for the real and the true betrays the extent of our alienation from the immediate world of experience. To be rooted in that latter world is to know that propositional assertions are limited by their living context: they are partial, perspectival and situated.

For Gadamer, the speculative power of the humanities resides specifically in their capacity to invoke and disclose the hidden dispositions of thought at play within understanding (*Dasein*). To be persuaded that language rather than drawing us further into that world somehow contains and states what is real indicates for Heidegger that we are 'fallen' beings that prefer the illusory stability that the definitions of the speech-created world afford as opposed to allowing language to initiate us more deeply into the uncertainties and hidden unknowns of understanding. For Heidegger, the issue is one of existential orientation. He recognizes that *Dasein* (our being in a totality of involvements) is always a being-towards-possibility. *Dasein* (humanity) is never a fact that is finished:[37] its mode of being is always turbulent and unsettled. We reside in the uncertainties of the possible. Why might a being-towards-possibility-and-risk be more hermeneutically suggestive than a mode of being seeking fixity and certitude? The issue is not about the scientific method versus rhetorical styles of reasoning but about the negative influence of those orientations which prefer the safe and controllable to the open horizons of actuality. It is questions of existential orientation towards change and uncertainty that underwrite the diminishment of the humanities. The substantive issue is not becoming alienated from the ontological totality of our life involvements but damaging their creative potential by regarding them as secondary. The cognitive devaluation of 'the totality of our involvements' withers the sources of meaningfulness informing our existence. Cultural nihilism (the loss of faith in the worthwhileness of creative action) ensues. The cultural alienation which Gadamer initially discusses only in relation to aesthetics also leads to the grievous denigration of how the worth of the humanities is perceived. This is the challenge that negative hermeneutics must overcome.

6. Nihilism and theory

The advent of nihilism impacts on how hermeneutics and the humanities are perceived. The humanities are in part responsible for their own demise in this respect. Nihilism does not arise *sui generis* but as a consequence of a disappointed quest for intelligible truth and meaning. Nihilism occasions the discrediting of the humanities by revealing the failure of their own norms of truth and meaning. This study defends the view that hermeneutics and the humanities gain their legitimacy from the norms of their own practice and not from any alleged metaphysical foundation.

Nihilism is a complex philosophical phenomenon. It assumes different forms some of which will play a strategic role in our attempt to articulate a non-foundational ground for hermeneutical practices. Negative hermeneutics is clearly nihilistic in that it entails a post-metaphysical rejection of intelligible truth and reality. Nietzsche and Wittgenstein sense that nihilism betrays an existential disposition, a 'passive nihilism', which questions the worthwhileness of any

---

[37] Heidegger, *Being and Time*, Part 5, Sec. 38.

practical intervention in life's activities. In later chapters, our defence of practice offers a forthright response to the life-denying aspects of passive nihilism.

The pervasive influence of metaphysical nihilism has certainly informed the popular view that within the humanities anything can be said about anything, that there are no decisive facts and that 'we are interpretation all the way down'. This conclusion encourages a nihilistic rejection of universal values and promotes in their stead forms of cultural relativism. In a climate influenced by cultural nihilism, the claim that hermeneutics is concerned with appropriating the 'meaning' of a text is met with derision. The collapse of belief in universal truths transcending both culture and language implies many truths or a proliferation of cultural monadisms. This raises deep concerns as to what the disciplines of literature and philosophy might legitimately address. Can the truth-claims of Oriental aesthetics be assessed in the same way as those propounded by Renaissance aesthetics? Cultural pluralism asserts the view that in matters of epistemology, religion and morality, not all roads lead to Rome and that the centre no longer holds. Due care is needed to negotiate these arguments. Their entailments are not as damaging to hermeneutics and the humanities as they might initially seem.

Nihilism is fundamentally a *via negativa*. It performs a metaphysical amputation, asserting that all truths appertaining to an unchanging intelligible world of Being are fictions. No such world exists: there simply is no meaning-in-itself which shapes and gives purpose to human existence. In this sense, there is no meaning to life. For Nietzsche, the *creation* of meaning is a key response to nihilism. Negative hermeneutics demonstrates that coming to terms with metaphysical nihilism (understood as a loss of faith in foundational meaning) is a necessary prelude for engaging in participatory forms of meaning which are always open to renegotiation, elaboration and enrichment. Nietzsche insists that nihilism in its psychological form is indicative of a lack of strength to create meaning. As we shall suggest, negative hermeneutics when combined with a participatory epistemology offers arguments capable of displacing the negativity associated with metaphysical nihilism. We will argue that understood as a sense-finding discipline, hermeneutics concerns the realization of those untried potentials for meaningfulness entailed within our language horizons. Engagement with sense-creating practices provides a powerful antidote to the dispiriting negativity of metaphysical nihilism.

When Nietzsche wrote there is 'No limit to the ways in which the world can be interpreted . . . plurality of interpretations a sign of strength. Not to desire to deprive the world of its disturbing and enigmatic character' (WP 600), he acknowledged what the humanities 'know' but cannot strictly say: human experience is so profoundly complex that no one theory can command its multiple registers. Thinkers as various as Stefan Rosenzweig, Gadamer and Rowan Williams understand that to honour the complexities of experience, disciplinary frontiers must be crossed. Intense and complex experience demands multiple registers of interpretation. Negative hermeneutics and its promise of a participatory epistemology offers a framework to integrate the multiplicities of interpretation without compromising their differences. And yet, as the drive towards professionalization and specialization shows, the allure of theory within the humanities is powerful.

A charge frequently levelled at the humanities (congruous with Gadamer's critique of alienation) is that they have 'sold out' to theory: literature and history are studied not in relation to contemporaneous experiences of the world or the effectiveness of how the past presently manifests itself in immediate experience but in conjunction with reflections on whether literature or historical events evidence a specific theory. Questions of personal application and assimilation are displaced by attempts at theoretical justification. In the bluntest of terms, we no longer take ourselves (our subjectivity) seriously and have lost the ability to trust (or have been led to formally distrust) our intuitions. The implication of this is that whereas speculative language tends towards dialogical expansion, the language of propositional assertion inclines towards restrictive stratagems of control. Speculative language is at the heart of both hermeneutics and the humanities and poses challenges which, if the current estrangement from these disciplines is to be overcome, must be effectively addressed.

The fact of mystical, religious or aesthetic experience is not at issue. Few except the most churlish would deny those revelatory moments when, for some inexplicable reason, understanding is transformed. A chance conversational encounter, an unexpected discovery in a book shop, a line of poetry taken out of context or an unusual turn of phrase can challenge what was thought to be understood and suddenly reorientate it. Such experiences are multi-registered involving shifts in intellectual, social and emotional orientation. They require a participatory model of truth rather than one based on propositional adequacy. The issue here is not about having to choose between 'speculative' insight and propositional understanding. Modes of propositional analysis depend on implicit frameworks of speculative ideas and values upon which the sense of their activity depends. Demands for propositional exactitude are equally important for probing the speculative understandings of what a text communicates but does not explicitly state. Error and misunderstanding occur when one side of the equation claims that because a text does not say what it says propositionally, it is not saying anything at all.

To be dejected by the uncertainties and open possibilities of this world and its refusal to comply with the demands of epistemological certainty is to fail to make a vital distinction between certainty and practical confidence. Theory may not achieve the formal certainty it pursues but sustained practices, artistic, social and historical, can generate a practical confidence in the world which derives from accrued experiences of engagement and participation (*Bildung*) albeit that these practices lack any formal grounding. The ability to overcome the *scepsis* sustaining alienated consciousness requires a practical trust in the life-world and its practices. As we shall argue in Chapter 5 this requires the development of a participatory epistemology.

If the humanities have sold out to theory, negative hermeneutics can be recruited to the opposition. Philosophical hermeneutics is resolutely anti-theoretical in its resistance to the subordination of experience to theory. Gadamer contends that hermeneutic philosophy is not a theoretical stance but a 'path of experiencing'. Its task is not to seize upon the particulars of experience vindicating a given explanatory model but rather to make us aware reflectively of what is performatively at play within experience. This does not deny the role of reflection in experience. To the contrary: 'reflection is brought into play . . . as we participate in the performance of life itself'.[38] We sustain reflection along with the performance of a task and not as any sort of objectifying confrontation. This reassertion of the primacy of experience does not constitute a return to a subjectivism but to subjectivity conceived in a Hegelian manner, that is, as an ontological reflection of what flows through it. If the humanities have sold out to theory, negative hermeneutics can redress the charge by denying any theory-experience binary and by expanding the notion of experience to include its reflective dimension. Hermeneutical *Erfahrung* is necessarily in the moment but is never just of the moment. It is connected to both memory and expectation. This integrative approach to theory and experience will form an important theme in the following discussions of practice.

Negative hermeneutics must allow for the reaccommodation of individual experience. Whereas the dominance of method within the humanities promotes scepticism towards personal responsiveness, negative hermeneutics encourages the opposite: the valuing of subjective experience as a gateway to

---

38 See the essay 'Hermeneutics as Practical Philosophy', in Hans-Georg Gadamer, *The Gadamer Reader,* ed. R. E. Palmer (Evanston: Northwestern University Press, 2007), 228–46.

the engaging with the objectivities that sustain it. Questions of individual responsiveness must return from the *margins* of epistemological concern to the centre of hermeneutical reflection. The pedagogical implications of this shift are significant. Participatory epistemology recognizes the particular and individual nature of experience. In order to be drawn out, the 'substantialities' it contains require constant questioning, dialogue and exchange. Participatory epistemology demands communities of questioning, communities which commonly confess their vulnerability to the address of key existential and cultural subject matters. Exchange with such communities encourages the expansion and growth of individual perspectives. To profess hermeneutically is to remedy the limitations of one's own subjectivity by engaging with those of others. Participatory epistemology concerns competent involvement, a sense of how the environments in which we participate are interdependent and an awareness of how in culture, language and history we are often codependent.

In addition to raising questions about the epistemological credibility of hermeneutics and the humanities, nihilism challenges any essentialist notion of the humanities and what it means to be human and seemingly condemns us to live within uncertainty.

7. The humanities in question

The collapse of faith in other-worldly religion, metaphysics and foundational truths fragments the world of humanism into pluralism, perspectivism and relativism. This suggests that like Oedipus we have become blind to who we are, where we have come from and to where we are going. If we are interpretation all the way down, have we lost our alpha and omega and no longer know our 'first and last things'? As Nietzsche commented, 'Ever since Copernicus mankind has been rolling from the centre towards x'.[39] Dieter Henrich and Helmuth Plessner remark that human beings are increasingly faced by what is unavailable to them. The ground from which they have sprung is unfathomable and appears to be withheld: 'we are but do not know what it is to be'.[40] From the perspective of negative hermeneutics this is not a cause for existential despair. It can be cogently argued that not knowing who we are is a defining characteristic of our mode of existence: 'to be' is to be in question. As Dilthey noted, what

---

39 WP Section 1.
40 Cited by Wolfgang Iser, *The Range of Interpretation* (York: Columbia Press, 2000), 155.

humankind is (or is capable of becoming) only the contingencies of history will reveal. In a similar context, Nelson Goodman observes that there is nothing solid underneath our ways of world-making: human beings live by what they produce and appear to be unending performances of themselves. From these remarks, the concept of 'humanity' emerges as indefinable. In Iser's language, the concept of humanity is a constitutive blank, a liminal space constantly filling and emptying with interpretations of itself.[41] We receive from history, literature and art, diverse understandings of what it might mean to be human. Viking warriorship is not consistent with Greek virtue, which in turn is not consistent with Christian duty. Each time one interpretation is applied, something will be omitted: not all predications will apply and this excess will drive and displace subsequent interpretations. The danger comes when a constitutive blank is colonized by a singular faith or ideology: *the movement of understanding ceases when we cease to be a question to ourselves.* Furthermore, a conceptual object which is metaphysically blank but historically fluid demands that cognition become multiform: such an object cannot be subsumed by one discipline alone. For such conceptual spaces to be colonized is to foreclose the creative possibilities held within them and to lapse into yet another master narrative of the human condition.[42] Wolfgang Iser hymns a life that cannot be frozen into hypostatizations of any of its aspects: life is basically unrepresentable and can only be conceived by means of its shimmerous, transient and self-produced figurations of understanding. Stefan Rosenzweig bids us to adopt 'an attitude of permanent vigilance against the temptations of certainty' because 'we have only the world that we bring forth with others'.[43] Non-essentialist approaches to the question of humanity are framed around the idea that the being of humanity always remains a being in question. As we shall see, practice becomes integral to unfolding the unseen possibilities within such questions. To adapt Michael Oakeshott's phrase, the conversations of humankind constitute what we are.[44]

Anti-essentialist thinkers such as Peter Sloterdijk hold to the view that whatever humanity might thought to be, it can only be conceptualized in terms of its own practices.

> Anyone who speaks of human self-production without addressing the human beings in the practising life has missed the point from the outset. Consequently, we must suspend virtually everything that has been said about human as working

---

41 Ibid., 158.
42 Ibid., 93–4.
43 Ibid., 158.
44 Michael Oakeshott, *Rationalism in Politics* (London: Methuen, 1981), 191–246.

beings in order to translate it into the language of practising, or self-forming and self-enhancing behaviour. . . . It is time to reveal humans as the beings who result from repetition. Just as the nineteenth century stood cognitively under the sign of production and the twentieth undershoot of reflexivity, the future should present itself under the sign of the exercise (practise).[45]

Sloterdijk's argument raises the question of how self-forming practices operate and whether what we refer to as human subjects are the result of practices known collectively as the humanities? Sloterdijk tends to the Nietzschean view that the human subject is the effect of interpretive practices. Gadamer's position is undoubtedly more ambiguous, oscillating between both essentialism and anti-essentialism. In essays such as *The Enigma of Health*, Gadamer speaks directly of an essential feature of being human and of behaving theoretically as being part of the practice of mankind. If essence means no more than family resemblance, then Gadamer's language is perhaps misleading. What makes his position more complicated is his reversion to neo-Kantian philosophical language. He speaks of 'reflection' as the highest form of freedom and of reflective practice as the exercise of 'real freedom'.[46] It is impossible to separate these notions from their Kantian provenance in which the language of freedom (expressed in the context of moral judgement-making) is linked to the romantic conception of a non-causal 'spontaneous' source of practical action. Contrary to the historical outlook which for the most part informs philosophical hermeneutics, the ghost of Kantian humanism appears to force Gadamer's notion of the human back into a form of essentialism. What is increasingly clear in the light of the objections made against both the humanities and hermeneutics is that the very notion of subjective agency needs to be rethought. Without a credible notion of subjectivity, the idea of hermeneutical experience (and learning) collapses.

These difficulties aside, Gadamer is right to associate the question of practice with the question of humanity. The repressed term in the equation is, of course, hermeneutics. Questions concerning what constitutes the human, the nature of practice and hermeneutics are clearly indissociable. Nevertheless, the ambiguity in Gadamer's position is instructive. It exposes the critical junction at stake in reasoning about these questions. The key conceptual triangulation concerns practice, essence and the human. The pivotal question concerns whether the term practice in this equation is to be read epistemologically or ontologically? If practice is read epistemologically and is understood as the acting out of what

---

45 Sloterdijk, *You Must Change Your Life, On Anthropotechnics.*, (London: Polity, 2013), 4 (Insert ND).
46 Hans-Georg Gadamer, *The Enigma of Health* (London: Polity, 1996), 45–60.

is essentially human, then Gadamer contradicts the fundamental historical outlook of his hermeneutics. If, however, practice is understood ontologically, it can be grasped as a generative process of interpretive engagement out of which what comes to be regarded as the human emerges. The epistemological reading presents practice as derivative, as an expression of an ahistorical essence. This is consistent with Gadamer's deep respect for both Aristotelian and Kantian essentialism: the human is regarded as the essential subject and practice as the expressive unfolding of its essential nature. According to the ontological reading, however, practice is primary, a mode of doing or engagement out of which the human and its existential possibilities emerge. Practice is the central agency and the human subject its effect of that activity. Indeed, the implication is that practice not only generates the subject but also empowers it.[47]

Much in Gadamer's hermeneutics tends to this ontological reading of practice. It is consistent with the historical basis of his philosophical orientation, and its advantage is that it permits a radically formative if not transformative account of practice, one that regards humanity not as an essential truth but as an emergent work in process. This study will argue that with regard to the questions of hermeneutics and humanity, the radical account of practice is the more productive. The ontological reading of practice sets its activities in the context of history, culture and tradition such that practices of interpretation become integral to the exploration of existential possibilities. Such interpretive explorations probe, question and extend what has been and might yet be understood as the human and as humanity. The ontological reading of practice reveals a key feature of Gadamer's thinking: triangulating the concepts practice, humanity and essence enables a shift from traditional metaphysical notions of essence to a more radical conception of essentiality. Whereas an essence in the classical sense precedes its historical expression, essentiality is built up in and through the historical. In response to the contingencies of its environment, a life form establishes *repertoires* of response out of which predictable patterns and narrative signatures of engagement develop. On the basis of this, a dialectic of continuity and disruption, a sense of hermeneutic identity or subjecthood emerges and, once established, becomes an effective though challengeable interactive agency in its own right. Essentiality involves the notion of an effective interpretative agency or *Dasein* emerging from metaphysically contingent processes of becoming allowing it to become, in Gadamer's phrase, 'more what it essentially is', that is, a consolidation of its actual and potential possibilities. This is where Gadamer's discourse on *mimesis* is so

---

47 This is also discussed in Chapter 5.

effective. The philosophical anthropology implicit in Gadamer's hermeneutical ontology of practice promises an account of the human and its relation to the humanities as mutually moderating (and potentially transformative) processes. The future legitimacy of the humanities requires such an account of inter-interpretive agency and offers a number of arguments in its favour.

8. Humanities, hermeneutics and transformative questions

To raise a question is, phenomenologically speaking, to anticipate an answer. If, as Wittgenstein suggests, a question exists only where an answer exists, to ask a question is to invoke the return to consciousness of what to a degree we already know: a sense of what a possible answer might look like. To bring the future of hermeneutics and the humanities into question is therefore to anticipate (draw out) future outcomes. This emphasizes, once again, the role of practice in our discussion for it is only by engaging more intensely in our practices that what is implicitly at play within our pre-understandings becomes apparent. With this in mind, this chapter will argue that the humanities and hermeneutics have to address the following three points.

1. The fate of both hermeneutics and the humanities is indissoluble. Although the legitimacy of many of their underwriting assumptions is in serious question, it is not so much a series of direct answers that are required but more questioning. *Being placed-in-question is not necessarily negative: questioning is the raison d'être of creative practices.* The key question is what the practice of questioning gives rise to. Being brought by questioning to see a subject matter differently is precisely what hermeneutics and the humanities undertake. The practice of questioning anticipates that the future will acquaint us more perfectly with what we presently know imperfectly. In philosophical hermeneutics, Socratic questioning loses the abrasive cynicism that Nietzsche feared and becomes a gentler, participatory way of hoping for more to become known.
2. To be true to its vocation of disclosing the meaningful, hermeneutics must not only constantly call the nature of its relationship to philosophy into question but also remain vigilant about keeping its own meaning in question. This study defends the view that hermeneutics is not a theory. Rather, it entails a wide range of interpretive procedures the default

outcome of which is hermeneutical experience, that is, a significant shift in the movement and orientation of an agency's understanding.

3. Radicalizing questioning processes in both hermeneutics and the humanities suggests that it is not how these disciplines are defined that matters but what they do, that is, what their effects are. If the fate of hermeneutics and the humanities is bound together it is because they embrace practices of keeping in and keeping open to question. These practices maintain the differential spaces of interpretation upon which understanding's movement depends. In the essay 'The Future of Hermeneutics', Vattimo argues that the discipline must transform itself into a practical philosophy, a philosophy of *praxis*.[48] It is an argument with which this essay is in part sympathetic, though much will depend on the meaning of *praxis*. Our argument will show how hermeneutic practices are operationally so constituted as to constantly call themselves into question. This negative capability is their transformative virtue.

This chapter has outlined and discussed the conceptual grounds on which hermeneutics and the humanities have fallen into question. It was noted that philosophical hermeneutics knows no systematic starting point for engaging in debates that are already underway. In hermeneutical practice, where one begins is not as important as that one begins for it is only by beginning that one meets with what has already started. Practices hermeneutically conceived are always eccentric: they stand outside themselves, rooted in an interrelational mode of being that impels them beyond their own centre.[49] Given the ontological setting of any hermeneutical engagement, reflective practice is immediately connected to what informs it. The speculative charge of such engagements concerns, as we have seen, their inferential capacity to illuminate the philosophical territory from which they spring.

If hermeneutics and the humanities are in question, clarity should be demanded about the nature of the questions in play. Hermeneutically speaking, these questions do not arise *ex nihilo* but always from an extant perspectival field which both contextualizes and guides reflective engagement. Wittgenstein's observation about philosophical sicknesses is pertinent. What if philosophical and creative engagement with actuality is 'sickened' by the very pre-reflective orientations which guide the engagement?

---

48 See Gianni Vattimo, 'The Future of Hermeneutics', in *The Routledge Companion to Hermeneutics*, ed. Jeff Malpas and Hans-Helmuth Gander (London, Routledge, 2015), 721–7.
49 Rowan Williams, *Being Human* (London: SPCK, 2018), 35.

> The sickness of a time is cured by an alteration in the form of life of human beings, and it was possible for the sickness of philosophical problems to get cured only through a changed mode of thought and life.[50]

The lead questions unsettling hermeneutics and the humanities are, perhaps, not themselves the central issue but are symptoms of a deeper malaise. It is, perversely, 'the devices and desires of our own hearts' which bring certain subject matters and ways of being into question, not that these predicaments are questionable in themselves. For thinkers such as Nietzsche and Wittgenstein, this perversity is a symptom of life's sickness, of its propensity to develop metaphysical and epistemological expectations which render existence questionable thereby estranging itself from its own actuality. The concerns which have brought hermeneutics and the humanities into disrepute are contemporary expressions of this malaise. The remaining part of this chapter considers the conceptual misunderstandings which have brought hermeneutics and the humanities into disrepute.

The methodological demands which bring the epistemological status of hermeneutics and the humanities into question concern (1) their lack of procedural certainty, (2) the finitude and incompleteness of their understanding, (3) the inability of interpretation to arrive at a final and decisive conclusion, (4) the absence of agreed methods and (5) the contestability of their appeals to universal meaning and truth. However, considered from an ontological perspective, none of these question areas are in themselves questionable. To the contrary, they reflect central aspects of our ontological predicament. They announce what Heidegger describes as our facticity, the factual condition or limitations of our existence. From an ontological perspective, these features describe what is the case and not, as Nietzsche would put it, what ought not be the case. Clearly, from an epistemological point of view, finitude, uncertainty and incompleteness of understanding reflect negativities and difficulties beyond formal resolution. And yet, considered from an ontological perspective, these issues operate as negative capabilities: the finitude of understanding allows it to become more, interpretation's lack of definitive closure permits the questions it addresses to remain open whilst the absence of foundational meaning permits the negotiable range of what can become meaningful to expand. Epistemological negativities tend to inhibit practical engagement and depress the movement of

---

50 Ludwig Wittgenstein, *Bemerkungen über die Grundlagen der Mathematik*, Remarks on the Foundations of Mathematics, ed. G. H. von Wright, R. Rhees, and G. E. M. Anscombe (Oxford: Blackwell, 1956), Vol. 11, 23.

understanding, whereas negative capability, considered ontologically, encourages deeper practical involvement and accelerates the movement of understanding. Wittgenstein's reference to sickness concerns the capacity of epistemology to demote what is ontologically primary (*Dasein* and its practical engagements) to a secondary world of appearance and to promote what is in ontological terms secondary (theory) to primary status. This gives rise to a central question. If factical existence is not at fault for being what it is, what brings it into question? What disposes us to regard the factical incompleteness of understanding as grounds for claiming the impossibility of understanding rather than as an invitation to achieve a completer though never complete understanding? In blunt terms, what is it that persuades us to see the key characteristics of hermeneutics – its incompleteness, its lack of conceptual transparency and the endlessness of its interpretation – as epistemologically negative rather than as ontologically positive? The issue here for Wittgenstein and Nietzsche is far from inconsequential. What is at stake is a potential cultural disaster. Their argument arises from a complex overlay of points which collectively form a genealogical critique of epistemology.

That which renders hermeneutics and the humanities questionable is a disposition towards an epistemological imperative that for a discipline to be taken seriously it must meet rigorous universal requirements regarding its truth-claims and the legitimacy of its methodological procedures. Irrespective of whether these disciplines should be asked to meet such criteria, it is plain that they could not be compliant. To insist that the claims of hermeneutical practices be susceptible to methods of universal verification is to demand something they cannot give. It is in their nature to be contingent, incomplete and finite and, what is more, their development depends on them remaining so. Achieving epistemological closure would halt the movement upon which finite understanding depends which, from a hermeneutical perspective, would be an ethical disaster. Nietzsche is alert to the underlying problem.

To ask that hermeneutics practices comply with conventional modes of epistemological and procedural verification derives from the implicit expectancy that they should. Nietzsche and Vattimo recognize this demand as flawed as it culminates in the despair of nihilism. Factive existence is incommensurable with the demands of epistemological certainty. About this Nietzsche is blunt: becoming and knowledge mutually exclude one another (*Werden und Erkenntnis schliessen sich aus*).[51] Rarely does it occur to the knowing subject that

---

51 WP 517.

its criteria of truth and meaning are at fault. More commonly, it is assumed that actuality itself is amiss because of its non-compliance. Nietzsche perceives that the damaging consequence of this faulty assumption is the de-incentivizing of practical engagement with factical existence and its practices. If factical existence is perceived as a false, apparent world (a direct consequence of prioritizing the epistemological over the ontological), why engage with the meaningless? The danger inherent within this epistemological prejudice is existential and cultural. (1) It promotes disregard for those contingent everyday practices upon which everyday engagement with actuality always has and always will depend. (2) The nihilistic demand that hermeneutic practices meet with unrealizable epistemological criteria undermines confidence in the contingent historical and linguistic practices that have not only shaped meaningful frameworks for our existence but have also provided those upon which the enhancement of future understanding depends. This is not to say that traditional practices should not be questioned. Questioning is essential to their mode of becoming. The issue is why are they being questioned? Are they being questioned to reveal further determinations of meaningfulness within the infinite potential they hold, or are they being questioned to determine their epistemic status? If the latter, only disappointment and alienation will result. The philosophical error here is to ask that factive life be judged by epistemological criteria that could never apply to it.

Understanding the grounds of this error is one thing but achieving such understanding changes nothing about factical existence. It remains what it always was, finite and uncertain. The decisive point concerns, what it is in our way of life that inclines us to adopt a way of thinking which estranges from the very actuality we would understand? Factical existence cannot be judged to be at fault for being what it is. Such understanding changes nothing and yet, it in another sense, it changes everything. It does not effect a change in the actuality of finitude and uncertainty but it can effect a change in how we come to think of our existential predicament and, in so doing, start to displace the conditions which promote a life-estranging nihilism. This opens the way to a complete rethink of the legitimacy of hermeneutics and the humanities. Wittgenstein comments in this regard,

> The way to solve the problem you see in life is to live in a way that will make what is problematic disappear.[52]

---

52 Ludwig Wittgenstein, *Culture and Value* (Oxford: Basil Blackwell, 1980), 27e.

What then has to change in our mode of thinking and being that might allow us to celebrate change, finitude and uncertainty and see in them the basis of expanding our engagement with actuality?

In a note of 1946, Wittgenstein offers a résumé of the difficulties.

> Getting hold of the difficulty deep down is what is hard.
>
> If it is grasped near the surface it simply remains the difficulty it was. It has to be pulled out by the roots; and that involves our beginning to think about these things in a new way, The change is as decisive as, for example, that from alchemical to the chemical way of thinking. The new way of thinking is what is hard to establish. Once the new way of thinking has been established, the old problems vanish; indeed they become hard to recapture. For they go with our way of expressing ourselves and, if we clothe ourselves in a new form of expression, the old problems are discarded along with the old garment.[53]

The problem is actually not 'deep' down but so close to the 'surface' that we often fail to see it. The problem is those unspoken frameworks of assumption that allow a question to emerge as credible in the first place. *We fail to see that that which renders what is in itself not a problem as a problem is itself the problem.* It lies in what Nietzsche describes as the metaphysics of grammar, that is, in the words and concepts we use to describe actuality as finite, incomplete and of indefinite meaning. These transmit unstated metaphysical and religious prejudices incompatible with the actuality they are used to describe. The problem, therefore, resides in the orientation of the philosophical and religious heritage *within* the words we use to describe actuality as finite and uncertain.

Our foregoing arguments suggest that at the root of the negative perceptions of hermeneutics and the humanities is a fear of the uncertain and finite which much philosophical and religious tradition has tried to placate with comforting fictions. The realization that it is this inheritance which nurtures a negative disposition towards factic existence does not, however, render it any the less finite or uncertain. The challenge is, as Wittgenstein suggests, to explore what it is in a way of life that disposes it to see as negative that which is not in itself negative. At this juncture, our argument turns away from hermeneutical practices negatively perceived towards a confident reaffirmation of their potentially culturally transformative worth.

Hermeneutical practices including the humanities can, on the one hand, analyse what in a way of life disposes it towards devaluing finitude and uncertainty as meaningless and, on the other, also imagine and experiment with ways of thinking that respond to finitude and uncertainty as positive invitations

---

53 Ibid., 48e.

to 'become more'. Contemporary negative perceptions of hermeneutics and the humanities may indicate the nihilistic consequences of disappointed metaphysical beliefs but, nevertheless, the ability of the humanities to create other ways of inhabiting both the uncertain and the finite is key to overcoming the nihilistic estrangement from actuality that undermines belief in the cognitive worth of hermeneutic practices. From an existential point of view, Nietzsche's experimentalism (his advocacy of not just different ways of thinking but also different diets and ways of living) assumes a therapeutic status. It emphasizes the priority of practice in exploring possible cures to that sickness which sees actuality as a problem when it is not.

From the broader perspective of our exploration of why hermeneutics and the humanities are negatively perceived, Wittgenstein's distinction between ways of thinking that problematize actuality and those which do not is useful for two reasons. First, it reveals, ironically, that it is the very insistence that hermeneutical practices should secure truth and meaning that renders them problematic. New ways of thinking are needed to overcome this negativity towards what are in fact life-forming practices. Second, more telling is that Wittgenstein's differentiation between problematizing and non-problematizing ways of thinking about actuality maps onto the primary distinctions that have structured Chapter 1 of this study. The following points are relevant:

1. Wittgenstein's distinction sharpens the contrast between the epistemological perspective, which prioritizes knowing (subjective) consciousness over being, and the ontological perspective, which prioritizes practical being (*Dasein*) over consciousness. The epistemological prejudice is a principle of deficit. Facticity from within the epistemological perspective always appears to lack something, to resist conceptual capture and to be always falling away from the truth. Actuality appears in consequence as deficient. However, when viewed from the ontological perspective, facticity emerges as abundant. Whereas the epistemological perspective problematizes actuality, the principle of ontological surplus recognizes that within finite existence there is always more to know and more to become.
2. The contrasting principles of epistemological deficit and ontological surplus are paralleled in Gadamer's aesthetics between discourses of *imitatio* (deficit) and discourses of *mimesis* (surplus). *Imitatio* equates to the aesthetics of representation (*Vorstellung*) and *mimesis* to the aesthetic as an emergent event (*Darstellung*). *Imitatio* considered as re-presentation

(making a copy) relates to deficit: in relation to its original, the image is necessarily imperfect. As with Plato's forms, the original is always ontologically independent of its copy. *Imitatio* problematizes images and the actuality to which they belong as being deficient in relation to the true world of being which they allegedly reflect. In contrast, the mimetic image (*Darstellung*) is the original and is not independent of its processes of coming forth. The image does not copy or reproduce an independent reality. The being of the mimetic image resides in the history of its effects, in the processes by means of which each new articulation of its nature allows it to become more. The essential contrast between *imitatio* and *mimesis* is now evident. Within epistemological frameworks of deficit, the multiplication of interpretation distracts from the original. In ontologies of surplus, it enhances and extends the actuality of the emergent original.

3. The correlations of *imitatio* with epistemological deficit and *mimesis* with ontological surplus demonstrate that Gadamer's analysis of key aesthetic categories is of greater consequence than he imagined. It points towards both a negative and an affirmative poetics of knowledge, each interpreting the same phenomena in different ways. Because of its non-compliance with what counts as truth, the poetics of deficit condemns the actuality of finitude as a false and apparent world, indeed, as something to be avoided and condemned as meaningless. By way of contrast, the poetics of surplus celebrates finitude and limitation as the basis of expanding the possibilities of understanding. Whereas the perspective of deficit (*imitatio*) expresses a poetics of loss, the ontology of surplus (*mimesis*) suggests a poetics of expectant growth, of potentials to be realized. The issue is, as Wittgenstein implies, not just with the words that we use to describe actuality but with how those words dispose us towards it.

4. Epistemologies of deficit and ontologies of surplus are built on another contrast at the heart of philosophical hermeneutics. It differentiates between subject-based epistemologies, which by giving knowing consciousness priority over being and its objects separate the knowing subject from the actuality it exists within, and interrelational epistemologies, which prioritize being over the subject. Epistemologies of deficit seek methodological control over their subject matter whereas ontologies of surplus endeavour to discover what ways a subject matter can become more. Ontologies of surplus affirm Gadamer's axiom that knowing consciousness (*Bewusstsein*) is more being (*Sein*) than knowing (*wissen*).

5. Unlike subject–object epistemologies which regard time as an objection to existence, interactive participatory epistemologies prioritize ontological surplus and esteem time as the medium within which new determinations of being arise. From within the perspective of epistemological deficit, time separates and distances the knowing subject from the intelligible reality it yearns to be one with, whilst within ontologies of surplus the hermeneutic agent is allowed to engage with the potentials within actuality more fully.
6. The axiom that knowing consciousness is more being than knowing is the basis of the hermeneutical principle of incommensurability expressed by the formula x equals x+. The principle encapsulates the summary differentiation between those ways of thinking that affirm actuality or which promote estrangement from factic existence. It simply asserts that in ontologies of surplus in which being always transcends knowing, no interpretation can exhaustively capture the totality of a subject matter. A subject matter is always more than its interpretation. The principle of incommensurability provides a litmus test for Wittgenstein's differentiation between ways of life that affirm factical existence and those that fear it. Does the principle of hermeneutic incommensurability represent an objection to existence by putting the truth of subject matters beyond our grasp, or does the differential gap between a subject matter and our knowing of it establish the conceptual space in which more of that subject matter can be known over time? In both instances, the givenness of incommensurability remains the same. What differentiates them is that whereas one framework of thinking sees incommensurability as an objection to factical life, the other celebrates it for inciting the quest to know more of our being.

Before considering the consequences of these points, it is worth noting the systemic symmetry between them. The negative reading of incommensurability aligns (1) with those epistemologies of deficit which regard truth as beyond human grasp, (2) with the aesthetics of *imitatio* which posits an image's original in a conceivable but unattainable world of intelligible being, and (3) with epistemologies of control that suppose that the knowing subject is cut off from and distinct from the world it seeks to know. The positive appraisal of incommensurability is clearly congruent with those ontologies of surplus that affirm the possibility of expanding horizons of knowing, with the aesthetics of *mimesis* and *Darstellung* which regard the image as adding to the being of its subject matter and with those participatory epistemologies which stress the interactive and interrelational nature of being. Though sound economic and political argument favours the broad civil value of the humanities, the deep prejudices informing the negative perception of hermeneutics and the humanities will not be dislodged until the 'way of life' sustaining them is dismantled. Before we discuss this, a further contrast between negative and positive presentations of incommensurability is pertinent.

The differing responses to incommensurability betray two contrasting modes of world orientation. (1) The negative evaluation of incommensurability reflects an inclination towards a dualist ontology involving the irreducibility of the knowing subject and the known object. (2) The positive evaluation tends to a monistic ontology in which the *act* is primary. In (1) the distanciation of knowing is primary, and in (2) the participatory act is central. (2) Enables us to affirm the ontological priority of possibility over the actual, a principle that is arguably implicit in Heidegger and Gadamer's thinking but which becomes more explicit in the hermeneutics of Paul Ricouer.[54] The following remarks about the ontological priority of the possible over the actual may seem remote from contemporary debates about the humanities but it is above all the nihilistic consequences of neglecting this principle that alarm Nietzsche, Rosenzweig and Wittgenstein.

Philosophical hermeneutics inherits from Heidegger an eventual ontology; Being manifests itself in its manifold *appearings*, in its comings-to-be and passings away. *Being resides in the actualization of its possibilities but can never be reduced to its actions.* The being of actuality is one of surplus: it always emanates from past future possibilities and already points towards its future unrealized possibilities. The argument is made clearer by a brief reference to the notion of the subject matter.

Subject matters understood as the key concerns or the concepts that draw our concern – health, justice, love, truth – are entities which like Plato's forms always transcend their particular historical instantiations. They do so because each instantiation offers only one historical perspective on the infinite possibilities for meaning that a given subject matter holds. In the case of a subject matter such as 'economics' the term has revealed potential meanings which ancient traders, Florentine bankers and nineteenth-century speculators could never have collectively imagined. Subject matters are logically speaking always in excess of their concrete instantiations. The transcendence of their historical

---

54 See James Fodor, *Christian Hermeneutics and the Refiguring of Theology* (Oxford: Clarendon Press, 1995); and Paul S. Fiddes, *The Promised End, Eschatology in Theology and Literature* (Oxford: Blackwells, 2000).

actualization is double. The actualization of a particular meaning does not exhaust other past possibilities for meaning that a subject matter will logically carry within itself. To the contrary, every actualized meaning carries into the present past possibilities for meaning yet to be actualized. On the same grounds, the actualization of a particular meaning cannot exhaust the range of future possible meanings a subject matter will hold. Indeed, a present actualization will bring the realization of certain possible future alignments of meanings closer. Ontologically speaking, the priority of possibility over act means that neither future nor past is remote from the present: both effect its possible choices and what those choices bring into being. The infinite (understood as the totality of past and future possibilities) co-inheres within the finite act. Put the other way around, it is the act that upholds the ever-present infinity of possibilities that both sustains and yet transcends all individual acts. This emphasizes once again the ontological importance of practice.

It is in and through the creative acts of practice that the past's effects and future's possibilities are maintained and generated within the present. By dissolving the epistemological dualism that sustains the negative reading of incommensurability, participatory ontology serves to dismantle the grounds of existential estrangement from actuality. Within participatory epistemologies and relational ontologies, actuality, agency and action are not separable. The actions of the practitioner are the actions of being and in being so continue to uphold and unfold the infinity of past and future possibilities co-inhering within every act. Nietzsche's and Wittgenstein's reasons for worrying about the de-habilitating effects of nihilism are clear. Anything that undermines confidence in practical action undermines how life and its possibilities unfold. The movement (actions) upon which the life of understanding depends is weakened. From an ontological perspective, the act holds open the differential space between x and x+ and in so doing, it allows the past and future being of possibility to co-inhere within it shaping the present. Though any act is dependent on the differential space between x (the finite determinations of a subject matter) and x+ (the infinity of possible meanings that reside within it), from an ontological perspective x and x+ are codependent. Life-denying nihilism, however, does not regard the incommensurable space between x and x+ as a space of possibility. Accordingly, the Platonic mind, the Christian soul and the Cartesian subject all feel barred from knowing the intelligible realm upon which the alleged truth and meaning of their existence depend. The incommensurability between x and x+ is not grasped as a space of possibility but is perceived as a disabling space, a place of exile which excludes the subject from ever knowing the truth of x. This returns us to the key question. Given that at the heart of both the negative and the positive readings of incommensurability lies the same differential space, what is it that inclines one form of life to see in it a space of possibility and another to see it as a space of disablement?

Both Nietzsche and Wittgenstein realize that a solution to overcoming the devaluation of finitude and uncertainty lies not in a change of philosophy per se (conscious reflection is after all but an effect of underlying interpretive orientations) but in a change of existential practices able to promote life-affirmative ways of thinking. Nietzsche's experimentalism tables a philosophical therapeutic intended to break addiction to metaphysical comforts. This implies that considerable and painstaking intellectual effort is required both to understand what aspects of our mode of life promote belief in metaphysical prejudices and which other aspects favour a positive orientation towards uncertainty and finitude. Both philosophers sense the need for a great 'unlearning', a dismantling of those intellectual and cultural habits which incline us towards a negative assessment of factical existence. These issues may seem remote from why the humanities and hermeneutical practices are currently perceived negatively. Yet, to the contrary, they are fundamental to exposing the 'world-picture' which pre-reflectively disposes us towards either a negative perception of incommensurability with its epistemologies of deficit or towards a positive affirmation of life in all its finitude and uncertainty.

The words finitude and uncertainty are not in themselves negatively weighted. They simply evoke the restless nature of factical existence. However, the continuing influence of certain linguistic, theological and philosophical traditions freights these words with negativity. For Gadamer it is not just the afterlife of religious values but an underlying contemporary ideological preference for technologies of control that devalues concepts of likelihood and possibility in favour of those of certainty and predictability. Wittgenstein fears that once the quest for certainty and predictability drives philosophical theory, our practices 'sicken unto death'. The very search for certainty in life will in all certainty estrange us from the practices upon which the movement of understanding depends. This exposes the deep irony within the negative perception of hermeneutics and the humanities. The demand for methodological and conceptual clarity stems from the worry that these disciplines lack any formal procedure to decide between competing modes of interpretation. Yet it is this presupposition that is problematic. Because of the demand that hermeneutic practices should be based on certain and confirmable procedures of operation that can never be met, the very drive to render the procedures of hermeneutics and the humanities more rigorous only renders them more opaque. *The cure for such 'metaphysical sickness' is to refrain from asking for justifications and truth norms where none can be given.* The finitude and contingency of existence must no longer be regarded as an epistemological negative but valued for providing the ontological grounds for maintaining understanding's movement and expansion. This requires both confidence in the practices that promote such movement and belief in the value of their transformative effects (*Bildung*). Achieving the final end is not what matters. The worthwhileness of such practices resides in the transformative outcomes their continual pursuit achieves. To insist that the humanities and hermeneutics submit to inappropriate and unrealizable methodological criteria only serves to undermine confidence in the worthwhileness of their practices and to weaken their transformative potential. The implication is clear. To overcome such negativity, subject-centred epistemologies need to be displaced by frameworks of thought that allow the hermeneutic agent or 'subject' to be integrated into its environment as a participant rather than removed from it as an epistemological sovereign in exile. Given the latent nihilism within subject-centred epistemologies, the case for adopting a regional ontology and a participatory epistemology is pressing. It would initiate the gradual displacement of those underlying epistemological prejudices which needlessly devalue the humanities. The impossible demands of epistemological justification should be 'knowingly' passed by. In this context, Wittgenstein's phrase, 'What we cannot speak about we must pass over in silence', acquires a life-enabling directness and simplicity.[55] Two suggestions will close our consideration of the factors which underwrite the negative reception of hermeneutics and the humanities. We need (1) a confident affirmation of the cognitive worth of hermeneutic practices and (2) a negative hermeneutics to establish a speculative philosophy of action (practice).

Regarding (1), the realization that actuality cannot be condemned as meaningless enables hermeneutical practices to identify and explore those linguistic, cultural and religious commitments which underwrite the belief that factical existence is meaningless. This allows the humanities and other creative disciplines to experiment with ways of living and thinking which embrace finitude and uncertainty as incentives to expand understanding. Once the epistemologies of deficit attached to them are abandoned, the very characteristics which have brought hermeneutics and the humanities into disrepute turn to their advantage:

---

55 Ludwig Wittgenstein, *Tractatus Logico Philosophicus* (London: Routledge & Kegan Paul, 1961), Sec. 7.

the finitude and uncertainty of factical existence allows these disciplines to unfold their as-yet-unrealized possibilities. Concerning (2), a speculative theory of practice is central to the development of negative hermeneutics. The speculative is relational by definition and ties the interpretive act not just to the spoken but also to the unspoken horizons of meaning upon which the intelligibility of the spoken depends. The interpretive act brings a totality of meaning into play, without being able to express it totally. Rowan Williams offers an almost Heideggerian account of the disclosive power of words. Words offer a coherent context for human living, a credible environment for action and imagination and plausible means of connecting narratives, practices and codes of behaviour. Words offer a world to live in.[56] Here we can insert a marker for an important aspect of our later argument.

Words do not just a bring world into being: their grammatical structures establish ways of being. A language world is not just an ambient space but sustains ways of travel towards purposes and goals. The Germanic origins of the noun 'world' (*w(e)oruld*) indicate a lived span within which the sense of a life unfolds.[57] Words structure ways of life. They enable the hodological mapping of a life-world, *hodos* from the Greek meaning way or pathway. These, as we shall argue, establish hermeneutical vectors or ways of travel with the attendant joys and disappointments of their trajectories. Gadamer insists that it is language's systemic anticipation of completion (*Vorgriff der Vollendung*) that structures the temporal projections of a such a life-world, giving it its sense of purpose and direction. 'Language is not just one of man's possessions in the world, rather on it, depends the fact that man has a world at all.'[58] 'To have a world' is to be bound into that world and its way of doing things. Language's anticipation of completion bestows a way of life (*hodos*) with its possibility for narrative shape and direction, allowing it to understand and come to itself through its forward projections. In establishing a world, words enable 'living in the broadest sense'.[59] In other words, words and their grammars of structuring temporal experience set the conditions of practice: 'practice means . . . the actuation of a way of life that is led in a certain way (*bios*)'.[60] Most important of all for our future argument, words and their anticipatory structures set the limits of a practice and establish the conditions for surmounting of its failures.

---

56 Rowan Williams, *The Edge of Words* (London: Bloomsbury, 2014), 52–3.
57 See Oxford Dictionary of English, 2nd edition, 2006.
58 TM 443.
59 Gadamer, 'Hermeneutics as Practical Philosophy', 230.
60 Ibid.

Picking up on a previous point, given the intimate connection of the finite and the infinite within linguistic meaning, the interpretive act inevitably opens new connections and possibilities. Confident involvement in language-being and its practices is key to opening such possibilities. However, it is not just movement within a language world that is important but what such movement facilitates within and between language horizons, that is, comparison, challenges to memory, alternatives to established ways of thinking, indeed, achieving the very conditions which render *Bildung* and the reflective character of hermeneutic experience possible. Gadamer's language ontology offers the basis for developing an account of the speculative act within hermeneutic ontology emphasizing once again why the notion of practice is so central to our argument.

The linking of the finite and the infinite within language-being cleverly undermines the ontological dualism which sustains existential estrangement from the finite and uncertain. Nietzsche, Wittgenstein and philosophical hermeneutics are clearly committed to a monistic ontology that affirms this-worldly change as the only actuality. This establishes a limit horizon for negative hermeneutics: there is no other intelligible infinity of being beyond this world of ceaseless change. Such arguments do not simply dissolve the question of the infinite but relocate it within their monistic ontology. This is made clear by the formal contrast between the negative and positive responses to the question of incommensurability. The negative response is built on the assumption that the finite being is incommensurate with the infinite being of metaphysics, a realm from which all finite beings are ontologically excluded. However, the positive reading supposes that although the finite and the infinite are epistemologically incommensurable, ontologically speaking they are not. The speculative character of language-being establishes the co-inherence of the finite and infinite. Neither are reduced to the other, and yet neither can be thought without the other. Without any relation to the speculative, finite utterances of words and concepts would fragment, lose their coherence across time and become incapable of invoking cross reference and inference. The speculative power of words makes manifest the infinite totality of meaning which binds each finite expression into bodies of actual and possible relations of meanings capable of infinite variation. This allows incommensurability positively read to be understood as an ever-dynamic differential space. In its continuous unfolding of finite meanings, every act of saying maintains the differential space in and through which the infinite (understood as a totality of possible meaning) sustains the every day. It is, in other words, in the ceaseless coming to be and falling way of finite meanings that the infinite play of speculative meaning maintains itself.

Within hermeneutic thought that act of invoking x always has speculative repercussions, that is, it invokes x+. This brings us to an important juncture of argument with regard to practice. When a subject matter is invoked, it is not just specific past determinations of meaning that are brought into the present but also those as-yet-unrealized possibilities for future meaning that past determinations of meaning to hold within themselves. The differential spaces opened by language's speculative unfolding not only connect past determinations of meaning with the present but also open the present to those actual but as-yet-unrealized possibilities for new thinking and ways of being that lie within past transmissions. The consequentiality of language's speculative being is of inestimable extent. Not only are present practices shaped by subject matters transmitted from the past but their future depends on the continued unfolding of the unrealized alignments and modifications of meaning and living within their transmissions. The speculative character of language-being not only allows the future possibilities of the past to inhabit the present but, at the same time, also permits the potentialities of the future to be logically prefigured in the present. From a hermeneutic perspective, it is not just the multiplication of different alignments of meaning that is important but also the comparative insights they make possible by bringing a multiplicity of ways of seeing into a greater (though never complete) coherence. False beliefs about the meaninglessness of human practices threaten to demotivate and prompt disengagement from the very practices that can transform existence. The movement of insights and concepts on which transformative understanding depends is jeopardized. It is, then, critically important to dismantle those religious and cultural frameworks of thought which instil a negative attitude towards the finite and the uncertain. This is why negative hermeneutics and the humanities are vital to overcoming the metaphysical sickness at the heart of the present estrangement from these disciplines. Of course, a positive reading of incommensurability does not diminish the ever-present finitude and uncertainty of existence. However, this is to misunderstand their importance. The finitude of understanding goads us towards a completer understanding, and the effects of uncertainty can be mitigated by growing that existential confidence that derives from engaging and trusting in life's practices. Does this not pose a contradiction?

Gadamer once suggested that we can never escape our shadows. The argument that in order to overcome the negative interpretation of incommensurability we need to displace those 'deep' religious and cultural ways of thinking that dispose us towards a negative understanding of finitude and the uncertain seems to suggest that an escape from the past is possible. Yet such a way of thinking would seem deeply un-hermeneutical, as if we could step away from our former shadows. If we could, we would become hermeneutically groundless, without orientation, in mid-air so to speak. Shadows at least indicate possible directions. However, the issue is, perhaps, not becoming un-hermeneutical but not becoming hermeneutical enough. As Heidegger appreciated it is a daunting task to think 'being' without the distorting influence of Christian metaphysics but, here, philosophical hermeneutics is arguably more tractable as a constructive rather than as deconstructive tool. What the past transmits to us as a subject matter is always a subject matter articulated in a specific and determinate way. This does not privilege the received interpretation since the latter is the actualization of one of many other logically possible interpretations. The important point here is that because of the speculative interrelationality of word and creative act, the transmission to the present of any one possible reading of a subject matter also transmits prefigurings of other logically possible entailments. These hold open the possibility of new alignments of meaning that might allow us to think about finitude and uncertainty differently. The past does not just shape the present but also presents it with its future options. It is, in other words, only by becoming more hermeneutical – seeing through historical limitations of received meaning – that hermeneutics can animate unrealized and critically potent alternative readings within any transmitted subject matter. In this respect the humanities and the human sciences are critically important to both maintaining and transmitting such cognitive possibilities and releasing what is at play within them through continued hermeneutical and creative practice.

9. Negative hermeneutics and the accentuation of the positive

A central claim of this chapter is that hermeneutical thinking is grounded in the constant interplay between foreground issues and background concerns. With regard to the distinction between intensive and extensive reference discussed in the Introduction, it is not enough to offer counterarguments against the negative perceptions of hermeneutics and humanities one opposes. Such negative perceptions do not arise *ex nihilo* but are underpinned by ways of life able to sustain their values by promoting conceptual frameworks sympathetic to their interests. Formal refutation of such positions does little to dismantle the existential circumstances which promote them in the first place.

What is necessary from the point of view of our argument is get to grips with the conditions which nurture a negative attitude towards hermeneutics and the humanities. The ontological and epistemological outlooks attached to negative hermeneutics are crucial in this respect. Within the ontology of language-being, negation is a device able to expose the existential frameworks which gird the surface arguments deployed against hermeneutics and the humanities. The effectiveness of negative hermeneutics at uncovering the underlying outlooks which sustain a formal position depends upon language-being's assertion of a totality of ever-changing etymological and conceptual relations. On the assumption of this truth, negative hermeneutics is wedded in part to a hermeneutics of suspicion: it is impossible to be definitive about any linguistic meaning. However, negation is welded to the positive principle that any meaning can 'mean more'. This breaks open attempts at conceptual and linguistic closure by ideology, blind faith or unthinking prejudice. Negative hermeneutics operationalizes the claim that there is always more to a meaning that one might suppose.

The claim reflects the foundational axiom of negative hermeneutics, namely, that all meaning has an ontological excess or, as we have expressed it elsewhere, x always equals x+. The axiom is pertinent to the distinction between *apophatic* and *apophantic* speech which, although it derives from Modern Theology, Gadamer inherits and adapts from Heidegger. The interplay between the *apophatic* and the *apophantic* is essential to the workings of negative hermeneutics. In this interplay, language-being assumes an enabling ontological primacy: the *apophatic* is primary and the *apophantic* secondary. The relation between the two is asymmetric. As noted earlier, Heidegger emphasizes that the *apophantic* language characteristic of subject epistemologies does not belong to a different language world to that characterized by the *apophatic* language of poetry and literature.[61] To the contrary, it is a derivative and hence dependent form of the *apophatic* but with all nuance, innuendo or poetic allusion removed for the sake of analytic discourse. The *apophantic* and the *apophatic* are not different language worlds but interpenetrate each other affording shifts in the movement of hermeneutic understanding. Within negative hermeneutics, the transcendence of the *apophantic* by the apophatic has a clear procedural implication: apophantic terms always mean more than they state. Negation becomes a device for opening the speculative dimensions of meaning that the *apophantic* tends to conceal. Negative hermeneutics negates all certainty in language by affirming the unavoidable incommensurability between a subject matter and its interpretations. Negation (the insistence that a subject matter can

---

[61] Heidegger, *Being and Time*. Part 5, Sec. 33.

always mean more) endeavours to break open sedimented meaning and lift the restraints of finitude on the movement of understanding.

The relation between *apophantic* and *apophatic* structures of meaning in language suggests a part-whole structure animated by three levels of negativity. The first level of negation is when either reflection or the movements of language itself reveal that what appears to be a fixed stable and self-enclosed meaning is not at all but part of a totality of other possible meanings. The second level of negation involves re-reading the particular as an instance of one of the many possibilities of meaning available within the horizon of language-being: the particular is negated by its status as a bearer of other possibilities for meaning within the whole. The third level of negation entails a reflective return from the abstractions of the whole back to the concrete circumstances of the particular synthesizing of levels one and two. The third level entails seeing a particular as *both* a carrier of a totality of meaning *and* a totality of meaning particularizing itself. This double perspective of seeing the particular pointing to the speculative and seeing a speculative whole particularize itself in singular instances is an achievement of the accomplished practitioner which will be extensively discussed in later chapters. However, the central question underpinning our presentation of negativity remains: if the negation of finite understanding is an unavoidable inevitability that practical existence must face, what differentiates those modes of life which respond to its challenge as an invitation to become more intensely engaged in the adventure of existence from those that regard it as slight on both the meaning of existence and the credibility of hermeneutics and the humanities? Negative hermeneutics exploits the negativity of experience in a positive fashion. It seeks to undo the negativity with which negativity is perceived. The stratagem is fundamental to any critical revaluation of hermeneutics and the humanities and endeavours to unfound those modes of thought that promote a negative perception of uncertainty and finitude rather than receiving the experience of negation as an invitation to the transformation of understanding. The positivity within this *via negativa* has a clear implication. Negative hermeneutics demonstrates that though failure within practices is inevitable, it is also necessary for any expansion of hermeneutical understanding. It is to the negative dynamics operating within practices hermeneutically conceived that we shall now turn.

3

The way of the negative

1. Negation's optimism

As both the negative and transformative aspects of hermeneutical reasoning are entwined, the following sections examine the function of negativity in hermeneutical thought and practice. How does negativity initiate transformative moments of hermeneutic experience? Exploring the grounds of hermeneutic negativity points towards a new philosophical legitimation of the humanities. In the previous chapter some of the principal factors governing the negative reception of hermeneutics were outlined. The finitude of understanding, the inconclusive nature of interpretation and the lack of formal methodology have undermined the theoretical credentials of hermeneutic practice. It would seem as if hermeneutics falls victim to a paradox of its own making: the enabling frameworks of hermeneutics prove to be disabling frameworks which prevent hermeneutics from achieving the understanding it strives for. However, this proves to be a matter of philosophical perspective. From one point of view, the incompletable nature of the hermeneutic project establishes the conditions which, when considered from another angle, promote the possibility of hermeneutic understanding. The lead argument of this monograph is that hermeneutical understanding is indeed possible but only as a matter of practical experience and not as a result of theoretical application. In many respects, negative hermeneutics shares with deconstruction certain negative epistemological outlooks but in order to establish the philosophical credibility of negative hermeneutics we must first make matters worse. One of the challenges of establishing a new justification of negative hermeneutics is not only to show that many of the deconstructive objections to the discipline are misunderstandings but also to demonstrate the need for a philosophical metamorphosis that will enable the impossible to be grasped as the condition of the possible. To set the context of this argument, we will consider how hermeneutics contributes to its own negative reception.

Hermeneutics has, indeed, an element of the tragic built into the framework of its operation.

On one level, the principle of hermeneutic surplus (x always equals x+) suggests the impossibility of hermeneutics. It implies that the truth of every assertion is always surpassed (or in Hegel's language negated) by what lies beyond it, that is, x+. X+ represents in Gadamerian terms the indeterminacy of meaning attached to a historically revealed subject matter which always transcends its particular instances. In *The Logic of the Humanities*, Cassirer contends that 'in the sphere of culture whether discovered in language, art, religion or philosophy', 'only within the actuality of the particular' and 'only in it' can a 'cultural universal find its actualisation'.[1] In other words, x+ can *only* infer itself speculatively through the different instances of x. In existential terms, x+ is the speculative totality of language-being which surrounds us: we live *within* it and because of that we can never know it completely. Though each particular can never reveal the totality of its possible determinations, such failure is fundamentally positive: each particularization also reveals the presence of the yet-more-to-be known. As a subject matter can only be known through its incomplete instantiations, new renditions of it are vital to disclosing its hidden potentials.[2] The uneasy space between x and x+ is *the* hermeneutical differential: there can be no understanding of x without an appeal to x+ and nor can there be any sense of what is entailed within x+ without given instances of x. This part of our chapter explores the 'way of the negative' that drives this seemingly irresolvable dynamic.

There is an obvious negativity in the hermeneutical perspective: its rejection of epistemological completeness and its denial of essentialist accounts of meaning are part of its philosophical signature. We shall suggest that it is only by allowing hermeneutic negativity to become more fully what it is that permits a constructive response to the negativity that drives hermeneutics. A defence of hermeneutics requires a reflective reconstruction of its negativity rather than a critical repudiation of it. It must illuminate 'the rationality of the rhetorical way of arguing, (and) show how hermeneutic reasoning works with arguments *and* with probabilities'.[3] Speculative reasoning must reflect not only on the unspoken

---

1 Ernst Cassirer, *The Logic of the Humanities* (London: Yale University Press, 1974), 25.
2 In his book *Hermeneutics: Facts and Interpretation in the Age of Information* (London: Penguin, 2018), John Caputo is rightly to admonishes the tendency of hermeneutic thinkers to become blind to the particular because of being overenamoured with a theoretical model. However, the particular without its theoretical background is inarticulate. What is, arguably, more important is the differential space between the particular and the general, the whole and the part, for it is that space which allows each element to reveal and moderate each other.
3 Hans-Georg Gadamer, 'Autobiographical Reflections', in *The Gadamer Reader*, ed. Richard E. Palmer (Evanston: Northwestern University Press, 2007), 27. Emphasis added.

aspects of meaning but also upon a *quasi*-Kantian principle in Gadamer's hermeneutics: *meaningfulness without meaning*, a principle in which the play of the negative is crucial.[4]

Hermeneutic negativity is intimately related to two other axioms discussed in this chapter: the *Vorgriff der Vollkommenheit* and the 'speculative' as an enveloping totality of potential meaningfulness. The role of hermeneutic negativity is to keep the differential space between x and x+ open and to maintain, thereby, the openness of hermeneutic experience itself. The principal claims in the forthcoming sections are:

1. Hermeneutic truth is related to its integrative function within experience.
2. Deconstruction's negative epistemological presuppositions prevent it from understanding that hermeneutical truth-claims can (and, indeed, must) be taken seriously for their capacity to offer new and existentially decisive interpretations of the 'totality of our involvements' that constitute our being-in-the-world.
3. The possibility of becoming open to new experience requires that a person *already* resides amongst hermeneutic horizons, the extent and import of which they are partially unaware of until revealed by the negativity of experience.
4. An interpretation's capacity for hermeneutic truth (its integrative function) can ease and settle the logical uncertainty about its cognitive status.
5. The impetus of interpretation towards achieving a completer, more profound sense of a subject matter requires a tractable distinction between 'aesthetic or summative completeness' and 'logical completeness'.
6. Negation in philosophical hermeneutics is not annihilation: what claims to be a truth cannot be the whole truth but only a determinate element of it.[5] The experience of negativity does not place a stop on understanding but opens the possibility of understanding more.
7. Hermeneutic negativity depends on a regulative presupposition of a completeness of meaning. What prevents hermeneutic negativity from collapsing into the constant attrition of claim and counterclaim is the overarching principle of linguisticality. It is this that blocks Gadamer's linguistic perspectivism from collapsing into relativism.

---

4 The explicit reference is to Kant's axiom of purposefulness without purpose. Whereas Kant argues that for an object to be perceived aesthetically it must be perceived as being purposeful without purpose, our argument will develop the theme that for an object to be perceived as hermeneutical it must be perceived as meaningful without meaning.
5 See Theodor Adorno, *Hegel: Three Studies* (Cambridge, MA: MIT Press, 1993), 77.

Considered as a hermeneutics of suspicion, deconstruction is inclined to regard *any* new claim to hermeneutic truth as an expression of manipulative cognitive interests and, in consequence, refrains from proffering constructive counterclaims. In contrast, when philosophical hermeneutics draws new configurations of meaning from the play of linguistic difference, its claim to truth is hermeneutical, that is, one which openly acknowledges the existential interests of a specific subject or subject community. Theoretical assertions about a given state of affairs are replaced with interpretive constructions charged with experience-opening possibilities. As a hermeneutics of suspicion, deconstruction is arguably fated to remain a tool of theory only able to generate further abstract possibilities for interpretation. Hermeneutics is not and never was about theory alone. Hermeneutics may utilize a range of theoretical devices but its aims and concerns are primarily dominated by existentially orientated *praxis*, that is, with how experience is to be understood and extended.

Although philosophical hermeneutics shares stratagems with deconstructive thought, it cannot be judged as a hermeneutics of suspicion but, rather, as one of expectation.[6] The difference concerns contrasting ends with regard to placing negativity into play. Deconstruction both utilizes and falls victim to a version of Hegel's bad infinity. It knows theoretically that claims to truth are vulnerable to being deconstructed *ad infinitum*. The process is one of bad infinity.[7] Everything is interpretation and endlessly so: there is no logical end to the indeterminacy of meaning. From the perspective of deconstruction, any claim to cognitive truth by hermeneutics cannot be but suspect. The validity of a truth-claim in hermeneutical terms, however, does not depend on determining its strict cognitive or epistemological status but upon, to use Wittgenstein's phrase, the wheels that it turns. Does it successfully render a body of experience coherent and meaningful? The fact that, logically speaking, there can be no final interpretation does not prohibit the possibility of other interpretations gaining legitimacy on the basis of their integrative capacity for bringing sense to the fragmented play of the life-world. The integrating capacity of hermeneutical truth-claims brings phenomenological closure to an experience and ends Hegel's worries about bad infinity. Nietzsche anticipates the point.

> The falseness of a judgement is to us is not necessarily an objection to a judgement: it is here that our new language perhaps sounds strangest. *The question is to what*

---

6 See Paul Ricoeur, *The Conflict of Interpretations* (London: Continuum, 2004), 97–119.
7 Such an infinity is not a goal, a totality of meaning to be arrived at, but is rather that which endlessly renews itself in each repetition of finite meaning.

> *extent it is life advancing* . . . and our fundamental tendency is to assert that the falsest judgements . . . are the most indispensable to us, that without granting as true the fictions of logic, without measuring reality against the purely invented world of the unconditional and self-identical, without continual falsification of the world by means of numbers, mankind could not live – that to renounce false judgements would be to renounce life.[8]

Deconstruction assumes falsely that hermeneutic claims to truth are valid if and only if they are also valid as cognitive claims about the world. This fails to acknowledge that apart from its cognitive status, a claim can be hermeneutically valid as a legitimate way of organizing experience of subject matters. Though the certainty of each and every hermeneutic claim to truth can be challenged, that challenge does not damage its operative value as a hermeneutical truth capable of rendering complex experiences coherent. This does not imply subjectivism. Wittgenstein's distinction between logical and psychological termini of interpretation is helpful.

> The intention seems to interpret, to give the final interpretation; which is not a further sign or picture, but something else – the thing that cannot be further interpreted. But what we have reached is a psychological, not a logical terminus.
>
> What happens is not that this symbol cannot be further interpreted, but: I do no (more) interpreting. I do not interpret, because I feel at home in the present picture. When I interpret, (I move) from one level of thought to another.[9]

Wittgenstein acknowledges that there is no logical terminus to interpretation and that interpretation is accordingly locked within a bad infinity. Unlike deconstruction, he grasps that what closes interpretation's bad infinity is its capacity for 'making me feel at home within the present picture'. An interpretation's capacity for hermeneutic truth (its integrative function) can ease and settle the logical uncertainty about its cognitive status. It can, experientially speaking, close the open door of logically possibility by rendering a subject matter truthful in such a way that it speaks to the interpreter as opposed to offering a 'true' representation of it.

Wittgenstein's solution to the problem of bad infinity within hermeneutical interpretation does not entail a cessation of the hermeneutic endeavour. To the contrary, 'I do no more interpreting' because I have arrived at an interpretation

---

8 Friedrich Nietzsche, *Beyond Good and Evil*, trans. R. J. Hollingdale (London: Penguin, 1973), 17, Sec. 4.
9 Ludwig Wittgenstein, *Zettel*, ed. G. E. M. Anscombe and G. H. von Wright (Oxford: Basil Blackwell, 1967), 234. Insert added.

of such hermeneutical truthfulness that the need for further interpretation is suspended. I have arrived at an interpretation (or, better, one has disclosed itself to me) that 'makes me feel at home within the present picture'. An interpretation emerges that integrates and renders coherent my fragmented experiences of a subject matter such that I can come to see them as a whole and see its truthfulness perhaps for the first time. The truth of that interpretation lies in its integrative function.

Wittgenstein's mention of a psychological terminus to interpretation suggests that such an end point is arbitrary and without logical compulsion. Deconstructive criticism is like-minded. Yet from the hermeneutic perspective that end point is neither arbitrary nor without rhetorical compulsion. The force of its hermeneutic truthfulness lies in its integrative capacity: its ability to render clear a complexity of experience in a meaningful and distinct manner. The impetus of interpretation towards achieving a completer, more profound sense of a subject matter is driven by what Gadamer calls the 'anticipation of completeness' (*Vorgriff der Vollkommenheit*). An experience of completeness involves coming to recognize what one's interpretive efforts have anticipated, presupposed and pursued. The capacity of an interpretation for hermeneutic truth depends upon its integrative function, on its ability to light up and render coherent the linguistic, historical and cultural factors *already at play* within my experience. These factors may be influenced by me but they are not dependent upon me. The processes at play within subjective experience cannot themselves be reduced to the subjective.

To defend philosophical hermeneutics against the logical *scepsis* that anything can be said about anything requires not a repudiation of the deconstructive position but a recognition of the procedural fact that the epistemological status of a truth-claim is not the same as the hermeneutical status of a claim to truthfulness. For negative hermeneutics there is a positivity within its own negativity. The educational and cultural significance of hermeneutics and its ability to transcend theory by *praxis* is dependent on this negativity. Any defence of hermeneutics must demonstrate that the negative impetus it shares with deconstruction does not just question and negate universal cognitive truth-claims but stimulates the emergence of hitherto unseen possibilities of interpretation. Within deconstructive thought the release of alternative readings surrounding a truth-claim renders its universality null and void: negation leads to annihilation. However, for philosophical hermeneutics negation is not nullification. Its critical procedures are undertaken not just in the interests of analysis but for the sake of extending our experience of the subject matters shaping our world. Negation is not just a matter of exposing difference but more a question of coming to see something differently. In other words, negation in hermeneutics entails transcendence. This becomes plain in Gadamer's account of the 'negativity of experience'.

2. The negativity of experience

This section explores the implications of Gadamer's claim that '"Experience" in the real sense, is always negative'.[10] Adorno astutely observed, 'Nothing can be understood in isolation, everything is to be understood only in the context of the whole, with the awkward qualification that the whole in turn lives only in the individual moments'.[11] Heidegger's distinction between apophantic and apophatic language initiates a significant development in the way part–whole relationships function in the hermeneutical tradition. As a particular linguistic representation of the world, a statement cannot represent the totality of linguistic relations (or life-form) from which it springs. Consequently, no statement can be understood in its fullness if isolated from the totality of linguistic involvements of which it is a part. Once placed in its 'speculative' environment, the limitations of the singular statement are revealed. Whilst hermeneutic critique can negate a statement (i.e. reveal that it is not the whole truth), it also reaffirms and reappropriates it as a way of regaining a sense of the totality of linguistic relations that lie behind it. Hermeneutic negativity has a clear positive speculative function.

The positivity of hermeneutic negation is expressed in the remark that 'the truth of experience always contains (an) orientation towards new experience'.[12] The negative moment is also implicit in the equation: 'if we have a new experience of an object, this means that we have not seen the thing correctly hitherto and now know it better'.[13] The negative moment challenges established expectancies not by nullifying previous experience but by revealing its limitations. The positive moment inheres in the negative: it is not that we have got it completely wrong about an experienced object but have come to realize that what we have experienced of it is a limited part of something more extensive than previously imagined.

10 TM 317.
11 Adorno, *Hegel*, 90.
12 TM 319.
13 Ibid.

> The negativity of experience has a curiously productive meaning. It is not simply a deception that we see through and correct but, more a comprehensive knowledge that we acquire. It cannot, therefore, be an object chosen at random in regard to which we have an experience, but must be of such a nature that we gain through it better knowledge, not only of itself, but of what we thought we knew before, i.e. of a universal. The negation by means of which it achieves this, is a determinate negation.[14]

The realization that what we have experienced of an object is not all that is there for us to experience of it opens the way to becoming aware that 'the truth of experience always contains an orientation to new experience'.[15] Gadamer observes that an experienced person has become so not just because of negative experience but because those experiences reveal what is true of all reflective experience; their truth points to and illuminates what lies beyond them, that is, further experiences of what we have come to know but only in a limited fashion. The experienced person is so not because of having experienced many things but because those experiences form an 'orientation towards new experience', that is, the sense that there is always more to come.[16]

> The perfection of [. . .] experience, the perfect form of what we call 'experienced', does not consist in the fact that someone already knows everything and knows better than anyone else. Rather the experienced person proves to be, someone who is radically undogmatic; who, because of the many experiences he has had and the knowledge he has drawn from them is particularly well equipped to have new experiences and to learn from them. The dialectic of experience has its own fulfilment not in definitive knowledge, but in that openness to experience that is encouraged by experience itself.[17]

The possibility of becoming open to new experience requires that a person already resides amongst hermeneutic horizons the extent of which they are unaware of until revealed by the negativity of experience. Experience can point to another dimension of an object's meaning only because that additional dimension was already a possible determination of meaning amongst those already known. 'Becoming open to new experience' is not a theoretical achievement but a consequence of practice, of being open to the unpredictable returns of experience which arise precisely because of participating in practices.

---

14 TM 317.
15 TM 319.
16 TM 319. Insertion added.
17 TM 319.

The nature of experience is conceived in terms of that which goes beyond it; for experience itself can never be a science. It is in absolute anti-thesis to knowledge and to that kind of instruction that follows from general theoretical knowledge.[18]

Four points arise from Gadamer's argument:

1. Formative exposure to experience's negative moments is shared by both the *Natur-* and *Geisteswissenschaften*. An experimental scientist is as subject to experiences running counter to professional expectancy as is any artist. After such challenges, any intuitive sense of what line of inquiry next to follow invariably arises from the hard-won lessons of experience rather than from theory alone. Once again, immersion in practical experience rather than theoretical expertise is key.
2. It is the force of negativity which impels us to question and to open ourselves to unexpected ways of thinking. Negativity simultaneously reveals the limitations of our understanding and what lies beyond it. The acquisition of previous experience is therefore crucial. The educative importance of maintaining one's reading in poetry or history resides in its capacity to enrich stocks of imaginative reference and acquaintance with unfamiliar patterns of reasoning. It is these that increase a hermeneutic subject's *repertoire* of responses when called upon on to navigate the unexpected challenges of negativity. It is not mere acquaintance with literary or philosophical canon that matters but the imaginative capacity to apply its varied grammars of thinking to new and unexpected circumstances.
3. Gadamer's approach to practice is central: one must already be immersed in a practice and its assumptions in order to be challenged by the negativity of experience. The positivity residing in this negativity is dialectical: the revelation of the limitations of established expectancies is synonymous with the simultaneous disclosure of what was *not* previously seen. This does not culminate in a negation of the practice but in an extension of its future possibilities. A cultural practice is essentially dialectical: the finitude of its very exercise will bring its expectations to critique and yet, precisely because of that, open it to the possibility of understanding more of itself.
4. *The negativity of experience reveals why philosophical hermeneutics is best conceived as a philosophical mode of reflection, as articulating a reflexivity*

---

18 Ibid.

central to practice rather than as a distinct method of interpretation. The negativity of experience is productive not just in the sense of opening unexpected horizons of meaning but also in that it brings a hermeneutic subject to self-consciousness. Following Hegel, Gadamer suggests that because of its negativity, experience allows the hermeneutic subject to establish a kind of unity with itself. This is the reversal that consciousness undergoes when it recognizes (or is made aware of) itself as being amongst the alien and different.[19] As Gadamer puts it, 'the experiencer has become aware of his experience, he is "experienced".'[20] The observation that 'every experience worthy of the name runs counter to expectation' implies that insofar as that experience makes me aware that it is my expectations that are being challenged, I am brought to an awareness of myself in a problematic environment. This, in turn, reaffirms that the dynamics of practice are central to the development of hermeneutical reflection.

Aspects of Gadamer's account of the negativity of experience are given independent literary shape by Nicholas Rothwell in his novel *Belomor*. The figure of Haffner, a survivor of a Soviet Gulag, gives voice to a negative epiphany. He describes how

> it has been clear to me there are moments in our lives when the world becomes unstable, when our visual field gives way: things break before us; they burst into fragments, disappear.[21]
>
> Shattered fragments; not just ruins. They also have their fate, their hidden order, their own narratives to tell.[22]
>
> If the world is pulverised, isn't it for us to piece together the broken shards? We have to sift, and search and gather up. To find the scattered pieces that belong together. To make our way through time, searching constantly, seeking for the echoes that come to us, the parallels; and then, maybe, patterns appear.[23]

Such negativity is described by the narrator in the following way:

> the shards – you said – what was left to us have been exploded, pulverised, reduced to rubble; no more order, nothing, no more structured harmony, no sequence – and the hardest things to find words that fit together.[24]

---

19 TM 318.
20 TM 317.
21 Nicolas Rothwell, *Belomor* (Melbourne: Text Publishing, 2013), 29.
22 Ibid., 30.
23 Ibid., 31.
24 Ibid., 215.

The character Haffner then points out:

> But there's one thing you don't seem to know. The game never ends: it doesn't balance up. Lives don't have shapes. There aren't grand encounters when everything comes into focus.[25]

Rothwell's invocation of a shattered world announces a theme that will become prominent in the latter sections of this chapter. The notion of a broken, disharmonious world acquires its force by making manifest the naïve pre-reflective assumption that everyday experience anticipates the possibility of a completeness of sense. The force of the negativity of experience depends upon the priority of that assumption.

The value of Rothwell's description lies in what it clarifies about the experience of negativity.

1. The negativity of experience is associated with the emergence of reflective individuation. In the antagonism between being confronted by a deeply puzzling world that resists our expectations and the image of a world that we believe complies with them, conscious individuation emerges. The negativity of experience draws consciousness from out of its pre-reflective slumber in which there is no difference between the world as experienced and the world as expected. The negativity of experience becomes the ground of hermeneutical experience in a double sense. The world as experienced no longer remains as it seemed, becomes strange and demands to be understood differently. Self-understanding requires remodelling as the negativity of experience reveals the vacuity of its developed expectancies. The emergent disjuncture between the disrupted world of actual experience and the world previously expected by experience reveals, to borrow Pippin's phrase, 'the world at work' within our prereflective judgements, the world of prejudices and pre-understandings at play in the formation of initial world outlooks.[26] The negativity of experience permits hermeneutics to catch itself out when its pre-understandings are exposed as inappropriate.[27]

---

25 Ibid., 217.
26 Robert B. Pippin, *The Persistence of Subjectivity, On the Kantian Aftermath* (Cambridge: Cambridge University Press, 2012), 68.
27 See John Caputo, 'The Wisdom of Hermeneutics', in *Conducting Hermeneutics Research*, From Philosophy to Practice, ed. Nancy Moules, Graham McCaffrey and Catherine Laing (New York: Peter Lang, 2015), ix–xii.

2. The negativity of experience is synonymous with an experience of limit. In bringing reflective consciousness to itself, the negativity of experience reveals the inadequacies of its presuppositions. This Gadamer names after Aeschylus *pathei mathos* – learning through suffering.

   > What a person has to learn through suffering is not this or that particular thing, but the knowledge of the limitations of humanity, of the absoluteness of the barrier that separates him from the divine. It is ultimately a religious insight – that kind of insight which gave birth to Greek tragedy.

   > Real experience is that in which a person becomes aware of his finiteness. In it are discovered the limits of the power and the self-knowledge of his or her planning reason.[28]

   The negativity of experience might be said to involve the world striking back at that human arrogance which believes it can straightjacket the ever-shifting complexities of actuality within the narrowness of its preconceptions. The resistance of actuality to our limited schemas of intelligibility is genuinely educative. Such negativity reveals the extent to which our judgements have been overhasty, neglectful of the intricate details of a problem or impetuous in the pursuit of a convenient solution. For Gadamer, genuine experience – the experience of negativity – is a coming to self-knowledge, a being prompted into a behaviour-changing recognition of the finitude of our capacities. Such tempered experience is formative. It confirms the hermeneutical virtues of not wilfully prejudging situations, of striving to remain open to the unexpected and of being receptive to what the uncertainties of experience might teach.

3. The negativity of experience prompts the emergence of reflective narratives. The power of negative experience discloses 'the world at work' within expectations and attitudinal postures. Such revelations may be singular but overtime they disclose a characterology. Emergent character patterns become manifest on the basis of a hermeneutic subject *already* participating in practices. Ontologically speaking, one's sense of who one is as a hermeneutic agent is not, strictly speaking, a condition of experience but the accumulative achievement of experience. This does not imply that an emergent narrative betrays the unfolding of an inner essence. What is carried from one engagement to another are acquired inclinations to act in certain ways that have accumulated as a consequence of experiential involvements. What emerges as a hermeneutical subject's

---

28 TM 357.

narrative identity is contingent, changing and open to new directions. The point, here, is that the continuity and difference in the unfolding of such a narrative is driven by the negativity of experience. It may establish overtime a clearer sense of the character we have become, but it also reminds us that our narrative identity is always provisional. The principal lesson that comes with the negativity of experience is that in being brought to the contingencies of our historical and cultural selfhood, we are reminded that we remain mysteries to ourselves.[29] The negativity of experience is fundamental to the collective and individual development of *Bildung* as a formative dialectical process.

Two further aspects of Gadamer's approach to the negativity of experience bear on our later discussion of the practical aspects of hermeneutics.

1. The negativity of experience contains its own principle of redemption. The negative moment is implicit in the formulation: 'if we have an experience of an object, this means that we have not seen the thing correctly hitherto and now know it better'.[30] The negativity of experience entails recognizing the limitations of our judgement. However, as such limitations become manifest against an expanding awareness of what we have overlooked, the recognition of our weakness of judgement brings with it possibilities for redemption, that is, seeking consciously to remain open and responsive to the possibilities inherent in new experiences of a subject matter. The negativity of experience has a clear ethical dimension. It is not simply a question of being brought by experience to an understanding of the limits of one's understanding but also of how one becomes reflectively disposed to that understanding and what it points to.
2. The argument that negativity is a prime mover within experience suggests an untimely philosophy of education which attributes an uncompromisingly positive value to the distanciation of reflection, to the disruptive capacities of experience and to becoming alienated from established custom and expectancy. The positivity inherent in negativity within education will be discussed in subsequent sections.

The gap between what we have come to understand and our understanding of what we have yet to understand brings us to the question of liminal space.

---

29 H.-G. Gadamer, 'The Hermeneutics of Suspicion', in *Hermeneutics: Questions and Prospects*, ed. G. Shapiro and A. Sica (Amherst: The University of Massachusetts Press, 1984), 57.
30 TM 319.

3. Liminal spaces

Post-structural and deconstructive criticisms of hermeneutics reflect epistemological concerns about the formally non-closable nature of hermeneutic truth-claims. Wolfgang Iser's analysis of interpretive practices appears to compound the case against hermeneutics.[31] Just as Schopenhauer's epistemological subject gets in the way of that which it seeks to know, Iser maintains that in its very pursuit understanding only succeeds in deferring its object. Yet there remains a positivity in such negativity.

It is an analytic truism that if the meaning of what is said is understood, there are other ways of saying it. If that meaning cannot be reduced to one of the many ways in which it can be said, a liminal space emerges between what is understood and how it might be said. Iser contends that interpretive practices open a liminal space between themselves and their subject matters such that the anticipated completion of understanding is always differed.

Iser makes three claims: (1) understanding is interpretation, (2) interpretation translates between different hermeneutic frameworks or registers and (3) understanding is always positioned *between* transmitting and receiving horizons of meaning. Hermeneutic practices endeavour to understand subject matters but these are never given neutrally. Not only do they appear in the specific modality of an age but the intellectual modality of our own period filters what can be received from a previous epoch. Because interpretive, understanding seeks to transpose what can be transmitted from one horizon into what can be received within another. This renders interpretation performative: it produces unintended effects by opening liminal spaces between a subject matter and the interpretative practices seeking to understand it. The space between a subject matter and its understanding 'contains a residual untranslatability that ... powers the drive to overcome it without ever being able to do so. Such a space – which can be qualified in terms neither of the subject matter to be interpreted nor of the register into which the subject is to be translated – turns out to be autopoietic in nature'.[32] The autopoietic character of interpretation will be central to our discussion of practice.

Iser rejects any transcendent or grandstand account of interpretation. If 'interpretation has to cope with the liminal space resulting from something being transposed into something else, then interpretation is primarily a performative

---

31 See Wolfgang Iser, *The Range of Interpretation* (New York: Columbia University Press, 2000).
32 Ibid., 195.

act rather than an explanatory one'.³³ In consequence, *hermeneutics cannot stand outside itself to explicate or justify itself*. The point underscores once again the importance of practice for our argument. It is through the figures of practice – circles of non-identical repetition, recursive looping and travelling differentials – that the productivity of understanding reveals itself. Yet here we stumble on one of hermeneutics' profound ironies.

Identifying the liminal space produced by the act of interpretation establishes understanding's impossibility. If hermeneutic differentials identify the irreducibility of the idioms from which a subject matter is transmitted and the registers into which it is translated, no interpretation can be commensurate with what it seeks to grasp. Hermeneutic reflection suggests that were writing to perfectly capture the thought pursued, not only would writing but thought would also cease. Thinkers as different as Nietzsche and Helene Cixous contend that writing works forwards and backwards, reversing past alignments of meaning as well as anticipating new ones. In other words, the practice of writing perpetually anticipates and undoes its origin and end. The practice of writing resists and disrupts the possibility of finality, upholds the differential space between the expression and the expressed and keeps the being of its subject matters in play. 'To write . . . is never to see the end: attempt after attempt, to begin again, to begin oneself again.'³⁴

Does not our discussion of the negative within hermeneutics imply that the practice of hermeneutics is an impossible one? Matters are further complicated by 'the anticipation of completeness' which seemingly drives hermeneutics towards irredeemable failure.³⁵ Despite its idealistic connotations of completeness, *Vollkommenheit* also suggests something about the undoing of understanding's projects, namely our projecting, anticipating and seeking out that which in formal terms can never arrive. Nevertheless, as we shall argue in later sections, understanding the dialectical movements which the *Vorgriff* initiates within hermeneutical experience is key to establishing a formal link between hermeneutics and the experiential structures of what we undergo in the humanities. They also suggest how 'experience' in the humanities is the equivalent to a dialectical form of learning. In the following sections, we will outline the role of the *Vorgriff* in the broader architecture of hermeneutic thought.

---

33 Ibid., 7.
34 Helene Cixous, *Rootprints, Memory and Life Writing*, trans. Eric Prenowitz (London: Rutledge, 1997), 168–71.
35 TM 293–4.

4. The fore-conception of completeness

The 'fore-conception' or 'anticipation of completeness' is an underplayed notion of considerable importance in Gadamer's analysis of hermeneutic experience. Astonishingly, the notion is cited only three times in *Truth and Method*, one being limited to a section title.[36] The pertinent remarks concern:

- Heidegger's disclosure of the fore-structure of understanding.[37]
- the understanding of (any) text remains permanently determined by the anticipatory movement of (the) fore-understanding.[38]
- The *Vorgriff* describes an element of the ontological structure of understanding.[39]
- the 'fore-conception' of completeness is a formal condition of all understanding. It states that only what constitutes a unity of meaning is intelligible.[40]
- the fore-conception of completeness that guides our understanding is, then, always determined by the specific content. [41]

Despite the simplicity of these statements, the *Vorgriff* has a considerable reach within hermeneutic operations. It structures performances of work, gives directional shape to how we understand works and ourselves overtime and emphasizes that the epistemological underpinning of hermeneutics is fundamentally participatory. Within an ontology of language-being with all its diversity and complexity, the 'anticipation of completeness' functions as a unitary device establishing similarities and continuities upon which knowledge can be built.

Gadamerian hermeneutics proposes that all linguistic and language-like practices are circumscribed by an ideal expectation of a completeness of meaning which though never realizable is nevertheless presupposed by each and every particular expression of meaning. This introduces a dialectical contrast between an infinity of possible meaning which all interpretations presuppose and endless finite meanings which interpretation strives to render clearer and more distinct. As a regulative idea, the 'fore-conception of completeness' has a double function: (1) It sets the framework which defines a work as the realization of one set of

---

36 TM 256–66, 293–4 and 524.
37 TM 265.
38 TM 293.
39 TM 294.
40 Ibid.
41 Ibid.

possible meanings against an infinite horizon of other possibilities. (2) The aesthetic completeness or identity of a work only becomes discernible against an anticipated totality of other possible meanings. However, the anticipated totality of possible meaning against which a work becomes discernible as a specific and limited completion of meaning also places limits on the adequacy of the work. The *Vorgriff* grounds the possibility of hermeneutic critique: it establishes why there is always something more to be said.

If Heidegger's notion of *Dasein* establishes an analytic of existential experience, Gadamer's concept of the *Vorgriff* grounds a hermeneutical analytic: it articulates the basic temporality of hermeneutical being. By opening a differential space between how we experience the world and think of its subject matters (forms), the concept establishes the negative space within which the movement of hermeneutical reflection becomes possible.

5. Completeness and meaning

The positivity within the negativity of hermeneutic critique becomes apparent if we consider the dialectical role of *Vollkommenheit* in Gadamerian hermeneutics. The dialectical and unitary functions of the principle must always be considered in relation to the ontology of linguistic being. As we shall see, the anticipation of completeness principle is central to Gadamer's account of image and concept formation.

Gadamer refers to the notion in the following terms:

> The circle, which is fundamental to all understanding, has a further hermeneutic implication which I call the 'fore-conception of completeness'. But this, too, is obviously a formal condition of all understanding.[42] It states that only what really constitutes a unity of meaning is intelligible. So when we read a text we always assume its completeness, and only when this assumption proves mistaken – i.e. the text is not intelligible – do we begin to suspect the text and try to discover how it can be remedied. The fore-conception of completeness that guides all our understanding is, then, always determined by the specific content. Not only does the reader assume an immanent unity of meaning, but his understanding

---

42 Despite its Kantian overtones the fore-conception of completeness is not grounded in the a priori expectation of an epistemological subject: It is rooted in linguistic being – Gadamer's extension of Heidegger's *Dasein* – in that the projective intentionality of language is what gives rise to and intends the possibility of completion.

is likewise guided by the constant transcendent expectations of meaning that proceed from the relation to the truth of what is being said.[43]

The principle of anticipation is transcendent not in the sense of being a Kantian subjective a priori but as something that emanates from the play of language itself. Two points merit comment: (1) When Gadamer speaks of 'a unity of meaning' with regard to a specific work he is not referring to any notion of a fixed meaning but to a (clearly variable) part-whole structure whose elements form a coherent, meaningful, yet elastic structure. The 'fore-conception of completeness' anticipates rather than designates the direction of an argument or performance. (2) The reference to 'transcendent' expectations of meaning does not imply that the *Vorgriff* is the equivalent of a Kantian logical a priori category of intelligible experience. Such status would be inconsistent with the broad ontological assumptions of philosophical hermeneutics and yet, as we shall see, Gadamer's *Vorgriff* clearly operates as a regulative idea within hermeneutical reasoning. The Kantian echoes are plain when Gadamer argues that the fore-conception of completeness is triggered (always determined) by a specific content.[44]

Fore-understanding is not just a matter of thinking within the fixed forms and files of tradition but a being guided by their inclinations and expectations. Long and deep immersion within a practice creates an expectancy such that when certain circumstances or themes come into play, discernible outcomes are disclosed as likely: the experienced navigator has come to 'know' what to avoid when running wild tides. The many failures of a practised cook indicate how to avert future culinary disaster. Philosophical hermeneutics views human experience as a temporal process. Significant, suggestive or profound, human experience is often an experience of passage. This is consistent with the claim that 'the true locus of hermeneutics' is a being in-between, a claim that can be variously confirmed.[45] The constant movement between the particular and the universal in language characterizes the in-betweenness of hermeneutical reflection. The ability of the imagination to sense or feel where an argument is going indicates an acquired ability to intuit from the experiences of like character what must

---

43 TM 293–4.
44 The parallel with Kant relates to the latter's remark that 'Intuition and concepts, constitute therefore the elements of our knowledge, so that neither concepts without an intuition in someway corresponding to them, nor intuition without concepts, can yield knowledge. . . . The understanding can intuit nothing, the senses can think nothing, Only through their union can knowledge arise' (see Immanuel Kant, *The Critique of Pure Reason* (London: Macmillan, St. Martin's Press,1970), B75–B76, A51–A52, 92 and 93).
45 TM 295.

have been already said and what in all likelihood will yet be said. Expectation is central to any sense of a living predicament. 'Reality always stands in a horizon of desired or feared or, at any rate, still undecided future possibilities' betwixt and between which we live.[46] Accordingly, it can be suggested that what accumulates and consolidates as acquired pre-understanding determines what is projected as an anticipated expectation of completion. Exposure to the ongoing buffeting of experience will lead to a constant review of projected outcomes. *In conclusion*, the anticipation of completeness opens the liminal space of the in-between in which life constantly moves between the 'no more' and the 'not yet'.

6. Completeness and envisioning identity

Gadamer implies that the anticipation of completeness grounds what is presupposed by every linguistic perspective, that is, the notions of a thing and of the world in itself. This suggests that the *Vorgriff der Vollkommenheit* is a regulative idea without which any sense of the continuity and coherence of objects of experience would be impossible. There is no actual thing-in-itself to be experienced, yet its formal presupposition is the very condition of experiencing a thing in the continuity of its appearances.[47] Gadamer's strong claim is that interpretation intends completion. This is not to say that the intention of completion anticipates the specific meaning of a text, only that a meaningfulness is anticipated such that its pursuit may lead to a completer understanding of it. With every amended understanding, the anticipated completeness changes and in changing, the direction of subsequent interpretations also changes. This infers that interpretation is an auto-poetic process in which the *Vorgriff der Vollkommenheit* constantly produces unexpected effects. This is reflected in Gadamer's veneration of spontaneous productivity within practice as we shall later see.

7. Formal completeness and aesthetic completeness

What does Gadamer mean by completeness? Clarification of the point will strengthen the distinction between analytic and hermeneutic styles of reasoning.

46 TM 112.
47 TM 447.

In the 'Transformation into Structure' section of *Truth and Method*, he comments on how in a reality of undecided possibilities, a particular art work can occasion the emergence of 'a meaningful whole (that) completes and fulfils itself [. . .] such that no lines of meaning scatter in the void'. Such a work presents itself as a closed circle of meaning.[48] Completeness in this passage invokes the idea that every part expresses something of the meaningful whole to which it belongs and that the character of that whole gains expression through its parts. Yet, this returns us to a defining tension within philosophical hermeneutics. Why, on the one hand, does Gadamer commit himself aesthetically to the notion of a completeness of meaning when his ontological commitments deny that any such completion of understanding is possible? Why must interpretation anticipate a completeness which it can never realize?

When Gadamer talks of completeness he is not thinking of epistemological completeness but of that rhetorical or aesthetic completeness the possibility of which is presupposed by interpretation understood as a sense-making process. Negative hermeneutics insists that though no final or complete understanding is achievable, hermeneutical or rhetorical truth is nevertheless possible. What is affirmed as art's truth is its ability to achieve an aesthetically integrated closed circle of meaning in which aspects of the complex elements of experience are brought together as an intelligible whole. Such completeness does not eliminate the logical possibility of alternative configurations. There is always another way of performing a Chopin nocturne. The question is, 'What interpretation offers the most transformative understanding of the subject-matter at hand?' Yet despite their transformative power, the achievement of rhetorical or aesthetic completeness is never immune from the challenge of finitude. An unexpected shift within the pattern of elements that constitute a transformative experience can sunder their erstwhile sense of completeness. In consequence, a formerly satisfying musical performance now jars or a signature gesture in a classic dramatic performance becomes staid. What once made perfect sense no longer does so.

The finality which transformative moments of meaningfulness achieve is hermeneutical rather than logical. They give sense, shape and significance to a sequence of experiences. In contrast, the order of everyday experience remains fragmented. Yet the expectation of completion and the fragmented nature of everyday experience are not at odds. Gadamer's position implies that precisely because the regulative idea of completion dominates the expectancies of

---

48 TM 112–13.

everyday experience, the latter is experienced as fragmented. The experience of reality always stands within the play of different strands of unresolved meaning. Yet, were it not for the regulative idea of completion, we would have little sense of where a certain sequence of events might point. Temporality within philosophical hermeneutics is not experienced as an atomistic sequence of moments but as shifting patterns of meaningful significance which gain or lose cohesiveness in relation to the expectations they inspire. Existence is experienced not as a meaningless flux of moments but rather as the constant waxing and waning of sequences of significance be they friendships, creative practices or religious commitments. The ingrained extent of our anticipations of completeness is demonstrated when actual experience runs contrary to expectation. The phenomenological experience of actuality as fragmentary already assumes a prior regulative intuition of completeness.

The power of the fragment to awaken a sense of completed meaning resides in its speculative ability to invoke through the stated or performed an anticipated but completeness of meaning. Compositions by Alban Berg and Anton von Webern excel in their capacity to allude to and insinuate a completeness of structure such that its anticipation becomes the condition of what is heard in performance.[49] A parallel pattern of reasoning shapes Gadamer's account of the speculative nature of linguistic meaning.

> Every word as the event of a moment, carries with it the unsaid, to which it is related by responding and summoning. The occasionality of human speech is not a causal imperfection of its expressive power; it is, rather the logical expression of the living virtuality of speech *that brings a totality of meaning into play, without being able to express it totally.*[50]

The particular word speculatively invokes the unspoken whole of which it is part. Theodor Adorno speaks of a 'fragmented transcendence'[51] and of how a single artwork is only a piece of the totality that it could be, that it anticipates but never will be.[52] The poignancy of a particular aphorism, the explosive charge of a certain poetic phrase and the sheer suggestiveness of the miniature lie in their collective capacity to insinuate the presence of an anticipated wholeness of meaning or structure. Anton von Webern's pieces for orchestra are a case

---

49 Alban Berg, *Fünf Orchesterlieder nach Ansichtskartentexten von Peter Altenberg op. 4*, Vladimir Ashkenazy, Deutsches Symphonie-Orchester (Berlin: Decca, 1993), CD 436 567-2 and Anton von Webern, *Five Pieces for Orchestra*, Robert Kraft (Naxos: Philharmonic Orchestra, 2009), CD. 8.557531.
50 TM 458, emphasis added.
51 Theodor Adorno, *Aesthetic Theory* (London: Routledge, 1984), 184.
52 Ibid., 299.

in point. The anticipation of completeness circumscribes an experience of suggestiveness and is indicative of our participation in forms of sensuous and cognitive movement.

The mutual mediation of part and whole strengthens Iser's contention that by seeking completion, interpretation succeeds (for the most part) only in deferring it. As we have noted, a change in the understanding of particulars alters our grasp of the whole they point to and that alteration changes how the particulars informed by that (now) altered whole are themselves understood. This is not to say that 'aesthetic' or 'rhetorical' completion is impossible. To the contrary, the interpretation is not an instance of an insatiable hermeneutic will striving to achieve an unattainable commensurability between the nature of a subject matter and its reading of that subject matter. Iser and Gadamer know that such logical commensurability is a nonsense. Here we return once more to the distinction between logical as opposed to rhetorical completeness.

Logical commensurability implies that interpretation can achieve a complete identity with its subject matter and, yet, remain discernible as an interpretation. Logically speaking, this is unattainable. However, though subject to the challenge of finitude, aesthetic and rhetorical completeness is attainable. The arrival of such a moment Wittgenstein describes as the point where I do no more interpreting. Gadamer speaks of such occasions as those in which interpretation cancels itself.

> The unfolding of the totality of meaning towards which understanding is directed, forces us to make conjectures and to take them back again. The *self-cancellation of the interpretation* makes it possible for the thing-itself – the meaning of the text – to assert itself. The movement of the interpretation is not dialectical primarily because the one-sidedness of every statement can be balanced by another side – this is [. . .] a secondary phenomenon in interpretation but because the word that interpretatively encounters the meaning of the text 'expresses' the whole of this meaning, i.e. allows an infinity of meaning to be represented within in it in a finite way.[53]

As we shall see when we discuss Gadamer's presentation of the *Wahrheitsanspruch*, the preceding passage affirms his belief that hermeneutical, aesthetic or rhetorical truth is possible. Yet is there not a paradox in this? What presents itself as being aesthetically complete is not, however, thereby rendered logically complete. Though a given performance of a musical work may seem both perfect and complete, that wholeness will never exhaust the logical possibilities for further performance that reside within the work. Furthermore, the mark of a masterful

---

53 TM 465.

interpretation of a Beethoven piano sonata is not only that it is distinct but that it also has the confidence to hint at other possibilities. This permits a distinction between the finished nature of a performance and the fact that a work in so far as it invokes a totality of meaning can never be complete.

As a regulative notion, the anticipation of completeness offers a promissory structure of completable meaning. Whereas for Kant, the aesthetic object anticipates a purposefulness without purpose, for Gadamer the hermeneutic object anticipates a meaningfulness without a determinate meaning. The anticipation of completeness, though it can never be the object of hermeneutic experience, is itself the condition of experiencing any hermeneutical object.

8. Truthfulness and completeness

The *Vorgriff der Vollkommenheit* operates as a regulative idea without which any sense of continuity and coherence amongst the objects of experience would be impossible. There is no actual thing-in-itself to be experienced and yet its presupposition is the very condition of experiencing a continuity of appearances as a thing.[54] In *Truth and Method*, Gadamer argues that the thing is not different from the views in which it presents itself: 'the thing-itself . . . is nothing but the continuity with which the various perceptual perspectives on objects shade into one another'.[55] The irony is plain. *The Vorgriff* allows us to think of the perceptual aspects we see as belonging to an anticipated thing without every allowing us to experience the thing itself. The negativity is once again clear: the *Vorgriff* appears to promise what it disallows.

The *Vorgriff der Vollkommenheit* understood as a regulative idea is embedded in Gadamer's presentation of a language world. Each word 'brings a totality of meaning into play, without being able to express it totally'.[56] This clearly presupposes that every meaningful utterance anticipates a completeness of meaning. Whereas for Kant an aesthetic object appears to us as being purposeful without purpose, *for philosophical hermeneutics a hermeneutic object is given to us as that which is indeterminately meaningful but without a determinate meaning.* As a culture concept, language does not refer to anything outside itself.[57] It does not make sense to ask for the 'meaning' of that totality. It has no meaning in

---

54 TM 447.
55 Ibid.
56 Ibid.
57 Cassirer, *The Logic of the Humanities*, 142.

itself but is the precondition of meaningfulness. For an object to be perceived as a hermeneutical entity presupposes a field of meaningfulness from which it can speak and in which it can be engaged as interpretable. This emphasizes that the *Vorgriff der Vollkommenheit* presupposes a participatory ontology in which the hermeneutic agent already participates. What saves Gadamer from the subjectivism he condemns in Kant's aesthetics is that the regulative idea of a totality of meaning is not the projection of a lone epistemological subject but is integral to every linguistic practice. This clearly suggests that the possibility of hermeneutics, art, poetry and music stands on a transcendental expectation of meaningfulness and completeness which has no meaning in itself. Hermeneutics understood as the quest for a completeness of meaning must, logically speaking, always fail. Nevertheless, as we shall argue in later sections, such negativity also confirms the anticipation of completeness as the formal condition of cumulative learning within hermeneutics and the humanities. *There may be no finality of understanding in hermeneutical disciplines but understanding is never final.*

The language ontology which underpins negative hermeneutics serves as a reminder of the fact that the pursuit of completeness within a practice always takes place in wider contexts of interrelational fields of meanings connected by etymology, conceptual entailment and personal association. Unresolved political and personal narratives, ongoing moral and professional dilemmas, unanswered questions in literary or philosophical practice as well as the ever-changing conundrums of personal relationships all are constantly at play within language-being in untold interconnected ways. The pursuit of completeness in one practice is but a part of a totality of ongoing quests for meaning and completeness across a full range of our existential commitments. That the pursuit of completeness in one practice is bound to fail is not the point. The demonstration that a particular reading is limited logically requires the revelation of other possibilities. These may lead to a completer understanding within the practice concerned but, most important and by default of their rootedness in a common linguisticality, they may also alter our grasp of what is at play in other commitments and practices. The key dialectical point for learning in hermeneutics and the humanities emerges. Without the pursuit of the anticipated completeness in one discipline, without the possibilities for understanding that emerge from its inevitable failure, there will be no tangential gains for understanding in others. In conclusion, the formal and unrealizable ideal of completeness emerges not only as the driver of understanding's disquiet but also as the philosophical condition of any hermeneutical openness to experience: completeness is the vigilant hope of hermeneutics. However, an important question remains.

Why are we committed to such a regulative principle given that it is an epistemological fiction? Hermeneutics suggests that the answer lies in language itself: the regulative idea of completeness derives from our embedded linguisticality. The idea of completeness is the condition of rendering objects of experience linguistically intelligible. Gadamer's contention that every spoken work anticipates a virtual totality of meaning implies that language itself presumes completable meanings. The notion that within language there is an 'infinity of meaning' to be explicated and worked out has a partner conception, that is, the fore-conception of completeness, which states that only what constitutes a unity of meaning is intelligible. Gadamer's Kantianism is explicit: the idea of completeness as the condition of rendering objects of experience linguistically intelligible is a regulative idea that governs the intelligibility of all linguistic objects.[58] The 'anticipation of completeness' might be described as an a priori expectancy built in to all language use. This is not to say that the principle is logically a priori but that given language's capacity for generalization, it has established itself as de facto a priori. The transcendental nature of regulative ideas requires brief comment.

Gadamer follows Cassirer in his suggestion that no perception of an artwork as a unity of meaning is possible without the idea of a completeness which cannot itself be derived from the perception of the empirical objects it enables. The *Vorgriff* is the precondition of any experience of a work as a work. It functions in a similar way to Kant's 'analogy of experience'. Kant declares,

> An analogy of experience is, therefore, only a rule according to which a unity of experience may arise from a perception or empirical intuition. It does not tell us how mere perception or empirical intuition in general itself comes about. It is not a principle constitutive of the objects, that is, of the appearances, but only regulative.[59]

Kant argues that we do not perceive an empirical *datum* (the work) to which we subsequently attach a number of descriptive predicates; rather, the work is nothing other than an empirically experienced set of descriptions or meaningful combinations conceived of *as if* it were an intelligible whole. This opens a liminal space between how artworks are rendered intelligible objects and how they are experienced as works. This liminal space is essential to the working of hermeneutic negativity. Though the anticipation of completeness applies to all things thinkable as hermeneutical objects, it does not determine the specific

---

58 Kant, *Critique of Pure Reason*, A178–A179, 210.
59 Ibid., A180–B223, 211.

meaning of a work. In itself, the anticipation of completeness has no determinate meaning: it is not a hermeneutic object but only provides the form of such objects whereby they become thinkable. In Kant's terms, the *Vorgriff* 'has no meaning and is completely lacking in content, though it may still contain the logical function which is required for making a concept out of any data that may be presented. . . . Apart from this, the axiom has no objective validity'.[60] A liminal space opens between the determinate nature of a hermeneutical object and the indeterminacy of its form, that is, the form of what is experienced is never exhausted by what is experienced. The *Vorgriff* functions as a limiting principle: only in relation to the anticipation of completeness do notions both of that which is incomplete and which can become more complete make sense. In other words, the adequacy, character and range of meanings actualized by the artwork become discernible precisely when set against the infinite horizon of completable meaning from which they are drawn. Philosophical hermeneutics cleverly inverts the pattern of reasoning in Baumgarten's *campos confusionis*.[61] Whereas Baumgarten argues that the clarity and distinctness of an artistic image is dependent upon the vagueness of its peripheral visual field, philosophical hermeneutics suggests that it is the artwork itself which reveals the realm of indeterminate possibility from which it arises.

The liminal space between a subject matter and its interpretation is not merely a differential space in which the incommensurable space between subject matter and an artwork becomes apparent but is also a space of experiential passage and transcendence. Gadamer's regard for the anticipation of a totality of meaning as a regulative idea of language makes this clear. Speaking involves a temporal movement: *speaking moves towards (anticipates) what wants to be said and comes from an unspoken recognition of something that needs to be said.*

The linguisticality of human experience involves a constant passage between unities of meaningfulness both lost and remembered and a completeness of meaning anticipated. Hermeneutics suggests that our unavoidable involvement in linguisticality implies that we are beings who are always drawn from a sense of incompleteness towards an anticipation of completeness. A dialectic of loss and hope is integral to our linguistic experience of being-in-the-world and indicates the transformative space of understanding. Crucially, the presence of the *Vorgriff der Vollendung* is disclosed by hermeneutic negativity which reveals the limitations of an understanding of a subject matter in relation to what it

---

60 Ibid., A239–B299, 259.
61 See Nicholas Davey, 'Baumgarten', in *A Companion to Aesthetics*, ed. D. Cooper (London: Wiley-Blackwell, 2009), 162–3.

can yet be understood as being. In so doing, hermeneutic negativity reveals the transcendental presence within language-being of that which both grounds and renders possible the experience of objects as hermeneutical. The *Vorgriff* is not just a figure of thought but configures what can be thought of as hermeneutic objects.

Hermeneutic objects are not just given in the way material objects are. The historical event is not 'out there' as something in the world to be reconstructed. Rather, as a hermeneutical object, the historical event emerges in and through the interactive process of understanding. The historical event considered hermeneutically is not an artefact that precedes interpretation but an object that arises from the practice of interpretation. To put the argument another way, if understanding is always an understanding of something, what nature must that something have for it to become a hermeneutical object? A key to this question lies in Gadamer's remark that the 'fore-conception of completeness' is obviously a formal condition of all understanding: only what constitutes a unity of meaning is intelligible.[62]

It is important to distinguish between an anticipation of formative completeness and a regulative anticipation of completeness. If formative, the appeal to completeness is paradoxical. In a realm of endless becoming there can be no final, definitive unity of meaning. If so, the principle of the 'fore-conception of completeness' establishes the formal impossibility of hermeneutics. If, on the other hand, the weighting is given to a formative anticipation of completeness, the outcome is more productive. For an object to become an object of hermeneutic consciousness, it must be encountered as an entity which *promises* to fulfil (i.e. must comply with) the hermeneutic subject's *expectation* of completeness. In other words, for reflective consciousness to engage with an object hermeneutically that object must suggest the possibility of a significant form, that is, point beyond itself towards the intimation of a completable meaning.

Gadamer is not suggesting that hermeneutic consciousness projects a meaning onto a meaningless object. Nor is he arguing that experiential objects have intrinsic meanings to be deciphered. It is a *leitmotif* of philosophical hermeneutics that the objects of everyday experience are invariably fragmentary in nature, clusters of undecided and contradictory future possibilities.[63] The meaning of such experiential objects is incomplete and unresolved. They have

62 TM 293–4.
63 TM 112.

not as yet been transformed into (a coherent) structure or unity of meaning. This is not to say that such objects lack meaningfulness: like all subject matters (*Sachen*) of experience, they remain ambiguous, open and unresolved in their meaning. The task of the hermeneutic imagination is to push forward and extend the entailments of such experience towards that anticipated completeness of meaning which reflection takes them to suggest. In other words the condition of experiential objects becoming objects of hermeneutical reflection is not that they present themselves as a unity of meaning to reflection but that their manifold elements are capable of being patterned by hermeneutic thinking in such a way that they promise to comply with its expectation of a formative unity of meaning. In conclusion, the condition of fragments of experience becoming potential hermeneutical objects is that their diverse elements (words, phrases, innuendos, entailments, etc.) *intimate* potentially completable unities of meaning. They are objects which invite involvement and participation in their unfolding. *The hermeneutical object is what a complexity of experience points to when thought of in terms of a possible unity of meaning.* It is something we move towards and something that emerges more clearly in our engagement with it. The expectation of completeness is the unifying form which when applied to a manifold of diverse elements allows it to emerge as if progressing towards a coherence as a unified work. This expectation permits a manifold to emerge and to be configured as that unity of meaning which the complexity of its elements implies. *Der Vorgriff der Vollkommenheit* considered as an ideal limit is the basis of the dialectical nature of negative hermeneutics.

These arguments appear to endorse the criticisms made of philosophical hermeneutics by deconstructive thinkers. Given the ontological circumstances in which it is applied, the more the *Vorgriff* strives to achieve a formal completion of meaning, the closer it approaches the formal impossibility of its realization: *hermeneutics assumes the impossible, strives after the impossible and will, ultimately, be broken by the impossible.* Yet, the formal argument against hermeneutics is inconsequential. It confuses epistemological truth with hermeneutical truth.

To defend philosophical hermeneutics against the logical *scepsis* that anything can be said about anything requires not a repudiation of the deconstructive position but a recognition of the procedural fact that the epistemological status of a claim to truth is not the same as its hermeneutical claim to truthfulness. Deconstructive criticism appears blind to the distinction and conflates the two. It supposes erroneously that the status of a hermeneutic claim to truth depends upon the epistemological status of its truth or, put in other words, the inability to determine the epistemological status of a claim nullifies the hermeneutic status that any claim may have. Deconstruction's denial of the plausibility of hermeneutic philosophy rests on a blanket negation of completeness. The deconstructive stance is clear: the hermeneutical pursuit of an impossible completion places the credibility of its quest into question. Yet the criticism fails to properly distinguish between the 'aesthetic' and the 'logical capacity' of language.

Words do not just stand for, refer to or configure linguistic objects. They also entail giving form and structure to those configurations.[64] However, what gives form to linguistic objects is plainly not itself a linguistic object. The *Vorgriff* is a logical form in and through which linguistic objects become intelligible as completable units of significant meaning. What makes it possible for hermeneutics to think about its objects as intelligible is not itself an intelligible object but only an intelligible form. Deconstruction's category mistake is to judge what is produced by language's logical capacity – the regulative idea of completion – as if it were a linguistic object. Here the mistake is compounded.

If all linguistic (aesthetic) objects are beyond formal completion so that their truth can never be rendered epistemologically complete, it would follow that if treated as an aesthetic object, the truth of the principle of completeness can never be arrived at. However, as the logical idea of language, completeness is not itself and never could be completable. The deconstructive criticism of hermeneutics effectively asks for the impossible: the truth of the principle of completeness is legitimate only if its truth can be formally verified. Not only is the quest unachievable but deconstruction fails to see that the truth of the principle does not depend on its epistemological verification but upon what it enables. *The truth of the principle lies in its hermeneutically integrative function, in its ability to bring objects of experience into meaningful relation.* Apart from what it enables, the principle has no truth: its truth lies not in any culminating moment of completion but in the rendering of experiential manifolds into albeit provisional units of intelligible meaning.[65] Its truth lies not in what it is but in what it does, that is, in its integrative function of bringing complex manifolds of experience into a hermeneutically intelligible structure. Deconstruction fails to see that the regulative idea of completeness which language anticipates is not an object of thought to be rendered ever more determinate but is, rather, the

---

64 The phrase derives from J. G. Hamann: see Cristina Lafont, *The Linguistic Turn in Hermeneutic Philosophy* (Cambridge, MA: The MIT Press, 1999), 9.
65 TM 293–4.

logical form under which objects of thought can be thought hermeneutically. The corollaries of this mistake are potentially damaging for the possibility of hermeneutic understanding within the humanities. This becomes plain if we consider the question, what does hermeneutic philosophy lose if the *Vorgriff der Vollkommenheit* is abandoned as a fiction?

From a hermeneutic perspective, whether the principle of completeness is formally realizable is not the point. The truth of the *Vorgriff der Vollkommenheit* lies not in the arrival of an anticipated meaning but in the bringing-into-structure that such an anticipation facilitates. As a regulative principle, the *Vorgriff* is the transcendental condition of objects being thought of as hermeneutical, that is, as objects whose structure anticipates the possibility of a completable meaning. To encounter a hermeneutic object is to experience an object that is illusive and suggestive, an object which presents itself as promising more than it presently shows of itself. To think of and to experience an object hermeneutically is to experience an object that invites engagement not for what it is but for what it might become. The *Vorgriff der Vollkommenheit* facilitates a structure of engagement in and through which a hermeneutic object is potentially always on the way to becoming more than itself. The *Vorgriff* establishes a framework of hope, the expectation of coming to know and understand more. In a language ontology whose *Sachen* are always in play, there are always meanings being lost and meanings awaiting recovery and discovery. The *Vorgriff* gives an intelligible structure to this constant play. It is never the 'meaning' anticipated but the structure of anticipation that is key. A number of points are pertinent to the argument.

1. Because of the finitude of both their transmission and reception, the subject matters of hermeneutic experience are never given in their entirety. The principle of hermeneutic surplus suggests that every disclosure of x implies the speculative excess of what is held in x+. The *Vorgriff* serves as an exploratory device: anticipating what the known aspects of a *Sache* point towards becomes a means for drawing out and actualizing its as yet unrealized determinations of meaning. The *Vorgriff* demands a reflective distance from what any disclosure of meaning reveals: that is, that whatever is disclosed can never be the whole story: there is always more to come. The achievement of reflective distance is a feature of what we call in Chapter 5 the accomplished practitioner and has the paradoxical quality of disinterested interest.

2. The *Vorgriff* grounds Gadamer's philosophical resistance to relativism. As a presupposition of linguisticality, the *Vorgriff* allows a constellation of diverse strands of meaning to be spoken of as if they were anticipating an intelligible whole. In other words, the *Vorgriff* does not anticipate a universal but a universality of field within which diverse perspectives of meaning become relatable. Such anticipations establish crucially the relatively stable emergent structures of a cultural becoming or *Bildung*.
3. Insofar as the *Vorgriff* stimulates interactive engagement with a *Sache*, it enables a hermeneutic agency to acquire a sense of having come to understand more. The *Vorgriff* conditions the possibility of both an unfolding self-understanding and participation in a hermeneutic adventure.
4. The anticipation of completion emerges as a transcendent condition of the possibility of the negativity of experience. The experience of negativity concerns a moment of recognition in which we are forced to realize that we have forgotten or overlooked the fact that a *Sache* can always be more than it has presently shown itself to be. The operative effect of assuming the completion principle to be true drives the essential negativity of hermeneutic experience, that is, that a *Sache* is always more than what it immediately shows itself to be. By insisting upon the finite nature of all understanding, such negativity anticipates the possibility of new and further experience.
5. As the condition of negative experience, the anticipation of completeness reveals itself to be a philosophical prerequisite of learning. The negativity of experience is generative of formative consequences. It establishes the possibility of a characterology: an understanding of the habits and circumstances which prompt a hermeneutic agency to hold the inadequate or limited expectations that it does. The negativity of experience does not just reveal a catalogue of misjudgements but also discloses the unseen dispositions and patterns of prejudice underlying them. There is an important corollary to this.
6. That negative capability is generative in that its formative consequences invoke what Gadamer refers to as the unfolding movement of a temporal structure (*die Zeitstruktur der Bewegtheit*).[66] This suggests that the anticipation of completion establishes not only a differential space but a temporal field within which the unfolding of a *Bildungsformat* can take

---

66 Hans-Georg Gadamer, 'Text and Interpretation', in *The Gadamer Reader*, ed. Richard E. Palmer (Evanston: Northwestern University Press, 2007), 189.

place. The unfolding articulates that temporal structure which holds in place its notional starting and end points. The negative moments of hermeneutical practice drive an emergent narrative structure forward by impelling it away from its starting point and towards its anticipated completion.
7. The anticipation of completion articulates the way of the negative and reveals the essential positivity of the latter. The anticipation of completion drives negative hermeneutics to question the adequacy of any given actuality and, in so doing, to reveal an infinity of other possibilities. The anticipation of completeness is not only the formal ground of negation within negative hermeneutics but demonstrates why the way of the negative is never itself negative. It always anticipates the possibility of more to come.
8. *The aim of the Vorgriff is not necessarily to arrive at an anticipated end but to organize the experience or performances of a work as if it had that end.* The end pursued can always be disrupted by the negativity of experience: it is not what is pursued that is of consequence but what the pursuit itself gives rise to, that is, those unexpected interpretations that can both change one's understanding of a given composition and (this is most important within the humanities) impact on unresolved issues at play in other areas of one's existential involvements. The anticipation of completeness is negentropic. Whilst it moves towards establishing intelligible order within one area of hermeneutic experience, its unavoidable connectedness with other linguistic fields of meaning means that it can quite unintentionally realign frameworks in other fields. The negentropic character of the *Vorgriff* discloses its negative capacity.

At the beginning of this section we argued that within an ontology of language-being with all its diversity and complexity, the 'anticipation of completeness' functions as a unitary device establishing similarities and continuities upon which knowledge can be built. This allows our argument to take a strategic turn: the relational nature of the *Vorgriff* emerges as central to Gadamer's account of image and concept formation and to how the hermeneutically transformative capacities of both concept and image can be understood.

The turn of our argument towards the image and the concept has an instructive impact on one of the key problems in Gadamer's aesthetics: what is meant by his use of the term 'representation'? We asked earlier why, having so vociferously criticized the original-copy relation in his earlier accounts of the image, does Gadamer revert in his later aesthetic writings to reworking the classical doctrine of *mimesis*? The underlying ontological prioritization of possibility over actuality offers an insight into this aspect of Gadamer's thinking. The anticipation of completeness offers an instructive account of how image and concept formation outline what the dynamics of 'understanding more' entail.

9. Images and coming to completion

Nowhere is the relationship between the intensive and extensive dimensions of a philosophical question more apparent than in the history of aesthetics that underpins philosophical hermeneutics. Not only does Gadamer question intensively the tradition of aesthetic thinking which reaches deep into the heart of philosophical hermeneutics but, by engaging with it, radically transforms it. The account of image formation (and specifically the effects of that formation) gives an insight into the transformative workings of understanding. Moreover, it offers an insight into how practice is able to transform our understanding of what is at play within experience. Nevertheless, the status of the image and the meaning of representation pose two paradoxical issues for philosophical hermeneutics.

With regard to the fixity of the visual image, how can it ever accurately represent the actuality of change and becoming? Will not any image be a re-presentation, a copy, a secondary appearance of such an actuality? Are not the concepts surrounding the language of the image and those associated with an ontology of change and becoming completely at odds? These two issues touch on the function of the *Vorgriff* in hermeneutical experience. Before we consider the issues at play, two contextual remarks are appropriate. Within an ontology of language-being the 'anticipation of completeness' functions as a unitary device establishing similarities and continuities upon which stable epistemological structures can be built. Both image and concept gain their hermeneutic significance from their transformative capacity within the obscure world of language-being. That the hermeneutic significance of image and concept depend on their relation to language-being emphasizes that hermeneutics is not a matter of distanced methodological analysis but one of participatory experience revealing the extent to which a hermeneutic agency *already* participates in that which is larger than itself. The hermeneutically empowered image or concept reveals precisely the extent of that involvement. Remarks made by Christian Lotz concerning the hermeneutic status of the image take us into the next area of our debate.

In his informative book, *The Art of Gerhardt Richter, Hermeneutics, Images and Meaning*, Lotz reminds us that the experience of art is, hermeneutically speaking, one of participation; that negativity in art always has a hermeneutic structure; that artworks do not simply occur in the mind of a viewer but involve a merging between viewer and work. Images are not stable unities but dynamic formations that are never fixed. Meaning is not something 'there' but emerges through participatory engagement. Images are 'apparitions', epiphanies and not derivative copies. The spectator is an involved-bringer-into presence of what lies within a representation.[67] Lotz's hermeneutical and aesthetic precepts depend upon the participatory relationship between concept, image and the world of language-being in which they operate. The question is how does the world of the static image inform the ever-changing realms of lived experience?

The hermeneutic subject does not of course emerge in the realm of *Dasein* without any mental capacities. *Dasein* rules out the *tabula rasa* account of mind. Continuous processes of linguistic and cultural attunement imply that the hermeneutic subject acquires images and concepts by virtue of its participation in language-being, indeed, that its being cannot be separated from language-being. A hermeneutic subject's repertoire of acquired images and concepts is fluid. Some inherited meanings are not fully formed, and others carry problematic and unrealized potentials for meaning that will haunt coming generations. Gadamer comments, 'speaking implies using (meeting with) pre-established words with general meanings, (whilst) at the same time, a constant process of concept formation is going on, by means of which the life of language develops'.[68] This is a reminder that for philosophical hermeneutics thinking and understanding are essentially movement: they entail participation in constantly shifting conceptual structures. Language and thought are conceived as structured processes of continuous adjustment to pressing experiences of the world.

Negative hermeneutics is anti-essentialist in its epistemological disposition. It sides with Hegel and Nietzsche in being wedded to the historical origins of images and concepts. It recognizes that in its emergence, language exhibits a propensity for generalization. Gadamer speaks of the life of language as 'lying

---

67 Christian Lotz, *The Art of Gerhard Richter, Hermeneutics, Images and Meaning* (London: Bloomsbury, 2017), 1, 19, 40, 45.
68 TM 229. Inserts and emphasis added ND.

in its logical productivity, (ie. in its) spontaneous and inventive seeking out of similarities by means of which it is possible to order things'.[69] The position is not unreminiscent of David Hume's argument that the concept of identity is derived from multiple experiences of the similar which the imagination then confuses as experiences of the same. Gadamer remarks, 'the common genus is derived explicitly from the observation of similarity'.[70] This suggests that the *Vorgriff der Vollkommenheit* is not a subjective a priori principle but a natural tendency within language towards grouping, ordering and classification. The parallels between concept formation in philosophy and image formation in art are striking. The *Vorgriff* offers an illuminating way of thinking about what the similarity entails.

Lotz argues that Gerhard Richter is an artist who emphatically sides with Heidegger and Gadamer in their advocacy of an aesthetics of *Darstellung* as opposed to one of *Vorstellung*. This has the consequence of suggesting that an image is something to be arrived at. In aesthetic theories centred on the concept of representation, something external to the artwork confers meaning upon the image. The artwork remains ontologically secondary to the original object that, in aesthetic terms, is re-presented (*imitatio*). However, in the case of *Darstellung* (presentation), the ontological relation between work and image is fundamentally different: the image is ontogenetic; it brings something into being. Nothing outside the image confers meaning upon it. Mimetic art in the sense that Gadamer uses the term is essentially performative and, hence, participatory. Through a combination of a number of elements, the meaningful image occasions itself in and through the presentation that is the artwork. Lotz observes,

> What is coming into presence in a representation (artwork) is what we should call in the proper sense an image. Images are not pictures (i.e. representations of something outside themselves), since they are dynamic they are never fixed but depend both on the spectator's formation and on the internal formation of the painting.[71]

If it is accepted that images are not pictures, that is, *re-presentations* of something outside themselves, must we not abandon the idea that painted images concern external objective referents (a known person or landscape) that all can commonly recognize? If so what is the artist drawing on when forming an image? How

---

69 TM 433. Insert added by ND.
70 TM 431.
71 Lotz, *The Art of Gerhard Richter*, 34.

does the *Vorgriff* function in the formation process? Gadamer's process ontology insists that the 'landscape' is not one thing but a sensuous manifold of different impressions, some calming, others violent, some bright, others sombre. Our experience of a portrait subject is similarly varied, sometimes joyous, sometimes withdrawn and, at other times, detached. This returns us to Rothwell's notion of the experience of a subject matter as a plethora of contrary and conflicting fragments. No subject matter is ever given to us in its entirety. The temporality and finitude of understanding means that 'subject matters' effectively break up before us. This is where the *Vorgriff* once again becomes pertinent. Remembering a significant family member or landscape is remembering a person or location that is 'one' only in word or image. What is held in memory of the 'subject' is, to the contrary, not one but diverse perspectival fragments without any general sense. Rendering them intelligible means finding patterns of meaningful relation between them. This does not mean returning them to a former unity that, ontologically speaking, they never had but rather seeking for them a coherence that would allow them the collective sense or narrative they originally lack. The implication is that in the act of talking about the broken and the fragmented, the tendency within language to anticipate association and completion impels the hermeneutic subject towards trying to discover a meaningful sense for fragmented and broken episodes and to render them intelligible, whole, if not healed. In what sense does an image endeavour to uncover a previously unseen unity in our experience of a subject matter? Here we can answer the question of what the portrait or landscape painter is seeking to summon into visibility given that the image is not of anything external.

The *Vorgriff der Vollendung* is clearly not an image itself. Yet, insofar as it anticipates an as yet to emerge unity for a manifold of fragments, the *Vorgriff* impels the painter's search for an image capable of endowing that manifold with a sense-giving pattern. The search is driven by an anticipation of the unity which the fragmentary and perspectival themselves point to, an image that brings the artist to see a previously unseen coherence within a body of experience. The image is not like a sign: it does not refer to a fixed person or geographical location existing independently of it. Lotz is eloquent on this point:

> A painting can only be an image because it internally builds up what it is about (its subject-matter) and thereby idealises (or, rather, essentializes) what it is about: it no longer refers to something in outer reality.[72]

---

72 Ibid., 51. Inserts added ND.

The image in effect gives expression to a temporal process. It is rooted in a body of inchoate experiences and brought forward by practice to order and articulate those experiences. The artistic image can then operate as a placeholder for such experiences and go on to achieve transformative effects well beyond the body of experiences out of which it was initially summonsed. In Gadamerian terms, being rendered into image allows a subject matter to become more what it is. The image synthesizes its elements into such a condensed form that 'something infinitely complex suddenly appears as something finite'.[73] A body of various and temporally distinct experiences which are not in-themselves one are brought together by the image and appear as 'one'. In short, the process of image making anticipates finding a visual form capable of unifying the complexity of an artist's experiences of a subject matter such that it becomes an intelligible placeholder for that diversity. Whereas in the aesthetics of representation the objective referent is external, in the aesthetics of presentation the referent is internal. It draws from and brings into articulate form what is at play within processes of participation, experience and memory. Whereas representation seeks an image to visually duplicate an external object, in the practical processes of presentation the image emerges from and speaks to the individual and collective world of temporal experience. The image is a coming into shape, a giving form to and a rendering thinkable of varieties of experience such that, when formed, it serves as a singular placeholder for bodies of experience which cannot themselves be reduced to singularities.

The dialectical character of image formation is notable. On the one hand, there is a formative impetus generated by the *Vorgriff* itself. The formation of an image allows a body of diverse but related experiences to be generalized under a certain visual form. The image 'essentializes' or 'idealizes' as one what is not one, that is, the body of resemblances it is drawn from. By establishing itself as a common referent, the image renders communicable a complex manifold of particulars which in themselves would be incommunicable. In the material form of a painted or sculpted image, isolated and fragmented experiences escape their particularity and become thinkable as part of the world of ideas. On the other hand, once formed, the image acquires applicative powers. The initial material roots of an image in individual experience allow the generalized image to be translated back into its particular instances.[74] In short, philosophy and religion

---

73 Ibid., 50.
74 Gadamer makes a series of related points: 'The general concept meant by a word is enriched by any given perception of a thing, so that what emerges is a new, more specific word formation, which does more justice to the particularity of that act of perception. However certainly speaking implies

need the materiality of the image for their ideas to both find a place in and to have an effect within the world. Lotz puts the point succinctly: 'formed images (*Gebilde*) are in between nature, theory and culture. They allow the possibility of seeing our ideas about the world in the world'.[75]

10. The *Vorgriff* and practice

What impels the practitioner towards wanting to form an image? What drives the belief that there is an image or concept able to make sense of conflicting bodies of intense experience? For negative hermeneutics the answer is clear: it is our being-in-language that impels us towards the clarifying concept or image. Such being-in-language is not a fixed state but entails immersion in a multiplicity of anticipatory processes. At play with the language world are sets of culturally inherited subject matters cross-hatched by ambiguities and unresolved tensions. Their meaning is always historically open, held within a nexus of etymological and logical entailments. Gadamer refers to the capacity of language to seek out the connected and the similar as 'its logical productivity'.[76] Each word means more than it says in any given context. This surplus is precisely that totality of meaning which every word invokes but can never express totally.[77] Subject matters such as democracy, race and gender can become highly problematic because of the conflicting alignments of meaning their transmission entails. The task of interpretation is to look to the excess that is x+ for those as yet unrealized but as yet possible alignments of meaning able to reconfigure the tensions in play. As Gadamer puts it in *Truth and Method*, thought can look to the stock of entailed ideas already within a subject matter to bring that subject matter to a fuller realization. In doing this, thought is guided by the *Vorgriff der Vollendung*. All concepts point to an infinite number of determinations, and the task of hermeneutic practice is to penetrate ever more deeply the unrealized possibilities for meaningfulness they contain.

The argument emphasizes that hermeneutics concerns participatory practice and involved agency rather than theory alone. The conflicts within an inherited subject matter can only trouble an agency that is concerned about

---

using pre-established words with general meaning, at the same time, a constant process of concept formation is going on, by means of which the life of language develops' (™ 429).
75 Lotz, *The Art of Gerhard Richter*, 7.
76 TM 432.
77 TM 458.

their implications. The image or concept that resolves inherited tensions within a subject matter does so by bringing a hermeneutic agency to see that what they had only known formerly as broken and fragmentary is now unified and cohesive. Of course, what the *Vorgriff* impels us towards is a realization of meaningfulness that was always logically possible only that the finite limitations of our understanding prevented us from seeing it. The *Vorgriff* emphasizes that hermeneutic experience entails a temporal trajectory of experience which, in Heideggerian terms, we undergo. This implies that our temporal quest to find patterns of sense within experience is structured by the *Vorgriff* and its anticipations. This argument about the anticipatory function of the *Vorgriff* links with the 'transformation into structure argument' presented in *Truth and Method*.[78]

Could there be an experience of hermeneutical understanding without the *Vorgriff*? If the *Vorgriff* were not the form of hermeneutic experience, it would be difficult to relate past, present and future interpretations of a subject matter's meaning. The form establishes the evolving continuity of non-identical repetitions upon which the transformative movement of understanding depends. Gadamer suggests that hermeneutics considered as a practice depends on a 'sensitivity for perceiving prior determinations, anticipations, and imprints that reside in concepts'.[79] If, furthermore, 'our thinking is never satisfied (and) constantly points beyond itself',[80] it is drawn towards what the *Vorgriff* implicitly anticipates, that is, those further as yet unrealized determinations of meaning that are already held within a given subject matter. Hermeneutic participation in a text or argument is not a matter of reconstructing its nature but rather of thinking with the movement of its terms and anticipating the as yet unrealized potentials for meaning that are already held within them. Let us now turn to the relation between the anticipation of completion and images.

If the *Vorgriff* were not the form of hermeneutic experience, it would be difficult to relate past, present and future interpretations of a subject matter's meaning. The *Vorgriff* is able to render these different moments of experience relatable under the same form. The genius of the image lies in its ability to turn the world that is not art into art and to see in art the fragmented world of experience rendered as if it where coherent and complete. Because of its ability to render disparate experiences seemingly whole and complete, the image allows us to see what we could not otherwise have seen. This is precisely where the surprise

---

78 TM 110–21.
79 Gadamer, 'Autobiographical Reflections', 21.
80 Ibid., 31.

emergence of an image can have such unexpected and transformative effects: it reorganizes a muddled complexity of thought and feeling into something graspable and brings us thereby to think about ourselves differently. The image enables us to see something which otherwise we would not have seen.

The *Vorgriff der Vollendung* considered as the procedural form of hermeneutical experience confirms that hermeneutics is primarily a form of participatory experience and not a philosophical theory. As the cognitive form of hermeneutical experience, the *Vorgriff* is an a priori structure that logically precedes thought in the sense that we find in it precisely what language has *already* prepared. The *Vorgriff* does not exist before language but emerges from within it and gives expression to the temporal form of *Sprachlichkeit* itself. It is a priori only in the sense that it invokes the way in which we as language-beings commonly structure and appropriate our experience.[81] This confirms hermeneutics to be neither a 'philosophy' nor a body of theory but a mode of temporally revealed meaningful experience. Though we cannot ask the meaning of this form, whatever is experienced as meaningful is so because it reflects the form of the *Vorgriff*. The hermeneutical element within hermeneutic experience is not an object of experience but concerns the form of that experience. A paradox at the heart of hermeneutics is now clear. If understood as the quest for the final truth, the hermeneutical quest is rendered impossible precisely by the very *Vorgriff* that enables it. Negativity is inherent within the anticipatory form of hermeneutic thinking. This paradox forces further reflection on the significance of art within hermeneutical thinking.

If it is specifically the image's capacity to synthesize and to unify which renders a temporal process of experience thinkable, what is the relation between seemingly illusory aesthetic representations of completion and the world from which they emerge where no completion is possible? If logical completion cannot be represented in the finite forms of art, what do images of completion represent if anything at all? This question returns us to the distinction between aesthetic and logical completion. 'Aesthetic completion' understood as the visible way in which an image successfully integrates a body of meaningful elements and 'logical completion' in which all possible determinations of meaning with a specific field of concerns are met, are manifestly not the same. Aesthetic completeness involves the sensible whilst the *Vorgriff* anticipates a formal completeness beyond determinate representation. Does this imply as critiques of the humanities and hermeneutics suggest that all artistic and literary representations of the world

---

81 See John Millbank, *The Word Made Strange* (Oxford: Blackwell, 1998), 128.

as whole and complete are illusions lacking in any cognitive content? Does this not empty the term 'representation' of any meaning? It can neither represent nor correspond to anything in the actual world. In a world where completion is impossible, what function would representation of the complete have?

Aesthetic representations of completeness are not of anything in the world but rather make a place for something that were if not represented would have no place in the world. Representations of completeness are representations of the possibility of things being other than they initially appear. Aesthetic renditions of completeness represent places of possibility: the factual can always be countered by other possibilities, and subject matters can always be more than they presently appear. Such representations demonstrate that transcendence is always possible within actuality. This strengthens an earlier observation that in hermeneutical thinking, the possible is ontologically prior to the actual. This brings the questions of representation and of negativity back into discussion.

As we have argued, understanding within philosophical hermeneutics entails an experience of movement, of a thinking with (*mit denken*) a subject matter whereby the practitioner is both shaped by and continues to shape the unfolding determinations of that subject matter. The *Vorgriff der Vollendung* as the form of our experiential involvement with a subject matter both guides and structures our participation in its movement. The history of a subject matter's unfolding meanings and the ambiguities they contain suggest future determinations of meaning that allow for a more comprehensive understanding of its implied meanings. The *Vorgriff* always points towards the possibility of an ever more complete meaning of a subject matter.

As the outcome of such thinking-with, the process of bringing into image is, simultaneously, a bringing to summation of what has been at play within a subject matter *and* a projection of what the *anticipated* outcome of that play is. The image represents not an actual world but an outcome of what is at play within a body of experience represented as a determinate world. It allows us to envisage as whole what in actuality we only experience in part. By showing what a body of experience anticipates or points towards, the image both represents and reminds us of the presence of possibility within the world. *The world is not art and yet the world requires art in order for us to discern what worldly action is possible.*

> The world can never become as complete and coherent as an artwork but the vision of possible completeness can inspire practical action towards making the incomplete more complete. It is not a question of translating the image into

actuality but of allowing that image to transform one's understanding of what is possible or plausible within actuality.[82]

Adapting one of Cassirer's arguments, only when realized by an artwork in an albeit limited way, can we become concretely aware of 'the living possibilities' present in a subject matter: 'prior to its realisation it (the subject matter or concept) is not restricted to a fixed and clearly delimited sphere of possibilities'. The task of an art image is precisely that of 'seeking and creating ever new possibilities',[83] allowing its subject matter to be represented in evermore innovative ways. However, for negative hermeneutics an important dialectical twist remains: in allowing us to see a body of experience as a meaningful wholeness, the image makes manifest that which though the condition of seeing cannot itself be seen.

Within negative hermeneutics the recognition of an artwork as an 'aesthetic whole' immediately invokes what that artwork is not, that is, a 'conceptual whole' or totality. However, it is precisely against such a horizon of indefinite possibility that the artwork gains its presence as a discernible determinate whole. Gadamer is sensitive to the ineliminable difference at the centre of this relationship: artworks offer 'aesthetic totalities' or 'closed circles of meaning' and thereby evoke a totality of meaning without being able to express it completely. Yet this negativity entails a positivity. Art's importance resides not in closing that differential space but in keeping it open. By maintaining the differential space, the artwork creates a space in which determinations of meaning other than those given in actuality can emerge. The artwork negates the immediacy of the ordinary and everyday in order to bring out the unnoticed possibilities they still hold. In this respect, the *Vorgriff der Vollendung* can be considered the driver of both artistic and hermeneutical practice. *The artistic image represents and makes manifests the place of possibility within the world.*

The foregoing remarks confirm the status of the *Vorgriff* as establishing the phenomenological constitution of the artwork or hermeneutical object. Recognizing this status has important dialectical consequences for our overall argument the least of which points to a paradigm shift in the way we think about the artwork. Negative hermeneutics moves away from the notion of art as an idea or as an object to be deciphered and towards the notion of art as a living, moving process that demands active involvement. As they influence the suggestion that our experience of art is an experience of reflective movement, the implications

---

82 Nicholas Davey, *Unfinished Worlds, Hermeneutics, Aesthetics and Gadamer* (Edinburgh: Edinburgh University Press, 2013), 134.
83 See Cassirer, *The Logic of the Humanities*, 76.

of this shift will be briefly outlined. They indicate what is fundamentally awry with the deconstructive critique of hermeneutics and the humanities.

That the *Vorgriff* can never achieve a formal completion of meaning suggests that the deconstructive critique of the implausibility of the hermeneutic quest for definitive meaning is indeed correct. The impossibility of rendering any understanding of an artwork complete means that there is no point at which we arrive at its truth. The very form which renders an artwork thinkable forever postpones its completion. Interpretation distances the work from understanding yet further. These points tend to support deconstructive critiques of hermeneutics. With no certain meaning to be grasped, nihilism appears to gain the upper hand. Any meaning anticipated by the *Vorgriff* is rendered meaningless in its pursuit. The negative judgement against hermeneutics and the humanities as lacking graspable cognitive content seems persuasive after all: there is no getting to the bottom of these disciplines as their bottom is denied. However, here our argument takes a significant turn.

The success of the deconstructive critique of hermeneutics and the humanities turns on the assumption that artworks and hermeneutics presuppose a bottom to be fathomed. However, if this essentialist assumption is abandoned in favour of a conception of the hermeneutical object as a process in which meaningfulness is always ravelling and unravelling, an altogether different account of the cognitive worth of hermeneutics emerges. It is not arriving at a terminal meaning that matters but the movement and collateral shifts of understanding that the process of pursuit enables.

The unfulfillable aspirations of the *Vorgriff* compromise claims to cognitive certainty within hermeneutics. In doing this it achieves a more fundamental negation: it exposes the deep Platonic prejudice in both the critique of hermeneutics and in much of the broad tradition of hermeneutics itself, namely that the artwork or hermeneutic object represent an hypostasised reality capable of being grasped. We shall argue to the contrary, namely that the artwork or hermeneutic object does not denote an intelligible essence but an experiential process whose being resides in its movement. Hermeneutic objects are not representations of an objective correlative. To the contrary, when we objectify them in language as 'works' they operate as placeholder terms for living participatory processes that unfold in and through interpretative engagement. This offers a new direction in hermeneutical aesthetics.

This argument transcends the notion that the task of texts and artworks is to represent or reflect established meanings or concepts. It passes to another and more fundamental position: artworks are conduits of hermeneutical movement.

Above all, it is the experiential movement that the artwork facilitates that is important. The object of our hermeneutic reflection is nothing other than the *living experience* that is the artwork. In this context, the term 'experience' (*Erfahrung*) conveys a reflective sense of being moved both intellectually and emotionally, of participating in something that has been, is and will be ongoing. Such movement is indicative of the 'truth-claim' (*Wahrheitsanspruch*) a hermeneutical object makes upon us, a claim which in the undergoing of it we experience a shift in the passage of our understanding. Once again the importance of the *Vorgriff* is emphasized. It establishes the differential space within which the transformational movement of insight (*Erfahrung*) can take place.

The differential space which the *Vorgriff* initiates allows understanding to pass between the *woher* and the *wozu* of a subject matter. This is consistent with Iser's notion that hermeneutical understanding involves recursive looping in which our engagement with a hermeneutical object constantly challenges both our received understanding of that object and our expectancy of what it makes possible. When we receive a hermeneutical object from the past we do not simply re-experience its past as it was. A shock of excited recognition seizes us when we are brought to see in that object the fulfilment of potentials that were not initially seen. The present comes to see the past not as inert but as a transmitter of possibilities which initiate further hermeneutical journeying.

Such a transformative movement is educational. The concept of education carries the etymological nuance of a continuous process, of being drawn out from a limited set of assumptions towards independent engagement with the unfolding of the potentials within a given practice. Being educated in the Gadamerian sense is to have become experienced and, as a consequence, to have attained confident openness to experience and its challenges. Such an education is to have undergone a transformational movement, to have recognized and responded to the emergence of possibilities within one's discipline. It is precisely the *Vorgriff* which in establishing the temporality of experience opens the differential space within which facilitates the transformational movement of insight. The power of the artistic or literary image resides less in its ability to represent a determinate subject matter than in its ability to articulate a sense of movement which is simultaneously retrospective and anticipatory. It is retrospective in that it reveals certain possibilities of the past as completed and anticipatory in that it also points to future possibilities yet to be realized. In this respect the hermeneutic dimensions of our experience of the image disclose something of the truth of our being, that is, that we have emerged from and live towards possibility. With 'its stress on temporal occurrence through us' art discloses more than itself, that is, that speculative totality of meaning which shines through art but which it cannot capture.[84] It opens our being to contemplation and reflection.

From the perspective of hermeneutical experience the importance of the unifying image in art, literature or poetry is what it incites, discloses and upholds beyond itself, that is, that sense of living movement upon which transformative understanding depends. Effective art incites participation in the possibilities that it reveals. The artistic image represents and makes manifest the place of possibility within the world. Insofar as it does so, the hermeneutic object or artwork excites by drawing us into *action*.

Nietzsche clearly understood the experience of art as a process of strengthening and enlivening.[85] 'All art works tonically, increases strength, inflames desire (i.e. the feeling of strength), excites all the more subtle recollections.'[86] The life-enhancing experiences of art excite and enhance our 'power of understanding'.[87] These remarks echo our comments about the effect of the hermeneutic object as both realizing past possibilities and anticipating future possibilities in understanding. Nietzsche notes that 'the effect of works of art is to excite the state that creates art – intoxication' and excitement.[88] This is a life-affirming call to action within a given practice.

Hermeneutically speaking, the artwork 'excites' for two reasons. First, the image reassembles bodies of fragmentary experiences as a unified whole in which we come to recognize with some excitement the fulfilment of possibilities of meaningfulness which, when at play within the past, we did not initially perceive. The image transforms what we thought we knew and represents in a new way what we thought was possible in a given practice. Second, by opening our eyes to the possibilities held in the past, the image points to what has now become possible. The image excites because it incites action and deeper involvement in the transformative movement of one's being. At this point, the 'way of the negative' achieves its most significant negation. It displaces nihilism itself.

Wittgenstein's poignant remark that the solution to a problem can be the disappearance of that problem is helpful here.[89] Given that the *Vorgriff*'s

---

84 John Millbank, *The Word Made Strange, Theology, Language, Culture* (London: Blackwell, 1997), 142.
85 WP 809.
86 Ibid.
87 WP 810.
88 WP 820.
89 Ludwig Wittgenstein, *Tractatus, Logico-Philosophicus* (London: Routledge and Kegan Paul, 1962), Sec. 6.52 and 6.521.

impossible pursuit of completion can promote a sense of despair, the suggestion that the *Vorgriff* displaces nihilism seems counter-intuitive. On the face of it, the opposite seems true. That the *Vorgriff* initiates hermeneutical movements which have no final resolution indicates that, perhaps, the deconstructive critique of hermeneutics is correct: there is no final truth to be arrived at. Nihilism appears unavoidable. However, this is to assume an essential truth or idea to be arrived at. Yet such a 'realist' assumption is incommensurable with the *Sprachsontologie* underwriting both negative and philosophical hermeneutics. When language addresses subject matters that transcend their individual articulations, it is not addressing objects outside language. Artworks and other hermeneutical objects are not simulacra for intelligible essences but experiential processes whose very being resides in their movement. If so, nihilism is dissolved: there is and never was anything intelligible beyond the language world. Subject matters may transcend particular interpretations but subject matters do not transcend interpretation. Rather, they reside in the historical and cultural movements of language-being. The fact that there is no end interpretation to a subject matter and that the finitude of our understanding is insurmountable proves irrelevant. If the movement of interpretation ceases so too would learning. Whereas nihilism laments our inability to bring the movement of interpretation to a conclusive end, negative hermeneutics grasps that the continued transformation of understanding depends on the perpetual movement of experience. The final understanding which the *Vorgriff* renders impossible guarantees that all learning and thinking is ongoing. The unquiet which the *Vorgriff* introduces into a practice insures that understanding within a practice continually transforms itself. The darkness that metaphysical nihilism is supposed to be turns out to be no darkness at all. By generating collateral incidental understandings, the pursuit of the impossible achieves life-transforming insights which simply displace the existential threat of nihilism. From an existential perspective, the unattainability of final understanding is exposed as irrelevant. Within the broad context of a Gadamerian language ontology, what is relevant are the consequential effects that pursuing completeness give rise to, that is, those accumulations of derivative insights arising from the formative negativities of experience which shape both the history and character of any practice. Hermeneutical understanding arises from the movement of experience and not the grasping of a subject matter's supposed timeless essence or truth. The temporal structure which the *Vorgriff* establishes for hermeneutical understanding not only displaces nihilism (by showing the irrelevance of essences or truths beyond the contingencies of the language world) but also demonstrates that everything of immediate significance for us derives precisely from the contingencies of the language world and *not* from anything beyond it. It is the movement which the temporal structure of the *Vorgriff* enables that shifts negative hermeneutics towards such a life-affirming stance.

The temporal structure of experience which the *Vorgriff* establishes demonstrates that hermeneutical understanding takes place entirely within the contingent movements of the language world and is not dependent for its justification upon any metaphysical grounding in essential certainties. If hermeneutical 'truth' can be spoken of, it lies in the integration of elements which establish the living movement of hermeneutic understanding. Two sets of arguments support this claim: (1) hermeneutical experience is structured by a meaningfulness without meaning and (2) the *Wahrheitsanspruch* of hermeneutical understanding integrates the retrospective and anticipatory elements of experience. Both arguments emphasize the clarification of ongoing experiential movement and not the attainment of any final truth. Within language-being, hermeneutical truthfulness and meaningfulness are grounded not in any claim to certainty but in their speculative environment, that is, in the horizons of meaning which they light up within a given practice. Lotz made clear that the power of the image is to render a fragmented body of experience a meaningful whole. It represents the disparateness of previous experience and renders it clear as if possessing a meaningful coherence that we initially failed to perceive. This not only enables us to understand past experience differently but also changes our anticipations of its future implications. In other words, the image reveals how we have both moved on and have more to understand with regard to a body of experience. The meaningfulness of the image, therefore, depends not on the uncovering of a hidden meaning but on its integrative power, upon its ability to illuminate past experience and to anticipate the possibilities that such transformed experience may yet point to. The notion of the *Wahrheitsanspruch* also has a retrospective (*woher*) and anticipatory (*wozu*) moment. This central concept of Gadamer's account of the experience of art does not refer to an epistemological truth-claim but to the experience of something 'truly' speaking to us through art or literature. This clearly invokes the speculative dimensions of language, that is, to how the meaningfulness of the said rests upon an integration of what has already been said with a sense of what has yet to be said. In terms of the argument given earlier, the experience of meaningfulness and of being addressed depend upon the temporal movements of retrospection and anticipation across the differential space made possible by the *Vorgriff*. If something addresses us it does so because in being addressed we are brought to recognize how something in our past understanding has indeed been transformed. That transformation then changes our anticipations of what possibilities are yet to emerge from such understanding. In other words, the *Wahrheitsanspruch* speaks to us because it allows us to recognize in the image or meaningful encounter the ever-changing shape of our own hermeneutical journey whose nature is never to arrive but to continually transform its sense of meaningful possibilities. Nihilism is displaced. A meaningful life depends on participating in practices that both give sense to past experience and open towards a future of enlivening possibilities. The philosophical significance of the *Vorgriff der Vollendung* within language-being cannot be underestimated. It establishes the differential space which renders the movements of practice and its transformative potential possible.

As the form of hermeneutic experience, the *Vorgriff* cannot of course be itself the object of such experience. Yet every hermeneutic experience will have its anticipatory structure. Every representation of completeness will offer a determinate representation of the indeterminate possibilities within a given form. Though such images may have a compelling aesthetic completeness, they will never exhaust the logical completeness which every *Vorgriff* anticipates. In this sense, the art image always fails: it cannot capture all the determinations of meaning its *Vorgriff* anticipates. It is with good reason that Heidegger argues that an artistic image hides as much as it reveals. Though a successful artwork has the sense of 'bringing something off', it can never exhaust the possibilities within its subject matter. In this sense, the successful artwork excites by intimating a sense of what is still possible within its form. As is so often the case in negative hermeneutics, negativity has a positive function. The *Vorgriff* establishes a negative space between itself and the artwork. It reveals the extent to which an artwork falls short, that is, it discloses possibilities for meaning which the work has excluded. Yet, this negative disclosure is also the basis of future artworks becoming more. In other words, by revealing the incommensurability between itself and the image, the *Vorgriff der Vollendung* establishes spaces of negative capability in which the possibility of things being otherwise can arise. The collision between the indeterminate possibilities of the *Vorgriff* and the determinate nature of the artwork marks the point where such possibilities are revealed. Within philosophical hermeneutics the way of the negative is invariably the route of understanding. The space between actual and anticipated meaning is the space in which previously unseen possibilities for meaning can be disclosed. In short, within the language ontology of *Sprachlichkeit*, the *Vorgriff* emerges not only as the form of hermeneutic experience but also as conditioning the appearance of hermeneutic possibilities for meaning beyond the initially anticipated. In short, it is the very disjuncture between the determinate meaning of an artwork and the totality of meaning it anticipates that brings other unseen possibilities for meaning into appearance. Within the language ontology of *Sprachlickeit*, the *Vorgriff* is not only the form of hermeneutic experience but also the precondition of the possibility of things being otherwise within that experience. The *Vorgriff* operates as a dialectical principle. Because within *Sprachlichkeit* it establishes the form of meaningful experience, it also conditions the possibility of its disruption. To conclude, the *Vorgriff der Vollendung* establishes the paradox at the heart of negative hermeneutics, a paradox which simultaneously drives the perpetual quest for meaning and at the same time sets the conditions for dissolving it. As the very form which drives the quest for the completion, it also impels that quest towards failure. Yet this negative turn shows that other alignments of meaning are possible. The disclosure of such possibilities requires the continuous actions of practice. In short, within language-being, the *Vorgriff der Vollendung* drives the negative dialectics which animates the life-giving movement of understanding. It establishes the form of understanding's disquiet. *The 'way of the negative' opens the path to hermeneutical experience. Hermeneutical life, it seems, always wants more.*

4

Towards a poetics of practice

1. *Sprachlichkeit* and practice

The primary mode of language-being (*Sprachlichkeit*) is movement. It maintains its being in the constant emergence and withdrawal of meaning, in the unfolding of experience and in the movement of understanding. In Nietzsche's conceptual language, *Sprachlichkeit*, considered as the totality of possible meaning, becomes and passes away but neither has it started to become and nor has it ceased passing away: it maintains itself in both.[1] This gives to hermeneutical practices considered as interactive processes a critical power of agency able to unfold from within its language world previously unarticulated alignments of meaning. Bringing new formations of meaning into being inevitably displaces others. As agencies of movement, hermeneutical practices maintain language-being itself. The interactive relationship between hermeneutical practices and the linguistic-being in which they are situated is dialectical. What characterizes the poetics of hermeneutical practice is movement in and between its ontological elements. Reflective movement is at the heart of any process of coming-to-understand.

Hermeneutical practices and their movement are distinct modes of language-being. Though each practice appears distinct, they are interconnected by actual and often unseen etymological and logical entailments. Precisely because of such connectivity, changes of meaning in one practice effect the stability of meaning in another. Though a practice may seek to steady the meanings that embody its concerns, because of logical and etymological links it also remains subject to the plays of meanings in adjacent practices. The effort to consolidate meanings within a practice can consequently push that practice towards other alignments of meaning capable of disrupting its project. Given the infinity of possible meanings held within language-being, the more a hermeneutical practice seeks to complete its unresolved frameworks of meaning, the more likely it is to

---

1   WP 1066.

disrupt and displace them. The agency of hermeneutical practices in extending the movement of their thought and understanding suggests that practices can be considered as hermeneutical vectors.

Practice considered as a vector (a way of travel) emphasizes how practices are essentially dynamic. In Heidegger's terms, they are projects both anticipating and being drawn towards their future possibilities. As modes of becoming, practices are necessarily incomplete. Commitment to a project requires bringing to fulfilment the subject matter a hermeneutical vector projects and navigates towards. The impetus towards completion is the attribute which renders such practice agencies capable of uncovering unrealized possibilities for meaningfulness within *Sprachlichkeit*. At the same time, revelations of unseen patterns of meaning can question the adequacy of how a practice has come to understand its presuppositions. Precisely because of its location in language-being, the forward impetus of a practice's drive to completion will prove the instrument of its deconstruction and failure. We will return to the question of a practice's hermeneutical agency later.

The foregoing comments confirm that hermeneutical practices involve a constant dialectical interplay between the language consciousness of a specific practitioner and the language-being in which that practice is grounded. Such dialectical interplay affirms how the intensive concerns of hermeneutics are embedded in their extensive ontological contexts. Such interplay is essential to the movement of a hermeneutical poetics. Once again, the efficacy of the hermeneutic axiom 'x always equals x+' is emphasized. The ability of x to have a hermeneutical effect depends upon its placement within a wider ontological environment of x+. The dynamics of these interactions will become the basis of our inquiry into how the 'telling image' and the 'listening word' serve as operative functions within their given hermeneutic environments. Having suggested that *Sprachlichkeit* is the ontological ground of all individual practices and their poetics, let us turn to the broad concept of practice itself.

2. The forgotten question of practice

The nurturing of radical questioning in both hermeneutics and the humanities suggests that it is not how these disciplines are defined that matters but what they do, that is, what effects they have. If the fates of these disciplines are bound together, it is because each embraces practices of keeping-in-question. In the essay 'The Future of Hermeneutics', Vattimo argues that hermeneutics must transform itself into a philosophy of *praxis*.² It is an argument with which this essay is in part sympathetic. Our concern, however, is to show how *hermeneutic practices are so constituted operationally as to constantly call themselves into question and that therein lies their transformative strength*. This will involve outlining a poetics of hermeneutical practice and identifying the effective elements within its economy.

Insofar as this chapter aims to restore faith in the cognitive content and the social and economic worth of hermeneutics and the humanities, it must place the notion of practice at the centre of its argument. It is through practice that these disciplines achieve their transformative effects. The current theoretical malaise in hermeneutics and the humanities reflects a lack of philosophical reflection on their educational effects. What are the mechanisms of such transformation? What are its preconditions and how is it nurtured? Reticence about addressing the question of practice in the humanities is inhibited by a fear of making what might seem imperious statements about this complex field of endeavour. However, *philosophical hermeneutics does not offer a theory of practice but more a hermeneutics of practice*, a skilled acquisition of learning how to reflect on and to take advantage of what is in play within its practices. *The negative capability of hermeneutic practices proves central to the movement of understanding.*

Ernst Tugendhat follows Heidegger and Gadamer in suggesting that the task of philosophy is not to discover new facts but to draw out explicitly what we implicitly know and act on.³ For Tugendhat hermeneutical reflection is not the explanation of something-not-understood but the clarification of what has been (in a certain sense) already understood. The notion that interpretation draws out what is already tacitly known follows the ontological priority Heidegger gives to *Verstehen* over interpretation or, in Gadamer's terminology, the priority of language-being over linguistic consciousness. However, the point that *any hermeneutic reflection is situated within and reflects projects that are already underway emphasizes that* thinking about practice is, therefore, no abstract exercise but an attempt to extrapolate from the circumstances in which it is explicitly used, the pre-reflective 'understanding' from out of which the concept of a given practice emerges. *Hermeneutic reflection seeks to render clearer the experiential processes speculatively invoked by that concept.* What philosophical

---

2   Gianni Vattimo, 'The Future of Hermeneutics', in *The Routledge Companion to Hermeneutics*, ed. Jeff Malpas and Hans-Helmuth Gander (London: Routledge, 2015), 721–8.
3   For an excellent discussion of Tugendhat's relationship with hermeneutic philosophy see Santiago Zabala, *The Hermeneutic Nature of Analytic Philosophy, A Study of Ernst Tugendhat* (New York: Columbia University Press, 2008).

hermeneutics strives to recover from a concept is not an explicit definition or proposition about what a practice is but rather an understanding of what the concept has come to entail through its effects.[4] The concept is not stipulative but summative that is, it concerns what the practice brings about or, rather, effects. In other words, any discussion of the meaning of the concept 'practice' should not be isolated from the processes it gives expression to.

The poetics of a practice involves at minimum interactions between a practitioner, the practised upon and practising itself, a process which in its unfolding potentially transforms each of its elements. A musical work speaks to a performer who in performing it not only changes what is understood as that work but also her own understanding of musicality, changes which in following performances can effect how both the work and the tradition in which it is set are received. A practice is, in effect, an established way of being that a practitioner enters into and whose discipline must initially be accepted. Initiation entails submission to what is in relation to the practitioner transcendent, that is, the historical conventions that have come to underpin any practice. The ontological complexity of a practice – its speculative extension – is such that it cannot be represented in its entirety conceptually. A practice is an 'immeasurable' which though open to analytical description nevertheless defies conceptual containment. Richard Sennet comments, with regard to the practice of drawing:

> The tactile, the relational, and the incomplete are physical experiences that occur in the act of drawing. (And yet) drawing stands for a larger range of experiences, such as the way of writing that embraces editing and rewriting, or of playing music to explore again and again the puzzling qualities of a particular chord.[5]

Accordingly, the nature of a practice has to be unfolded from within: it must be participated in, its effects mapped and felt. The concept is not a mental representation of a singular reality but a placeholder term for complex processes which exceed conceptual capture. Gadamer insists, nevertheless, that despite this incommensurability, reflecting on a practice and pursuing it are not at odds. Rather, bringing the practice under the concept that its involvements have generated is a way of gauging the ungraspable totality of involvements underpinning that practice. Hermeneutical reflection upon the concept of

---

4   This does not imply that the meaning of a concept can be exhaustively reduced to the conditions of its emergence. Arguably, Gadamer would be sympathetic to Habermas's rejection of Foucault's reductive genealogy of concepts, a rejection that is based on the premise that once a linguistic concept has emerged, its logical entailments can transcend the circumstances of its initial emergence and meaning.
5   Richard Sennet, *The Craftsman* (London: Penguin, 2009), 44. (Insert added. ND).

practice has nothing to do with getting clearer about set definitions but with becoming more profoundly aware of the processes at play within the involvements that generate the concept in the first place. Philosophical hermeneutics does not offer a theory of practice but a hermeneutics of practice, a way of understanding what is at work within it.

3. Practical steps

Gadamer claims hermeneutics is a philosophy of practice but given our previous remarks, it would be better to argue that his thought *points* towards a hermeneutics of practice. As the forgetfulness of Being is a signature theme in Heidegger's thought, so the forgetfulness of language is a core theme of Gadamer's *Sprachsphilosophie*. If linguistic communication is itself primarily a practice, it is in the nature of most practices that, hermeneutically speaking, they too forget themselves. Part of the task of a poetics of practice is to recover an awareness of its forgotten but nevertheless operative elements.

We shall argue that a strong distinction needs to be made between hermeneutic practices that are carried out reflectively and hermeneutical praxis that is animated by reflective experience. Similarly when it comes to a literary or musical practice, what is consciously undertaken depends upon what that practice, historically speaking, has already taken up and established as its effective traditions. *The activity of the practitioner is ontologically dependent upon the prior 'doing' of the adopted practice.* The 'way of practice' is therefore prior to and greater than the willing and doing of the practitioner who embraces it. Such a way is a 'way of being', a 'way of life' entered into and embraced. As such, 'a way of practice' is invariably forgetful of the enabling orientations which ground and transcend it. A hermeneutics of practice seeks to recover and bring to light the 'forgotten' orientations of a practice but not for the sake of mastery. No practice can, hermeneutically speaking, be mastered: it is always in excess of itself. A hermeneutics of practice aspires to the hermeneutical, that is, to further extend, enable and participate in the subject matters of its concerns.

Underpinning Gadamer's approach to practice is the thought that Being is prior to and exceeds knowing. Being cannot be theorized and made subject to 'metaphysical' capture. However, practices remain rooted in and reflect our mode of being as hermeneutic agencies operating within the shaping horizons of language and tradition. As such, our being and the practices through which it is made manifest are incomparably 'more' than we can conceive. Yet it is precisely our groundedness in the ontic dimensions of practice that initially surpasses thought that enables a practice to bring to reflection ever-new dimensions of its being. Hermeneutic agency is in a permanent state of recovery, seeking not so much to recapture the forgotten and overlooked but rather to recover the hidden possibilities within received ways of thinking.

Being, practice, participation and experience have ontological precedence over reflection: practical engagement is both the ground of and gateway to hermeneutic reflection. Before we pass to a fuller discussion of practice itself, let us briefly summarize the importance of practice in our current discussion.

1. Post-Gadamerian hermeneutics needs to develop an ontology of practice to establish how the humanities achieve transformative changes in outlook.
2. Practices achieve their transformative effects because of the differential spaces they generate. Opening liminal spaces within understanding enables practices to establish the conditions necessary for recursive looping to take place. This allows the development of accumulative understanding, for the emergence of a practitioner's characterology, and the narrative patterning associated with *Bildung*.
3. Being open to new experience is not a theoretical achievement but a consequence of practices being vulnerable to the negativity of experience and its unpredictable turns.
4. To be challenged by the negativity of experience and the opening of the future possibilities contains, presupposes that a hermeneutic subject already participates in established practices. *Hermeneutical experience presupposes ontological participation.*
5. Philosophical hermeneutics does not offer a philosophy of practice but ways of articulating the reflexivity central to *praxis*. It endeavours to promote an awareness of what is performatively at play within practical experience. Philosophical hermeneutics is not a theory of practice: to the contrary, its theoretic stance *accompanies* the 'lived performance of a task' and seeks to articulate what is already underway within it.
6. Practices mobilize the differential spaces between works and their subject matters keeping the relations they permit open and fluid. As an event, *hermeneutic truth is a practice-based emergence.*
7. Practice not only moderates the subject matters it transmits but, in so doing, can also transform the practitioner's self-understanding. The transformative effects of immersion in practice constitute the much underestimated social and economic value of the humanities.

8. Engagement with sense-creating practices provides a powerful twofold antidote to the dispiriting negativity of metaphysical nihilism. First, theory may not achieve the formal certainty it pursues but sustained practices, artistic, social and historical, can generate a practical confidence in the world that derives from accrued experiences of engagement and participation (*Bildung*) albeit that these practices lack any formal grounding. The ability to overcome the *scepsis* sustaining alienated theoretical consciousness requires a practical trust in the life-world and its practices: it assumes participation and engagement. Second, practices in their respective pursuit of fulfilment and completion set the conditions for the emergence of hermeneutical truth and its integrative function. Hermeneutic practices are not concerned with the issue of universal truth in the classical epistemological sense but with what 'rings true' within them and with what makes sense amongst their horizons.

The foregoing remarks establish why practice is central to our reflection and indicate what must be further clarified concerning the hermeneutical significance of practice within the humanities.

From a hermeneutical perspective, practices share a similar ontological predicament. All are prone to overarching ambition, to narrowness of judgement and the limitations of their perspective. And yet practices are not isolated. They serve as nodal points not only for what is at play within them but also for what can pass between them. Being rooted in and between practices is a precondition of the emergence of any transformative insight. Furthermore, practices not only moderate the subject matters that they transmit but, in so doing, can transform a practitioner's self-understanding. The transformative effects of immersion in such practices determine the underestimated social and economic value of the humanities. Before this claim can be properly established, the nature of practice needs closer examination.

Since the operations of language and the transmission of meaning are inseparable from the practice of the humanities, it is inevitable that the generative dynamics of dialogue will be a major point of reflection in the coming discussion. As forms of 'sense-making', practices represent different ways of organizing the indeterminacies of human experience. Such practices assume and pursue a completion (*Vollkommenheit*) of meaningfulness be it in the culmination of a creative piece or in the successful outcome of a yoga or dance exercise. However, it is not what is pursued that matters but the formative consequences of the pursuit. The pursuit of interpretation's completeness is but a means of inducing the collateral effect of achieving that transformation of understanding which is the end of hermeneutic engagement. This suggests three additional points.

1. The generative effects of practice underpin the interdisciplinary value of the humanities. In terms of the achievement of transformative effects, it is not what a practice aims at (aesthetic completeness) that is of primary importance but, rather, what that quest brings into play and keeps in play across horizons.
2. A hermeneutical approach to practice can dissolve many of the distinctions that sustain the arts-science differentiation. The sooner educational strategists and political administrators grasp that the arts-science distinction is one of degree and not kind, the better.
3. Theory may not achieve the formal certainty it pursues but sustained practices, artistic, social and historical, can generate a practical confidence in the world that derives from accrued experiences of engagement and participation (*Bildung*) albeit that these practices lack any formal grounding. The ability to overcome the scepsis sustaining alienated consciousness requires a trust in the life-world and its practices. This demands a participatory epistemology which can trace its roots to ancient *theoria*.

Our proposed ontological reading of practice illuminates Gadamer's triangulation of the concepts, practice, humanity and essence. It marks a philosophical passage from the traditional (metaphysical) notions of essence to a more radical conception of essentiality. Whereas in much classical philosophy, essence precedes its historical expression, for Gadamer essentiality is built up in and through the historical. In response to the contingencies of its environment, a certain life form establishes a set *repertoire* of responses out of which predictable, repeatable and sustainable patterns and narratives develop. A dialectic of continuity and disruption, and a sense of hermeneutic identity or subjecthood, emerges and, once established, becomes an effective agency in its own right. Essentiality involves the notion of a being or *Dasein* emerging from metaphysically contingent processes and becoming more essentially what it is by consolidating and extending the narratives and existential potentialities inherent in its emergence.

The philosophical anthropology implicit in Gadamer's hermeneutical ontology of practice promises an account of the human and its relation to the humanities as mutually moderating (and potentially transformative) processes. The future legitimacy of the humanities requires such an account, and this chapter offers a philosophical outline of the arguments in its favour. 'Becoming open to new experience' is not a theoretical achievement but rather a consequence of practice, of being open to the unpredictable turns and returns of experience which arise precisely because of participating in practices.

> The truth of experience always implies an orientation toward new experience.[6]

> The dialectic of experience has its proper fulfilment not in definitive knowledge but in the openness to experience that is made possible by experience.[7]

It is participatory practice rather than theory that drives the dialectic of experience. This is a pertinent reminder of a key point that underlies our argument. The argument that understanding is an event of Being successfully relocates the question of understanding in ontology rather than in epistemological consciousness. Though the event of understanding may be arbitrary, it does not arise *ex nihilo*. The question 'How is understanding possible?' becomes an ontological question of determining what the event of understanding presupposes. What are the elements in play that govern the possibility of understanding ontologically conceived? A poetics of practice suggests a way of unravelling the ontological presuppositions governing the possibility of understanding's emergence.

The term 'poetics' has clear hermeneutical overtones. It suggests that a literary or artistic work is constituted by constant interactions between part and whole. Consistent with a participatory epistemology, the concept implies that there is no 'essence' or 'true meaning' to a work. Rather, its meaningfulness is accumulative and subject to perspectival shifts. Changes to parts alter the grasp of the whole, and an altered understanding of the whole promotes a different understanding of its constituting elements. To argue that a work resides in the 'economy' of its elements aligns comfortably with the notion of a poetics as involving an effective interplay of those components that contribute to the emergence or event of understanding. The ancient Greek term *oikonomia* (economy) has two components: *oikos* (house) and *nemein* (to manage): a well-kept house is one in which all of its components allow the whole to integrate and function collectively to the optimum of its capacity. Such an economy is never fixed but dynamic, always responding to and regulating the needs of circumstance. When considered in conjunction with Heidegger's conception of language as the 'house of Being', the strength of the analogy with poetics becomes apparent.

---

6   TM 355.
7   Ibid.

The living structures of those works which house us within a tradition, as well as the living structures of hermeneutical experience and understanding, are dependent on continuous movement. Gadamer's remark that the 'essence of what is called spirit lies in the ability to move' is prescient in that the underpinning ontological structures of experience, reflection, understanding, education and practice plainly involve and are sustained by the continuous movement of their constituting elements.[8] A poetics of hermeneutical understanding is central to any defence of hermeneutical practice. To understand the scope and limits of hermeneutical practices it is necessary to understand both what comes into play within the movement of understanding itself and how such movement is enabled by the differential spaces established by language. To this end, before passing to a fuller discussion of hermeneutical practice and the poetics that forms it we need to consider further aspects of the concept of practice itself.

4. Practice: A historical problematic

In talking of practice in relationship to hermeneutics, we are not talking about practical philosophy as conceived by Kant. To speak of a philosopher's practical philosophy is generally to draw attention to their moral philosophy. Robert Pippin's book on *Hegel's Practical Philosophy* makes it clear that 'by practical philosophy most philosophers would mean an account of the distinct sort of events for which we may appropriately demand reasons or justifications from subjects whom we take to be responsible for such events.'[9] If the principal content of practical philosophy appeals to ethics Gadamer has little to do directly with such debates. Matthew Foster asks why Gadamer remains seemingly 'silent about much that is critical and important to the viability of practical philosophy?'[10] An illuminating answer is suggested by David Cooper. Speaking of Heidegger and Wittgenstein in the context of Ancient Chinese Philosophy, he makes a remark that is also telling of Gadamer.

> No doubt these writers have their individual reasons for apparent hostility or indifference to moral discourse. I suspect however that they all share the sense, indicated by the remark from *Tao Te Ching*, that so to speak, *ethics comes too*

---

8   Hans-Georg Gadamer, *The Relevance of the Beautiful and Other Essays* (Cambridge: Cambridge University Press, 1986), 10.
9   Robert Pippin, *Hegel's Ethical Philosophy, Rational Agency as Ethical Life* (London: Cambridge University Press, 2008), 1.
10 Matthew Foster, *Gadamer and Practical Philosophy* (Georgia: Scholars Press, 1991), 240.

late: something has already gone wrong with our lives when pre-occupation with good versus evil, with rights and values, sets in. The Way is already lost, the experience of mystery already forgotten. Be that as it may, and despite these hostile remarks, it is clear that none of these writers is without a perception of how our lives should go. Moreover, there is surely an agreement among them that there should be lives in awareness of the 'things that cannot be put into words'.[11]

In certain respects Forster is right. Gadamer is for the most part silent about what is conventionally understood as normative ethics. However, to understand hermeneutic thought as a practical philosophy and to bring its normative dimensions to light, we need to look more closely at the various ways practice has been conceived historically. These differentiations allow the distinctness of Gadamer's position to become apparent.[12]

Like Pierre Hadot, Gadamer insists that questions of practice do not apply to ethics alone but concern all aspects of philosophy.[13] Navigating the ambiguities of what a practice means is itself indicative of what reflective practice is. Gadamer remarks that hermeneutics is primarily a practice: 'hermeneutics refers, first of all, to a practice [. . .], hermeneutics is a practical art'.[14] In this practice 'what one has to exercise above all is the ear, the sensitivity for perceiving prior determinations, anticipations, and imprints that reside in concepts'.[15] Accordingly, translation exemplifies hermeneutic practice in that it wrestles with the unclear and ambiguous.[16] Translation is exemplary because of its ontological presupposition of *Sprachlichkeit*, a being-in and a being-in-between languages and their differential spaces. Crucially, being-in-a-language does not mean that one creates the meanings of its words or their fields of nuance. Rather, being-in-a-language entails having a sense of placement in a

---

11 David Cooper, *The Measure of Things, Humanism, Humility and Mystery* (Oxford: Clarendon Press, 2002), 353. There is one aspect of Gadamer's aesthetics that approximates the intuition that 'ethics comes too late'. A passage in *Truth and Method* suggests that with regard to the question of literary and artistic meaning, hermeneutic judgement also comes too late. 'Someone who understands is always already drawn into an event in which meaning asserts itself. [. . .] When we understand a text, what is meaningful in it already captivates us just as the beautiful captivates us. It has asserted itself and captivates us before we can come to ourselves and be in a position to test the claim to meaning that it makes [. . .] In understanding we are drawn into an event of truth and arrive, as it were, too late, if we want to know what we are supposed to believe' (TM 490).
12 For an excellent introduction to the intellectual history surrounding the concept of practice, the reader is recommended to read Etienne Balibar, Barbara Cassin, and Sandra Laugier on '*praxis*' in *Untranslatables, A Philosophical Lexicon*, ed. B. Cassin (Princeton: Princeton University Press, 2014), 820–32.
13 Pierre Hadot, *Philosophy as a Way of Life* (London: Blackwell, 1995), 24.
14 Hans-Georg Gadamer, 'Classical and Philosophical Hermeneutics', in *The Gadamer Reader*, ed. Richard E. Palmer (Evanston: Northwestern University Press, 2007), 44.
15 Ibid., 21.
16 Ibid., 331.

verbal landscape of great variety, familiar, yet capable of constant surprise. *One may have a command of the language of one's being but never a command of the being of one's language.* The distinction between linguistic consciousness and linguistic-being is crucial.

Linguistic consciousness already presupposes linguistic-being but linguistic consciousness can never capture its transcendent ground in language-being. Language's infinite horizon of possible meaningfulness precludes any meaning within it from complete and definitive statement, yet this preclusion opens it to ever completer renditions. Linguistic-being is the excess which reaches beyond linguistic consciousness. It enables linguistic consciousness to transcend itself. Competent practice in language is more than a working acquaintance with its lexicography. It is, in addition, having an acute sense for what is at play within its received determinations of meaning and, more so, for what they anticipate of as yet to be articulated alignments of meaning. Being a practising (reflexive) participant within a language is to be situated between what has been said and what has yet to be said. Learning another language is hermeneutically instructive not so much for an extension of linguistic competence but because of the discernment that strains to navigate unaccustomed patterns of meaning. It is precisely because one already participates in a practice that its explicit application can draw out what is implicitly in play within it. In summary, translation exemplifies practice hermeneutically conceived on the following grounds.

1. Translation presupposes a prior ontological situatedness in horizons of meaning which are not of the translator's own making. Linguistic-being is always more than linguistic consciousness.
2. Translation is not the substitution of one term with its foreign equivalent but more a sensing of how what is at play in language game might be expressed in another. It is more the anticipation of what is possible rather than the reiteration of anything fixed.
3. As a reflective practitioner, the translator stands in between what is possible within one language and what can be said in another knowing that one cannot be reduced to the other. The practitioner in effect actualizes the potentials within received meanings and sets them into play in new and unexpected ways. Not only does participation in a foreign language allow one to hear one's own language differently, but it also permits the grafting of foreign terms on to a home language with transformative effect.

4. Translation, as with any other practice, requires ontological immersion in its operating horizons. Being orientated within a horizon – or in Wittgenstein's terms 'knowing one's way around' – does not presuppose that one is ever fully 'at home' in that practice. As we have seen, the indeterminacy of linguistic meaning drives the search for completer meaning. It is this restless search which, by default, gives rise to the emergence of unanticipated meanings in adjacent practices. Such adjunctive aleatoric effects are central to the transformative effects of practice within the humanities.
5. Translation exemplifies hermeneutic practice in that what it brings about is made possible by being situated within in, by participating in and by drawing out what is already at play within its horizons of meaning. Here one may talk of the ingenuity of hermeneutic practice: the drawing out of unexpected insights or nuances of meaning from what is already at play within a practice.

The preconditions of translation mirror the systemically related components influencing the emergence of meaning as an event. Ontological situatedness and operating between the differential spaces of personal, shared and differing cultural horizons also animate the movement of the poetics informing practice. Practices are clearly enabled and informed ways of doing. How hermeneutic practices relate to, reflect and are informed by the broader history of the term we must now consider.

Gadamer's invocation of the concept practice is by no means clear. What is clear is that his invocations of classical, Kantian and Hegelian strands of thought have productive consequences beyond what he anticipates. Practice is, broadly speaking, what Adorno intuits as a constellar concept: it gathers together a cluster of associated but by no means identical meanings which become more complex as newer meanings traverse older ones. Barbara Cassim's discussion of *praxis* is exemplary in this respect: it does not try to systemize the approaches to practice articulated by Aristotle and Kant but maps their systemic relations.[17]

---

17 Barbara Cassim, *The Dictionary of Untranslatables, A Philosophical Lexicon*, ed. B. Cassim (Princeton: Princeton University Press, 2014), 820–32.

5. Cassim and *praxis*

The ontological domains of *poiesis* and *praxis* have important implications for the nature of hermeneutical and practical judgements. Considered as faculties, both act on and produce contingent objects. They do not produce generalities. Neither do they concern what Platonists grasp as timeless (geometric) objects belonging to the realm of intelligible necessity. *Poiesis* and praxis produce finite objects whose very contingency renders them unstable, always subject to being rethought or reconfigured. The implication is that in the realms of *poiesis* and *praxis*, knowing and judging can only be on a case-by-case basis. Practical wisdom whether in the arts, medicine or the law cannot be concerned with universal objects or rules alone. *Poiesis* and *praxis* are not therefore disciplines of pure theory (*episteme*) alone but concern application to the particular.[18] This distinguishes them from the realm of *episteme* 'which deals with the necessary and the general'.[19]

The restriction of *praxis*, hermeneutical or aesthetic, to the particular case does not however limit its knowing to the singular, contingent and arbitrary. The knowing characteristic of *praxis* may not be of the same necessity as *episteme*, but it is a knowing that arises from a plurality of particular cases and circumstances. The practice of law is plainly exemplary. Such 'knowing' is won by hard experience and, as in the case of tradition, becomes part of the tacit orientation of any practitioner. It is a knowing that although in strict Platonic terms is groundless (i.e. does not reflect or represent intelligible forms or universals), is nevertheless founded upon the non-identical repetitions of subject matters (*Sachen*), repetitions which cumulatively constitute the historical continuity of a practice. More important, such non-identical contingently grounded repetitions open the logical spaces within which new determinations of meaning concerning the subject matters of any given practice can emerge. Gadamer speaks accordingly of practices as processes of becoming which through their exercise acquire a greater being.

Cassim implies a subtle connection between *praxis* and *episteme*. As the constant regeneration of itself through its works (*energeia*), a *praxis* tends to nothing other than the constant improvement of its own activity. In this respect, each class of practice approaches *episteme*, that is, it anticipates the

---

18   Ibid., 822.
19   Ibid.

perfection of its form.[20] On one level, this is misleading. It suggests that, as is the case in Platonic thought, the form or theory of a practice ontologically precedes its expedition. Practical knowing is rendered mimetic: a repetition of a pregiven form. However, in Gadamer's thought the form of a practice is emergent, its perfection anticipated and revised by each repetition. As a mode of *Werdensphilosophie*, philosophical hermeneutics insists on the historical genesis of all cultural forms and regards the form of any *praxis* as a contingent historical emergence.

The absence of any prior epistemic grounding does not mean that *praxis* emerges *ex nihilo*. To the contrary, practices both emerge from and are dependent on established patterns of cultural commitment and engagement. They are a consequence of the historical forms of life (*Lebensform*) that ground them. *Praxis* reiterates the key axiom of hermeneutic logic: it is always more than itself, simultaneously capable of being transformed by and indeed of transforming the speculative horizons in which it is set. However, the knowing that such transformation affords has nothing to do with a proximate imitation of a prior underlying form but with processes of practical accumulation consequent upon the pursuit of the practice itself.

The nature of *praxis* is inherently paradoxical. On the one hand, no teleology or divine genesis governs its emergence. This is why *praxis* in Kantian thought is judged to be a free or independent principle: nothing external determines its nature. Related assumptions fuel the romantic notion that in moral and artistic practice, humanity comes to express the free and spontaneous unfolding of its non-determined nature. Yet, as a self-emerging historical form, *praxis* is clearly a dependent principle. Though not *sui generis*, it is ontologically dependent upon the linguistic and cultural horizons which enable its operations. As we shall see, the unavoidable tension between the independent and the dependent within *praxis* drives the inherent instability of its quest for ever better or 'truthful' articulations of its ends.

It does not follow that if the emergence of a *praxis* is utterly contingent, metaphysically speaking, then the reasoning within it is equally so. To the contrary, the principle of ontological dependence suggests the genesis of a *praxis* is dependent upon the linguistic and cultural horizons out of which it emerges. Its reasonings will also be shaped by its enabling horizons. A *praxis* will develop its own *rationale*. Judgements of what is appropriate or possible

---

20 Cassim, *The Dictionary of Untranslatables*. The anticipation of perfection by a practice is consistent with our presentation of the *Vorgriff der Vollendung*.

within that *rationale* depend on a grasp of what its forms of reasoning point to. A *praxis* cannot develop in *any* logically possible direction. How it unfolds will be dependent upon what is contingently possible within the rationale of its horizon. In other words, though reasoning within a *praxis* is not formally constrained by an external teleology, it is constrained by what is contingently possible within its horizons. This is not to say that modes of reasoning that belong to different cultural traditions have no bearing on each other. To the contrary, the issue is whether such traditions exhibit a logical congruence such that each can inform the other by analogy or family resemblance. The argument underscores a key contention within negative hermeneutics: there is no universal form of reasoning within the humanities but only various modes of practical reasoning which by virtue of their placement within the universally emergent horizons of *Sprachlichkeit* are able to mediate one another. The Enlightenment myth of a universal reason is replaced with a universality of practical reasonings each robust and with distinct patterns of coherence and meaningfulness. It is the overarching notion of *Sprachlichkeit* which prevents such a plurality of reasonings from collapsing into a relativism.

Gadamer's observation that hermeneutic *praxis* requires a special skill states the obvious. Hermeneutical thinking involves particular practices with an extensive intellectual history. The substantive philosophical point concerns why hermeneutics is exemplary for understanding the interpretive practices that constitute the humanities? Philosophical hermeneutics eschews appeal to a universal form of reasoning and interdicts any possibility of subsuming all forms of interpretation under a universal system. The *Werdensphilosophie* which underpins Gadamer's position prohibits the claim that hermeneutics is a universal method. As we shall see, the concern is not the universality of method (the illusion of Dilthey's *Geisteswissenschaften*) but the universality of a shared ontological predicament the negativity of which humanities practices are capable of transforming.

In his chapter 'Hermeneutic', Wolfhart Pannenberg argues that it is only because the words of a language are *incompletely* defined that propositions can be formulated with precise definition. He cites Liebrucks's remark that each individual word and concept is surrounded by an 'undefined range of possibility'.[21] The parallel with Gadamer's notion of the speculative horizon of a word's meaning is plain. It reflects Heidegger's philological tactic. Though as a

---

21 Wolfhart Pannenberg, *Theology and The Philosophy of Science* (London: Darton, Longman and Todd, 1976), 217.

hermeneutical strategy *Deconstruktion* may seek to strip a philosophical term of the encrustations of its historically institutionalized meanings, it does not betray an antiquarian quest for original meaning. To the contrary, it aims to recover what is at play within a field of meaning so that its potential lines of thought can be reanimated and extended. In this context Cassim's reflections on *praxis* are telling. They implicitly pursue Pannenberg's thought that the meaning of a word can be more precisely formulated when its field of meaning is brought into relation with others. Cassim's linking of *praxis*, *poiesis* and *episteme* reveals aspects of *praxis* that a lexicographical analysis would fail to reveal. As a mode of doing, *praxis* is clearly a form of making and yet it is not to be defined by what is made. In its making, *praxis* brings to light the various hermeneutic vectors that ground its being but which it does not itself make. Yet it is only in its making that these horizons are brought to light. This offers a better understanding of the disclosive power of hermeneutical practice. *Praxis*, considered as an inexhaustible generative process, reveals itself not in what it makes but through its making. *Praxis* and *poiesis* are codependent: neither can be reduced to the other and yet neither can exist without the other.

Equally significant is the asymmetric relation between *praxis* and *episteme*. *Praxis* as a mode of making involves a degree of 'knowing that' and 'knowing how'. The craftsperson must know how metals behave under stress. Such knowledge is acquired through constant engagement with the pliability and tolerances of her materials. Though a *praxis* may involve technological knowledge in its execution, *praxis* in art, music or medicine is not itself a technology. It requires personal engagement with subject matters. *Practice entails a knowing unknowing grounded in the tacit epistemé of a tradition* and its heritage of different ways of working. In Heideggerian terms, *praxis* assumes an ontologically prior orientation to being-in-the world and its projects. Such *episteme* is no eternal archetype. It is metaphysically contingent, an inexplicable historical emergent that tacitly shapes the way a community of practitioners work with and relate to the world. Neither can the possibilities within an enabling *episteme* be grasped in their totality. However, they can be known partially and accumulatively when disclosed by the works which they enable. As a mode of becoming, a *praxis* and the *episteme* which grounds it are in August von Cieszkowski's words an 'auto-activity' (*Selbsttätigkeit*), a 'liberation of action' that opens up (an) historical space of transformation, a term which anticipates Wolfgang Iser's conception of interpretation as a form of auto-poeisis.[22] Hadot too speaks of practices seeking

---

22 Cassim, *The Dictionary of Untranslatables*, 825.

a transformation and metamorphosis of vision and personality. Once again the primacy of movement is emphasized in hermeneutical practice.

Returning to the main point, a *praxis* and its inherent possibilities cannot be grasped as a theoretical object. Its nature only becomes apparent through its historical effects. In this respect, coming to know what a *praxis* is demands participation in a way of doing which though it may shape our being cannot, because historical, be fully known. The hermeneutical importance of *praxis* is clear. It enables that which cannot be fully known to be known more fully. It is an emergent auto-activity which when engaged with releases its inherent possibilities.

Of the many cognate terms Cassim discusses alongside *praxis*, there is a notable omission which concerns the relation between hermeneutical *praxis* and *theoria*. On one level, the conjunction is misleading appearing to privilege theory over practice. The notion of a body of hermeneutic theory antecedent to objects of interpretation is anathema to Gadamer. Yet, if the classical Greek term is stripped of its modern connotations relating to theory, *theoria* emerges as fundamental to the operation of hermeneutical *praxis*. To think of hermeneutic *praxis* in terms of a theory-practice binary fails to place the elements of *praxis* in their right order. Whereas the binary supposes that the epistemological subject is set over and against the interpreted object, hermeneutical *praxis* demands a participatory epistemology which assumes the prior existence of a world of interpretive practices which we are already (pre-reflectively) engaged in. This suggests that hermeneutic *praxis* is a mode of reflective-engagement-with and a philosophical drawing-out-of what is prior to hermeneutical consciousness. Gadamer argues that though 'hermeneutics has to do with a theoretical attitude toward (both) the practice of interpretation' and 'the interpretation of texts', it is also concerned with the experiences interpreted in them, and with the questions they raise.[23] Experience is not reduced to theory but to the contrary, theory is subordinated to the elucidation of what comes into play within experience. Gadamer puts it as follows: 'this theoretic stance (hermeneutic praxis) only makes us aware reflectively of what is performatively at play in the practical experience of understanding.'[24] Nor does hermeneutical *praxis* entail the application of a specific philosophy of understanding. It uses philosophizing in a distinct way: it

---

23 Hans-Georg Gadamer, 'Hermeneutics as Practical Philosophy', in *The Gadamer Reader*, ed. Richard E. Palmer (Evanston: Northwestern University Press, 2007), 245.
24 Ibid. The point does not of course deny that abstract reasoning is possible in its own right. Metaphysical speculation, astronomy and physics all entail modes of pure theoretical reasoning. The issue for Gadamer concerns the extent to which such abstract reasoning can illuminate ordinary experience.

teaches how to exercise the ear and to acquire the sensitivity for perceiving those prior determinations of meaning already at play in words and concepts.[25] This constitutes the right ordering of hermeneutic *praxis*. Hermeneutical *praxis* is not a premeditated method of understanding which anticipates specific results but 'seeks an event of understanding that is transformative, although not as directly pointed to as a desired action'.[26] Indeed, although a hermeneutic *praxis* might anticipate a specific reading or interpretation, the end product is not key. Rather, it is those serendipitously arrived at moments of transformed understanding which arise as a consequence of pursuing a certain reading or interpretation. This suggests that hermeneutic *praxis* entails a trained disposition, a specific way of reflectively soliciting and putting oneself in the way of the unexpected.

6. *Praxis*, ontology and the way of understanding

Gadamer regards the exercise and expediting of practices as a way of life, as indicative of a certain *bios*. He remarks, 'Practice formulates the mode of behaviour of that which is living in the broadest sense. Practice, as the basic character of being alive, stands between activity and situatedness.'[27] 'Practice means the actuation of life (*energeia*) of anything alive, to which there corresponds a life, a way of life, a life that is led in a certain way (*bios*).'[28] Gadamer distinguishes (not unproblematically) between the human and the animal in this context.

> Of course, there is a decisive difference between animal and human being. The way of life of human beings is not fixed by nature like other beings. This difference is expressed by the concept of *prohairesis*, which can only be predicated of human being. *Prohairesis* means 'preference' and 'prior choice'. Knowingly preferring one thing to another and consciously choosing among possible alternatives is the unique and specific characteristic of human being.[29]

Without becoming entangled in the complex assumptions of this passage, Gadamer clearly follows Nietzsche in regarding human beings as the least determinate of animals. If human beings lack essential characteristics, it follows that their contingently developed mode of being is a consequence of their

---

25 Hans-Hans-Georg Gadamer, 'Autobiographical Reflections', in *The Gadamer Reader*, ed. Richard E. Palmer (Evanston: Northwestern University Press, 2007), 21.
26 Hans-Georg Gadamer, 'Hermeneutics as Theoretical and Practical Task', in *The Gadamer Reader*, ed. Richard E. Palmer (Evanston: Northwestern University Press, 2007), 247.
27 Gadamer, 'Hermeneutics as Practical Philosophy', 230–1.
28 Ibid.
29 Ibid.

social and historical practices. Though Kant's essentialist humanist notion of free will is close to the surface of Gadamer's argument, the parallel should not mislead. Gadamer's implied argument is not that there is a human essence which possesses a free will prior to its actions but rather that the actions and outcomes of a certain form of life (better, the interactions a form of life is involved in) have consequences for how that hermeneutic agency comes to understand itself. The argument here is subtle and suggests why problems associated with *praxis* in hermeneutics and the humanities are both complex and easily overlooked.

A dialectical tension between principles of independence and dependence underwrites a strategic distinction between practices and *praxis*. This underpins a counter-intuitive insight: practices are, collectively speaking, ontologically prior to the hermeneutic agents that engage in them. To put it another way, there is an ontological asymmetry between practices and their supposed agents; a practice cannot be understood through an analysis of an agency's grasp of that practice alone. Gadamer shapes two arguments that pursue this line of reasoning. (1) Ontologically speaking, any game will be larger than a player's sense of what she is playing and (2) the being of an artwork will always exceed the conscious grasp of its creator. This asymmetry characterizes the relationship between *praxis* and practice; the exercise of a *praxis* (Gadamer also talks of practical rationality) is dependent upon the cultural practices that ground its possibility. The pursuit of a specific spiritual or meditative *praxis* whether Jesuit or Zen would be unintelligible were it not for the noviciate's *prior* submission to the grounding historical and linguistic practices that underwrite their individual *praxis*. This re-emphasizes that for philosophical hermeneutics subjective consciousness is not the initial driver. The adoption of a musical or historical *praxis* is dependent upon an initial acceptance and surrender to a historically established 'way' of doing things. A *praxis* is ontologically dependent on the practices that precede it.

> The Greek word they used about this whole realm is that word which is now no so foreign to us – *pragma* – a word that means the realm in which one finds oneself involved in the practice of life. This realm of practice does not stand over and against us as something to be overcome, but as something in which one moves around and does things.[30]

Though the grounding practices of a culture or way of life might be characterized as metaphysically contingent (there is no teleology that drives their unfolding),

---

30 Hans-Georg Gadamer, 'Greek Philosophy and Modern Thinking', in *The Gadamer Reader*, ed. Richard E. Palmer (Evanston: Northwestern University Press, 2007), 270.

they nevertheless determine the range of options that someone born into or who adopts them will confront. *Praxis* understood as coming to reflective judgement about the perceived options within a practice can *perhaps* be considered as an act of free choice. *Praxis* responds to the options that established practices preselect. If practices are ontogenetic in that they articulate the nature of a certain being-in-the-world, *praxis is ontoreflective in that it clarifies what is at play within the practice underpinning it.*

Philosophical hermeneutics presents tradition and linguisticality (*Sprachlichkeit*) as the grounding that articulates being-in-the-world. The sustaining role of ontologically antecedent practices betrays an ancient sense of dependence upon that which inhabits and yet transcends one's being. A parallel with the texts of Lao-Tzu is helpful. They speak not of ontologically prior practices per se but of 'the Way' that gives 'creatures life and brings them to fruition and maturity'.[31] The concept is variously deployed in early Chinese texts. Confucian thinkers refer to the 'way of a true King' whilst Lao-Tzu alludes both to the 'way of a sage' and to the 'way of a warrior'. These deployments are arguably closer to *praxis* than to practice in so far as any conscious involvement in the martial arts, poetry or government presupposes prior immersion in their enabling practices.

Lao-Tzu's offers an analogy to the relationship between practice and *praxis* in hermeneutics. Reflective *praxis* is nurtured and supported by the broader existential and cultural practices that bear it along. Section 45 of the *Tao Te Ching* proposes in famously enigmatic terms that:

> The way that can be spoken of is not the constant way,
> The name that can be named is not the constant name,
> The nameless was the beginning of heaven and earth.[32]

Lao-Tzu's articulation of 'the Way' compliments Gadamer's logic of the speculative relation $x = x+$. The way that can be articulated (i.e. 'x') is not 'the constant way' for no statement of $x+$ can exhaust its historical possibilities. And yet the prior existence of $x+$ grounds the possibilities of propositions about x. Indeed, whatever $x+$ might be thought of depends upon statements about x and what they cumulatively point to.

The dialectic of naming that which cannot be named suggests how that which is beyond naming grounds and effects what is named in hermeneutical

---

31 Lao-Tzu, *Tao Te Ching* (New York: Everyman's Library, 1994).
32 Lao-Tzu, Tao Te Ching, translated by D. C. Lau, (New York: Everyman's Library, 1963), xxi.

dialectics. It establishes how the 'ways' of tradition and language both support and set the parameters of their reflective *praxis* but yet cannot be reducible to them. This explains why the ontological basis of philosophical hermeneutics and the practices it sustains cannot be theorized. Acknowledging that such 'ways' do indeed 'surpass all understanding' does not culminate in the nihilistic conclusion that the basis of hermeneutical *praxis* is arbitrary and dependent upon arbitrary nominalism and subjective preference. To the contrary, the effective grounds of hermeneutical agency transcend the subjectivities they sustain. Both the ancient Chinese conception of 'the Way' and Gadamer's notion of the grounding horizon of tradition are 'immeasurables' that are not amenable to exhaustive epistemological description.[33] This does not render them indiscernible. To say that x is an immeasurable is not to say that it is beyond intelligent discernment, only that it cannot be instrumentalized by monological methods. To recognize tradition as an 'immeasurable' accepts that only a proliferation of viewpoints can unfold its 'likely' (anticipated) nature. Immeasurables demand that cognition become multiform.[34] By deploying multiple modes of perspective, it can be more fully understood. It is arguments such as these that allow negative hermeneutics to provide a clear *rationale* for interdisciplinary engagement. What is at stake in the practice–*praxis* relation now becomes apparent.

Any *praxis* supposes an underpinning practice, and yet the full scope of that practice and its speculative entailments cannot be captured by the *praxis* it gives rise to. In Daoism, the primacy of tacit knowing establishes 'the Way' that guides the concerns of explicit knowing or *praxis*. As Richard Sennet points out, that tacit knowing is inarticulate does not mean that it is unintelligent for what we can say in words is often more limited than what can actually be shown in non-verbal practices. Zen philosophy appreciates this. The master practitioner is an enigmatic teacher who 'enlightens' by showing, by invoking patterns of tacit acquaintance, rather than by telling.[35] If we accept that the cultural and linguistic practices enabling our engagement with the subject matters of art and science constitute a 'way' of understanding, then, as tacit, much of that understanding will be an unknowing knowing.[36] This is made plain in Gadamer's pivotal distinction between linguistic consciousness and language-being.

---

33 Wolfgang Iser, *The Range of Interpretation* (New York: Columbia University Press, 2000), 128.
34 Ibid., 141.
35 Sennet, *The Craftsman*, 95.
36 The phrase is indebted to the Medieval Classic, *The Cloud of Unknowing*, see *The Cloud of Unknowing and Other Works*, trans. A. C. Spearing (London: Penguin, 2001).

Language-being transcends linguistic consciousness. The latter, though shaped by language-being, cannot grasp the totality of its entailments. This does not render linguistic-being a noumenon. To the contrary, linguistic consciousness is ontologically dependent on the ontological priority of language-being. As Hana Videeen's recent study of the Anglo roots of modern English has shown, etymology and philology repeatedly demonstrate how everyday speech idioms extend into networks of meaning we as individuals are barely conscious of.[37] Philological recovery in hermeneutics is not an antiquarian project but seeks to discover how forgotten nuances of meaning open new ways of thinking about contemporary subject matters. In Gadamer's formulation the word is 'the advance achievement of thought'. Put more radically, the achievements of language-being already run ahead of where thought (linguistic consciousness) has to go. In struggling towards a debate's resolution, thought meets with what language has already projected as one of its implicit conceptual possibilities.

This emphasizes why the canon in the humanities and the classics must continue to be taught. This has little to do with any conservative defence of tradition. The ontic priority of language-being suggests that in the received language worlds of the humanities lie potential ways of thinking awaiting actualization by hitherto unanticipated cultural challenges. *Praxis* can be considered as a way of drawing out what is implicitly at play within a practice. Abandoning tradition is the hermeneutical equivalent to self-harm. The notion of a speculative ground to understanding establishes a philosophical basis for openness. No interpretation can be exhaustive. The possibility of alternative readings can never be foreclosed. Hope for understanding's renewal and transformation is, ontologically speaking, fully warranted. The ontological actuality of *praxis* as agency maintains such openness.

7. Practice and *Dasein*

The ontological priority of practices over *praxis* is implicit in the temporal entailments of Heidegger's conception of *Dasein*. Whilst Lao Tsu invokes a 'way' of understanding, Heidegger speaks of its paths. Gadamer's notions of tradition and *Sprachlichkeit* also shape the horizons of hermeneutic agency. All three philosophers emphasize the facilitating priority of that which transcends individual subjectivity. The hermeneutic subject does not choose her enabling

---

37   Hana Videen, *The Word Horde* (London: Profile Books, 2021).

horizons and yet, as Heidegger's notion of 'thrownness' (*Geworfenheit*) emphasizes, the hermeneutic practitioner is subject to what is at play within them. *Dasein* is its practices, comes to itself through its practices and does not exist apart from them. The transcendent ground of each *Dasein* reaches beyond its reflective grasp though that ground has each *Dasein* in its grasp. Practices are projects: hermeneutical vectors are rooted in an indefinite past and extend into a future shaped by expectation. The 'ecstatic' temporality of every *Dasein* lies in its projects extending between an unrecoverable past and a future yet to arrive. Its being is always *unterwegs* moving along the projected vector which it is. *Dasein* is being-subject to a variety of vectors not all of which are mutually consistent.

The ontological trajectory of each *Dasein* is always towards the new possibilities for being that its practices dispose it towards. Considered as a project, each cultural practice establishes its *Woher und Wozu*, its *open* narrative of where it has come from and where it is going to. It is not just that the temporal projections embedded in a cultural practice propel it towards an envisaged future but that the forward momentum of each practice can potentially re-envision both its future and its past. We shall argue that *praxis* is capable of initiating such re-envisioning.

8. MacIntyre, tradition and practice

Praxis can be considered as a way of drawing out what is implicitly at play within a practice. Heidegger considers that *Dasein* lives in a condition of possibility, future possibilities being part of its being. *Dasein* as a form of life continually places its enabling sense of past and future into critical review. Now that the connections between *Dasein*, practice, possibility and projection are clearer, the relevance of Alasdair MacIntyre's approach to practice can be discerned.

What resounds in the following quotation is an alignment of ideas congruent with the thinking of Heidegger and Gadamer. MacIntyre does not make a strong distinction between practice and *praxis* though the moral orientation of his thought suggests that his invocation of practice includes *praxis*. The conceptual link between these three thinkers concerns the discernment of possibilities situated within practice. MacIntyre writes:

> An adequate sense of tradition manifests itself in a grasp of those future possibilities which the past has made available to the present. Living traditions, just because they continue a not-yet completed narrative, confront a future

whose determinate and determinable character, in so far as it possesses any, derives from the past.[38]

A cultural example of situated practice resides in the musical idiom of 'theme and variations'. Beethoven's piano variations on Mozart's *Ein Mädchen oder ein Weibschen* or Brahms's 'Variations on the St. Anthony Chorale' are renowned instances. What is hermeneutically exemplary about them is that although most audiences believe they know the lead theme, the composer sets out to show by means of ingenious variations that they don't. In such practices, Richard Sennet suggests, there is 'a constant interplay between tacit knowledge and self-conscious awareness, the tacit knowledge serving as an anchor, the explicit awareness serving as critique and corrective'.[39] This mirrors the relation between intensive and extensive questioning guiding our overall argument. The very constraints of an inherited motif define the context within which an artist's creative powers come to expression. The brilliance of such works lies in their capacity to surprise. Sennet comments, 'Surprise is a way of telling yourself that something you know can be other than you assumed.'[40] It is at this point Sennet suggests that we begin to experience wonder: tradition holds possibilities surpassing initial expectation. Such works excite because they permit sight of the familiar in new and surprising ways and thereby remind us of our blindness and deafness. The musical form of 'theme and variation' is an aesthetic embodiment of negative hermeneutics: the form continually catches out the listener's expectancies. From the artist's perspective, revealing the hidden potentials within a traditional form gives confidence to their practice. The key point remains: the experience of such a work's brilliance and the wonder of what it reveals are ontologically dependent upon prior immersion in the tacit practical dimensions of existence. This makes cogent the dialogical relation between practice and *praxis* which we will discuss more fully later.

Before we consider MacIntyre's position further, let us summarize three of the key arguments that have arisen.

1. The ontological priority of practice over *praxis* gives to the latter a key role in drawing out and bringing to reflection the unarticulated possibilities within the practices that underwrite its operation. This echoes Heidegger's argument that 'interpretation' is a drawing out of the unfilled possibilities

---

38   Alisdair MacIntyre, *After Virtue* (London: Duckworth, 1982), 223.
39   Sennett, *The Craftsman*, 50.
40   Ibid., 211.

within understanding.⁴¹ This also emphasizes the strategic role of *praxis* within hermeneutics and the humanities: only by means of reflective engagement with what is at play within the horizons of a practice can they be moderated and extended.

2. The ontological priority of practice over *praxis* confirms the fundamental negativity of philosophical hermeneutics. Neither hermeneutics nor the humanities can be theoretically grounded. Both transcend method and defy reduction to being objects of theoretical articulation alone.
3. That the sustaining horizons of practice are in theoretical terms beyond formal articulation does not render them unintelligible. Many practices are based on skills and knowledge that are beyond the powers of verbal explanation.⁴² That a practice is in certain sense beyond words does not mean that we cannot use better and more careful words to point to what is entailed within it.

MacIntyre expresses his gratitude to Gadamer's reworking of tradition. 'I take it to be unquestionably true', that 'to become aware of the historically conditioned character of our philosophical enquiries is not to have escaped from it'⁴³ but rather to be in continuous engagement with the open-ended subject matters that inform it. It is not MacIntyre's discussion of tradition that concerns us but how his approach to practice illuminates what is implicitly in play in Gadamer's reflections upon the practical.

MacIntyre follows Heidegger and Gadamer in proclaiming that ontologically speaking practice precedes the individual practitioner. In *After Virtue*, MacIntyre announces:

> By a 'practice' I am going to mean any coherent and complex form of socially established cooperative human activity through which goods internal to that form of activity are realised in the course of trying to achieve those standards of excellence which are appropriate to, and partially definitive of, that form of activity, with the result that the human powers to achieve excellence, and human conceptions of the ends and goods involved are systematically extended.⁴⁴

---

41 Martin Heidegger: 'Interpretation is grounded existentially in understanding; the latter does not arise from the former. Nor is interpretation the acquiring of information about what is understood; it is rather the working-out of possibilities projected in understanding.' *Being and Time*, trans. J. Macquarrie (Oxford: Blackwell, 1960), 189.
42 Sennet, *The Craftsman*, 94.
43 Alasdair MacIntyre, 'On Not Having the Last Words: Thoughts on Our Debts to Gadamer', in *Gadamer's Century, Essays in Honor of Hans-Georg Gadamer*, ed. Jeff Malpas, Ulrich Arnswald, and Jens Kertscher (Cambridge, MA: The MIT Press, 2002), 158.
44 MacIntyre, *After Virtue*, 187.

The invocation of standards of 'good' internal to a practice will be an important element in our discussion of *praxis*. Practice is a historical achievement and is prior to any individual decision to engage with it. This re-enforces the idea that a practice is a 'way' of doing things and insofar as it is socially established and historical, it transcends any initiate who subsequently engages with it. The process of becoming an artist or writer is not a question of pleasing oneself or of acquiring easy self-expression. The adoption of a discipline involves the disciple in initially accepting what its precepts entail.

> A practice involves standards of excellence and obedience to rules as well as the achievement of goods. To enter into a practice is to accept the authority of those standards and the inadequacy of my own performance as judged by them. It is to subject my own attitudes, choices, preferences and tastes to the standards which currently and partially define the practice ... we cannot be initiated into a practice without accepting the authority of the best standards realised so far.[45]

To engage with a practice is therefore to submit to a 'way' of doing things that precedes one.

> To enter into a practice is to enter into a relationship not only with its contemporary practitioners, but also with those who have preceded us in the practice, particularly those whose achievements extended the reach of the practice to its present point. It is thus the achievement, and *a fortiori* the authority of a tradition which I then confront and from which I have to learn.[46]

Given the ontological priority of practices over practitioners, there is a sense that it is not I who decide to become a practitioner of a given practice but rather that the authority of an established musical or medical practice calls me to it. The call draws me irrespective of my willing and doing. This is not an act of passive acquiescence but one of knowing acceptance. In Heideggerian terms, a mode of *Dasein* (a hermeneutic agency) senses in the call of tradition the *promise* of its own possibilities. It is not the 'I' that is effective here but the push and pull of a given *Dasein*'s ontological placement. MacIntyre concurs in this respect: the realm of practices rules out all subjectivist and emotivist analyses of judgement.[47] To become engaged in a practice is to transcend one's subjectivity. In practice, the practitioner recognizes that they do not belong to themselves alone and because of that can always become more than themselves.

---

45 Ibid., 190.
46 Ibid., 194.
47 Ibid., 190.

> What I am (as a practitioner) [. . .] is in key part what I inherit, a specific past that is present to some degree in my present. I find myself part of a history and that is generally to say, whether I like it or not, whether I recognise it or not, one of the bearers of a tradition. [. . .] Practices always have histories and [. . .] at any given moment what a practice is depends on a mode of understanding in it which has been transmitted often through many generations.[48]

By invoking the ontological priority of tradition, it might seem that MacIntyre is laying claim to an essentially conservative position. On a certain level this is true. The living actuality of traditions effectively constrains the scope of actions they enable. Ernst Cassirer is clear on this point.

> Every language exhibits a determinate vocabulary, which it did not create instantaneously, and the same holds for all modes of creative activity in the plastic arts. There is a reservoir of formal elements for the painter, the sculptor, the architect, and there is a very real syntax for each of these fields, much as there is syntax in any language. All this cannot be spontaneously invented. It is here that tradition forever maintains its claims.[49]

The enabling tradition of a practitioner encapsulates their every action and submits them to the strict necessity of what is possible within its parameters.[50] Since every creative tradition has its syntax, it is almost inconceivable for a practitioner to operate outside the *Weltanschauung* that it defines. For an Anglo-Saxon poet pondering the world's edge, Haiku is not an option. However, though a tradition may appear restrictive, none is closed. Tradition is better thought of as a field of possibilities. For Gadamer, freedom and spontaneity are not opposed to tradition but are found in the working out of what it contains. The important task is to find a free space within it and to seek out its inherent possibilities.[51] The seeking out is the task of the productive practitioner.[52] Traditions uphold fields of possibility which enable the practitioner to discover their own. Cassirer argues that tradition and creativity are not exclusive: 'only through it (tradition) can that continuity of creative activity be realised and captured which is the basis of intelligibility in the plastic arts'.[53]

---

48   Ibid., 221.
49   Ernst Cassirer, *The Logic of the Humanities* (Clinton: Yale University Press, 1974), 200.
50   Ibid., 18.
51   Hans-Georg Gadamer, *On Education, Poetry, and History* (Albany: State University of New York Press, 1992), 59.
52   Cassirer, *The Logic of the Humanities*, 37.
53   Ibid., 201.

This does not mean that traditions and the practices they sustain are immune from internal criticism. They are communities of difference and debate. The concept of tradition in English political theory is unfortunately associated with a conservative endeavour to maintain continuities of political and cultural identity. MacIntyre is well aware of this Burkean prejudice.

> We are apt to be misled here by the ideological uses to which the concept of a tradition has been put by conservative political theorists. Characteristically such theorists have followed Burke in contrasting tradition with reason and the stability of tradition with conflict. Both contrasts obfuscate.[54]

As an open structure, tradition cannot of course be fully defined. Attempts to do so will inevitably distort its totality. Uncritical approaches to tradition can perpetrate its hidden irrationalisms. Wolfhardt Pannenberg challenges such negligence. Far from being immune to criticism, artistic or political traditions can criticize their past and present performance not against an external criterion of truth but against what they themselves claim to as their projected truths and goals. On the assumption that all reasoning takes place within the context of some traditional mode of thought, criticism and invention *can* transcend the limitations of what has hitherto been reasoned. Tradition and reason are not mutually exclusive. To the contrary, rational debate can occur within and between traditions over whether their actual performances match declared aspirations. MacIntyre argues, 'When a tradition is in good order it is always partially constituted by an *argument* about the goods the pursuit of which gives to that tradition its particular point and purpose.'[55]

> So when an institution – a university, say, or a farm, or a hospital – is the bearer of a tradition of practice or practices, its common life will be partly, but in a centrally important way, *constituted by a continuous argument* as to what a university is and ought to be or what good farming is or what good medicine is.[56]

MacIntyre's key insight is that

> Traditions, when vital, embody continuities of conflict. Indeed when a tradition becomes Burkean, it is always dying or dead.[57]

MacIntyre's rejection of the Enlightenment myth of universal reason debunks the customary opposition between tradition and reason. The move allows regional

---

54   MacIntyre, *After Virtue*, 222.
55   Ibid.
56   Ibid.
57   Ibid.

practices to recognize, recover and restore the integrity of their own (situated) reasonings. It also weakens any strict demarcation of theory and practice. The 'thrown projection' of a practice will have already theorized to a degree the *rationale* of that practice, its sense of *wozu* und *woher*. This questions the assumption once again that theory is a supplement to creative practice. Theory is no add-on but precisely that reflective element (*theoria*) which both thinks with and draws out what is at play within a practice. *Theoria* is not an activity external to a practice but an integral element of its unfolding.

MacIntyre's appeal to the situated nature of practical reasoning provides a singular riposte to non-interventionist modes of education that privilege naivety and spontaneity in the novice. These modes deprecate tradition as a distorting ideological power moulding the student to its prejudices and frustrating their 'inner spontaneity'. This romantic conception posits a false dichotomy between continuity and spontaneity. Not to teach the principal canons of a practice is nihilistic: it de-situates students and disenfranchises them from their possible futures. To use Gadamer's term, there are no 'free spaces', no neutral zones to be found independent of historical practices. To the contrary, such openings only reveal themselves within living practices. The point is to engage reflectively and critically with canon and tradition in order to discover the articulable possibilities that reside within them. If all seeing and thinking is situated, then, to shield students from tradition in the name of spontaneity is to exclude them from those relational spaces able to allow their creativity to assume meaningful shape. Participating in and critically reflecting on the tradition that engenders one's practice is to nurture the conditions that extend its possibilities. It is to transform potentially both the history of that practice and one's understanding of it. With such transformation, how one is situated in the world undergoes a formative reconfiguration.

Within negative hermeneutics *practices denote ontogenetic processes* that produce the forms which come to symbolize and represent them. For Cassirer, a culture and its practices 'are not the product of fixed physical factors'. Its emergence is non-dependent, a 'mysterium' of spontaneous emergence which always solicits a better, closer understanding. In Heideggerian terms, such epiphanies open a world and keep it abidingly in place. McIntyre's discussion of practice and the virtues it generates proposes that practices are self-forming, generate their own internal goods and in the pursuit of such goods evolve the values able to judge exemplary practice, engender debate over what exhibits virtuous performance and serve to enliven and invigorate that practical tradition. MacIntyre supplements Gadamer's broad approach to tradition with a more detailed outline of its practices and their operation.

Practices are contingent historical emergences. Of course it is the case that certain practices emerge in response to the desire for certain 'goods'. A composer is commissioned to write music for a coronation or an artist is employed to produce a portrait. These 'goods' are external to the practices. In Gadamer's mind, such practices employ regular and repeatable techniques (*technē*) in that their end (the good) is external to them. MacIntyre's key point is that in the pursuit of its external goods, a practice evolves its own internal goods raising the question of whether the execution of the composition is well done. Does a composer have an integrity of voice or do they wilfully borrow from the achievements of others? Are the motifs or materials selected appropriate to the subject matters handled? The answer to such questions lies in the historical unfolding of a practice. Its community of practitioners build the performative criteria according to which exemplary practice can be ascertained. To what degree does a particular work embody the internal goods of that practice? Does it bravely face up to its subject matter? Is it 'truthful' in its response?

Gadamer's hermeneutics reflect similar norms. How open is a reader to her text? Is an interpretation 'tactful' in that it respects the otherness of contrasting cultural values? The notion of practice generating its own constantly debated performative norms links Heidegger's conception of project with Gadamer's idea of what a practice anticipates. In each instance, a 'form of life' or a *Dasein* generates from within itself its own revisable goals and norms of excellence. This further strengthens the idea of practice as an auto-poetic ontological structure.

For MacIntyre, to be a practitioner is both to be shaped by the tradition of a practice and to partake in a historically extended, socially embodied argument about the goods which constitute that tradition. To acknowledge indebtedness to the past of one's practice is not to be confused with any form of conservative antiquarianism. To the contrary, critically engaging with one's tradition and gaining an adequate sense of its character manifests itself in a grasp of the future possibilities which the past has made available to the present.[58] A practice enslaved to its past is blind to its future possibilities. A sense of foreboding lingers in MacIntyre's response to the question of what is it that brings practical traditions to an end? 'What weakens and destroys them?'[59] It is a question that Gadamer

---

58   Ibid., 223.
59   Ibid., 222.

might have asked: a tradition or a practice declines when the conversation that it started begins to fade. What brings this about?

> The answer in key part is: the exercise or the lack of exercise of the relevant virtues [...] Lack of justice, lack of truthfulness, lack of courage, lack of relevant intellectual virtues – these corrupt traditions, just as they do those institutions and practices which derive their life from traditions of which they are the contemporary embodiments.[60]

Negative hermeneutics offers similar reasoning. A tradition or practice maintains and renews itself so long as its defining questions command the interest and concern of its participants. Ontologically speaking, it is the dialogue about its core subject maters that upholds, mediates and potentially transforms the future of a practice. However, MacIntyre's position fights shy of a key point. The 'virtues' sustaining a practice do not just rise and fall de facto. They demand commitment and attunement to the hermeneutical dimensions of a practice, namely an acceptance of its transcendent dimensions, a recognition that there is always more to understand, that no work can exhaust it and that other perspectives are always available. For negative hermeneutics, the future of a tradition rests on keeping the questions which drive it open for it is in that openness that the as yet undisclosed possibilities for a practice disclose themselves. The vitality and openness of both a tradition and the practices it sustains are dependent upon the commitment of its practitioners to hermeneutical transcendence. As we shall see in later sections, it is in the willingness to act upon and to believe in the worthwhileness of its precepts that the future of a practice depends. This is why the (nihilistic) demand for epistemological certainty within practice is so dangerous. However, the main value of MacIntyre's observations is that they emphasize, first, the creative instability of practice and, second, that its norms are ontogenetically developed from within practice itself and, third, that the being of practice is a forever restive reaching out to extend its possibilities.

9. Hadot, Sloterdijk and anthropologies of practice

In conjunction with our discussion of practice, Pierre Hadot's text *Philosophy as a Way of Life* and Peter Sloterdijk's two books *You Must Change Your Life* and *The Art of Philosophy* remind us that philosophy is a practical matter. Whereas

---

60   Ibid., 223.

Hadot speaks of philosophy as the 'exercise of a life',[61] Sloterdijk refers to the discipline as reflecting different ways of 'practicing existence'.[62] The descriptions are pertinent reminders that philosophy is not a matter of school or of doctrinal exposition but involves practical training and exercise. Hadot is aware of how recent philosophy has not seen itself as the embodiment of a form of life. This is connected with philosophy's transition from oral to written discourse. Being written as an *aide memoire* enables descriptions of a spiritual practice to become disassociated from their author, to assume the status of texts in their own right and to acquire the status of autonomous statements of doctrine. Provisional spoken guidelines to practice become canonic assertions of dogma. When distanced from the 'way of life' that nurtured such exercises, the connection between philosophy and its practice can easily be forgotten.

Hadot's argument that for the Ancients, philosophy itself was thought of as a spiritual exercise[63] is valuable for two reasons. It is a timely reminder that philosophy is not just a matter of conceptual analysis but a life exercise.

> (Philosophy) considered as spiritual exercises were exercises because they were practical, required effort and training and were lived, they were spiritual because they involved the entire spirit, one's whole way of being.[64]

Hadot like Nietzsche before him accords ontological priority to the form of life that philosophy as practice gives expression to. He implies that philosophy is a therapeutics, a way of gaining clarity about what is at play in a mode of being. Philosophy considered as a practical exercise is a second-order response to an ontologically prior predicament. Furthermore, if we recall that *Dasein* is not raw existence but a way of life, the parallel between Hadot and Heidegger becomes clear. Not only is philosophy rooted in and reflects *Dasein* but as a practice it establishes meditational spaces (clearings) which allow that which is at play within *Dasein* to become apparent. Hadot makes additional points relevant to our analysis of practice concerning both repetition and *theoria*.

Regarding repetition, any practice requires being exercised and such working outs are subsequently consolidated into methods. A practice is a set of exercises prescribed (though never fully described) by certain rules. Repetition is key. By definition, any spiritual exercise entails repetition (*askesis*). The point of repetition is not the endless and mindless recurrence of the same. Returning to

---

61 Hadot, *Philosophy as a Way of Life*, 24–8.
62 Peter Sloterdijk, *You Must Change Your Life* (London: Polity Press, 2013), 5/6.
63 Hadot, *Philosophy as a Way of Life*, 126.
64 Ibid., 21, insert added.

the same activity across time establishes a certain rhythm to a practice and allows sameness and difference to become discernible within a rhythmic span. Hadot knows that hermeneutical experience shares with spiritual exercises experiences of change and movement between part and whole, distanciation and participation as well as between remembering and forgetting. The importance of repetition is not the repetition of the same itself but the differences that repetitions of the same occasion. Non-identical repetitions are epiphanic. Sennet writes of this dimension of practice that:

> 'We all know it; it is *rhythm*. Built into the contractions of the human heart, the skilled craftsman has extended rhythm to the hand and the eye.'[65]

> 'The repeats are steadying, but in religious practice they are not stale; the celebrant anticipates each time that something important is about to happen.'[66]

Rowan Williams comments similarly: 'The nature of ritual repetition [...] invites the unsettlement that will make the difference.'[67] This is true not just of religious practices for what is key is what the exercising of such practice occasions. As *Bildung* and its processes of formation reveal, it is the pattern of non-identical repetitions which are hermeneutically revealing.

Hadot's discussion of *philosophy* as a practice leads us to Peter Sloterdijk's analysis of both the form and hermeneutical consequences of practice itself. If Nietzsche's eternal recurrence returns endlessly to the same, repetition in hermeneutically conceived practice endlessly produces the different. Where Hadot's notion of philosophical practice as immunology seeks stability in the face of destabilizing truths, Sloterdijk's account of practice is dialectical: it is practices' pursuit of the excellent that generates instability. Non-identical repetition produces difference; difference establishes distance. In this context, the conditions of hermeneutical experience begin to emerge.

For Sloterdijk, the defining indeterminacy of human beings finds expression in their primary cultural practices which demand that the pursuit of the good and the true is undertaken as an imperative. Commenting on Sloterdijk, Eduardo Medieta argues that 'humans are creatures of the distance from themselves, from others, from the world, from their own world schemas'.[68] Whereas Hadot speaks to the tensions of practice, Sloterdijk emphasizes the distances which define

---

65   Sennett, *The Craftsman*, 175.
66   Ibid.
67   Rowan Williams, *The Tragic Imagination* (Oxford: Oxford University Press, 2016), 7.
68   Eduardo Mendieta, 'Peter Sloterdijk, *You Must Change Your Life*', *Notre Dame Philosophical Reviews* 7 (2014): 18.

them. Put another way, human beings endure and reside within the distances and differences that their cultural practices make possible. For philosophical hermeneutics, it is within such distances that we live: the human being is self-grounded in the pathos of the distances generated by its practices.

Sloterdijk develops Nietzsche's observation that 'every elevation of the type "man"' 'depends on a pathos of distance which involves' a 'looking up' and a 'looking down', 'the constant exercise of obedience and command', a 'holding down and a holding at a distance', in short, a 'continual self-overcoming'.[69] Whereas MacIntyre notes that practices develop their own 'internal goods', Sloterdijk analyses the effects of their pursuit, that is, the generation of differential spaces. Like Nietzsche, he understands that to accept an ethical imperative entails submitting to disciplines of transformation, to an '*askesis* of self-overcoming'[70] which presupposes the differential space between the 'away from which' and the 'towards which'.

> What is the human being if not an animal of which too much is demanded? Only those who set up the first commandment can subsequently present Ten Commandments. In the first, the impossible speaks to me: thou shalt have no other standards next to me. Whoever has not been seized by the oversized does not belong to the species of *homo sapiens*. The first hunter in the savannah was already a member: he raised his head and understood that the horizon is not a protective boundary but rather a gate for the gods and dangers to enter.[71]

Ideals of excellence can, of course, only be approached. The achievement of a present standard only extends expectations of future performances. Sloterdijk contends that 'humans can only advance as long as they follow the impossible'.[72] The argument has clear parallels with Gadamer's invocation of the *Vorgriff der Vollendung* which as a language construct is accorded powers of ideal projection and anticipation. The capacity of human practices to project distance-producing ideals suggests that humans are 'structurally superior to themselves, and carry within themselves an asymmetry in which they mould and are moulded'.[73] The projection of such ideals means that the human being is 'inescapably subject to vertical tensions', always dwelling in contests of achievement and accomplishment, always seeking a better reading or a more convincing performance. This requires, as Nietzsche understood, the pathos

---

69   Friedrich Nietzsche, *Beyond Good and Evil* (London: Penguin, 1973), Sec. 257.
70   Mendieta, 'Peter Sloterdijk, *You Must Change Your Life*'.
71   Sloterdijk, *You Must Change Your Life*, 443.
72   Ibid., 442.
73   Ibid., 328.

of distance, distances without which judgement and discernment would not be possible.[74] It is not that humans create practices but rather that the animal which develops practice creates the differential space out of which the human arises. The dynamics of practice shape Sloterdijk's contemporary articulation of a romantic *Bildungsphilosophie*. Four pivotal points emerge from this account of practice.

1. Insofar as human beings are born of the differential space which constitutes practices of excellence, they are creatures of distance and excess.
2. The differential space generated by such practices makes human beings inescapably subject to vertical tensions.[75] The impetus towards better more perfect performance always expresses dissatisfaction with the standard accepted. All improvements in practice whether spiritual or physical start with negation, with a 'secession from the ordinary'.[76] The asymmetry between the achieved, the to-be-achieved and the to-be-surpassed is an effect of the differential space produced by practice. Sloterdijk conjectures that humans are 'structurally superior to themselves', constantly reproducing the conditions of overcoming themselves and becoming more.[77] Residing in the in-between of the differentials from which they emerge, humans are both the subject of and become subject to the tensions of their practical eccentricities.
3. Humans require practices of constant overcoming to implement and maintain the unstable differential spaces upon which their being as creatures of perpetual transformation depends. Humans are accordingly creatures of repetition. Sloterdijk announces, 'It is time to reveal humans as the beings who result from repetition. Just as the nineteenth century stood cognitively under the sign of production and the twentieth under that of reflexivity, the future should present itself under the sign of the exercise.'[78] *Homo repetition* is a creature of habits and practices who pursues the exceptional, the excessive and the outstanding. In ontogenetic terms, it is the differential hermeneutic space opened by creative and

---

74 Friedrich Nietzsche, *Genealogy of Morals* (Cambridge: Cambridge University Press, 1997), Part 1, Sec. 2.
75 Sloterdijk, *You Must Change Your Life*, 13.
76 Ibid., 217.
77 Ibid.
78 Ibid., 4.

aspirational practices that establishes the limits within which the unlimited pursuit of excellence adventures.
4. Repetition is not the mindless reiteration of the same but has ontogenetic capacities. The expanding and accumulative learning derived from the continuities of non-identical repetitions (*Bildung*) generates stability and confidence within a practice. Repetition also establishes formative differences between performances.

The productive power of repetition manifests itself in social and individual forms. On the level of the social, the stabilizing repetitions of practices are central to cultural formation. Sloterdijk honours Nietzsche when he suggests:

> The term 'culture' refers to grooming systems for the transmission of regionally essential cognitive and moral principles to subsequent generations. Because this transmission is always the source of serious intelligence work, all actually successful cultures sufficiently capable of reproduction develop a form of central ontological organ that passes judgement on the vital or non-vital status of 'things' – six thousand feet beyond the philosophical distinction between the substantial and the accidental.[79]

Establishing a musical practice's norms of excellence, contemplating their various performative modes and comparing them to those of other musical practices allow a wider musical culture to develop, a culture in which excellence is always a simultaneous source of inspiration and dispute. As we have argued earlier, the differential spaces established by practice are maintained by competition and contest. The production of key points of difference – alternative modes of performance or composition – provides the coordinates whereby formative advances within a discipline can become discernible. Such points serve the development of cognitive norms. The differences produced by exercising the same allow comparison, judgement and development. They establish, in Sloterdiyk's words,

> science in progress, there are real knowledge gains, there are expeditions in which we, the epistemically committed collective, advance to hidden continents of knowledge by making thematic what was previously unthematic, bringing to light what is yet unknown, and transforming vague cognisance into definite knowledge.[80]

---

79 Ibid., 271.
80 Ibid., 7.

As we shall see, by articulating the dynamics of practice, Sloterdiyk effectively sets the basis for answering in the affirmative Gadamer's question, 'Is there to be no knowledge in art?'[81] Sloterdijk echoes Nietzsche's thesis that language's ability to create identities and stabilities where there are none regulates the differences and non-identities of actual experience in such a way as to create the semblance of a knowable world. A practice's ability to map, organize and stabilize differences permits it to establish self-referential continuities and traditions. The repetitions of practice allow the emergence of a cultural world. It is into such practice-established worlds that individuals are born and become subject to their 'axiological tensions'. The power of practice to create such worlds allows humans to 'step out of the river of life and take residence on the shore,'[82] establishing an existence beyond the everyday. Human existence (*Dasein*) is a matter of being practised. Philosophical hermeneutics' seminal notion of *Sprachlichkeit* is pertinent: 'the shore' bounding Heraclitus's river is the speech-created world (*Sprachsgeschaffene Welt*) which grounds writing, reading and the possibility of memory.

On the individual level, the disciplined repetition of the same provokes formative differences within a practice. The repetition of key exercises, protocols and procedures enables a practice to chart its different responses to the same subject matter. Furthermore, such revealed continuities and differences ground the emergence of subjectivity. A musical performer becomes aware of their performance style by appraising its variations in repeated performances of the same piece. The distinctness of a performance style emerges in and through the different repetitions of a performance style. Through the differentials of iterated practice, a sense of subjective competence arises. A basis for orientating ourselves towards the challenge of the new and unexpected is accordingly established. In Sloterdijk's words, 'we are the performers of practices and exercises that subjectivise us.'[83] Practice emerges as an *auto-poesis*, a productivity based on repetition's productive capacity to generate differences out of which continuities of sense and self can tentatively emerge. Rosenzweig aptly refers to these continuities as processes of selfication.[84]

Differentials are key to hermeneutical operations. In the case of the *Vorgriff der Vollendung* the differential space between the 'away from which' and the 'towards which' demarcates the space within which endless movement of hermeneutic

---

81   TM 97.
82   Sloterdijk, *You Must Change Your Life*, 217.
83   Mendieta, 'Peter Sloterdijk, *You Must Change Your Life*'.
84   See Iser, *The Range of Interpretation*, 133.

reflection occurs. This returns us to the claim that negative hermeneutics does not offer a theory of practice but a hermeneutics of practice, a reflective practice that grows out of and mediates our practical involvements.[85] Hermeneutical reflection is indeed a product of practice, emerging from and indicative of the movement across the differential spaces that constitute a practice. This strengthens Gadamer's claim that hermeneutic reflection is not an adjunct to but part of any intelligent practice. This suggests that strictly speaking, there is no hermeneutics of practice, only a hermeneutical experience arising out of the differential spaces that constitute a practice.

With their expectations of completion, practices generate their 'betwixt's and between's'. They establish the differential spaces which drive their performance. This re-enforces the logic of incommensurability at the root of hermeneutical experience. Hermeneutical differentials establish the experiential space which makes reflective movement possible. What demarcates these differential spaces as hermeneutical is that they disclose passages of movement in our subjectivity. They mark a hermeneutic transition – a coming-to-a realization – that we have been brought to see our blindness or the shallowness of our perception. These articulations form part of what Gadamer describes as the negativity of experience.[86]

Hermeneutical experience is not the experience of a fixed neutral object beyond the interpreter but an experience of movement which involves the interpreter. Such experience is less an experience of meaning per se and more an experience of movement which leads me to see the blind points in my seeing more clearly. The object of hermeneutical understanding lies not in my experience of a text or image but in the pattern of changes in my experiences of that text. The argument derives from the claim that practice itself establishes the differential structures which enable experiential movement.

What we understand as a painting changes not because we have altered our viewpoint of an otherwise stable object but because our image of it is formed in the changing shifts of our experience. In his study, *The Art of Gerhard Richter*, Christian Lotz argues with specific reference to Gadamer that:

> The constitution of meaning is fixed neither on the side of the subject nor on the side of the object. Instead the image is formed between the subject and the object and constitutes itself through this process as independent from subject and object. This ongoing shift of the same is what we should call the 'image'.[87]

---

85 Nicholas Davey, *Unquiet Understanding: Gadamer's Philosophical Hermeneutics* (Albany: SUNY Press, 2006), 242.
86 TM 353–4.
87 Christian Lotz, *The Art of Gerhard Richter* (London: Bloomsbury, 2017), 35.

Nietzsche and Wittgenstein remind us not to succumb to grammar's metaphysical snares by thinking of the image as an object independent of our interpretation. To the contrary, what we call the image is constantly being formed in the flux of experience. The image 'is not something static that can be immediately identified and modified. Rather, it emerges into being and remains "fluid" throughout'.[88] This has three implications.

1. An image is not a thing or object but a type of becoming that can be better understood by extending and repeating the experiential circumstances that generate it. Only then, to use Gadamer's phrase, can it 'become more' and be differently understood: temporal passage and the recursive moments of repetition in practice are key to extending the understanding that an image makes possible.
2. Understanding the meaning of an image is not a question of projecting an interpretation on to a neutral object but of tracing patterns of coherence and significance across the range of non-identical but cumulative repetitions of experiences through which the meaningfulness of the image arises. Understanding such meaningfulness is more a question of understanding something fluid, of what it has come to mean and might yet mean.
3. The object of hermeneutic reflection is, then, not a painting or sculpture conceived as a material object independent of me but the experience of meaningfulness which arises codependent with the image.

The object of hermeneutic reflection is not the meaning of the painting itself but what my engagement with that painting has brought me to see. As Christian Lotz puts it, 'Meaning is not something "there" (as if) "externally independent" [. . .]; instead, we should look at it as something that becomes.'[89] The object of hermeneutic reflection is, then, an experience of cognitive movement, an experience of having been discernibly 'moved on' in one's thinking such that I have come to think of both the painting and myself differently. This movement of cognitive difference sharpens both our emergent subjectivity and the narrative shape of its agency. Such movement is the *raison d'être* of humanities education. Understanding what hermeneutical experience entails cannot be accommodated within the Cartesian epistemological paradigm. What is required is, to the contrary, a participatory epistemology capable of articulating the movements of

---

88 Ibid.
89 Ibid., 33.

hermeneutic experience as processural interaction. If the object of hermeneutic reflection involves coming to understand that my orientation to an artwork has changed, what prevents that understanding from being anything other than subjective? The answer is paradoxical: the objective constitution of hermeneutic response allows my hermeneutical experience to be grounded in something other than just my subjectivity.

What, then, do we mean by the claim that the objective constitution of hermeneutic response allows the object of hermeneutical experience to be grounded in something other than subjectivity? Heidegger's notion of ontological difference offers useful assistance here. That which I come to understand is not a world hypothesized as independent of me but a world I am *already* deeply involved in. Gadamer's argument that *Bewusstein* (consciousness) is more being (*Sein*) than knowing (*bewusst*) is apt: our knowing is rooted in interactions that both enable it and yet transcend it. The object of my knowing is then a 'coming-to-mind'. In being brought to mind by an image, we become conscious of ourselves as the 'concernful' beings that we already are. Poetry and literature transform into intelligible form that prior inchoate knowing whose anxieties and concerns repeatedly flow through everyday experience. Heidegger alludes to the ontological priority of *Dasein* over interpretation in his remark concerning 'the intelligibility of something as always having been articulated, even before there is any appropriative interpretation'.[90] The images of art and literature bring us to recognize that which we had not really grasped 'understandingly'. Lotz's argument reminds us that 'we would do well to take paintings not as simple objects of interpretations but as *interpretations* themselves. Because of this, they offer us intelligible views upon our world'.[91] In so doing they reveal us not as objects in the world to be gazed at but as beings whose own concernful looking discloses them as concerned beings in the world. The hermeneutical content of the image is, then, not the object the image presents for us to look at but a visible entity which in being looked at reveals us to ourselves. The hermeneutical content of the image emerges, then, as a conscious passage of experience: the transitive experience of being brought from seeing the world in an image to seeing in that image a reflection of ourselves as concerned beings in the world. Looking catches us out as onlookers. Seeing images makes hermeneutical seeing possible. They offer a view of our objective ontological predicament as concerned beings deeply involved in cultural practices long before we are aware of being so. In referring

---

90 Heidegger, *Being and Time*, 203.
91 Lotz, *The Art of Gerhard Richter*, 203.

to ourselves as concernful beings we allude to Heidegger's conception of *Dasein* as a mode of anxiety and assurance, expectation and disappointment. These are not self-cancelling opposites but contrasting poles defining a differential space in which continuing engagement with the defining concerns of existence reveals ever-new aspects of their relation. It is not just the unpredictable nature of experience but also the unintended consequentialism of practice which prompts such dialectical turns. First, we are pushed towards a practice by the grounding concerns of our being: a poet seeking expression in what expresses itself to her. Second, once drawn into a practice we are prone to the constant ambush of the unexpected. Such turns are productive. When a practice reveals a failure in a line of thought there may be disappointment but failure as Nietzsche well knew is always potentially productive.[92] It can disclose other ways of doing and reclaim for the future a temporarily disabled practice. Practice is always faithful to unseen possibilities. Not only are we subject to the negative turns of experience but they subjectivize us. It is practising that creates both the practice and the practitioner. Negative turns are productive because humanizing: they uncover the finitude of existence. The committed practitioner knows that he will never grasp the fullness of a subject matter. Making mistakes bring us to realize that we clearly do not know it all. Practice is humbling: it demands that we confront our weaknesses and be honest with ourselves. As MacIntyre implies, to shy away from the painful demands of practical judgement impugns the integrity of the practitioner. Practice humanizes us not by making us better human beings but by forcing us to realize that there are occasions when we will be called on to act without any certainty of outcome and to take responsibility for the unknown consequences of such actions. Practice demands the courage of facing up to a consequentialism of unknown effects. Rowan Williams notes: 'the search for the reasonable and safe course of action in a practice will always "bring disaster sooner or later" since it "presses us to ignore the unavoidable costs" of timidity and compromise'.[93] Practice turned into a mere mechanics of action is practice bereft of commitment, risk and humanity.

The fact that we are drawn to certain subject matters in art, music and literature does not reduce our responses to the merely subjective. The subjective response has a twofold objectivity. It is an objective occurrence: we do not choose our initial responses; they happen contrary to our willing and doing. Also, and more important, that we respond betrays our prior and deep involvement in

---

92 Friedrich Nietzsche, *Untimely Meditations*, 'David Strauss, the Confessor and Writer' (Cambridge: Cambridge University Press, 1983), 3.
93 Williams, *The Tragic Imagination*, 14.

the structures of concernful being (*Dasein*). Our responses disclose that we are *already* deeply disposed towards the vital concerns of our mode of existence and its cares. The hermeneutic dimension of such responses lies in what they bring us to see – the objective structures of care, of vulnerability, of knowing and forgetting, which shape our existence. It is the objective constitution of hermeneutic response – its rootedness in concernful being – that allows my hermeneutical experience to be grounded in something other than just my subjectivity. There is, of course, a turn in the argument. The objective structures which ground a practice and impel it forward also threaten its cohesion.

10. Practice and re-earthing of theory

Before we consider the poetics of practice in more detail, we should consider the extraordinary shift in foundational philosophical ideas that enable Gadamer to insist that philosophical hermeneutics is 'not pure transcendental reflection'[94] but arises 'from practice itself'.[95] 'Reflection is brought into play in such a way that it accompanies the lived performance of a task.'[96] The rationale of Gadamer's approach is the outcome of a historical revaluation of those philosophical commitments which prioritize metaphysical questions (theory) over those of practical existence. Opposing the prioritization of the theoretical, philosophical hermeneutics does not so much analyse practical activity as participate in it, think with it and engage with what is at play within it. This has several implications:

1. If practice is prior to theory, the relationship of philosophy to the arts and humanities changes. Theory can no longer operate as conceptual policemen within the humanities but must serve as a Socratic midwife drawing out cooperatively what is at play within their practices.
2. The prioritization of practice over theory reiterates that hermeneutics needs to embrace a participatory epistemology able to escape decisively from modern philosophy's Cartesian heritage.
3. The development of a participatory epistemology restructures what is meant by hermeneutic understanding. If the objects of hermeneutic

---

94 Hans-Georg Gadamer, 'The Heritage of Hegel', in *The Gadamer Reader*, ed. Richard E. Palmer (Evanston: Northwestern University Press, 2007), 334.
95 Gadamer, 'Hermeneutics as Practical Philosophy', 231.
96 Hans-Georg Gadamer, *The Enigma of Health* (London: Polity, 1996), 53.

experience are not cultural artefacts but what engagement with them occasions, that is, movements in orientation and perspective, it follows that the object of hermeneutic understanding is not a text or scientific procedure but the experience of transition and transformation.

4. If by hermeneutic understanding is meant the methodological examination of texts by various reading techniques, then there is no such thing as *hermeneutical* understanding. Hermeneutical understanding is gleaned only when the many techniques of engagement with a text force a radical reorientation of the reader's sense of being-in-the-world. In other words, hermeneutical understanding is an experience of temporal transition when it *becomes evident to reflection that one's being in the world has undergone a radical realignment*. This emphasizes that the poetics of understanding does not concern the external application of schemas of interpretation to a body of experience. Rather such a poetics involves the spontaneous rearrangement of understanding within the differential spaces established by language. Metaphysics is effectively removed from the equation.

These, in outline, are the implied consequences of shifting philosophical hermeneutics towards a participatory epistemology. In order to appreciate the potential of this for our argument we should consider the changing significance of practice within the historical transition from classical metaphysics to recent modes of life philosophy. This is far from a historical detour. Whether it is a question of their ability to generate their own differential spaces or whether it is a matter of enhancing their inner creative tensions, our argument has gradually unfolded the autonomous ontology of practice and its powers of *auto-poesis*. The debate about 're-earthing' theory is in effect an argument that concerns the claim that practices justify themselves according to their own norms and are not dependent upon any form of external validation.

11. Platonism and worldly estrangement

Many practices are carried out unthinkingly without due care and with dull habit. Some practices aim at the unthinking. A dance movement, a particular stretch of piano phrasing and a specific combat response are practised repeatedly so that they become automatic. However, a *praxis* as opposed to a practice deliberately seeks an awareness of the implicit cultural and historical assumptions inhabiting the practice it is rooted in. It is not the case for Heidegger that sensuous life has to be suspended in order to reveal the underlying form of its objects. To the contrary, *Dasein* understood as a realm of embodied commitments is, ontologically speaking, already a realm of socialized practice. Sloterdijk puts it elegantly: the consequence of Heidegger's conception of *Dasein* is that 'the whole enterprise of theory' is 'literally "earthed" again from scratch'.[97] This permits Gadamer to argue that philosophical hermeneutics is not pure transcendental reflection:[98] as a mode of theoretical reflection, it arises 'from practice itself, and with all the typical generalisations that it brings to explicit consciousness, (must) be related back to practice'.[99] In the book *The Enigma of Health* Gadamer strengthens the point: 'Reflection is rather brought into play in such a way that it accompanies the lived performance of a task. [. . .] What properly belongs to an action which we call intelligent is just this capacity to sustain reflection *along with the performance* of a task, and not any sort of objectifying confrontation.'[100]

The characterization of classical philosophical theory as a mode of non-involvement in practical matters strengthens our critique of deconstructive approaches to hermeneutics. Deconstruction emerges as a classic instance of theory, that is, as a 'permanent agitation' against the truth-claims of regional 'meaningful positions and authentic, energetic (local) perspectives' in favour of an abstract criterion of truth and meaning that can never in actuality be complied with.[101] Whereas deconstruction deploys Nietzsche's epistemological scepticism to undermine any pretence of universal truth and meaning, it fails to note how it too is dependent upon such pretension, that is, *no* universal truth is possible. Meaningful local perspectives are condemned because of deconstruction's adherence to a fable. For all its playfulness, deconstruction is anti-life: it favours abstract demands for conceptual certainty over the productive uncertainties of interpretive practice. Negative hermeneutics remains in Nietzsche's phrase 'true to the earth': it seeks realizable possibilities within practices irrespective of their lack of formal foundation.[102] Deconstructive criticism involves what Sloterdijk might have called 'a necromantic acrobatics' which refuses to be sullied by the living commitments of practice. To grasp why deconstruction fails in its account

---

97 Peter Sloterdijk, *The Art of Philosophy* (New York: Columbia University, 2012), 26.
98 Gadamer, 'The Heritage of Hegel', 334.
99 Gadamer, 'Hermeneutics as Practical Philosophy', 231.
100 Gadamer, *The Enigma of Health*, 53 (emphasis added).
101 Sloterdijk, *The Art of Philosophy*, 41.
102 See Friedrich Nietzsche, *Thus Spoke Zarathustra* (London: Penguin, 1969), Zarathustra's Prologue, Section 3.

of the hermeneutic theory/practice relationship is *eo ipso* to understand the strength of the hermeneutical account of that relationship.

Deconstruction's apriori rejection of truth-claims in hermeneutics commits it to the erroneous view that attempts at hermeneutic truth are the equivalent to stating what the *definitive* truth of a text or text analogue is. Hermeneutic claims to truth are demonized as the expression of a will to power that seeks to stifle all plays of meaning within a work by corralling them within a fixed conceptual framework. Because no such claims are epistemologically confirmable, deconstruction implies that there are no circumstances in which they ever could be taken seriously. Deconstruction betrays itself as an armchair academicism. It persuades itself on (strangely) universalist grounds that as no claim to meaning and truth is formally possible, it cannot and need not contribute to the creative discourses from which local claims to meaning arise. The need for involvement in such discourses and practices is ruled out. The 'idols' of reason are preferred to confidence-building involvement in everyday practices.

Such agnosticism is indicative for Nietzsche of the nihilistic life-despising orientation of classical philosophical theory. Deconstruction measures the possibility of hermeneutics against the absence rather than the presence of meaning-in-itself. It accords theoretical entities, albeit negative ones, greater reality than the everyday objects of practice for it is against the abstractions of theory that the meaning and value of everyday objects is judged. Nietzsche understood the consequence of this: the everyday living world of contingent practices is condemned as apparent and meaningless.[103] The question for Nietzsche is what type of life prefers to honour the fictive world of intelligible being as real instead remaining 'earthed' in the actual world of everyday concerns and practices?

The notion that philosophy understood as the formal pursuit of intelligible essences is a type of mental sickness is prominent in Wittgenstein's thought. The metaphysical quest for the essential is presented as a hopeless compulsion based on a misunderstanding of the capabilities of language. Words and concepts do not refer to universals that allegedly exist beyond the language world. Rather, the meaning of general terms arises from perceived similarities and not from identities amongst clusters of resemblance. Philosophy can only be cured of its essentialist addictions if confusions over meaning are referred back to and resolved within the particular practices that deploy them. It is, then, the practice turn which cures philosophy of its metaphysical sickness. Once questions of meaningfulness can be settled in regional practices, the metaphysical pursuit of

---

103 WP 507.

essential meaning can in all good conscience be abandoned as absurd. Nietzsche's voice echoes in Wittgenstein's prescient remark:

> The sickness of a time is cured by an alteration in the form of life of human beings, and it was possible for the sickness of philosophical problems to get cured only through a changed mode of thought and of life.[104]

Negative hermeneutics and its grounding in life practices are indicative of just such a 'changed mode of thought and life'. Martin Heidegger was not alone in wanting to bring philosophy and thinking (*Denken*) back to earth.

When Heidegger speaks of the 'The End of Philosophy', he articulates the consequences of a position already articulated in *Being and Time*, namely that *Dasein* and its commitments are ontologically prior to conscious reflection. The development of theoretical language is presented as an abstraction of what is given in a more primary linguistic acquaintance with the world: 'Dasein-with is already essentially manifest in a co-state-of-mind and a co-understanding. . . . Being-in and its state-of-mind are made known in discourse and indicated in language by intonation, modulation, the tempo of talk, "the way of speaking"'.[105] When we make assertions (propositions) about things 'we take a step back from that which is already manifest' and place the entities we engage with in *Dasein* into a form that 'can be passed along'.

The apophantic realm of language is in Nietzsche's terms 'an arranged and simplified world'.[106] The act of describing everyday objects of concern in language attributes them with linguistic predicates subsequently mistaken for features of the objects themselves: description supplants the described. The further reduction of such descriptions into conceptual schemes establishes a speech-created world which can then be elaborated as and mistaken as a world-in-itself. The illusion arises that with language human beings acquire the key to the essence of all things. Nietzsche prefigures Heidegger's narrative on the history of metaphysics.

> The aberration of philosophy is that, instead of seeing in logic and the categories of reason means towards the adjustment of the world for utilitarian ends, (basically, toward an expedient falsification), one believed one possessed in them the criterion of truth and reality.

---

104 Ludwig Wittgenstein, *Remarks on the Foundations of Mathematics* (Oxford: Blackwells, 1978), 132.
105 Heidegger, *Being and Time*, 205.
106 WP 568.

> And behold, suddenly the world fell apart into a 'true' world and an 'apparent' world: and precisely the world that man's reason had devised for him to live and settle in was discredited.
>
> This was the greatest error that has ever been committed, the essential fatality of error on earth: one believed one possessed a criterion of reality.[107]

Nietzsche's 'history of an error' anticipates Heidegger's gloss on the history of metaphysics. Both depend upon key juxtapositions. In Nietzsche's case, the world of everyday practical existence which reason and language adjust so that 'we are able to live in it'[108] is devalued as soon as reason is esteemed the key to a supposed essential reality beyond the adjustable everyday. For Heidegger, the pertinent juxtaposition is linguistic: it concerns the distinction between what is essentially only articulation and description as opposed to an assertion of essence. In the 'End of Philosophy' Heidegger speaks not of the end of philosophical reflection per se but of the demise of philosophy understood as classical theory which, after Nietzsche's epistemological amputation of the unconditioned, is forced to 'return to earth'. Philosophical theory as metaphysics has to be replaced with the more modest aspirations of philosophical reflection (*Denken*) whose task is to articulate what is at play within the practical world of *Dasein*. The issue concerns not the correctness of Heidegger's Nietzsche-inspired historical narrative concerning the demise of metaphysics but how it decisively strips philosophical theory of its metaphysical pretensions and repositions it in the poetics of practice, that is, in the world of everyday practices from whence it initially emerged. Whereas deconstructive criticism manifests the continuing infectiousness of a hybrid form of the old metaphysical 'sickness', negative hermeneutics repositions theory in relation to practice and abandons any transcendental pretension. To repeat, considered as a mode of theoretical reflection, hermeneutical thinking arises 'from (within) practice itself, and [. . .] all the typical generalisations that it brings to explicit consciousness, (must) be related back to practice'.[109] Gadamer brings the historical narrative of Nietzsche and Heidegger full circle. His hermeneutics of practice is heir to Heidegger's re-earthing of philosophy in the concerns of *Dasein*. Nietzsche's and Heidegger's deconstruction of metaphysics reverses the traditional priority given to theory over practice. Negative hermeneutics goes further and reconstructs the position of theory *within* practice. This allows a new participatory epistemology in which

---

107 WP 584.
108 WP 306.
109 Gadamer, 'Hermeneutics as Practical Philosophy', 231.

practice and theory are mutually informing aspects of the same interactive processes. This brings us to the key notion of *theoria*.

12. Theoria: Participating from a distance

We are, however, left with a problem. If negative hermeneutics is a post-metaphysical philosophy hostile to the alienating distanciation of analytic methods, why does Gadamer make explicit appeal to the role of distanciation within reflection? The distanciation of reflection prises open those differential spaces within which the elements of a practical poetics can forever realign themselves.

> 'The spectator is set at an absolute distance, a distance that precludes practical or goal orientated participation. But this distance is aesthetic distance in a true sense, for it signifies the distance necessary for seeing, and thus make possible a genuine and comprehensive participation.'[110] (TM 128)

> 'Distance with respect to various possibilities is what is closest to us as human beings, *it is the distance within which we live.*'[111]

Within negative hermeneutics how are participation and distanciation reconciled? Our previous discussion of metaphysical theory and the contingencies of empirical existence now comes to fruition. Doubling is a notable figure of hermeneutical thought: *di-* is a standard prefix applied to words of a Greek origin and implies a doubling, a making twice. The prominence of such terms as di-alectics, di-alogue, di-fference, di-fferentials, di-stance and di-stanciation within negative and philosophical hermeneutics is beyond question. Practices are dependent upon the hermeneutical differentials that constitute them. They emerge from the in-between spaces such differentials generate. In classical metaphysics, distance and distanciation mark the gulf between reality and appearance. The distanciation invoked is metaphysical concerning the difference between the intelligible world of concepts and the realm of sensuous appearances. By implication, negative and philosophical hermeneutics collapse this two-world differentiation. Distance is no longer the gulf between two distinct ontological realms but that in-between space which emerges from within actuality itself. Philosophical hermeneutics transposes

---

110 TM 128.
111 Gadamer, *The Enigma of Health*, 58.

the differential space which articulated the reality and appearance distinction into the heart of Being itself. Differentiation emerges as an event of Being. Practices generate from within themselves the distanciating spaces which make reflection upon their processes possible. It is not so much that the production of differentials is an event of Being but rather that Being maintains its *being* in the endless proliferation of its differential spaces.

If theory and reflection are not external to practice but integral to it, how does the distanciation of theory operate within a practice and enhance it? If philosophical reflection does not appraise matters of practice from the 'outside' as it were, how does it partake in and function from within a practice? To understand how philosophical reflection performs a transformative role within practice, a paradox needs confronting. If alongside the embodied world there is no 'metaphysical platform' from which the Heracleitan flow of the everyday can be surveyed and structured, are we not condemned to the blindness of the momentary? Yet, if theory does not distanciate itself from the everyday, theory can neither map nor guide it. If theory can distanciate itself how does it avoid becoming alienated from practice once again?

> The word theory, *theoria*, is Greek. It exhibits the distinctive characteristic of the human being – this fragile and subordinate phenomenon in the universe – that in spite of his slight and finite measure he is capable of pure contemplation of the universe. But from the Greek standpoint, it would be impossible to construct theories. That sounds as if we made them. The word does not mean as it does from the vantage of a theoretic construct based upon self consciousness, the distance from beings that allows what is to be known in an unbiased fashion and thereby subjects it to anonymous domination. Instead, *the distance proper to theoria is that of proximity and affinity.* The primitive meaning of *theoria* is participation in the delegation sent to a festival for the sake of honouring the gods. The viewing of the divine proceedings is no participationless establishing of some neutral state of affairs or observation of some splendid demonstration or show. Rather *it is a genuine sharing in an event, a real being present.*[112]

The passage establishes that the distance necessary to reflection is not a consequence of a knowing consciousness being set over from and apart from what it comes to know. To the contrary, the distance that makes knowing possible is an opening within (and of) Being itself. Hegel's greatness in Gadamer's eyes resides in the fact that he grasps distanciation as an event of

---

112 Hans-Georg Gadamer, *Reason in the Age of Science* (Cambridge, MA: The MIT Press, 1990), 17–18. Emphasis added.

Being itself.[113] Far from blocking the epistemic subject from knowing beings, the space of distanciation allows such beings to emerge as knowable. It is through the opening of differential spaces that language-Being reveals (and maintains itself) as a process of perpetual disclosure.

Gadamer emphasizes that the distance proper to *theoria* is that of proximity and affinity: visiting religious spectators witness and thereby become part of a religious event. The spectators are not indifferent to what they observe: as celebrants of their own gods, they have an interest in how another community represents its gods. By distancing themselves from their own divinities, witnessing the religious practices of others allows strangers to see their own gods through different eyes. *Theoros is a standing-back in order to stand-nearer*, 'participation by distancing'.[114] It extends to the othering of oneself within acts of self-reflection, to distancing oneself from one's practices in order to critically engage with what is at play within them. This reaffirms the ontological priority of practice over reflection. Furthermore, the continued vitality of a cultural tradition and its practices depend on upholding and maintaining the differential spaces and creative tensions opened by reflective distanciation. Reflective distanciation is key to keeping the elements of a hermeneutical poetics in motion. The next step in our argument is to consider how reflection can distanciate itself from a practice in order to deepen and extend its involvement in that practice. To answer this we must turn to the parallels between concept and image formation in philosophical hermeneutics.

The poignancy of these parallels emerges from the suggestion that distanciation is an event of being. This implies that reflection is not distant from or alienates the subject from an otherwise independent being. To the contrary, reflection as an event within being opens differential spaces which not only allow particular subject matters to become visible but also reveal being itself as an endless process of disclosure. Reflection accordingly opens the distances that enable the movement of thought, distances which for Gadamer span the spaces in which we live. How is this to be articulated, and what is the role of concept and image formation in delineating such distances?

First of all we should remember that our thinking is always situated. As Adam Sandel argues, 'the world is the basis of taking up, questioning, or revising any particular practice' so that our understanding is always a situated kind of

---

113 Ibid.
114 Lotz, *The Art of Gerhard Richter*, 65. I have discussed *theoros* at greater length in my book *Unfinished Worlds* (Edinburgh: Edinburgh University Press, 2014).

understanding.[115] This is not a matter of a human subject seeking out its place in an alien world but rather of finding that our practices have already articulated the world that we find ourselves in. Second, we need to remember as Vattimo argues that we are always already 'situated in an opening of truth'.[116] It is in these distances of reflection that the world in which we are implicitly already involved in explicitly opens towards us. As events of Being, such openings disclose themselves in the movements of reflection. Third, Heidegger's phrase *Aus der Erfahrung des Denkens* (From Out of the Experience of Thought) points to just such an 'opening of truth'. Reflective experience is always an experience of passage, a coming to know that whereas once I used to feel a certain way about a subject matter, I now not only feel differently about it but also can articulate the difference. Hermeneutical understanding involves the experience of such movement. This movement takes place within the temporal arc of a practical project, an arc articulated by the trajectory of its away-from-which and its towards-which, that is, that differential space created by the act of practical projection. Hermeneutical thought is a conscious experience of being swept up by thought, of moving between thoughts such that one comes to an awareness of having been moved on in one's thinking. What then is the role of concept and image formation in delineating the distances (spaces) in which we live? The question is informed by another: how does reflective *praxis* engender alterations within a practice?

13. Differential spaces

If reflective *praxis* engenders alterations within a practice, reflective *praxis* has effects. To understand how these effects come about we need to understand the interactive spaces in which practices operate. In this endeavour, two themes are important: (1) The dialectical relationship between language-being and linguistic consciousness and (2) the differential movement between them which prompts shifts in hermeneutic experience. With its reference to the temporal patterns of acoustic experience, musical language often provides insightful ways of approaching certain hermeneutic figures of thought.

'Prelude' refers to that which introduces the main body of a composition. It announces that which is to come but, of course, that which comes to be heard

---

115 Adam Adatto Sandel, *The Place of Prejudice: A Case for Reasoning Within the World* (Cambridge, MA: Harvard University Press, 2014), 102 and 107.
116 Gianni Vattimo, *Of Reality, The Purposes of Philosophy* (New York: Columbia University Press, 2016), 53.

is often dependent upon that which has already been heard. Composers such as Luigi Berio and Leos Janacek are expert in bringing audiences to hear in what is performed what they are already deeply familiar with – reservoirs of popular song – even though the songs might not figure directly in what is performed. This introduces a subtle and appropriate shift to the meaning of *praeludium*: it becomes a hearing of, a drawing out of, what went before. The musical experience becomes not a reliving of a past sound world but a hearing of the formative voices of that previous world within a contemporary performance. Whilst a prelude anticipates acoustically how a composition is to unfold, in a hermeneutical sense, it also opens what a composition is drawing from, how its sense of direction gathers together and makes audible what has gone before it. In this context, a musical experience entails an acoustic opening towards both what a compositional figure anticipates and what that figure has itself drawn from. This offers a pertinent parallel with philosophical hermeneutics.

Gadamer's language ontology emphatically places language-being before consciousness: being exceeds knowing; consciousness is inescapably more being than knowing. Consciousness is always more than it thinks of itself as being and its being always more than it can think. Within philosophical hermeneutics, language-being operates as a transcendent principle. Language-being functions within philosophical hermeneutics as the ontological whole in which all individual parts (language users) are grounded. The differential relation between part and whole in language-being is fundamental to Gadamer's correlation of thought and motion.

The notion that language-being is more being than knowing is emphasized by the argument that knowing consciousness always turns to the stock of implicit ideas that language-being has already built up. Gadamer refers to this as the advance work that language undertakes for reflection. This does not mean that in language-being reflection meets fully formed ideas. Were this so, reflection would only meet with what it already knows. The element of movement central to the hermeneutic experience of thinking would be missing, and thinking would be reduced to an endless repetition of the same. Language is clearly temporal: speaking, writing and thinking unfold in time. Passage and movement is a feature of them all. Language-being considered as the totality of linguistic and cultural relations is clearly a shifting totality. Here the 'advance work' that language-being undertakes can be glimpsed. Language-being does not predetermine the ideas and concepts that reflection subsequently recovers but establishes the basic syntactic and semantic frameworks from which possible idea sets can be derived. Hermeneutic engagement with a philosophy involves 'thinking along with it', not merely recovering or repeating its key concepts but moving them on, subjecting them to further development. Listening for what is held within language-being is not a case of seeking to decode a 'totality of thought determinations' but rather of attempting to sense possibilities for new configurations of meaningfulness held within it. Language-being might imply such a totality but it is not reducible to a singular logic. Language-being is a manifold which, though it can be thought of as one, is not one. In a lucid essay on Hegel's system, Gadamer implies that such speculative structures do not unfold according to a general logic but according to their own *rationale*. Each structure is circumscribed by its own logic, by its own discrete reasonableness and plausibility. Only in this sense does Gadamer imply that language-being is logical. This has consequences for how philosophical hermeneutics can defend not 'reason' in the humanities but the inherent reasonableness of such disciplines.

From the perspective of philosophical hermeneutics, it is a mistake to think of language-being as simple or single entity. Considered as a manifold, it is closer to Heidegger's notion of *Dasein*, an infinite network of interconnected pre-reflective practical orientations that sustain being-in-the world. Language-being is transcendent in that it precedes and yet grounds each language practice. When Gadamer contends that Being that can be understood is language,[117] he does not mean that if things and creatures are to be understood they must speak through a linguistic idiom. He qualifies the remark by arguing that 'that which can be understood is language'[118] and that the language at issue is 'any language that things have'. There is no universal language in language-being, only the languages of the beings of that world have. All beings within language-being can be understood within the terms of their own language games.

The manifold nature of language-being implies a rich veining of language horizons. The language horizon of a cultural locale may be interwoven with the languages of different disciplines whether practical, theoretical and professional. Linguistic meaning is both indeterminate and relational: configurations of meaning in one horizon can be destabilized by proximity to another in which similar terms are used in a different context. Changes in cultural and ideological usage question established usages. Interaction is facilitated by the sharing of similar (though not identical) concepts. Such placeholder terms operate as points of intersection between different hermeneutic vectors. Whereas one language

---

117 TM 474.
118 Ibid.

community may associate a certain set of predicates with a placeholder, another will attribute a different set. This renders the specific usage of a placeholder term in one language horizon vulnerable to being changed by the proximity of different usages in another. In such exchanges meanings attached to placeholders different to my own are transmitted into my horizon with the possible effect of extending, disrupting or transforming what I thought I understood by them. Because any statement within my own language horizon is also a communicative act within the totality of language-being, its content and meaning is continually subject to realignment by its proximity to different configurations of meaning at play within the whole. This gives rise to two points.

First, the dialectical movement between part and whole within language-being formally underpins what Gadamer understands as hermeneutic experience. The differential space between part and whole opened by that movement is the temporal space of experience. Second, the reflective dimensions of practice which seek connection with the underpinning totality of engagements of which the practice is a part do so with the deliberate intention of critically exposing its operating assumptions to wider alignments of meaning within language-being. Reflective practice risks itself for the sake of transformation and renewal. Negative dialectics is central to the experience of practice hermeneutically conceived. The differential spaces established by a poetics of practice make these transactions possible.

'Thinking with' a position means developing an intuitive sense of what as yet lies undeveloped within it, acquiring the practical skill of hearing from where a position is coming from and conjecturing what may still lie within it and anticipating its direction of travel. Such 'thinking-with' would be impossible unless one was already embedded in if not hefted by the language-being underpinning its development. Language-being holds the possibilities that linguistic consciousness (reflection) can subsequently develop. The importance of engaged practice is once again emphasized. Only by being involved in a language-related practice can the possibilities held within it become *post factum* apparent to reflection.

Practice's dialectical refiguring of its enabling ground is not unique to philosophical hermeneutics. The musical form of 'theme and variation' often reaches back to an original note cluster so that the 'possibility and probability' of its subsequent development can be judged. The return, however, is never to the same. When the original note cluster is repeated one can hear in it what a first hearing often withheld, that is, its developmental possibilities. Such hearing is dependent upon the opening of a differential space across which the movement between 'implicitly sensed' and 'explicitly heard' can be experienced. In his discussion of Jacques Maritain's aesthetics, Rowan Williams refers to an equivalent notion in painting and poetry, namely the intuitive pulsion. This is described as 'something like units of imaginative sense, clusters of feeling or even knots of imagery and cross reference, which can never be captured simply in the music of sounds' or imagery. Such pulsions precede the creative act and indeed drive it for like language-being 'they always give more' and are always in excess of what they enable. The *praeludium* motif suggests then, hermeneutically, the experience of an opening, a sense of entering the differential space between what a composition is drawing from and where it is heading. The analogy with musical language is important: it reminds us that when we talk of hermeneutical experience we are talking in terms of a first-person experience, the actual experience of a temporal sequence unfolding. Hermeneutical experience occurs within the trajectories of patterns of sense working themselves through. Aesthetic and literary references to what has gone before and is already in play serve as a philosophical *praeludium* to thinking what formal philosophy often inexplicably overlooks – *the experience of thinking itself*. Grappling with this is a fundamental challenge for philosophical hermeneutics. Several guiding qualifications are appropriate.

For philosophical hermeneutics, the experience of thought is essentially the experience of movement. *The Relevance of the Beautiful* asserts that 'the essence of what is called spirit lies in its ability to move'.[119] The experience of thought as movement is an experience of opening. Nietzsche is acutely aware of the autonomous movement of language-being: 'a thought comes when "it" wants, not when "I" want'.[120] Nietzsche's notion of a thought approaching anticipates Heidegger's eventing (opening) of truth. Nietzsche's sensitivity to the prior effects of grammar offers a useful key for our general argument.

For Nietzsche too thinking is the experience of a disclosive opening. In *Twilight of the Idols*, Nietzsche remarks, 'I am afraid that we have not got rid of God because we still have faith on grammar.'[121] Indeed, his philological hermeneutics reduces the 'metaphysics of grammar' and its vocabulary – the concepts of subject, unity, identity and substance – to convenient linguistic fictions. Nietzsche's pronouncement of the death of God is the logical outcome of his repudiation of the apophantic aspects of philosophical language.

---

119 Gadamer, *The Relevance of the Beautiful*, 10.
120 Friedrich Nietzsche, *Beyond Good and Evil* (Cambridge: Cambridge University Press, 2002), Part 1, Sec. 17.
121 Friedrich Nietzsche, *Twilight of the Idols* (Cambridge: Cambridge University Press, 2015), 170.

However, without knowing it, Nietzsche's critique of theology reveals the ability of networks of meaning within language-being to undermine those belonging to a related language game or horizon. The recognition that language does not communicate by means of propositions and statements alone but also through its disclosive or expressive capacities suggests how the speculative can invoke networks of meaning without stating them out right. However, though different, the apophantic and aletheic operations of language are not mutually exclusive. A propositional statement can bring to mind aspects of meaning associated with, rather than asserted in, an utterance. Nietzsche's language of negation is caught out by this duality of function. As a linguistic act, Nietzsche's negation of God as the subject of theological statements unwittingly relocates the question of God within the aletheic function of language itself. The historical effect is to prompt something quite contrary to his original intention, namely a renaissance in the philosophy of religion. As a linguistic act, Nietzsche's apophantic denial of God unavoidably subverts its own negation by stimulating and affirming speculatively the world-disclosive powers of language. By default, the linguistic framework of Nietzsche's negations both evokes and sets in play a sequence of ideas that operates not only independently of his intentions but also contrary to them. As the activity of his linguistic consciousness, these negations reveal the reality of that linguistic-being that exceeds his thinking and subjects it to movements contrary to his initial willing and doing. Nietzsche's negations inadvertently reveal the autonomous language-being which circumscribes the moving space of hermeneutic experience and to which we are all subject.

Nietzsche's predicament exemplifies the wider ontological dimensions at play within thought's movement. His assertion that thoughts come of their own accord acknowledges that disclosure and displacement are part of a poetics in which unanticipated alignments of meaning can arise. His example demonstrates how participation in a practice can of itself promote unpredictable effects. Because of the ontological priority of language-being over linguistic consciousness, it is impossible to anticipate the extent to which a practice is connected to and rendered vulnerable to other alignments of meaning. This gives further emphasis to two points of our argument. First, only continued engagement in a practice can disclose the extent of its vulnerability to other as yet undisclosed alignments of meaning. Second, the centrality of experience in negative hermeneutics is once again emphasized as participation in an ontological opening. A finite mind can of course conjecture theoretically about the extent of its limitations but in reality these only become known in the immediate experience of negativity. The negativity is inherent in the poetics of practice. This does not imply that theory plays no part in practice hermeneutically conceived. To the contrary, it is a key driver in provoking the negativity of experience required by hermeneutical learning. How then do the aleatoric features of a practice promote its aletheic functions? This question allows us to return to the poetics of practice we have been anticipating and to further explore how practices within the humanities 'work' by achieving their transformative effects.

14. A poetics of hermeneutic practice

Jonathan Culler argues that poetics can be distinguished from hermeneutics because its primary focus is not on the meaning of a text but on the examination of how a text's different elements come together to produce certain effects on the reader.[122] Negative hermeneutics disputes this distinction: the meaningfulness of a text or image lies in its effects. Such meaningfulness does not depend on the intentions of an epistemological subject but upon the transactions within engaged practices. To understand such meaning-constituting transactions demands a grasp of the poetics operating within its ever-shifting economy of elements. This brings the ontogenetic capacity of a hermeneutical practice into discussion.

When Gadamer asks after the philosophical preconditions of hermeneutic experience he is pursuing an explanatory poetics for the hermeneutical. The implied poetics is not a grammar of the fixed elements of hermeneutic experience but an attempt to understand how its economy of elements interlinks, moderates and transforms itself. Identifying the elements of such experience has led us to discuss the distinctions between language-being and language consciousness, historical horizons, subject matters and anticipations of completeness. None are stable and nor are they graspable apart from one another. As we have stressed, hermeneutic understanding involves an experience of movement, that is, the living interplay of its constituent elements. This emphasizes that the ontology of hermeneutic experience is a complex of interactions made possible by the porosity of language worlds. Language worlds are not enclosed monadic structures but are logically, philologically and etymologically porous enabling translation and transmission between them. Without such porosity, the economy of elements

---

122 Jonathan Culler, *Literary Theory* (Oxford: Oxford University Press, 1997), 139.

sustaining hermeneutic experience could not occur. In this respect, the interplay across linguistic horizons and language games is ontogenetic.

The indeterminacy of meaning contained within a language horizon is of an infinite extent. There is no way of predicting what hidden potentials it holds. Because of their porosity, the collision of one language horizon with another can occasion numerous emergences of unanticipated meaning. The primacy of *Sprachlichkeit* and the interdependence of language worlds establish the interconnectivity on which a poetics of practice depends.

Practices considered as hermeneutical vectors do not exist in a vacuum. The space of language-being is not empty but a fluid environment dense with the intercrossings of multiple vectors. A participatory epistemology clearly supposes the possibility of exchange across and through language horizons. However, exchange requires movement between horizons. Such animation is stirred by the incompleteness and instability within any linguistic practice, by the *Vorgriffen der Vollendung* explicitly seeking completeness of understanding for their language horizons and by the fact that because it takes place within the wider context of *Sprachlichkeit*, a practice's search for completeness will because of the porosity of its boundaries both effect and be affected by contiguous horizons of meaning. Lines of exchange and interaction map the interactions which constitute a poetics of practice. The relational ontology underpinning this hermeneutical movement is further illuminated by the concept of practice as a hermeneutical vector.

Practices are hermeneutic vectors. They can be conceptualized as 'Feldwege' or pathways which presuppose points of departure and arrival. Vectors span the *woher* and the *wozu* of a given practice. Vectors are passages of travel already *unterwegs*, travelling towards their anticipated end. Lotz points out that Heidegger's use of 'Feldweg' is closely related in German to notions of leaving, moving away from and moving towards.[123] That which brings a constellation of activities into a coherent practice is its focus upon a given subject matter. Every practice seeks to discern the possibilities within its objects of concern. The trajectory of a vector anticipates how a grounding practice can be brought to greater completion. The *Vorgriff der Vollendung* propels a practice along its vector and animates the poetics of practice by keeping the economy of its elements in play. A living practice will be haunted by the incompleteness of its aspirations and primary subject matters. Yet such incompleteness renders it vulnerable to other passing vectors animated by similar concerns. The ontological primacy of

---

123 Lotz, *The Art of Gerhard Richter*, 199–200.

the language world is crucial: it constitutes the 'linguistic atmosphere' through which different vectors continually pass. By pursuing its own completion within the wider environment of the *Sprachswelt*, a hermeneutic vector will inevitably encounter, pass through and cause turbulence for others. These encounters hold the possibility of changing a vector's direction of travel, altering how it grasps its subject matter and transforming its self-understanding. Thus the more a practice pursues its completion, the more likely it is to collide with other hermeneutical vectors and undergo a challenge to its understanding of its subject matters. Three interjections about 'hermeneutic windows', 'subjective experience' and 'the incompleteness of interpretation' are now pertinent.

First, Lawrence Kramer in his text *Music as Cultural Practice* introduces the term 'hermeneutic windows' by which he refers to those 'pressure points' within a composition where multiple lines of contesting cultural association and significance begin to manifest themselves.[124] An artwork is not so much subject to a multiplicity of interpretations but embodies a conflict of interpretations. The hermeneutic window is reflective permitting us to see beyond our everyday perspective (vector) and grasp the extent to which other unnoticed ways of seeing have shaped our perspective. Gadamer's *pathei mathos* opens one such window making visible the prejudices that have contorted our judgements of a situation.

Second, colliding vectors are inseparable from subjective experience. In so far as they reveal the inadequacies of our understanding, their occasion sharpens our sense of being an involved and vulnerable agency in the practices that constitute our being. This implies that an empowered notion of subjective agency must be at the heart of humanities education. Without it, the transformative power of education ceases to make sense. This is why this study argues for the primacy of hermeneutical experience over hermeneutic theory. The collision of vectors is central to the negativity of experience and the transformative possibilities it prompts. Furthermore, as we shall suggest, this collision effects the transition from practice to *praxis*. Nevertheless, this must not disguise the need for a more fully worked-out notion of subjective agency within hermeneutics.

Third, the notion of a hermeneutic vector like the *Vorgriff der Vollendung* is a *form* of thought, a way of thinking about what a practice presupposes. Practices without projected goals internal or external are inconceivable. Practices are defined by the goals they anticipate rather than what they achieve. And yet, as previously stressed, it is not achieving the envisaged end that matters but what its pursuit gives rise to, that is, serendipitous collisions with other hermeneutical vectors.

---

124 Lawrence Kramer, *Music as Cultural Practice* (Berkeley: University of California Press, 1990), 10.

How then do images and concepts operate in this hermeneutical poetics? What role do they play in the economy of its exchanges. If, as T. S. Eliot notes, 'Words move',[125] the movement that concerns us is between the linguistic orientation of the individual practitioner and the *Sprachswelt* in which his or her practice takes place. The movement of hermeneutical understanding involves a constant interplay between the foreground questions preoccupying a practice and the background issues that frame them. indeed, the effectiveness of an image very much depends on the unseen operation of its constituting elements. How do words, images and concepts facilitate interplay and transaction within the economy of components that constitute a practice? For negative hermeneutics concepts and images are not static but engaging and effecting processes. The phrase 'image formation' is telling.

A poetics of practice focuses not on the genesis of the image alone but on what it brings into formation. Concepts and images are often presented as devices of restraint – a straightjacketing of complex experiences into simplified forms. Nietzsche is eloquent in this context: simplification is mummification by concept.[126] Negative hermeneutics is less concerned with fitting experience into the pre-established forms of language and art than with giving an account of how image and concept develop their form-giving capacities of bringing-into-relation and establishing transformative structures. Concept and image making are indicative of participatory ontological processes. Lotz suggests that 'making an image of something is identical with the transformation of a complex phenomenon into a condensed and understandable form'.[127] Experiences are living processes involving formative shifts of pattern, of memory and of anticipation. The transitive process of bringing something into image is an invaluable way of bringing clarity to what is at play in the confusing multiplicity of experience. Yet must we not distinguish between the process of forming an image and what an image itself gives form to?

Lotz argues that 'formed images are dialectical: they are in-between nature and theory and they allow us to enjoy our own rational activity and the possibility of seeing our ideas about the world in the world'.[128] Living experience involves an active thinking-with-and-through such temporal passages in an effort to discern their sense. As we have argued, looking, seeing and thinking are all anticipatory

---

125 T. S. Eliot, *The Four Quartets, Burnt Norton, Verse V, The Complete Poems and Plays of T.S. Eliot* (London: Faber and Faber, 1969), p.175.
126 See Friedrich Nietzsche, 'Reason in Philosophy', in *Twilight of the Idols*, ed. Aron Ridley and Judith Norman (Cambridge: Cambridge University press, 2005), 167.
127 Lotz, *The Art of Gerhard Richter*, 55.
128 Ibid., 7.

processes which strive to discern what is being indicated in their disclosures. When Lotz argues that meaning is only possible through essentialization he refers precisely to image making as a process of simplifying the complexities of visual experience in order to render its implied, sensed or intuited pattern visible.[129] The process is aided by the impetus within thought towards grasping the general and the tendency of language to strive towards completion. In other words, the emergence of the image and its ability to communicate meaningfully depend upon all the discussed elements within the poetics of practice – horizons, differential spaces, anticipations of completeness – being brought into play.

The hermeneutical task of the artistic image is not to represent the visual world per se but to render visible that which is at play within experience which without art's intervention would not be discernible. Such an image is not ontologically secondary in relation to a supposed original referent: it is not a copy or a reproduction. Much rather, the image adds to its referent, allowing its cognitive content to become more. The *Vorgriff der Vollendung* is once again pertinent. In struggling to bring an image into form, the artist essentially anticipates the outcome of certain lines of travel. This is precisely the function of the hermeneutical imagination, to bring into unity that which is ordinarily only known as a perplexing manifold. The image is invariably that which an artist is working towards rather than working from. An artist may be with a sitter but only as a reference point to draw out and to anchor what overtime comes into form as an ever more complete image of the sitter.

The argument confirms that the anticipatory powers of the *Vorgriff der Vollendung* are driven by the hermeneutic imagination. The finalized likeness does not achieve a completeness of viewpoint. Such a notion is a contradiction in terms. Rather, the *Vorgriff* anticipates what such completeness might be like. The artist no longer sees the image as a stand-in for a physical person. Rather, the artist is brought by the emergence of the image to see, perhaps for the first time, the complex, contrary, living manifold that he has been acquainted with but has never consciously seen so comprehensively. In other words, the image translates into visible intelligible form that which if unmediated by art would remain intangible.

This implied poetics of hermeneutical practice establishes that image formation is genuinely transformative. It brings into communicable and interpretable form processes of experience which otherwise would remain shapeless and inconsequential. The cognitive power of art is also clearly asserted. The formation of images renders tangible passages of experience which would otherwise slide from memory and comprehension. The process

---

129 Ibid., 87.

of image formation emerges as genuinely hermeneutical: it makes me aware of a passage of experience in myself. When I look at a portrait image of a friend I am not looking at a painted duplication of what that friend once looked like. Rather, what the image brings me to see is a vision of what is not normally visible. The image serves as a placeholder for that body of transient experiences known as friendship. It allows me to internally visualize a body of experience and grasp it in new ways. The image is what may be described as a 'thought-image', a visual coalescence of a range of experiences which in being rendered visible are rendered thinkable.[130] This also emphasizes that images are vehicles of non-identical repetition rather than just facilitating repetitions of the same. The more I return to an image, the more the formative experiences associated with it are brought under review. The ongoing educative function of the image is clear: it initiates a transformative movement, prompting me to reassemble what I misleadingly thought I had understood. Whereas the artist assembles from his experiences a unificatory image of his sitter, the image, once formed, bids me to think on, to reassemble and to give form to the diversity of experience held within myself. *Image formation is a process both summative in its anticipatory movement and formative when applied recursively to experience.*

Before we examine the poetic dynamic of an image's summative force we should look more closely at an image's interrogative dimension: its ability to return our gaze and to look into the complexity of our own experience as if striving to discern its sense and pattern. When an artist 'essentializes' a marine environment in an image of a seascape, she has not captured the singular essence of ever-shifting waters but, rather, has discerned in its myriad changes a pattern or order that renders its complexity a visible simplicity. Meaning for both Lotz and Gadamer is achieved not by capturing an irreducible essence but by processes of bringing-into-relation. In this respect, the image brings a manifold to a summative unity *as if* it were one. This we have previously identified as the centripetal impetus of the hermeneutic imagination which brings an image into existence. The emerging image is, from the artist's perspective, both dimly anticipated in his manifold experience of its subject matter and by the *Vorgriff der Vollendung* projected by his practice. Once its aesthetic autonomy is achieved, the image functions independently of the artist and is capable of exerting a formative influence on its spectators. Formed from the fragmented, it heals fragmentation. The image returns me to myself, initiating a reassembly of my dispersed self. Memories of shoreline walks, tides and storms are brought back to mind and remembered as part of a half forgotten or unremarked

---

130 Gerhardt Richter, *Thought Images* (Stanford: Stanford University Press, 2007).

narrative. The image becomes not just a placeholder for what I have come to know of the fluidity of its subject matter but a focal point for formative changes (clarifications) in my own self-understanding. In other words, in reception the image operates formatively: it has the interrogative power to assemble and to bring under review long separated experiences, reawaking some and linking others in unanticipated ways. The image throws me back on previous experience, brings the latter into focus within the forms of its own visual logic and allows me to see, perhaps for the first time, aspects of what shows itself as my ever-changing narrative.[131] For this to happen all the diverse elements of the poetics underpinning the emergence of the image have to be in due alignment.

The interplay of dialectical elements within the poetics that constitutes a given practice is now clear. We have considered the impetus of a body of experience striving towards a unifying image and how when formed that image can bring dispersed aspects of experience into a more cohesive unity. It would be a mistake to think of such movements between part and whole in too linear a fashion. It is as much a question of movement across part-whole clusters or vectors as within them. The consequentialism of unintended effects within hermeneutics depends precisely upon the possibility of these multiple movements. The relational ontology and participatory epistemology of philosophical hermeneutics facilitate such exchange. Such an ontology is implied by both Lotz and Gadamer and is of obvious consequence for the poetics we are outlining. First, Lotz and, then, Gadamer.

> The idea must appear in the work itself and come to presence in it. Meaning, we could say, is ultimately bound to its material form and therefore any reflection on art is forced to come back to the 'this-ness' – to the 'here and now' of the individual work. Otherwise it could not be reported. Thought is forced to the gaze, the ears, the hands and the tongue, in order to find itself in the external world.[132]

> (Aristotle) showed that all *aisthesis* (perception) tends towards a universal, even if every sense has its own specific field and thus what is immediately given in it is not universal. Both the specific sensory perception of something as such is an abstraction. The fact is that we see sensory particulars in relation to something universal.[133]

---

131 For a discussion of the hermeneutic economy of elements that allow an image or a concept to function, see my essay 'Dialogue, Dialectic and Conversation', in *The Gadamerian Mind*, ed. G.-J. Van Heiden (London: Routledge, 2021).
132 Lotz, *The Art of Gerhard Richter*, 7.
133 TM 90.

Both passages invoke the oscillating movement between sensuous materiality and conceptual thought. The form of argument is Kantian: intuitions without concepts are blind and concepts without sensuous content are empty. Indeed, for Lotz it is precisely this transitionary movement that constitutes the spiritual in art: 'the spiritual moment . . . does not simply exist; rather, it is in every work of art the becoming and forming moment'.[134] However, the transitionary movement between a sensuous manifold coming to form in an image (the centripetal) and an image achieving embodiment in the world (the centrifugal) is but one pattern of movement within the hermeneutic poetics we are outlining. Shifts in hermeneutic understanding depend not just on reciprocal movements between the materiality of sense and the intelligence of the concept but also on those across and between different material and conceptual horizons. *The formal exchanges of sense and meaning enable the transformative movements within understanding.* The insights of Lotz and Gadamer establish the essential coordinates within which transformative movement that between horizons can occur. On the one hand, images, meanings and concepts not only find a place in the world through their material embodiment but in finding that place they enter a space that potentially links them to every other thing in the world. On the other hand, by being linked to the realm of ideational content, the sensuous dimensions of the image are loosened from their material bounds allowing their content to enter the world of intelligence (*Geist*). Transformative movement within hermeneutic understanding is clearly dependent upon the transitionary movement between sense and intelligence.

In our experience of the world, just as the sensuous cannot be completely severed from the ideational, nor can ideas of meaning become fully disembodied from the material. What is key is the porosity of both intellectual and material horizons. An image may for reasons of personal history or broader tradition be tied to particular times and spaces. However, though its meaning depends as Lotz argues on being embodied, the image is not logically tied to any specific embodiment. Other temporal and spatial instantiations are possible. In the same way, because an image is attached to and gains its meaning from a specific concept does not prevent it from being exposed to other concepts. Because of both the interconnectivity of linguistic meaning within *Sprachlichkeit* and the embodied nature of its meanings, the meaning of images and concepts is always subject to spatio-temporal transposition and transformation. Lotz and Gadamer come close to Wittgenstein's argument that 'we must think of perception

---

134 Lotz, *The Art of Gerhard Richter*, 7, 22.

as containing a thought-element' and 'thinking of thinking as containing a perception element'.¹³⁵ The hermeneutic impurity of image and concept (the fact that they cannot be disassociated from other frameworks of meaning) allows both to serve as portals for times and places of meaning other than our own. The lines of movement required by a hermeneutic poetics are now clear. Practices emerge from and intensify these movements. The importance of educational practices as sites for facilitating hermeneutical transformations could not be better emphasized.

---

135 Mary Warnock, *Imagination* (London: Faber and Faber, 1976), 192. Warnock argues that all perception is to a degree thought imbued. See p. 151.

5

The provocations of practice

Provocation c. 1400, from Old French provocacion *(12c.) and directly from Latin* provocationem *(nominative* provocatio*) 'a calling forth, a summoning, a challenge', noun of action from past participle stem of* provocare *'to call out'.*

1. Introduction

Chapter 4 examined the arguments against the formal possibility of hermeneutics considered as a universal method of interpretation. The following factors mitigated against its success: no interpretation can be fully adequate to its subject matter; subject matters are always in excess of their interpretation; all understanding is both finite and perspectival: there is always something more to be said; and no interpretative understanding can be complete or achieve full methodological transparency. These factors underpin a central claim of 'negative hermeneutics': hermeneutics considered as an epistemology of interpretation will fail. Such failure is both inherent in and made inevitable by the structure of hermeneutical practice itself. The *Vorgriff der Vollendung* is instrumental in provoking this demise. However, nihilism is its consequence *only* if such negativity is taken to betoken an epistemological failure. If hermeneutical transactions are treated ontologically, negativity provides the impetus for a practice to seek deeper engagement with its subject matters. Though negative hermeneutics formally blocks the possibility of complete knowledge, it opens the way to ever completer knowledge. The emergence of negative hermeneutics is far from catastrophic: it is a fundamental stimulus to further hermeneutical reflection, to the enhancement of engaged subjectivity, and to the growth of subject positions all of which bring our arguments to their affirmative summation.

In this final chapter, we shall consider how negative hermeneutics highlights the dialectical consequentiality of hermeneutical practice. The more a practice explicitly seeks to understand its subject matters and to clarify its own norms and assumptions, the more it journeys into its *Sprachswelt* exposing itself to other potentially disruptive configurations of meaning. Their presence within the *Sprachswelt* renders hermeneutical practices ontogenetic by provoking unexpected alignments of meaning. Understood as a formal refusal of any final terminus for interpretation, negative hermeneutics actually constitutes a repudiation of nihilism. In its rejection of fixity, negative hermeneutics gives ontological precedence to possibility over Being. Because of their ontological placement in the *Sprachswelt*, the constant unease and tension between practices maintains the ever-open possibility of transformative understanding. How does the pursuit of completion within a practice both *provoke* the failure of a project *and* condition the possibility of its transformative renewal? Here we beg the central question: how do practices function hermeneutically? How does involvement in a practice open the differential spaces upon which the transformation of its understanding depends? The justification of the preceding discussion of the poetics of hermeneutic practice is now evident.

The poetics establishes the architectonic structure within which the moderating movements of hermeneutic understanding occur. The tensions between language-being and linguistic consciousness, on the one hand, and the infinite expectations of completion versus the eternal recurrence of understanding's fragmentation and disruption, on the other, constitute the essential preconditions for a hermeneutical poetics and its movement. However, we must now turn from the preconditions of such a poetics to what generates its movement and transformative capacities. In what does the provocative capability of a practice reside and what links it to the pursuit of completion? What becomes evident is that a negative poetics is also operating within hermeneutics: the conditions which bring the illuminating image and the transformative word into being are the self-same conditions capable of displacing their insights.

Drawing from Georg Simmel's essay 'The Concept and Tragedy of Culture', Ernst Cassirer contends that formal structural oppositions within cultural practices prove their demise.[1] The pivotal opposition concerns the perpetual tension between the indeterminacy of expectation and the determinacy of achievement within a practice. Cassirer argues that

---

1 Ernst Cassirer, *The Logic of the Humanities* (New Haven: Yale University Press, 1974), 184.

the real tragedy of culture . . . in contradistinction to one which is pitiable or comes as destruction from external causes – (is) one in which the destroying forces are not only directed against a being but originate in the deepest recesses of this very being; it is a fate in which a destiny is completed in a self destruction which is latent and, so to speak, the logical development of the very structure by means of which that being has attained its positive existence.[2]

The relation between a culture and its practices is not just a formal dialectic but is lived out as a drama. By implication,

it is no simple event, no peaceful unwinding (but . . .) an act, which is forever necessary to begin anew; and its goal is never certain. . . . All that it has created it continually threatens to tear apart again with its own hands. Accordingly, when considered solely in the light of its products, it always contains something unsatisfactory, something which is profoundly questionable.[3]

All practices are differentiated by their specific forms which are of an indeterminate nature such that justice, harmony or beauty can be determined in an infinite number of ways. Each practice seeks the perfection of its form which can only ever be provisionally realized. Cassirer argues that the created work never fulfils the full scope of the practitioner's creative intuition and as a result the short fall of the work intimates what might yet be possible within that practice. Cassirer continues:

The further the cultural process develops, the more the created shows itself to be the enemy of the creator. Not only can the individual not fulfil himself in his work; in the end, his work threatens to destroy him. What life truly and inwardly strives for is nothing other than its own movement and the streaming fullness of it. It cannot bring forth this inner fullness, it cannot enable it to become perceptible in specific creations, except that these very creations become limits for it – firm embankments against which this motion streams and on which it breaks itself.[4]

The notion of *Sprachlichkeit* and its anticipation of completion offer a more positive account of how practices regenerate themselves through challenge and failure. It is the anticipatory impetus of *Sprachlichkeit* that drives the provocative capacity of practice. This capacity drives the negative hermeneutics enabling it to surpass Cassirer's tragic outlook. We will, accordingly, divide Chapter 5 into two

---

2   Ibid., 187.
3   Ibid., 190–1.
4   Ibid., 191, emphasis added.

sections: those which outline the 'negative' impetus of hermeneutical practices and those which explore the transformative dynamic of negative hermeneutic operations.

2. Negative moments: Practice and the instabilities of understanding

Ontologically speaking, the *Sprachswelt* is the *cantus firmus* upon which hermeneutic practices and their effects rely. If 'the Word' was 'in the beginning' ambiguity has been in language from the start. Ambiguities inherent within the *Sprachswelt* drive each practice towards clarifying its operating terms and expectancies both of which are under constant pressure from the ever-changing circumstances of their deployment. The *Vorgriff der Vollendung* anticipates an ideality of meaning which promises to rid a practice of its ambiguity and yet the *Vorgriff* is instrumental in bringing a practice to discover further alignments of meaning it is implicitly and explicitly linked to.

Considered as a *Sprachsontologie*, negative hermeneutics perpetuates the dialectical circumstances that render stability of meaning for any practice problematic. Precisely because the *Vorgiff der Vollendung* launches its movement towards clarity within the *Sprachswelt*, it risks exposing its alignments of meaning to the questioning of others: *the impetus towards clarification conspires in its own undoing*. The dialectical value of negative hermeneutics lies in the production of such instability. Negative hermeneutics sets a negative poetics in play capable of dissolving the cohesiveness of word and image. Furthermore, if the core meaning of words and concepts can never be rendered fully determinate, their meaning will always remain to a degree ambiguous.

By providing its transcendent form, *der Vorgriff* galvanizes and gives direction to a given practice. Because it does so within the wider context of *der Sprachswelt*, it is able to intervene in and disrupt horizons of meaning other than its own. The ability of *der Vorgriff* to achieve consequential effects across various horizons of meaning emphasizes the tactical importance of this Kantian figure of thought within negative hermeneutics. The constructive and destructive functionality of the *Vorgriff* is made apparent by Kant's dual axiom: 'thoughts without content are empty, intuitions without concepts are blind'.

> It is, therefore, just as necessary to make our concepts sensible discernible, that is, to add the object to them in intuition, as to make our intuitions intelligible,

that is, to bring them under concepts. The understanding can intuit nothing, the senses can think nothing.[5]

Although Kant stresses the distinctness of concepts and intuition, the phenomenological foundations of philosophical hermeneutics dispose it towards emphasizing the constant interplay between the sensuous image and its concept within hermeneutic understanding. Kant's axiom is structurally fundamental to the hermeneutical dimensions of *Erfahrung*. The latter involves the constant interplay between sensuous experience striving for intelligible content (its subject matter) and subject matters (concepts or forms) seeking meaningful incarnation in sensuous particulars. The account of concept and image formation offered by Gadamer and Lotz is similar: an artist clarifies a body of diverse experience by finding an appropriate image whilst the philosopher attempts to simplify a manifold of impressions under the unity of a concept. Here the function of image and concept coalesces as 'placeholders' or 'thought-images' for manifolds of complex experience. As placeholders they transcend the circumstances of their formation and render the world beyond those circumstances thinkable within their own forms and categories. The movement of hermeneutic understanding can in part be thought of as the constant struggle of both sensible intuition to overcome its 'blindness' and concepts endeavouring to achieve an embodied presence.

Though useful, the Kantian figure of thought oversimplifies understanding's movement. Kant assumes it to take place within the cognitive subject. Taking Hegel's *Geist* as his precedent, Gadamer replaces the epistemological subject with an ontological subject, that is, the *Sprachswelt*. The scope of understanding is no longer limited to the horizons of meaning within individual consciousness but extends to traversing the multiple horizons of language-being. Openness to horizons of meaning other than those of a 'home' practice is itself a consequence of the instability of understanding's movement.

The movement between intelligible concept and sensuous embodiment is beyond being quieted: a concept can never dissolve into pure perception, and sensuous content can never ascend to unadulterated conceptuality. This movement in part accounts for the unsettled nature of hermeneutic practices. Gadamer does not deny the possibility of thinking in terms of pure concepts but only its relevance. What is the value of such an abstract exercise for

---

5   Immanuel Kant, *The Critique of Pure Reason* (London: Macmillan, St Martins'sPress,1970), 93, A 52, B 76.

understanding embodied experience?[6] In Sloterdyk's terms, such thinking has become 'unearthed'.

This implies that for philosophical hermeneutics concepts cannot achieve any final determination of meaning. Just as no image can be striped of all intelligible content, no empirical concept be entirely released from its material embodiment. This confirms Wittgenstein's observation that we should think of perception as having a thought element and of thought as having a perceptual element too. This implies that if a concept can never fully dissolve into perceptual embodiment and if sensuous content cannot completely ascend into the purity of the concept, both retain traces of each other in themselves. Such traces indicate the critical points of porosity facilitating the transmission of conceptual and sensual elements within hermeneutical experience.

The plurality of linguistic horizons within the *Sprachswelt* suggests that the horizons of meaningfulness through which the movements of understanding pass are many and various. Both the infinite determinations of meaning attached to a concept and the openness of embodied meaning to endless interpretation guarantee the permanent instability of understanding. The porosity of terms attached to a *Vorgriff* means that, as part of a hermeneutical vector moving through the complexities of the *Sprachswelt*, they are inevitably subject to shifts in their constituent meanings. It is both the fluidity and interconnectedness of all these elements that enable *Vorgriffen* to provoke the emergence of unexpected dimensions of meaning. The provocative power of the *Vorgriff* derives from its alternating dialectical capacity: though the *Vorgriff der Vollendung* anticipates an ideality of meaning which strives towards ridding a practice of its ambiguity, the very pursuit of that ideality only generates further ambiguity.

3. Practice and repetition

Practices do not emerge *ex nihilo*. They are grounded in the language-being their operations presuppose. A practice can neither draw out nor provoke hidden alignments of meaning from within the indeterminacy of language-being unless already housed within a determinate framework of meaning. *Implicit alignments of meaning in language-being could not destabilize a practice's*

---

6   Like the tradition of Kantian thought which preceded it, philosophical hermeneutics is deeply sceptical of exercises in metaphysical or purely theoretical thought. The latter have significance only as tools for analysing the complexities of human experience. They have no capacity for revealing the nature of reality independent of human consciousness.

established configurations without mutual ontological participation. Indeed, it is a practice's placement within the *Sprachswelt* that allows repetition to be productive by generating non-identical repetitions as opposed to mechanical repetitions of the same. Richard Sennet's remarks that in practice repetitions are telling: 'the repeats are steadying, [...] in religious practice they are not stale; the celebrant anticipates *each time* that something important is about to happen'.[7] In other words, the ontogenetic capacity of repetitions (their ability to disclose ongoing formative narratives exemplified by such processes as *Bildung*) requires the instability of meaning and the movement of understanding it can provoke.

Practices follow clear and regular protocols. They may change in technique and technology but they remain disciplined modes of engagement with clear cultural and spiritual concerns. Practices offer predictable and reliable schemas of engagement with the ontological endowments of language-being even though the outcomes of such engagement are serendipitous. From a hermeneutic perspective, repetitions are not orientated towards the production of the same but the induction of the different and the unexpected. Creative practices can embrace technology but they are not technologies. Their outward protocols may involve the reliable sameness of preferred working environments and equipment but their impetus is towards soliciting from the speculative dimensions of language-being the surprising and the unpredictable.[8] Practice protocols galvanize and render predictable the dispositions, tools and circumstances in which the uncertain can be navigated. The repetitions of yoga or tai chi exercises are not to recapture the same body posture but to enter into it more deeply and, what's more, to sense both ongoing and previously unnoticed changes in physical aptitude and muscle memory. A reading practice may depend upon stable structures of assimilation, but we do not read poetry and literature to meet with what we already know but rather to be challenged by what we don't as yet know. Difficulty is essential: it turns a practice outward, forcing it to reappraise its engagement with the unexpected. Texts for hermeneutics have a Heracleitan quality: the same text can never be read twice.[9]

Practices may require predictability and stability but the broader historical and linguistic circumstances in which they operate are not stable. Their environments have a propensity for movement and change. There is always a

---

7   Richard Sennet, *The Craftsman* (London: Penguin, 2008), 177.
8   This point is invariably overlooked in the traditional art and craft debate.
9   'One cannot step twice into the same river, nor can one grasp any mortal substance in a stable condition, but it scatters and again gathers; it forms and dissolves, and approaches and departs.' Heraclitus, *The Art and Thought of Heraclitus*, ed. Charles H. Kahn (Cambridge: Cambridge University Press, 1989), 53.

potential mismatch between a practice's expected outcomes (projections derived from established experience) and those unexpected outcomes which arise from changes in the broader operational circumstances in which a practice operates. Political managers often find themselves undone by shifts in the *Zeitgeist* they aspire to manage. Military stratagems borne of previous success can be compromised by unseen aspects of new technology. The reverse also happens. A piece of equipment designed for a theatre of operation where its expected performance disappointed can prove astonishingly successful in circumstances for which it was not intended. Technology transfer is frequently serendipitous and its effects, both positive and negative, unpredictable. Meditation and drawing practices may follow very precise and regularized procedures but they are intended to make both visible and navigable unnoticed changes in the ongoing movements of their subject matters. This suggests that creative practices are productive precisely because of an incommensurability between what a discipline envisages as its scope of action and the actual but untried possibilities that exist for it in the cultural horizons sustaining its being. A productive breakthrough involves that moment in which a practice surpasses its expectations and brings to light unseen possibilities within the ongoing tradition guiding its operations. Precisely because practice operates in the instabilities of *der Sprachswelt*, the repetitions of its operations can bring alterations in that world to light. The repetitions of practice are provocative precisely because of that practice's grounding in the *Sprachswelt*. *Cycles of repetition have the capacity to mark previously unremarked shifts in the broad horizons of meaning from within which they operate. The marking of such differences allows a practice to form a narrative sense of where it has come from and where it is going to.*

The ontological excess of what is actually possible over and against the limited extent of what is imagined as possible brings to light the dialectical counter-thrust within Gadamer's justifiable scepticism concerning the spread of bureaucratized teaching and learning systems within higher education and the corrosive influence of predictive methodologies upon the human sciences themselves.[10] Gadamer is profoundly aware that all planning and execution take place within an unstable equilibrium so that whatever is planned is constantly under threat: 'the experienced person knows that all foresight is limited and

---

10 'We should have no illusions, bureaucratised teaching and learning systems dominate the scene'; see Hans-Georg Gadamer, *On Education, Poetry and History, Applied Hermeneutics*, ed. Dieter Misgeld and Graeme Nicholason (Albany: State University of New York, 1992), 59). Writing at the end of 1959, Gadamer commented, 'even the classical historical *Geisteswissenschaften* were undergoing a reorientation toward new statistical and formal methods, so that the pressure toward scientific planning and the technical organisation of research was unmistakable' ('" 551).

all plans uncertain'.[11] For philosophical hermeneutics, this is, ontologically speaking, an unavoidable truth which can only be grasped in the accidents of experience. However, a dialectical twist in the argument saves the knowing practitioner from nihilistic despair. The ontological conditions which disrupt the chances of a plan succeeding also establish the conditions for arriving serendipitously at unexpected outcomes. This does not refer just to the 'truth' known to every military commander since Classical times, that is, that when hostilities commence every plan 'goes out of the window', but also to its more important corollary, namely it is precisely the emergence of the unexpected that can offer unplanned ways of disarming one's opponent. From a hermeneutical and educational perspective what is key is that the practitioner should have acquired a sufficient stock of practical knowledge not only to recognize in the unexpected unpredicted opportunities but also how to take advantage of them when they arise. The knowing practitioner is not the one with an inflexible faith in their plans but one who, despite its challenges, keeps faith with their practice because they know it contains more possibilities than can be presently imagined. The negativity of experience within a practice has a negative capability: keeping faith with a challenged practice brings its redemptive possibilities closer.[12]

A plan is always of its time and circumstance. It is impossible to predict all the contingencies capable of disrupting a practice other than knowing that certain circumstances will likely prove its undoing. Yet, contrary to expectancy, this does not render all planning and organization futile. An environment of ontological excess renders focussed planning even more consequential. Though the pursuit of targets may induce unforeseen circumstances which prove the plan's demise, bringing about the unexpected can give rise to unforeseen future possibilities. Furthermore, insofar as the pursuit of a plan can stimulate the emergence of unforeseen ideas and consequences, that pursuit can serendipitously provoke solutions to problems in adjacent horizons. Neither outcome could come about without the pursuit of a plan. It is, after all, not what the plan aims at that is important but what its pursuit in a realm of infinite possibilities can bring about, that is, the emergence of hitherto unforeseen possibilities for a given practice.[13]

---

11 TM 357.
12 Such optimism is underwritten by the supposition that whatever challenges an individual language consciousness or agent may be presented by their practice, there are within language-being more possibilities for that practice than any single linguistic consciousness can fathom. The question is how to open them up.
13 The completely unpredictable insight can prove world-changing. A quick witted test pilot, when asked to examine the underperforming North American Mustang fighter, noticed that the distance between the front of the cockpit and the propeller nose was exactly the same as on the Mitchell Spitfire. This insight led to the Mustang being fitted with the Spitfire Merlin engine

This implies the emergence of a practical virtue. In a world of infinite possibilities, the hermeneutic practitioner should be both committed to the determined pursuit of an interpretive stratagem and yet remain sufficiently detached from the tactics of that pursuit to take advantage of any new circumstances it may give rise to. In philosophical hermeneutics, the pursuit of the impossible gives rise to the emergence of the possible.

4. Practice and speculative movement

Their ontological placement within the *Sprachswelt* renders the operations of practice potentially provocative. For creative and reflective practices to achieve their transformative effects requires that they operate in language-being. Their effects are manifest in a repatterning of relational fields of meaning. To argue that practices operate in language-being is not to claim that they are reducible to words. It is, however, to make a claim about the ontological placement of practices, that practices reciprocally affect and are effected by language-being. Language-being transcends the linguistic. As Gadamer puts it, 'we speak not only of the language of art but also of a language of nature – in short, of any language that things have.'[14] Language-being includes anything that can be expressed and remembered in terms of signs and symbols whether mathematical, musical or architectural. It embraces anything that *speaks* to us in terms of significant patterns – darkening clouds betokening a coming storm or increasing unemployment hinting at forthcoming political insecurity. As the realm in which we live, language-being is of an infinite extent and embraces endless possibilities for meaning and significance within our individual and collective being. Furthermore, ontologically speaking, language-being is not a singular entity but a network of interconnected semantic fields. Gadamer implies this in his presentation of the speculative dimension of meaning. Static essentialist accounts of meaning are rejected. Meanings, he insists, are the spaces in which things are related to one another.[15] The porosity of meaning allows

---

the consequence of which was such an improvement in speed, range and aerodynamics that the course of aerial warfare during the second half of the Second World War was altered in favour of the Allies. See Paul Kennedy, *Engineers of Victory* (London: Allen Lane, Penguin, 2013), 122. In addition, the serendipitous products of plans and research are well discussed by Richard Sennet who noted that how Motorola made it a policy to archive unexpected design solutions that might prove useful in confronting problems not yet arrived at. See Sennett, *The Craftsman*, 33–5.

14   TM 475.
15   TM 433.

different meanings to penetrate and disrupt each other. The relational nature of meaning is emphasized by its speculative character. Two key passages in *Truth and Method* merit lengthy quotation.

> There is another dialectic of the word, which accords to every word an inner dimension of multiplication: every word breaks forth as if from a centre and is related to a whole, through which alone it is word. Every word causes the whole of the language to which it belongs to resonate and the whole world view that underlies it to appear, Thus every word, as the event of a moment, carries with it the unsaid to which it is related by responding and summoning. The occasionality of human speech is not an imperfection of its expressive power; it is, rather the logical expression of the living virtuality of speech that brings a totality of meaning to play, without being able to express it totally. All human speaking is finite in such a way that there is within it an infinity of meaning to be explicated and laid out.[16]

> Language itself, has something, speculative about it ... not only in the sense Hegel intends, as an instinctive prefiguring of logical reflection – but, rather the realisation of meaning ... Such a realisation is speculative in that the finite possibilities of the word are orientated toward the sense intended as toward the infinite.

> To say what one means ... means to hold what is said together with an infinity of what is not said in one unified meaning and to ensure that it is understood in this way.[17]

Beneath the argument that linguistic consciousness (*Bewusstsein*) is more being (*Sein*) than knowing (*Wissen*) lies the hermeneutical axiom 'x always equals x+'. Language-being is accordingly the reality sustaining every language user.[18] That which both transcends and grounds individual linguistic consciousness is the vast and ungraspable network of etymological meanings and conceptual associations which influence every word. Each word 'causes the whole of the language to which it belongs to resonate'. It is tied to extensive networks of meaning which reach beyond its particular language location. Most European languages are replete with philological borrowings from Greek, Latin and Sanskrit forms. Linguistic networks are not fixed, and their movement is vital to sustaining new directions of thought. This underlines another axiom of hermeneutic thought: the meaning of a word or concept cannot be historically foreclosed; it is always possible to say something more about it and that 'more' can provoke further unanticipated twists of understanding.

16 TM 458, emphasis added.
17 TM 471.
18 TM 449.

At any given time, a concept or a word holds within its combinatory power the potential for more of its presently unseen determinations of meaning to unfold. The inheritance of a language tradition is not just received meaning but the promise of future meaning. *To dwell in language is to dwell in its ontological endowments.* This reaffirms the primacy of practice in our argument. Any transformation of understanding is dependent upon a practice having the capacity to unfold its unseen potentials of meaning. Precisely because they are grounded in language-being, practices can initiate such speculative movements. The consequence can also be negative. A practice can meet with alignments of meaning detrimental to its own. What then impels a practice towards its own undermining? Considering this question will extend the role of the *Vorgriff der Vollendung* in our debate.

5. The negativity of provocative expectations

The history of human practices is replete with negative consequences: unforeseen elements in a practice undo its expected outcomes. The surprise of being outwitted or wrong-footed forces a review of the expectancies guiding practical commitments. As Gadamer comments, 'Every experience worthy of the name thwarts an expectation.' Experience is a process which is essentially negative.[19] How, then, does a practice's pursuit of its anticipated outcomes provoke its demise? Numerous circumstantial factors prompt practices to question the adequacy of their presuppositions. The relational nature of meaning exposes them to unforeseen historical shifts of meaning in language-being. The negativity of experience is a direct consequence of how a practice projects its *Vorgriff* across the *Sprachswelt*. Every practice is focussed upon defining clusters of its key concerns. These emphasize that the defining preoccupations of a practice are not concepts alone but distinctive ways of engaging with the world. 'Expression' is a central subject matter of musical performance practice. The term requires a degree of conceptual understanding (it has clear connections with notions of tension and release) and also demands practical know-how about how to use performance environments to best effect. The meaningfulness of such a subject matter oscillates between its perceptual instances and its conceptual connotations. The fluidity of elements within that meaningfulness mirrors the movement of part and whole within hermeneutic connectivity. Each perceptual instance offers a concrete perspective on its generalized conceptual content, whilst the latter often

19 TM 353.

only makes sense when given in distinct and memorable exemplifying instances. Philosophical hermeneutics implies that part–whole relationships maintain their being by the infinity of finite movements within them. Echoing Kant's axiom of empty concepts and blind intuitions, a subject matter can neither be definitively represented in concrete form nor exhaustively defined conceptually. Its being resides in the unease of that constant movement between part and whole which sustains linguistic beings. Such finitude introduces that element of uncertainty which is key to provoking a practice into action.

There is a clear affinity between Gadamer's use of the term subject matter and the Heideggerian notion of a practice as a temporal project. Conceptions of health and well-being give reason and purpose to the practice of medicine. Subject matters do not just articulate the conceptual framework of how a practice is thought out, they establish a framework that is lived out. By framing the direction of a practice, they articulate a mode of interaction with the world.

In seeking to clarify the instabilities and opaqueness of meaning within its subject matters, a practice presupposes a fore-conception of completeness. The fore-understanding – the projected direction and anticipated outcomes of a practice or in Nietzschean terms its *wozu* – governs that practice's self-comprehension. As has been argued, 'the fore-conception of completeness' is treated within philosophical hermeneutics as a formal condition of all understanding: only what constitutes or aspires to a unity of meaning can be understood. A practice becomes explicable in terms of what it is aiming at.

The projection of completeness takes place within the wider context of the *Sprachswelt*. This ontological placement grants the *Vorgriff* its *provocative power*. Its application exposes the assumptions of that practice to unanticipated questions. The context in which the *Vorgriff* operates accords it with a dialectical efficacy capable of working against the grain of its own assumptions. Though it emerges from within a practice as an attempt to clarify the latter's direction and purpose, the *Vorgriff* is a provocative driver of negative experience. The dialectical nature of the *Vorgriff* is clear.

In Chapter 3 we offered an analytic of how the 'anticipation of completeness' governs both the formal possibility and impossibility of hermeneutics. On the positive side, it was established:

(1) Within a language ontology, the anticipation of completeness functions as a unitary device capable of establishing similarities and continuities upon which knowledge can be built.

(2) The principle of anticipation grounds the possibility of hermeneutic critique: the ideal of completion establishes the horizon against which there is always something more to be said.
(3) The anticipation of completeness opens the liminal space of the in between enabling a life to move constantly between its 'no-more' and its 'not-yet', and a practice to move from its *woher* to its *wozu*. That liminal space is a space of tension (*Spannung*) which, hermeneutically speaking, spans a life.

On the negative side, however, it was noted that

(1) There is a fundamental incommensurability between the assumptions of completeness and the continuous flux of existence.
(2) The anticipation of completeness is negentropic: whilst it moves towards establishing intelligible order within one area of hermeneutic experience, because of its unavoidable connectedness with other linguistic fields of meaning, it can unintentionally realign and disrupt frameworks of meaning in others.
(3) If understanding is both unitary and differential, the achievement of completeness would bring understanding to a stop. Its being depends on *movement* towards completeness, not its achievement. There can be no formal closure to hermeneutical understanding.
(4) The placement of a practice within language-being renders its galvanizing impetus towards completion seemingly futile. Within the openness of language-being, the anticipation of completeness initiates a path to an inevitable confrontation with failure.

The conceptual analytic of hermeneutic practice exposes the antinomy between the formal aspirations underwriting the impetus to completeness and the ontological character of the circumstances in which it operates. Were philosophical hermeneutics a conventional epistemology, the antinomy would prove fatal. However, philosophical hermeneutics concerns itself not with formal proofs but with the interactive process of something coming to experience. The antinomy marks out what is in phenomenological terms a passage of travel, a hermeneutic vector passing from the unreflective acceptance of the assumptions governing a practice's impetus to completion to a reflective experience of the failure of those assumptions. This is not a question of appreciating the formality of a logical incommensurability but a question of experiencing how the assumptions of one's practice collide with the nature of actuality in which they are applied. The reflective nature of this experience renders it hermeneutically provocative.

In seeking to clarify ambiguities of meaning and direction within its subject matters, a practice projects a certain conception of its anticipated development. Because it emanates from a practice within the language world, that projection can have unpredictable effects. The ontological priority of language-being over linguistic consciousness means that it is formally impossible to anticipate the extent to which a practice can be connected to other alignments capable of either extending or disrupting its own. Furthermore, no matter how a practice seeks to reduce the ambiguities of meaning within its subject matters, they remain porous. In seeking to complete its projects, a hermeneutical practice will inevitably provoke collisions with other frameworks of meaning and postpone the possibility of its completion. Wittgenstein's distinction between core and peripheral meaning illuminates the predicament.

6. Regulative completeness and hermeneutic displacement

Consider, first, the implications of Wittgenstein's distinction between core and peripheral meaning which emphasize a central feature of the ontological priority of language-being over linguistic consciousness. Whether a practitioner is aware of it or not, a practice's core terms are tied to peripheral meanings which implicitly reach into frameworks of meaning beyond those with which a practitioner is initially acquainted. If meaning is relational, the core meaning of a subject matter can never be *essentialized*. It will be tied to fields of peripheral meaning from which it cannot be fully separated. It is inevitable, then, that the core meaning of subject matter will remain to a degree ambiguous. In seeking to rid itself of such unclarity, a practice will endeavour to simplify the meaning of its core terms. The drive to such clarity forces a practice to confront its peripheral meanings bringing accepted meanings and aspirations into question once more. Interpretation's drive to simplicity only serves to reveal the unanticipated complexity of unnoticed peripheral meanings around a core term. The search for a distinctness of definition always threatens to displace it.

In Chapter 2 it was argued that the *Vorgriff der Vollendung* contributed to disrupting interpretation's endeavour to achieve a finality of meaning. It opens a liminal space between the determinate nature of a hermeneutic object and the indeterminacy of its form. Indeed, that liminal space proves to be the open space of hermeneutic experience itself such that the achievement of any finality of meaning would, ironically, close the possibility of hermeneutic experience. The dialectical capacity of interpretative stratagems to defer understanding is closely examined in Wolfgang Iser's book *The Range of Interpretation*.[20] Each stratagem reveals the proactive, disruptive nature of interpretation.

Iser's study declines to offer any theoretical proclamation of what interpretation is and prefers instead to approach interpretation though its applications and effects. Three stratagems are discussed: (1) hermeneutical differentiation, (2) recursive looping and (3) hermeneutical mapping. Each represents different modes of navigating the fundamental ambiguities of existence within processes of continuous change and flux. In Chapter 1 of this study we saw how according to deconstructive criticism the success of interpretation is continually frustrated by the incommensurability of its epistemological ambitions and its ontological circumstances. Every attempt to engage with tradition only further distances an interpretation from its object, and every attempt to recapitulate an interpretation only serves to alter the nature of the repeated. What we must now understand is that interpretation does not just suffer these problems but it actually generates them. The burden of much of the present part of this study is to show how because of its ontological structure, practice generates the negativity which is at the heart of its activities.

With regard to hermeneutic differentiation, any attempt by interpretive practice to clarify a grounding subject matter inevitably opens a liminal space between itself and the subject matter with which it is concerned. This brings a central problem of interpretation to the fore: 'interpretation creates a liminal space between the received subject-matter to be interpreted and its translation into a different more contemporary register?'[21] The problem here is twofold. To translate a subject matter into a contemporary register is to adopt the prejudices and expectations of that register. Inevitably, not all aspects of the received subject matter will be or can be selected. This invites the question of how comprehensive the new interpretation might be? By exposing neglected areas of a subject matter, the liminal space between a subject matter and the practice which interprets it is increased and the possibility of achieving a completer understanding of it deferred. Iser notes 'that the reception of a past is dominated by a desire to classify but such dominance screens off all the details that defy integration into the organising patterns . . . (details) which are bound to emerge again when the horizon of expectation changes'.[22] The drive of the *Vorgriff* to rid

---

20 Wolfgang Iser, *The Range of Interpretation* (New York: Columbia University Press, 2000).
21 Ibid., 19.
22 Ibid., 183.

itself of ambiguous meaning is defeated by the liminal space it produces. Being grounded in language-being, the impetus towards any completion of meaning generates further hermeneutic differentials. Similar difficulties confront the application of recursive looping within hermeneutical practices.

When confronted by a problematic meaning, hermeneutic practices often return to the origins of an argument, reviewing and repeating its lines of development or going back to how grounding conceptions were formerly conceived. These tactics are associated with the use of recursive looping to rediscover a lost direction of argument. If recursion aims at recapturing a continuity of thought within a practice, the consequence is to render clarity of meaning even more difficult to obtain. Recursion undermines and defers the possibility of reformation. Recovering and repeating the terms of a practice are never neutral acts innocent of ontological consequences. Such reiteration 'functions as the reference for recursive looping, which issues into an ever expanding range of thick descriptions'[23] of the practice which initiates it. Recursive looping further complicates the practice for which clarity of meaning is sought: 'the more deeply it goes, the less complete it is'.[24] Within a practice, recursive looping is the act of a self-perpetuating differential.

The third of Iser's stratagems concerns the auto-poietic consequences of mapping. Trying to 'read' existence and map its difficulties reflects the fact that 'we are always in the midst of life and continually seek to lift ourselves out of (its) entanglements'[25] by making the ways of commitment and practice navigable. However, the practice of mapping a territory to render it better known only complicates the aspiration. Without intending to do so, mapping makes clear the territory unavailable to it. Mapping the known necessarily produces uncharted territory not specifiable prior to the mapping. Hermeneutical mapping 'adumbrates the conditions under which the not-yet-existing may be conceived'.[26]

Interpretive projections seek completion and closure in a world of endless change which ceaselessly proliferates the conditions for new alignments of the meaningful. Given their ontological context, such projections defer the certainty they seek. This endorses the earlier claim that considered as a mode of epistemological theory, hermeneutics is bound to fail. The projected criteria for achieving a definitive and complete interpretation can never be formally met.

---

23 Ibid., 99.
24 Ibid.
25 Ibid., 157.
26 Ibid., 156.

In this context, nihilism might seem the unavoidable consequence of practice's interventions.

The difficulty posed by Iser's stratagems is not their inherent capacity for failure but what they assume in the first place. The anticipation of completeness presupposes that something is meaningful if and only if it meets with the criterion of completable meaning. With this expectation, it sets out to meet the expected but given the character of the world in which it is applied, failure is inevitable. In a realm of becoming, the *Vorgriff* operates as an agency of negative hermeneutics. This is not necessarily problematic as we shall see. Just as the *Vorgriff* has a negative destructive function, it also has a constructive capability. To move towards a consideration of the positive function of the *Vorgriff* we need to distinguish between two senses of the term 'completeness'.

It is not the context of anticipation that is questionable but the expectation underpinning it and, more specifically, how that expectation conditions a practice's response to that inevitable moment when its grounding expectation of completeness is undermined. Is the pursuit of completeness indicative of an attempt to 'regulate' and shape the processes we interact with or is it to verify the truth of a constitutive idea within a text or historical event?

7. Integration and completeness

If the pursuit of completeness is regulative, it is indicative of an unending and infinitely varied attempt to give shape and significance to a body of experience. Because unending, the process lends itself to becoming known more completely. The regulatory framework is not inhibited by a lack of final truth. Completeness considered as regulative ideal regards truth not as definitive verification but as a criterion of experiential integration. It underpins the idea of hermeneutic truth as an integrative function which renders what is known of a text or artwork more complete by integrating into it new experiences of their focal subject matters. A regulative ideal of completeness can aspire to become 'ever more true' but never to be the complete truth. The notion of truth as integration emphasizes that hermeneutical knowing is part of an ontological continuum. A practice which regards completion as regulative is not devastated by the negation of its key expectancies since it knows that precisely because the final truth is unattainable, other interpretive possibilities always remain. For practices which uphold completeness as a regulative ideal, the experience of negation is an invitation to enhanced engagement. However, for practices which regard completion as constitutive, the emergence of nihilism remains a threat.

Iser's stratagems of interpretation mark out the inevitable dialectical failures that undermine their application. The anticipations of completeness driving these stratagems (whether regulative or constructive) fail for the reasons noted. However, it is not the context of their application that is questionable but, as suggested, the expectations underpinning them. These expectations condition a practice's response to that inevitable moment when expectations of completeness are frustrated. In short a practice committed to regulative completeness will not regard the provocation of negation as calamitous but as an opening towards extending its understanding. However, a practice driven by a commitment to constitutive completeness will regard the challenge of negativity as a potentially devastating disruption of its presuppositions.

Nearly all the thinkers discussed in this chapter are deeply concerned about the dehabilitating effects of nihilism. Anything that undermines confidence in practical action undermines how life and its possibilities unfold: the movement (actions) upon which the life of understanding depends is weakened. Gadamer and Nietzsche know that for linguistic beings living in language-being, a confrontation between actuality and how we think and speak about it is inevitable. The question is, then, are our underlying philosophical commitments welcoming to the challenge of negativity (i.e. regard it as an opportunity to extend our acquaintance with actuality) or are they fearful of any further engagement with the uncertainties of existence?

Negative hermeneutics is clear that within the *Sprachswelt* practice's pursuit of either regulative or constitutive completeness drives practices towards an inevitable confrontation with nihilism. If knowing and becoming mutually exclude one another, why do we persist in applying the regulative idea of completion even though we know of its inapplicability? The answer leads to a key dialectical turning point in our argument about negative hermeneutics: what appears as a moment of absolute negation actually confirms the possibility of 'hermeneutical' knowledge.

The realization that the categories of reason and grammar do not apply to existence actually confirms the degree to which we are wedded to them as schemas of interpretation. The moment of negation discloses that we are creatures disposed to seeking out patterns of sense within existence's irregularities. The anticipation of completeness considered as a regulative idea betrays the ways we interact with and render intelligible to ourselves the processes we are engaged with. Without it, the continuity and coherence of objects of experience would be impossible. The idea of completeness governs the condition of rendering objects of experience intelligible to us. The hermeneutic object is what a complexity of experience points to when thought of in terms of a possible unity of meaning. It is both something we move towards and something that emerges more clearly in our engagement with it over time. The expectation of completeness is the unifying form which when applied to a manifold of diverse elements allows it to emerge *as if it were* progressing towards a coherence as a unified work. What allows the hermeneutic object to emerge into consciousness is an experience of diverse elements brought into an intelligible unity by the regulative expectation of completeness.

Hermeneutic understanding supposes that its objects are intelligible if and only if they can in principle be thought of as unifiable part-whole structures. Such understanding anticipates and projects back into a sensuous manifold's play of elements, a completeness of meaning that it intuits from that play. As a regulative idea, the *Vorgriff* cannot itself be realized. Its anticipated unity of meaning is not an object of experience but only a form in which objects of experience become intelligible to us. The notion of hermeneutic truth as integration, suggests that the truth of the *Vorgriff* lies not in the arrival of its anticipated meaning but in the bringing-into-structure that it facilitates. As a regulative idea, it is a cognitive precondition of ever-shifting processes being rendered interpretable. It would seem that our mode of understanding is such that it finds things about which no story can be told unintelligible. They do not fit into any framework of expectancy. This does not mean that we have to know what the expected end is, only that one can be envisioned. The fore-conception of completeness anticipates rather than designates the direction of an argument or performance. In other words, the *Vorgriff* is an ontological framework which renders an object intelligible by placing it within an unfolding framework of *wozu* and *woher*. To encounter a hermeneutic object is to experience an object that is always underway, illusive and suggestive precisely because in its unfolding it withholds something of itself. The notion of the withheld is unintelligible without the expectation of a completion of meaning yet to come. As far as our mode of existence is concerned, where there is life, there is expectation. Our form of life is such that in order to render them intelligible, it is disposed to fitting processes of becoming into narrative structures with envisionable ends. The *Vorgriff* is the precondition of understanding an object hermeneutically, that is, as something whose being is its temporal unfolding. The *Vorgriff* establishes the living span of every hermeneutical being: it opens the differential space spanning the *wozu* and *woher* of every life practice.

The *Vorgriff der Vollendung* emerges nevertheless as a driver of negative hermeneutics. Given that all hermeneutical practices are grounded within the *Sprachswelt*, that the horizons of meaning within that world are open and porous and that the instability of meaning within a practice impels it towards a completer grasp of its subject matters, the movement of that practice towards completion within the ever fluid context of the *Sprachswelt* will inevitably guide a practice towards contrary and disruptive assumptions concerning the meaning, direction and purpose of its key subject matters. Confrontation with the negativity of experience becomes inevitable. From the moment a *Vorgriff* is projected into the *Sprachswelt*, an entire fatality establishes itself. The incommensurability of the *Vorgriff* with the mode of existence it was meant to enlighten becomes apparent. Nevertheless, though the incommensurability between the forms of our thinking and the character of our existence may make formal knowledge impossible, it does indeed set the conditions for the possibility of hermeneutical knowledge. To this possibility we shall shortly return.

The regulative pursuit of completeness is a hermeneutical fiction which upholds the galvanizing momentum of a practice. If the being of a practice depends upon the continual movement of reappraisal and renewal, the realization of its expectancies would in fact condemn that practice to a sclerotic entropy. In other words, as with thought and understanding, movement is the being of a practice: it maintains itself so long as it does not, eschatologically speaking, arrive. Rejuvenation and revival are dependent upon a practice maintaining its momentum by means of constant experimentation and critique. The regulative ideal of completeness and the constant pursuit of an ideality of meaning render all practices unquiet, forever seeking a fuller comprehension of themselves. A practice's being is its doing, and its doing is a movement animated by the dialectical functioning of the pursuit of completeness. Part of the positive educational heritage of hermeneutics is its demonstration that negativity and disruption are inherent to the unfolding of any practice.

8. The positivity of negative outcomes

Though it may seem a disaster from an epistemological perspective, the absence of final truth and definitive meaning in a world of constant processual change is positively advantageous from an ontological viewpoint. The negative moment in hermeneutics challenges established expectancies not by nullifying previous experience but by revealing its limitations. The positive moment inheres in the negative: it is not that we have got it completely wrong about an experienced object, only that what we have experienced of it is a limited part of something more extensive than previously imagined. Indeed, the very incompleteness of experience gives good reason to suppose that there is always more of a subject matter to be experienced. Negative hermeneutics is clearly driven by the realization that there is no *final* truth or ultimate meaning to be had. Yet, what is it that allows negative hermeneutics to be a driver for more or for a completer understanding?

The argument 'there is no truth, only interpretation' can solicit a nihilistic response: there is no point to interpretation as there is no ultimate truth to be grasped. On the other hand, the argument draws from negative hermeneutics an affirmative pragmatic response: increasing interpretation multiplies our grasp of what the 'truth' of subject matter might be. What then is it that inclines one readership to see negative hermeneutics as a hermeneutics of loss and bereavement and another to see it as extending the potentials for new and more extensive understanding?

If, as argued earlier, the root of the nihilistic attitude towards hermeneutics and the humanities is a fear of the uncertain and finite, the cultural challenge, as Wittgenstein and Rosenzweig surmised, is to explore what it is in a way of life that disposes it to see as negative that which cannot in itself be negative. The philosophical and existential challenge is to accept that uncertainty enables and drives practice. From the perspective of traditional idealist philosophies, the disappearance of 'an intelligible beyond' makes the world of actual being appear unsafe, shrouded by emptiness and the absence of truth. Yet, from a Heideggerian perspective, the experience of emptiness turns into an affirmation of yet-to-be-realized possibilities for being and understanding. For traditional metaphysics the world one dwells in is, indeed, *nothing*: this floating uncertain world is all.[27] Everything that our existence has hitherto depended on – language, history and tradition – is an element of that uncertain world. Indeed, it is what is within that world that has nevertheless sustained and nurtured what we value as meaningful. That our world has not and will never meet received epistemological criteria for truth and certainty has no bearing on its evident ability to sustain us. The problem lies with us and not in the nature of actual being. What negative hermeneutics reveals is that we

---

27 See Nicholas Davey, *Unquiet Understanding, Gadamer's Philosophical Hermeneutics*, (Albany: State University of New York Press, 2006), 96.

have mistaken the form of experience (regulative completeness) for its content (constitutive completeness). The dialectic at the heart of negative hermeneutics suggests that within language-being, the more a practice seeks to realize its constitutive completeness, the more it will fail. Not only does the finite nature of understanding conspire against the possibility of grasping such completeness but the ability of language to constantly disrupt renders the completeness which understanding craves impossible to achieve. For negative hermeneutics, the implication is clear; if we persist in pursuing the constitutive truth of subject matters, nihilism and disbelief are inevitable. In other words, negative hermeneutics asks that we suspend our disabling epistemological faith in certainty and learn to trust and have confidence in the enabling 'uncertainties' of language and tradition that sustain us. It follows Heidegger and Gadamer in accepting the impossibility of going behind language to examine its hermeneutic credentials. Negative hermeneutics argues that if we can abandon our metaphysical and epistemological faith in intelligible truths and essences we can come to see that the world lacks nothing: it remains a plethora of ever-changing possibilities and perspectives. If we are able to renounce our epistemological preference for certainty, we will come to see that meaning and truth do not depend upon constitutive essences which populate metaphysical being but upon ever-shifting frameworks of interpretation which render the changing orders of experience intelligible to us. Negative hermeneutics reveals the habitual error underpinning our intercourse with actuality: if we confuse the intelligible form of our experience with its supposed actual content, nihilism is inevitable. However, just because thinking of things hermeneutically requires an anticipation of completeness does not mean that the truth of what we are thinking about requires completion. For reasons we have given, to pursue that requirement within language-being cannot but lead to nihilism. Within the continual flux of language-being, the 'truth' of a hermeneutic object (i.e. its full epistemic determination) cannot but remain uncertain. To insist within a *Sprachsontologie* that knowing the truth of such an object is dependent upon knowing its fully determined state leads nowhere. Negative hermeneutics, however, points to a participatory epistemology, an epistemology of relations.

The anticipation of completeness is the form under which transient hermeneutic objects (texts, performances or compositions) become intelligible to us by suggesting unfolding meaningful patterns. These allow narrative structures to emerge. This enables a body of relations to link with others. In other words, the truth of the anticipation of completeness lies not in the realization of any supposed end state but in what the form enables, that is, the development of historical and cultural relations from which our sense of meaningful existence derives. There is no certainty here, only the provisional and the temporary. Negative hermeneutics holds that to insist that the truth of anticipation depends upon the realization of anticipation's final content will lead to nihilism and, in consequence, to a completely unnecessary if not dangerous devaluation of those contingent relations that a meaningful existence depends on. Language, history and tradition are needlessly undermined. However, the positivity of negative hermeneutics is clear. Just as it reveals that the pursuit of completeness within the *Sprachswelt* will (because of the very porous nature of language) lead to nihilism, it also discloses that everything that accords our existence with meaning and value depends upon the uncertainties of the language world. In consequence, negative hermeneutics indicates that a practical response to the isolating effects of uncertainty would be to expand dialogical involvements and multiply viewpoints of a subject matter. The challenge for negative hermeneutics is to gauge the extent to which the humanities can abandon the demand for epistemic certainty and accept that our being and its practices are shrouded in uncertainty. How does the hermeneutic practitioner live courageously in the face of metaphysical nihilism? Here we return to the question of the confidence won from practice and its movements.

9. The confidence of practice

Gadamer argues that 'the certainties of science are different from the certainty acquired in life' and, what's more, 'the unsureness of life is to be overcome by the experience of life that the experience of life provides'.[28] What are these non-epistemic sources of certainty and how does life provide them? The key to these questions lies in the expedition of practice itself.

Gadamer claims tradition as a non-epistemic source of certainty or, rather, of confidence: 'Tradition in the form of morals, religion and law, rests (in contrast to methodical doubt) on a knowledge that life has of itself.'[29] Individual uncertainty may be assuaged by initiation into the broader structures of inherited thought: it is practice-acquired-confidence that displaces the (unrealizable) epistemic quest for certainty. Practice-acquired-confidence emphasizes an aspect of the term's Latin root *fide* (to have faith in) or, rather, to bind together that which

---

28 TM 238–9.
29 TM 238.

one has faith in (*con* + *fide*). It indicates how in negative hermeneutics an epistemological appeal for certainty can be displaced by a confidence born of historico-ontological engagement. From a historical perspective that key claims to the certainty of truth and meaning never can be validated for all time has no bearing on the fact that the contingent and unverifiable claims to meaning within tradition have indeed enabled us de facto to find sense and purpose within existence. That they have evidently done so gives good reason to have confidence in the paths of semantic engagement they open. Such confidence allows the transformative movements of understanding to further unfold, whereas the unfulfillable demand for epistemic certainty stifles such movement. As Gadamer puts it, 'Does what has always supported need to be grounded?'[30] We cannot go beyond or behind language to examine its hermeneutic credentials. To ask for certainty where none can be given suggests a loss of confidence in the historical and linguistic traditions that have made life possible.

Confidence in life is not simply acquired by immersion in tradition and language. *The certainties of life are won*: they are achievements, expressions of participation and involvement. The certainties of life or knowing how to go on as Wittgenstein might put it are those emergent certainties acquired and tempered through confident engagement with various practices. The argument is of a piece with other elements in our overall contention, namely that practice forms the practitioner and that practice is an ontogenetic process central to the concept of *Bildung*. Practice is indeed the vehicle of the practitioner's selfication.[31] If practical confidence is inhibited such formative processes are stifled.

These points emphasize the role of confidence derived from practical involvement, that is, that hard-won confidence of knowing what to do in moments of crisis. Negative experience is intrinsic to practice. Confrontation with limit experiences is both unavoidable and intrinsic to processes of revaluation and renewal. For the experienced practitioner the provocation of negation offers not just a challenge but an invitation to open towards unseen possibilities for understanding. The dialectics of practical engagement provokes the confident practitioner to embrace negativity as an invitation to expand the practical experience.

Negative hermeneutics suggests that hermeneutics considered as a form of philosophical theory should be displaced by an account of the 'hermeneutical' as a mode of being. The principal claim is that what is termed 'hermeneutical

---

30 TM xxxvii.
31 Iser, *The Range of Interpretation*, 133–4.

awareness' is a consequence of the negativity of experience, that is, of the collapse of a certain body of interpretation. Consequently, hermeneutical consciousness is the product of and not the initiator of the provocative dimensions of practical engagement. It is the negativity of experience within a practice that opens the possibility of hermeneutical knowledge. The following points are pertinent:

1. The negativity of experience draws consciousness out of its 'pre-reflective slumbers' in which there is no difference between the world as experienced and the world as expected.
2. The negativity of experience permits hermeneutical consciousness to emerge, 'to catch itself in the act' by exposing its pre-understandings as limited.
3. The experience of negativity is 'a coming to self-knowledge' fundamental to the emergence of agency considered as an individuated *Bildung*'s process.
4. Only because we are already committed to, predisposed towards and have concerns about the anticipations of completeness attached to a practice, are we vulnerable to and can learn from the challenges to our expectations.

Because it is fundamental to the development of hermeneutic consciousness, the negativity of experience returns the question of subjectivity to hermeneutic debate. This emphasizes the idea of the hermeneutical as a mode of experience in which the past and the future of an agency's self-understanding come into question. The return of 'subjectivity' to hermeneutic debate is surprising. Gadamer usually adopts a negative attitude towards the concept. He speaks of 'the impotence of subjective particularity'[32] and attacks the psychologistic supposition that meaning resides in what a subject 'intends' or imposes. Subjectivist accounts of meaning are *not* as they (and indeed, romanticism) proclaim: spontaneous acts which bring meaning and colour into a meaningless world. To the contrary, 'all self-knowledge arises from what is historically pre-given, what with Hegel we call substance because it underlies all subjective intentions and actions. . . . What we need to discover in all that is subjective, is the substantiality that determines it'.[33]

Gadamer's underplaying of the subjective is unusual. The negativity of experience and the collapse of hermeneutical expectations cannot be but

---

32 TM 489.
33 TM 302.

personal. Indeed, hermeneutical engagement makes no sense without an appeal to embodied subjectivities. This implies that a consequence of emphasizing practical engagement in hermeneutic thought is that the subjectivity of experience must be taken seriously. If it is not, neither hermeneutical exchange nor a hermeneutical education arguing for a change of outlook makes sense. So what is the reflective self-knowledge at issue?

Gadamer's account of Aeschylus's *pathei mathos* (learning through suffering) concerns the emergence of a subjectivity that gains self-awareness through an unexpected confrontation with its limitations, inadequacies and mistakes.[34] 'It is ultimately (as Gadamer suggests) a religious experience.'[35] 'Profound' experience is far from inconsequential: it involves the experience of one's own finitude. 'Hermeneutical experience' is felt as a contested space where conflicting interpretations in which we are complicit collide. Such experience is participatory and is only undergone by engaged subjectivities. On this stands a key claim of philosophical hermeneutics: subjective awareness only arises as a consequence of deep prior practical involvements (*Dasein*): it 'always involves an element of self-knowledge and constitutes a necessary side of what we called experience in the proper sense'.[36] Indeed, it is precisely because we are embodied subjectivities with living concerns and frustratable expectations that negative experience can, by thwarting them, throw them into stark relief. Central to *pathos mathei* is an overwhelming sense that we have misjudged situations and persons. Expectations prove naive, forecasts overshoot the mark and political planning is exposed as short-sighted. No practice is immune from the challenge of such negativity. Precisely because we are subject agencies with primary concerns and interests (*Aufgaben*), we are vulnerable to the challenge of negativity.

The coming-to-hermeneutical awareness integral to negative experience involves the displacement of one set of expectancies by another: 'only something different and unexpected can provide someone who has experience with a new one'.[37] Learning occurs only when negative experience becomes dialectical. New experience not only displaces the assumptions of previous experiences but also restructures former knowledge in such a way that we can now both predict what was previously unexpected and understand what it was within an initial outlook that led to what we now understand as its blind points. This dialectical aspect of negative experience renders it 'hermeneutical'. Insight into our short-sightedness

---

34 TM 356.
35 TM 357.
36 TM 356.
37 TM 353.

'always involves an element of self-knowledge.... Insight is something we come to'.[38] Insight cannot be taught by theory. It arises only through the challenges and sufferings of practical engagement. This is consistent with the argument that hermeneutic reflection does not concern an object – understood but achieving a reflexive awareness of having undergone a significant movement within one's understanding. The objects of hermeneutic understanding are not cultural artefacts per se but what engagement with them occasions: movements in self-orientation and perspective. The understanding attached to the negativity of experience concerns an experience of repatterning, realignment and reconfiguration. What makes such understanding 'hermeneutical' has nothing to do with grasping a singular meaning but rather with experiencing the realignment of various meanings into a new and significant pattern. Part of the shock of negativity lies in its exposure of unseen implicit relations. Becoming aware of an inadequacy operating within an interpretive practice is all the more embarrassing when it emerges that other interpretive regimes have been overlooked. In short, precisely because it does not occur in an ontological vacuum, the negativity of experience uncovers a hermeneutic window that looks out on how 'one interpretive pathway after another opens up'.[39] In other words, the experience of negativity is synonymous with the disruptive disclosure of other ways of thinking about key terms in one's practice. Hermeneutical defenestration emerges as the consequence of exposure to alternative modes of thinking.

10. The provoked self

The experience of negativity provokes the emergence of hermeneutic consciousness. It awakens in the practitioner a consciousness of movement, of having left one way of responding to and thinking about a work to embrace another. The experience of negativity also disrupts a practitioner's view of a text by challenging established perspectives of reception. Such disturbances open a work's unnoticed possibilities. The provocation of negation is not calamitous. It enables moments of opening towards unseen interpretations allowing a practice 'to become more'. In this context, the accomplished hermeneutician or practitioner comes to know the value of 'regulative' completeness as an ideality

---

38   TM 357.
39   Lawrence Kramer, *Music as Cultural Practice, 1800–1900* (Berkeley: University of California Press, 1990), 8.

of meaning. It serves as a critical check against political or religious claims to closure and impels a practice towards discerning further determinations of its withheld meanings. *The impossible pursuit of completeness within becoming emerges as a transcendental condition of maintaining the movement of a practice's being and hermeneutic expansion.*

Negative moments prove productive. They establish groups of non-identical repetitions allowing the character of a practitioner to become discernible. In this respect Sloterdyk rightly emphasizes the productive capacities of a practice.[40] The gradually established but never completed character of a hermeneutical agency emerges from constant practical repetitions. Over time, the pattern of such an agency becomes recognizable though not necessarily predictable. Catherine Pickstock argues:

> the mark of the strength of a thing as an engrained habitude would be its spontaneity and adaptability, since a strong disposition is not merely fixed and stubborn but capable of originality and improvisation. This observed truth concerning human beings can be extended to ontology or geology because it has been concluded that the perdurance of a thing consists in its non-identical repeatability and a certain style that can persist through different and unpredictable variations.[41]

Pickstock's remarks enforce the argument that the hermeneutical self is an ontological emergent, the product of interaction with other interpretive beings. The being of such a hermeneutical agency (its effective character) lies in the pattern of its non-identical repeats. Iser notes, 'the self never consolidates into an identifiable, let alone ultimate shape. Instead it passes through endless configurations of itself.'[42] We might add that the 'selfication' of the practitioner proliferates in its continual reconfiguration. 'Each individual manifestation of such an unfolding sequence of selfing is nothing but a transition, leading to another shape of the self that the practitioner is set to become.'[43] This emphasizes once again the 'negative capability' associated with *der Vorgriff der Vollendung*. For a subject agency to acquire a sense of self from the history of its inclinations and dispositions is, of course, for it to anticipate a self that is completable. Yet there is no end station for such a being. In Heidegger's terms, *Dasein* is always a being in question. The hermeneutically aware subject is not completable but, rather, an unfinishable adventure. The being of a such a subject agency resides in the perpetual inconclusiveness of its non-

---

40 See Peter Sloterdijk, *You Must Change Your Life* (London: Polity, 2013), 6–7.
41 Catherine Pickstock, *Repetition and Identity* (Oxford: Oxford University Press, 2013), 31.
42 Iser, *The Range of Interpretation*, 133–4.
43 Ibid.

identical repetitions. Though the anticipation of future completion is implicit in each practical act, each act in fact defers the completion and resets the conditions whereby the subject agency can 'become more'. If 'hermeneutical agency' entails the idea of a completable self, the dynamics of a practice can be said to provoke and anticipate the emergence of its practitioners: practitioners are always on the way to their practice but never fully arrive. Their emergence is a response to an emergency. The capacity of negative experience to provoke the emergence of hermeneutically aware subject agencies reveals the 'way' of hermeneutical practice itself. Once again, Nietzsche is a pertinent guide.

He insists that becoming and knowledge rule each other out. An ontology of becoming is incommensurable with the traditional categories of knowledge: there are no 'things' to be known, no beings with intelligible essences. Nietzsche's ontology prohibits any metaphysical completion to becoming: there is no end state able to redeem the ambiguities and opaqueness of existence. His ontology is incompatible with any appeal to a *Vorgriff* that supposes an end state for becoming. Yet Nietzsche's thinking plainly does not rule out the regulative use of completeness. Within becoming, knowledge in the loose sense of the term rests on the supposition that *Vorgriffen* function regulatively. If by knowledge we mean the formation of predictable and memorizable patterns of non-identical repetitions, knowledge within becoming is provisionally possible. Furthermore, the pursuit of such repetitions within language-being exposes the subject agent to unexpected alignments of meaning that can have both constructive and destructive implications for that agency's self-understanding. Nietzsche's position concedes that though the *Vorgriff* is without metaphysical significance, this has no bearing upon its status as a necessary category of understanding within a world of becoming. As we have established, the application of the *Vorgriff* places processes and interactions within a structural framework of *woher* and *wozu* permitting the character and identity of 'things' and agencies to be discerned as patterns of non-identical repetition.

This preceding argument has three consequences.

1. It encourages the strong claim that within an ontology of becoming, the *Vorgriff* functions as a transcendental condition of possible knowledge. This is pertinent to the development of a participatory epistemology within relational ontology.
2. It implies that as a consequence of immersion in the dialectics of practice, the accomplished practitioner is brought to and indeed comes to embody

a knowing awareness of *both* the limits and possibilities of their practice. Immersion in the inevitable negativity and facticity of experience weathers the outlook of the accomplished practitioner and renders it hermeneutical.
3. In addition to the claim that the non-identical repetitions of a practice induce the formative emergence of a subject agency, the argument implies something about the 'way' of a hermeneutically astute agency.

In conclusion, the theme of hermeneutical defenestration lends a further perspective to our main theme; without involvement in the negative dynamics of practice, hermeneutical conscious would not be provoked into being.

11. The way of hermeneutical practice

Hermeneutical practice emerges not as a method or analytic but as a mode of existential discernment, a discernible style of interactive engagement with the subject matters of a practice. Hermeneutical practice, like the style or character of the hermeneutic agency it displays, is an ontological emergent. However, whereas the character of an agency emerges from within and is maintained by the non-identical repetitions of practice, considered as a mode of attentive discernment, hermeneutical practice exhibits a knowing mindfulness of subject matters. Such mindfulness is an experientially acquired awareness that without denying its compelling particularities a subject matter can always reveal more of itself. Tempered by the negativity of experience and mindful of its return, the accomplished practitioner recognizes that within the negative there is a shaded positivity. Distanced involvement characterizes the knowingness of the accomplished practitioner. The capacity of negative experience to disclose the presence of hidden or overlooked aspects of experience is made possible by the excess of our *being*, by the fact that ontological speaking we are always more than we are conscious of being. Practice uncovers that excess: in bringing us to ourselves, practice takes us beyond ourselves.

The principle of hermeneutic excess guarantees that within language-being things can always be otherwise. Precisely because in language-being the totality of meaning relations exceeds those of any determinate interpretation, any negation of a particular interpretation cannot necessarily negate other possible interpretations that surround it. That we cannot grasp such possibilities in advance does not speak against them. The accomplished practitioner has come to know that the unexpected disclosures of meaning provoked by negative experience give concrete grounds for faith in the possibility of future emergences. This emphasizes the hermeneutical axiom that language-being is always in excess of linguistic consciousness: negative experience uncovers its own positivity; things can always mean more.

Negativity within hermeneutics can never be absolute: there are always other possibilities. Such optimism fosters a restrained scepticism. If, logically speaking, no claim to meaning can be absolute, neither can a new interpretation claim completeness. Despite its compelling novelty, a fresh paradigm of practice will invariably overlook or withhold some dimension of its subject matter. In other words, the language ontology of hermeneutics sustains a dialectics of excess and lack: just as there is always more to be said within a practice, what is said can never be all that can be said. In listening to what a practice addresses, the accomplished practitioner strives to hear in what is said what has not yet been said. As we have argued, the life of understanding and practice is movement. Such movement manifests the unquiet nature of understanding and the restless sense of incompleteness that drive a practice. In the immediate tensions of practice, the accomplished practitioner discerns the constant coming-to-be and the passing away of its past and future possibilities. The immediacy of practice and what mediates it beyond its immediate boundaries are not ontological opposites. In being committed to actual practice and in seeking to fulfil its present demands, the accomplished practitioner is also committed to discerning what transcends that practice and will make it 'more'. What transcends a practice's immediate concerns does not negate them but rather expands them, that is, allows them to be seen in a new light. The accomplished practitioner knows that to pursue what is beyond a practice is not to go beyond that practice but to strive to realize the beyond that is within that practice or, in more formal terms, to discern $x+$ within x. The being of what transcends a given practice and the being of that practice are codependent. Here, the accomplished practitioner can attain a practical hermeneutical wisdom. This does not entail the completeness of a project but achieving a qualitative 'completeness' of outlook, a practically attained wisdom that depends on the continuous movement of practice. Such wisdom understands that a practice requires a transcendent perspective and that such a perspective is always positioned *within* a practice. In conclusion, 'the way of the hermeneutics' discerns the transcendent in the immediacy of practice and considers the immediacies of practice as the outcome of possibilities within the transcendent. Understanding their codependence, the accomplished practitioner inhabits both perspectives. It is, however, only passage through the provocations of negative experience that allows the practitioner to arrive at such a dialectical understanding of practice.

12. Negative hermeneutics and the redemption of the negativity

An important implication deriving from the provocative dimensions of practice is that negative experience should not be regarded negatively. The dynamics of negative hermeneutics suggest that the term 'negation' has less to do with experiences of restriction, delimitation and curtailment and more to do with transcending perspectives that have held us in their thrall. The provocative character of practice implies that we be open to the negativity of experience welcoming its arrival as an announcement of new possibilities for experience and not just as a hindering of long-held expectancies. The transformative aspect of negation is entailed within the reflective moment of self-implication that the experience of negativity entails. The grounding of negative experience within a language ontology enables such experience to point beyond itself and in so doing to transform itself into an affirmation of unexpected possibilities. Within the provocative dynamics of practice, such transformation demonstrates the negative capability of negation.

As we have argued, negative hermeneutics does not annihilate hermeneutics but promotes a transformative hermeneutics of practical involvement. Within the perspective of language ontology, negation operates transformatively, a function that is clearly indicated by the etymology of the term. The concept is not merely tied to notions of denial and lack but also to ideas of neglect and negotiation.[44] These nuances are implicit in Gadamer's concept of the 'negativity of experience' in which the power of the negative has little to do with disproof and repudiation but with the ability to achieve a shift of perspective and an altered way of knowing. The experience of negativity is transformative because it entails a knowing experience of self-implication.[45] This Hegelian motif is implicit in the suggestion that 'experience is initially always *an experience* of negation: something is not what *we* supposed it to be'.[46] Such moments confront a subject agency with an immediate awareness of the finitude of its understanding. Negative experience

---

[44] See *The Oxford Dictionary of English Etymology*, ed. C. T. Onions (Oxford: Clarendon Press, 1961), 606.
[45] Catherine Keller, *Cloud of the Impossible* (New York: Columbia University Press, 2015), 23–4.
[46] TM 354.

is instructive not only because it renders us conscious of the extent to which we have been taken in by a certain perspective but also because it discloses how our belief in the truth of that outlook has also prompted us to overlook and neglect alternative ways of thinking about its subject matter. Negative experience entails what Catherine Keller describes as a moment of knowing 'self-implication'.[47] Gadamer substantiates the point: 'only through negative instances do *we* acquire new experiences (and come to think differently about ourselves). Such insight involves an element of self knowledge'.[48] In this moment of self-implication, negative experience indicts us as participants in our own shortcomings. Yet the experience of negation also implies a moment of transformation. Although the experience of negativity may entail a process of decentring which deprives a hermeneutic agency of a stable conception of itself, that self-same process also initiates that agency into other existential possibilities.

The capacity of negativity experience to turn from the disruptive to the transformative is enabled by the ontological priority of language-being over an agent's linguistic consciousness. The rootedness of linguistic consciousness in language-being allows that consciousness to become more than itself, that is, to be implicitly grounded in historically received ways of thinking that extend far beyond what that consciousness can initially grasp. The positivity within negative experience – its negative capability – is that within which we meet the possibility of becoming more than ourselves. The ontogenetic capacity of provocative practice is once again emphasized.

To arrive at a conscious acceptance of the limited nature of our understanding entails the recognition of alternative concepts to our accepted ways of thinking. This implies that within ourselves we are *already* tacitly acquainted with the possibility of transformative perspectives. The argument reflects the apophatic entanglements of our language-being. Precisely because of the relationality of the latter, a subject agency's individual language consciousness always has the speculative capacity to point beyond itself. This enables a more substantial observation.

The negativity of experience demonstrates that that which renders our hermeneutical understanding of self and world limited is not any awareness of infinite mind or being beyond language. Wittgenstein's caveat is pertinent: 'to set a limit to thought, we should have to find both sides of the limit thinkable.'[49]

---

47 Keller, *Cloud of the Impossible*, 288.
48 TM 356 (insert added).
49 Ludwig Wittgenstein, *Tractatus Logicao-Philosophicus* (London: Routledge & Kegan Paul, 1961), 3, Preface.

Yet for negative hermeneutics there is no beyond language, no absolute mind, no infinite being that limits language. That which limits a certain perspective and renders it finite is not a metaphysical conception of something other than language but an infinity of other possible finite perspectives. There is nothing beyond a linguistic perspective or outlook that renders it finite other than language-being itself. Beyond a given linguistic orientation lie only more words. As Wittgenstein argued, only language sets the limits of language.[50] This is made clear by negative experience itself.

When a grounding conception of self or world is rendered empty by the challenge of negative experience, it may seem that existence has been reduced to a nothingness: everything we thought gave meaning and purpose to our being proves limited and inadequate. However, the collapse of a specific body of beliefs does not leave 'nothing' as a remainder. To the contrary, beyond the negated linguistic framework of thought lie other ways of thinking. Language-being always transcends what a particular linguistic consciousness grasps as its world. As we have argued, any conscious acceptance of what negative experience demonstrates (i.e. the limited nature of what we understand as world and self) must *already* entail a logical *recognition* of alternatives to established concepts. Gadamer insists that 'thinking is always moving beyond every particular limit'.[51] In short, the nihilistic collapse of pivotal existential concepts may dislodge linguistic consciousness from its sense of being at the centre of its world but it does not cast us into the abyss: we do not meet with nothingness but only with other aspects of language-being which our previous convictions prevented us from seeing. This emphasizes the apophatic relationality of language-being. Affirming the relational ontology of negative hermeneutics means that as finite language-beings we are already part of the infinite relatedness of language-being. Whether we like it or not, negative experience reveals the extent to which we as finite language-beings are *already* enfolded in the infinite, that is, within that infinity of other possible ways of constructing ourselves linguistically held in language-being. Viewed from an epistemological perspective, negative experience may seem a moment of breakdown in which our understanding is rendered crushingly limited but from an ontological perspective that experience emerges as a moment of both breaking into and breaking open the numerous other ways of constructing self and world. Negative experience entails a *Bildungsprozess* which passes from a renunciation of what we thought

---

50   Ibid.
51   Hans-Georg Gadamer, 'Autobiographical Reflections', in *The Gadamer Reader*, ed. R. E. Palmer (Evanston: Northwestern University Press, 2007), 35.

we knew about both ourselves and our world to an ecstatic affirmation of the endless possibilities of what we can yet become within language-being. Put another way, negative experience initiates a process of unlearning in which the certainty of philosophical, political and theological commitments is undone. Such a negation of previously cherished certainties returns us to a condition of unknowing in which we once more become a question to ourselves. Yet, critically, as the argument about recognizing limits implies, such unknowing is not the same as an ignorance. The hermeneutical subject that has both come to be knowingly unknowing of its essence and attained a full awareness of being a question to itself grasps that it can only come to know more of itself by exploring the essential possibilities in which it resides. The unknowing hermeneutical subject knows that because of its apophatic entanglements in language-being, it is already enfolded in constellations of possible meaning that stretch beyond its immediate consciousness. By showing us what we are not, negative experience opens us to the question of what we can yet be. The process of 'unknowing' that negative experience initiates 'never lessens or reduces knowledge but (actually) makes new knowledge possible'.[52] Viewed from an ontological perspective, there is an inherent positivity within negative experience: the negativity of experience within language-being does not render our knowing of ourselves empty or as nothing. To the contrary, it reveals our being to be a plenitude of possibilities and gives us philosophical licence to explore them.

The latter argument is congruent with the notion of the accomplished practitioner discussed earlier. Repetitions of negative experience form a reflective awareness that any level of a successful practice is both defined by its limits and by the anticipation of what that practice has yet to achieve. In this respect, negative hermeneutics offers a constructive response to Wittgenstein's observation about the limits of language. In contrast to his monistic approach to language games, negative hermeneutics stresses the interrelationality of language-being. This emphasizes the ontological priority of language-being over linguistic consciousness and provides philosophical grounds for why the negativity of experience demonstrates that because of our apophatic entanglements, we are always more than ourselves. To recognize the claims of negative hermeneutics is to grant that we are connected to an infinite body of linguistic and conceptual frameworks the totality of which is beyond our cognitive grasp. Accordingly, within negative hermeneutics the infinite is a placeholder neither for an absolute mind nor for an objective correlative to finite understanding but for a limitless

---

52   Keller, *Cloud of the Impossible*, 23.

relations-world of interconnected linguistic perspectives. The very moment negative experience exposes our established conceptions of world and identity as limited in relation to other conceptions, other possibilities for how we might conceive of ourselves and our world become apparent. Negative experience reveals the extent to which we have become negligent of other possible ways of configuring ourselves within language-being. It is against a growing awareness of these other possibilities that the finite nature of our understanding is uncovered. By revealing the finite limitations of our initial mode of understanding in relation to language-being as a whole, negative experience discloses that individual linguistic consciousness is already more than itself. In this respect, *the negativity of experience redeems its own negativity*. That which exposes the limited nature of our understanding also reveals the unlimited nature of its possibilities. There is no metaphysical transgression here. The negativity of experience leads to a deepening and extension of one's finite engagements and to an acceptance of movement and change as the route to becoming more. It does not lead to a condemnation of the finite and limited in the name of a metaphysical absolute. The ontological priority of possibility over actuality emphasizes how negative hermeneutics upholds the precedence of existence over essence. Any pursuit of fixed notions of substance, essence and identity metaphysically conceived is suggestive of a will to death. Any privileging of essence or identity as 'transcending' the relational nature of language-being places such notions beyond the very finite movements of words and concepts upon which the life of meaning and understanding depends. Negative hermeneutics returns the genesis of such notions to the movements of language, movements which always hold the promise of new life and insight. The negativity of experience not only negates nihilism but also offers an affirmation of that life form (*Dasein*) which seeks through negation to become ever more itself. The question becomes how to draw out and articulate these transformative possibilities. In this respect, negative experience entails an anti-nihilistic posture which does not take no for an answer. This takes us one step beyond Keat's presentation of negative capability. The issue is not just how to reside contentedly within uncertainty but how to go beyond it, that is, how to draw out the inherent possibilities it may hold. Gadamer's appeal to the imagination makes a striking contribution to the argument.

The paradox of negative experience is that it brings us to see and to dwell more fully in the realm of our possibilities. The question is how to become more open to and be guided by what such possibilities contain. Gadamer's appeal to the imagination neither evokes a Kantian cognitive doctrine, which deploys the imagination to mediate between a concept and its particular material exemplifications, nor does it appeal to a creative capacity which bursts forth spontaneously *ex nihilo*. Gadamer's references to the imagination (*Phantasie*) are rare. There are only two in *Truth and Method*[53] but when they appear in other essays, they have a strategic importance: they are orientated towards enhancing understanding as the basic being-in-motion of *Dasein*'s existence.[54] His references emphasize the imagination's hermeneutical function[55] and context. Within language-being the imagination's function is to develop a sense of the unforeseen constellations of ideas at play within a given practice.[56] Its task is in effect to go beyond what is presently understood and to accelerate the movement of thought which constitutes the basic being-in-motion (*Bewegtheit*) of existence.[57] Consider the following passage:

> The true philosopher awakens the intuitive power already resident in language: every linguistic zeal or even linguistic violence, can be in place only if this can be accepted into the language of those who want to think along with the philosopher, think further with him, and that means if his words are able to push forward, extend or light up the horizon of communication.[58]

These remarks connect the function of the imagination with the anticipation of completion. The projection of possible outcomes for a cultural practice is dependent upon thinking with and beyond a practice. However, the hermeneutical function of the imagination is not just limited to anticipating where a text or argument is going. More important is its role in responding to impasses, difficulties and breakdowns in practice. Gadamer openly states that the 'imagination naturally has a hermeneutical function and serves the sense for what is questionable. It serves the ability to expose real, productive questions.'[59] Odo Marquard celebrates the imaginative capacity of the humanities to construct alternative visions of the world which not only contrast with but also critique the limiting aspects of a dominant ideology. Marquard proposes that the humanities

> help us to emigrate from a world that is only objectified or whose story is only the story of progress; and because they do this, the human sciences have to do with education – because education ensures one's capacity to emigrate.[60]

---

53 TM 46, 53.
54 Hans-Georg Gadamer, 'Classical and Philosophical Hermeneutics', in *The Gadamer Reader*, ed. R. E. Palmer (Evanston: Northwestern University Press, 2007), 56.
55 Hans-Georg Gadamer, 'The Universality of the Hermeneutic Problem', in *The Gadamer Reader*, ed. R. E. Palmer (Evanston: Northwestern University Press, 2007), 85.
56 Gadamer, 'Autobiographical Reflections', 37.
57 Gadamer, 'Classical and Philosophical Hermeneutics', 56.
58 Gadamer, 'Autobiographical Reflections', 36.
59 Gadamer, 'The Universality of the Hermeneutics Problem', 85.
60 Odo Marquard, *In Defense of the Accidental* (Oxford: Odeon, 1991), 102.

Gadamer's appeal to the imaginative function is less binary. It does not seek to supplant one conception of actuality with another but to transform and find alternative constellations of ideas *within* what has become broken or questionable. In negative hermeneutics, the role of the hermeneutic imagination is genuinely productive not in the sense that it aims to create *ex nihilo* but in the sense that it seeks to dwell within a problematized subject matter and draw out different ways of understanding what is at play within it. This emphasizes an ontological truth central to creative practice. Its defining subject matters contain more possibilities than have ever been actualized within the history of that practice. A subject matter and its possibilities always exceed its known realizations. When a practice breaks down or when its precepts fall into question, the task of the hermeneutic imagination is to listen acutely for what is at play within the questionable and to draw out its undisclosed possibilities. *Even a problematic term points beyond itself.* No matter how questionable a subject matter might become – gender, race, justice – it can never be completely negated. Finite critical thought can never exhaust the infinite potential meaning within a subject matter or concept. The task of the hermeneutic imagination is to discern how a meaning can become more than what presently limits it.

The hermeneutic imagination is integral to sensing the infinite dimensions of understanding that limit its finite modes. It is also fundamental to the movement of thought itself. As we have argued, the interrelational movement of words in a language-based ontology is both centrifugal and centripetal. The adequacy and stability of meaning attached to a key subject matter can be put under intense critical pressure when the excess of other possible meanings for that term is brought to bear on it centripetally. At the same time, because the meanings attached to a subject matter do not reside exclusively in the practice in which it has been problematized, the question of what the subject matter in question might yet come to mean also has a centrifugal thrust forcing hermeneutical thought outward towards a consideration of other possibilities of meaning held within language-being.

13. Vectoring the immeasurable

This chapter concerns the workings of hermeneutical understanding. Chapter 3 presented the elements comprising a poetics of hermeneutic practice. This chapter has explored how practice brings these elements into play and provokes unexpected realignments of meaning. *The provocation of practice resides in its anticipation of completeness.* Practices without goals either internal or external are inconceivable. Practices are defined by the outcomes they anticipate rather than achieve. How does the anticipation and pursuit of completeness disrupt and defer understanding? Exactly, how is a practice provocative? The response to these questions is both existential and ontological.

Existential concerns and commitments draw us more deeply into the language worlds to which we initially belong. Such worlds hold clues as to how the unresolved social and historical narratives we are born into might play out. Language worlds house the hodological maps of individuals and their communities, articulating practices characteristic of the modes of *Dasein* they sustain. Heidegger is attuned to how the language of practice is always ahead of itself, always inclined towards future potentials and possibilities of meaning.[61] Though the worlds of meaning inscribed in art and literature attribute patterns of sense to existence, such attributions remain, hermeneutically speaking, incomplete always intimating something as yet unrealized. In Gadamer's terms, they offer a 'promise' of completion. What allows a practice to provoke unexpected alignments of meaning? The dialectical interplay between a given language world and the totality of language-being is crucial.

Language-being (*Sprachlichkeit*) transcends its constituent language worlds. It has the status of what Rosenzweig calls an 'immeasurable', an inexpressible this-worldly transcendent. Language worlds infer the totality of language-being but cannot render it in words. On this stands one of hermeneutics' regulative axioms: each language world is ontologically dependent on horizons that lie beyond it. No language world can be closed off from any another. Their porous etymological boundaries allow movements of understanding both vertical and horizontal: vertical in the sense that past and future meanings of a term can never be exhausted and horizontal in that the etymological roots of a term stretch into other languages. Attempts to 'colonize' the meaning of a term have the effect of closing off its past and future potentials. Established meanings in a practice can also be destabilized by the contingent contiguities of meaning in related practices. Yet such negativity remains hermeneutically positive. Though the edges of a word's finite meaning delimit and define its distinctive sense, its porous edges leave that word open to other fields of meaning within language-being. It is the porous edges of linguistic meanings which render them open to meaning beyond themselves and that enable movement between practices. Such movement is at

---

61 Martin Heidegger, *Being and Time*, trans. John Macquarrie (London: Blackwell, 1960), 279, 281, 307.

the core of hermeneutical experience. It draws out and provokes the disclosure of hidden alignments of meaning contained within the totality of language-being.

The notion of a practice as a 'way' of travel or vector emphasizes how practices as modes of *Dasein* are essentially dynamic. Not only the aspirations of their supporting traditions but their commitment to defining subject matters place practices ahead of themselves. Practices are always projects, ways of being whose being is to be thrown forward. However, practices do not operate *ex nihilo*. They are subject to the pressures and circumstances of their broader cultural environments. The incompleteness of meaning within a hermeneutic vector renders it vulnerable to the proximity of different meanings in adjacent vectors. Negative hermeneutics identifies 'the dialectic of the word' as the theatre of engagement in which the anticipations of practice are tested by the unseen undercurrents of meaning in the speculative totality of language-being itself.

Every practice focusses on central 'matters of interest'. Subject matters matter. The defining preoccupations of a practice are not just concepts but articulate distinctive ways of engaging with the world. The meaning of a subject matter oscillates between its perceptual instances and its conceptual connotations. Its significant content echoes the movement of part and whole within its hermeneutic framework. If a subject matter cannot be definitively represented in concrete form and if it cannot be exhaustively defined conceptually, its being resides in the infinite unease of its modes. The constant movement between part and whole sustains its being. The movement is dialectical: a new rendition of an art form can prompt a rethinking of what is possible under that concept whilst such a rethinking also expands the field of what is perceivable under its purview. In ontological terms, such movement is possible because both its perceivable and cognizable content is open to endless development. This introduces an element of uncertainty into a practice. If the subject matter which guides a practice can only ever be seen and understood partially, the doubt arises as to whether the direction posited by a subject matter has been appropriately grasped. However, it is only further application and experiment that can fashion an answer. This implies that the ontological structure of a subject matter – its past determinations and present anticipations – impel it towards its envisaged completion. Within language-being, the forward impetus of a subject matter renders inevitable a collision of anticipated meaning with other alignments of actual and possible meanings that transcend it both vertically and horizontally. This is not necessarily negative. Other horizons of meaning become apparent to a practice precisely when they challenge its primary assumptions forcing it to review its sense of past and future direction.

The negative dialectic of understanding's movements depends, first, on a practice's place within the totality of language-being and, second, upon a practice being driven to bring its subject matters to their anticipated completion which renders its incompleteness of understanding vulnerable to other alignments of meaning. As the impetus towards completion is incommensurable with the openness of language-being itself, the pursuit of completeness serves as a provocative hermeneutical fiction which maintains the forward momentum of a practice. The being of any creative and reflective practice depends on the continual movement of reappraisal and renewal. Actual completion would condemn a practice to a sclerotic entropy. The continual provocation of hermeneutical movement is the very being of a practice: it maintains itself and its possibilities so long as it does not, eschatologically speaking, arrive. Rejuvenation and revival are dependent upon constant experimentation and critique. Yet in terms of hermeneutical knowledge, what a practice pursues is not as important as the pursuit. It is a practice's pursuit of completion which provokes unexpected alignments of meaning.

Hermeneutical vectors understood as projections of completion do not cross empty spaces. Within language-being they pass through other vectors. Hermeneutical vectors not only traverse language-being individually but in their collective movement bind and uphold themselves within the totality of relational meanings they form. It is the subsumption of linguistic consciousness within language-being that establishes the participatory ontology which allows the vectoral projections of practices to provoke and interact with one another. Such a relational ontology implies that practices are always interacting, converging and diverging from one another. Interaction is its mode of collective being.

The provocative nature of a vector is implicit in Gadamer's account of the speculative movement of language. Language and thought are not strictly separable: the process of thought is the process of explication in words. In thinking something through we meet with 'the logical achievement of language'.[62] 'Thought can turn for its own instruction to that which language has built up'.[63] In so doing, thought meets with language's ontological endowment. In following a movement of thought, we discover ourselves to be already taken up by and to be operating within pre-established networks of meaning. The ontological priority of language allows reflection (linguistic consciousness) to summon and provoke pre-established networks of meaning in which it is

---

62   TM 429.
63   Ibid.

already located. The interconnecting patterns of meaningful relations within *Sprachlichkeit* do not point to anything beyond themselves only to other patterns of meaning on which they are dependent. It is this relationality that Gadamer has in mind when he refers to 'the living virtuality of speech that brings a totality of meaning to play, without being able to express it totally'.[64] The ontological placement of a hermeneutical vector within *Sprachlichkeit* establishes its provocative capacity. Practices are subject to shifts of meaning precisely because of the relational nature of meaning. Hermeneutic practices induce transformational shifts in understanding because of the porous nature of their linguistic fields. Negative hermeneutics accepts that transformative understanding is not only possible but also a given in existence. Whether it be summative in bringing to fruition themes at play within an existential orientation or disruptive in the sense of *pathei mathos* when the presumptions of a judgement are exposed as inadequate, the effect of such understanding is such that we are abruptly brought to see ourselves and the world we inhabit differently. Without such transformative possibilities and the risks they pose, the humanities are rendered futile.

Practice provokes the emergence of new understanding but does not produce it. Hermeneutic practices are not technologies of predictable let alone repeatable outcomes. Yet the seemingly spontaneous emergence of transformative understanding is by no means arbitrary. Because of the relationality of language-being, the execution of a practice cannot help but initiate changes of meaning in its own horizons as well as within the wider cultural frameworks in which it is placed. Because a practice is connected to other alignments of meaning in unpredictable ways, it is impossible to get to the bottom of a practice: its possibilities are endless. Only continued engagement in a practice can induce the emergence of what is yet possible within it. In conclusion, it is the movement of concepts, images and nuances of meaning within a practice that is provocative. Provocation is generic to practice. The indeterminate nature of practical understanding means there is no foretelling of what lies in the conceptual framework sustaining its operation. Within negative hermeneutics, incompleteness has a positive ontological capacity: it drives a practice to become more. A practice's vectoring of the immeasurable has productive effects in that it provokes the emergence of hitherto withheld possibilities for meaning from within language-being.

---

64   TM 458.

14. Recursion and repetition

The combinatory power of metaphor informs the provocative capacities of recursive reading. Metaphor indicates that the fields of meaning associated with a word are sufficiently indeterminate so as to allow penetration by other fields of meaning. To navigate further the question of how recursive readings of the same text can produce different understandings we need to bring a two related concepts to bear, that is, Wittgenstein's notion of core and peripheral meaning and further aspects of Gadamer's concept of linguistic consciousness.

The ability of recursive reading to produce new alignments of meaning presupposes a certain looseness or porosity of meaning that permits new semantic combinations. Wittgenstein's differentiation between core and peripheral meaning is pertinent. In the *Blue and Brown Books* he defends the porosity linguistic meaning:

> Many words ... then do not a strict meaning. But this is not a defect. To think that it is would be like saying that the light of my reading lamp is no real light at all because it has no sharp boundary. [65]

The core determinations of meaning required by language to function are established by the metaphysically contingent conventions that govern a language game and not by the preferences of individual language users. Yet, set meanings are always subject to variation allowing them to adapt to ranges of circumstance. Core meanings invariably shade into fields of peripheral meaning. It is the open areas of meaning that facilitate the greatest hermeneutic movement. The looseness of a subject matter's semantic periphery permits it to function as a placeholder term *across different discourses*. History, literature and philosophy all deploy the concept 'narrative'. The term's formal indeterminacy means that its use in one discipline is vulnerable to different meanings deriving from others. My chance reading of a philosophical approach to narrative can offer a profound challenge to the narrative structure of my historical horizon. Reading can be a risky matter. The indeterminacy of core meaning allows different notions of narrative to infiltrate and alter one another. Semantic indeterminacy is a formal condition of those metaphoric transfers that facilitate changes in understanding. Disruption and negation is a necessary and unavoidable part of education's negative capability.

---

65   Ludwig Wittgenstein, *Blue and Brown Books* (Oxford: Blackwell, 2003), 27. See also Wittgenstein's *Philosophical Investigations* (Oxford: Blackwell, 2003), Sec. 62.

Wittgenstein's distinction between core and peripheral meaning suggests that if the core meanings of words and concepts are never fully clear, recursive looping has little to do with the recovery of the same but more to do with achieving new and potentially less ambiguous determinations of meaning. Recursive looping extends the meaning of what was only ever partially understood. The stratagem relies on the loose relationship between core and peripheral meaning. Because the life of language is never fixed, the practice of reading can bring to light unnoticed shifts of meaning in language horizons. Recursive looping can never achieve the same reading of a text. It discloses the extent to which a reader's expectancy of meaning has changed. By generating different readings of a core subject matter, recursive looping uncovers the play of continuities and differences which constitute the ever-changing narrative of an individual's understanding.

Recursive looping is a tactic that allows hermeneutical consciousness to become aware of itself. Gadamer's language ontology offers a variation of the extended mind thesis. 'In language,' he writes, ' the reality beyond every individual consciousness becomes visible.' The formulation that consciousness is more being than knowing claims that there is 'a world at work within my understanding' that reaches beyond my understanding. It is a world whose operations can be caught in the act. The relevance of Gadamer's notion of linguistic consciousness to recursive looping is clear. Any reading of a text involves the receiving horizon of the reader being open to the transmitting horizons of the text. Yet neither are static. Both are subject to ever-changing streams of meaning. This suggests, once again, why it is that no reading of a text can in phenomenological terms be repeated: the horizons of meaning within which I return to a text and the horizons of meaning to which I return within that text are constantly shifting. This clarifies the value of recursive reading. The differences between initial and subsequent readings of a text, which recursivity provokes, can disclose subtle changes of orientation within both receiving and transmitting horizons.

Recursive looping can achieve serious knowledge gains. It advances the hidden contents of knowledge by making thematic what was previously unthematic. It brings to light the as-yet-unknown and transforms vague cognizance into definite knowledge showing that contrary to Nietzsche's insistence, becoming is not incommensurable with all types of knowledge. It is the porosity of meaning within language-being that makes the practice of reading provocative, productive and precarious. A reader's understanding of a subject matter's meaning is formed over time by a pattern of non-identical repetitions. Because of language-being's openness, the practice of reading other texts and literatures adds to the patterns of meaning established in one's own cultural horizon. At the same time, the practice can also be disruptive introducing new elements of meaning to established understandings.

The value of the disruptive capacity of reading lies not in the production of differences per se but in establishing a continuity of differences that allows that which has no essential identity to make its emergent character more discernible. The non-identical repetitions of practice are the ground upon which the continuity of an agent's narrative is built. Nietzsche's anticipation of a process epistemology is helpful.

> A world in a state of becoming could not in a strict sense, be 'comprehended' or 'known'.[66]
>
> We would know nothing of time and motion if we did not in a coarse fashion believe we see what is at 'rest' beside what is in motion.[67]

Though the world(s) at play within the endless stream of our language horizons are not formally speaking knowable, they do not amount to an unintelligible flux. Rather, as Gadamer's phenomenology suggests, we directly experience the claims that a subject matter makes on us. What is not immediately perceptible are those subtle shifts of belief and attitude that are ongoing within and around us, shifts which alter the character of one recursive reading from another. The relatively stable points of 'rest' which constitute each reading make shifts in hermeneutic orientation manifest. The worlds at play within the ongoing stream of our understanding are caught in the act, as it were, by the differences between recursive readings. These render discernible the shifting narrative structures that come to constitute the continuity of a subject agent's being. In other words, recursive reading sets the conditions for the emergence of a self other than the one which undertook the first reading.

15. The returns of aesthetic completeness

The previous sections have established the provocative and productive powers of practice: its internal dynamics impel it towards moments of crisis and breakdown. Because of both the speculative structure of language ontology and

---

66 WP 517.
67 WP 520.

the incommensurability of any subject matter with its interpretation, practices striving to extend their competence will always be liable to disrupting and deferring their understanding. This confirms the *Vorgriff der Vollendung* as one of the principal drivers of negative hermeneutics. The deconstructive side of negativity is plain but what of the constructive?

Despite the negativities which disrupt practice, philosophical hermeneutics manifestly emphasizes the power of art to speak directly to us, to disrupt our everyday experience certainly but, also, to present deeply persuasive and meaningful realignments of even the most traumatic experiences. Gadamer's commitment to the humanities (*Bildung*) and to the transformative power of aesthetic truth makes little sense without a belief in the power of art to 'speak' meaningfully of the world in which we exist. Here we touch on a fundamental tension in negative hermeneutics. Whilst committed to the power of the negative, hermeneutics openly advocates the transformative power of art to restructure fragmented fields of experience into meaningful wholes. The *Vorgriff der Vollendung* is, once again, central to this tension.

As a regulative principle, the *Vorgriff* conditions the possibility of understanding by placing manifolds of experience in projected intelligible wholes. This presupposes the possibility of regulative completion. And yet, within the *Sprachswelt*, the pursuit of such completion conspires against its attainment. However, to conclude that philosophical hermeneutics offers little more than an endless and inconsequential dialectic of assertion and counter-assertion would be a serious error. It is the consequential effects of these dialectical motions that are crucial for the emergence of hermeneutical insight. This will become clear when we discuss the 'returns' of aesthetic completion per se.

Gadamer's undeniable affirmation of the power of aesthetic experience to unify our fragmented experiences of actuality is vulnerable to criticisms of art's claim to truth made by Nietzsche and Adorno. If art's semblances of completion are illusory and do not represent the world as it is, their beauty distracts us from confronting and resolving the existential challenges which fuel the need for such illusion in the first place. However, these criticisms suppose what Gadamer does not foster, namely, the supposition that the actual truth of the world is beyond all representation and that any artistic claim to truth is but a distortion of actuality masquerading as its truth. And yet, epistemological correspondence theories of truth are not applicable to negative hermeneutics. As we have argued, the power of hermeneutic truth resides in its integrative capacity and not in its mimetic function. The problems concerning the relation of Gadamer's aesthetic to negative hermeneutics are indeed complex. Let us briefly return to a precept central to negative hermeneutics: all understanding is movement. With this in mind, what is the role of aesthetic completion in a world in which regulative completion is formally impossible?

The disruptive dialectics of practice are premised on the possibility of continuous movement. As events, hermeneutic and aesthetic understanding occur, that is, they 'come about'. They are epiphanic, emerging from the unexpected, transforming and displacing expectations unexpectedly. The forward impetus of this movement derives from the anticipation of completeness. This brings us to a pivotal question.

If the anticipation of completeness is of infinite extent and therefore poses an unrealizable quest, how is the achievement of hermeneutical movement ever possible? If the anticipation of completeness is formally unrealizable, how can we assess whether we have moved closer to its realization. If we cannot the criterion of improvement is seemingly lost. Similarly, if completeness is formally inconceivable, how can particular interpretations of a subject matter be criticized as incomplete? Without formal comparators, the movement which sustains a process of *Bildung* becomes impossible. The transformative project of philosophical hermeneutics is placed in jeopardy. To so reason, however, is to make the same mistake as those critics of hermeneutics who charge that hermeneutic or artistic claims to truth involve an illegitimate appeal to conceptual completeness. The charge confuses regulative completeness with summative completeness and confounds the possibility of seeing the dialectical interplay between them. We shall argue that the seminal relation concerns a hermeneutical differential: the regulative principle of completeness conditions the possibility of summative completeness.

Though the determinate visions of summative completeness presuppose indeterminate regulative completeness, the latter can never be reduced to determinate visions of the summative. The asymmetry between the pursuit of regulative and summative completeness drives the movement of hermeneutical practices. Though the pursuit of regulative completeness may be wilfully pursued, the emergence of summative completeness in the medium of the 'living word' or the 'vital image' *happens* to us, occurs as it were, as a collateral effect of the pursuit of regulative completeness.

It is a *leitmotif* of negative hermeneutics that the objects of everyday experience are given to us in fragmentary fashion, as clusters of undecided future possibilities.[68] The 'meaning' of such objects is not yet transformed into a fully coherent whole or structure. The task of interpretation is to sense the future

---

68   TM 112.

direction of such processes and to anticipate their completeness. Within the indeterminacies of existence, the quest for summative or aesthetic completeness emerges as a quest for intelligible sense, giving shape and pattern to the ambiguities of being. The quest for aesthetic or summative completeness is a quest for sense, not a metaphysical quest for the meaning of existence as a whole. Aesthetic completeness seeks to render aspects of existence 'limited wholes'. What is brought to summative completion is not the infinity of possible meanings underwriting a body of experience but singular aspects of a subject matter woven into a 'meaningful whole' which can be seen as 'aesthetically complete'. The transformative achievement of aesthetic or summative completeness is the creation of seemingly 'closed circles of meaning' so that 'more becomes known than is already known'.[69] This offers further insight into the dialectical interplay between formal and summative completeness.

In pursuing the completeness of its projects, a practice seeks summative completion for its concerns bringing them into meaningful alignment within itself. And yet the indeterminate principle of regulative completion which drives a practice towards a summative form of completion is always in excess of the summative, always implying that there is more to hermeneutical manifold than an interpretation suggests. Precisely because of its indeterminate nature, the anticipation of formal completion forces summative completion to overshoot itself. Whereas formal completion is always in excess of its determinate applications, summative completion remains finite in relation to the infinite capacities of the regulative. The irony is twofold. Although the regulative principle which impels a practice towards the summative completion is responsible for disrupting it, it is also the principle which impels a practice to restructure its disrupted elements into a new summative synthesis. There is always more to understand of a manifold. When practices fail, it is precisely the formal anticipation of completion that also drives them towards reconfiguration and renewal.

No matter the power of art and literature to achieve summative closures of meaning, what artworks bring into meaningful unity by no means exhausts other possibilities for meaning within the manifolds they unify. Each manifold x is always in excess of itself. Precisely because subject matters serve as placeholders across a plurality of discourses, the achievement of summative completeness in one practice is not immune to logical challenges from others. As Wittgenstein insisted, the meaningfulness of a term depends upon the contexts and

---

69 TM 114. This is Gadamer's transformation into structure argument.

conventions of its use. If all possible instances of a term's meaning had to be established before usage, nothing could be communicated. However, summative reasoning can never demonstrate that its interpretations of a subject matter are formally complete. It can only persuade us that its renditions of a selected manifold are as compelling as practically possible.

The following section defends the dialectical thesis that the unrealizable pursuit of regulative completeness provokes the rise and fall of patterns of summative completeness in art and literature along with the transformative motions of hermeneutical understanding they induce.

The anticipation of completeness implicit in the *Vorgriff* initiates a dialectic movement sustained by the constant tension between its destructive and creative moments. The interdependence of these movements suggests that it is the provocative dimensions of a practice that establish the conditions whereby that practice can turn towards a creative realignment of itself. Viewed through the lens of negative hermeneutics, negativity within the humanities is profoundly educative.

Whilst it exposes a practice's formal anticipation of completeness as unattainable, the provocative nature of practice also uncovers the conditions under which new forms of summative (aesthetic) completeness become possible. Without the prior assumption of regulative completeness, summative completeness would not be perceivable in art or literature. Furthermore, without the perceivability of summative completeness, that which is not perceivable – the idea of regulative completeness – would not itself become thinkable. The dialectical interplay between regulative and summative completeness is an effect of language-being. In the framework of negative hermeneutics, words and concepts do not represent different worlds. Both are different aspects of language, and it is within language-being that the asymmetrical relation between words and concepts is productively maintained. Within this schema, regulative completion belongs to the formal realm of concepts whilst summative completion relates more to words and images. However, it is the relation between them that is central to their interplay. Whilst it is evident that the realm of words is not the world of concepts, concepts can neither be reduced to words nor can they be explained without them. Just as words cannot exhaust what a concept entails, words are dependent upon concepts for their clarity of meaning. Gadamer's remark that 'language is . . . uncannily near our thinking'[70] suggests that to speak a language is to implicitly invoke the formal possibility

---

70   TM 378.

of a completeness of meaning without which summative completeness and the related notion of a hermeneutical object unfolding between its *woher* and *wozu* would not make sense. Without language we would have little sense of reason and without reason's powers of configuration, words would lose their sense. Yet, the asymmetry that differentiates words and reason renders them mutually dependent. The argument echoes Nietzsche's remark that 'we cease to think when we refuse to do so under the constraint of language'.[71] The implication is that when we think of a practice hermeneutically we cannot help but think of it as a *woher/wozu* structure that infers the possibility of a completable whole. However, once a practice is thought of as a formally completable whole, the dialectical fatality of negative hermeneutics comes into play. The act of thinking of itself as a practice anticipates a completeness that practice is bound to pursue but will never attain.[72] Practice always falls short of its anticipations.

Implicit in these points is the argument that understanding the elements of a text in relation to how they might comprise a whole is 'permanently determined by the anticipatory movement of fore-understanding'.[73] Such anticipatory movement is implicit in the idea that hermeneutical objects whether persons or artworks are intelligible in that they have to be thought of as a dynamic structure ever unfolding between its *woher* and anticipated *wozu*. In other words, a part–whole relationship cannot be thought of without a formal anticipation of completeness. The possibility of such completion is what all meaningful experience presupposes even though it might not be attained. This gives direction and purposefulness to understanding's movement. However, the formal structure of completeness has no determinate content of its own. It is the form of both thinking about and bringing into to structure the shifting manifolds of experience. Gadamer emphasizes how the fore-conception of completeness is always determined by the specific content of the practice that projects it.[74] The fore-conception is, therefore, both provisional and correctable. A corollary to the argument that practice will always fall short of its aspirations is that 'the true meaning' of a hermeneutic object can never fully emerge. 'The discovery of the true meaning of a text or a work of art is never finished; it is infact an infinite process.'[75] Does not the anticipation and pursuit of what is in

---

71 WP 522.
72 'Hermeneutics has the task of revealing a totality of meaning in all its relations' (TM 471).
73 TM 293.
74 TM 294.
75 TM 298.

fact beyond completion mean that nihilism and despair are the unavoidable result?

Nihilism is not the inevitable result of this dialectic. To the contrary, the impossibility of regulative completion establishes the conditions whereby the emergence of new modes of summative completion becomes possible. The paradox of aesthetic and hermeneutic understanding is that neither can attain that formal completion the assumption of which governs the possibility of their activity. Both forms of integrative understanding are made possible by the antinomic play within language-being of two modes of completion which drive the consequentialism of unintended effects underpinning hermeneutic understanding. Without a prior assumption of the possibility of regulative completeness, summative completeness would not be perceivable in art or literature. Indeed, the reverse also applies: without the perceivability of summative completeness, that which is not perceivable – the idea of regulative completeness – would not be thinkable. The two notions of completeness are codependent. As is so often the case in negative hermeneutics, it is their interplay which is key.

We have argued that regulative completeness is not an object but a form of thought which gives hermeneutical shape to objects of experience. This strengthens earlier objections to deconstruction's critique of hermeneutics: because the meaning of a hermeneutic object is never completable, hermeneutics cannot be condemned for failing to complete that which is beyond the possibility of completion. The life of understanding is movement and so to demand complete certainty for a practice's precepts would be to stymie their movement. However, it can be argued that we understand words and images not because they offer a complete meaning but because they anticipate a direction of meaning. This implies that articulable understanding is possible because incomplete, because of what it is understood to be pointing to rather than directly asserting. With regard to the anticipations of completeness within regulative forms of reasoning, the words of Eavan Boland are apt: 'and all of it unfinished in this form'.[76] The discovery of what remains unfinished gives summative completeness the task of drawing out further aspects of the infinite potential for meaningfulness that a given form or subject matter contains. Within the language ontology of negative hermeneutics, regulative and summative understandings are codependent.

---

76 Eavan Boland, 'An Irish Georgic', in *A Woman Without a Country*, ed. Eavan Boland (Manchester: Carcanet, 2014), 49.

This emphasizes that in aesthetic and hermeneutic understanding the summative and the regulative stand in relation to each other *within* a part-whole structure. It has been a theme of our argument that everyday experience is often broken and incoherent: conversations arise and break off inconclusively. 'Reality' always stands in a horizon of desired or feared or at any rate still undecided possibilities.[77] The fragmented nature of experience drives mutually exclusive expectations not all of which can be realized. And then, quite unexpectedly, something is said, something is found in a poem or in an image which *speaks* and when it does 'a context of meaning closes and completes itself'. A moment of summative or aesthetic completion is achieved when an emergent word or image suddenly pulls together and renders intelligible related elements at play within a field of experience that in themselves make no discernible sense until brought together as a cohesive unity. The 'truth' of summative completeness is clearly hermeneutically integrative: a diversity of experiential elements suddenly make sense when brought together as a coherent whole. It is important to stress that the 'revealing image' and the 'living word' are not the deliberate achievement of a methodology within practice.[78] To the contrary, they arise as a consequence of an artist's participation in a practice and not as the result of wilful design. Summative completeness presents itself within practical engagement. This is precisely the unifying and integrating role that Gadamer and Lotz attribute to the revealing of word and image in art and literature. This emphasizes that summative understanding in hermeneutics and aesthetics cannot be taught: it is not a theorizable object to be learned. Rather, it arises only in and because of practical engagement.

For Lotz, making an image of something is identical with the transformation of complex phenomena into a condensed and understandable form. *Images render complexities of experience thinkable.* 'They introduce new relations, new reflections and new forms of the world itself by mediating sensual presence with rationality in the universality of an image.'[79] The recursive capacity of both image and concept permits both to shine back into experience across passages of time revealing unnoticed patterns and relations. In such circumstances, concepts and images forge memory and experience into summative wholes of pattern and sense. Though such moments may be momentous in how they both integrate

---

77   TM 113.
78   Gadamer would argue that the emergence of the revealing image or the living word is the action of the thing itself. On this point see my chapter: 'Can Art Make Anything at All', in *To Understand What is Happening, Essays in Historicity*, ed. Jan Ivar Lindén (Brill: NL, 2021).
79   Christian Lotz, *The Art of Gerhard Richter, Hermeneutics, Images, Meaning* (London: Bloomsbury, 2017), 29.

thought and experience in new ways within a practice, they remain finite and open to challenge.

No matter how perfect an artistic composition may seem, it remains a composite entity always logically vulnerable to having its constituent elements realigned. There is nothing logically compelling about a summative whole other than the evident fact that it makes sense of a body of experience in a persuasive, consistent and compelling manner. Summative understanding in art and hermeneutics is never a matter of rational proof. It is a question of the reasonableness of what is revealed. The 'revealing image' and the 'living word' do not prove the character of existence but they can 'show' it to us in ways that would be churlish to deny. We will return to the implications of this point in later comments on Wittgenstein remark that we can be brought to understand something without necessarily being able to put it into words.[80] And yet, the ontological truth remains: no matter how compelling the summative unity that a poetic or painted image may achieve, it is always subject to disruption and challenge by the finitude of existence. Why is it that the anticipation and pursuit of formal completeness in hermeneutical disciplines does not collapse into nihilism when it is realized that the inaugurating quest of a practice is unrealizable? The following sections argue that the dialectical turn which makes the avoidance of nihilism possible is, in effect, a consequence of Gadamer's language ontology. The regulative principle which impels a practice towards completion is not only responsible for disrupting the summative quest but also for provoking a practice to restructure its disrupted elements in a new summative synthesis. The antinomic play between the regulative and summative in hermeneutical reasoning is driven by the logical instinct of language for completeness.

16. The dialectic of word and concept

For negative hermeneutics the essence of speaking and thinking is that movement agitated by language's inherent impetus towards completion.[81] This movement is constituted by the dialectical relationship between word and concept. Language is impetuous: it wants to move on. It senses that there is always something more

---

80   Ludwig Wittgenstein, *Tractatus Logico-Philosophicus* (London: Routledge and Kegan Paul, 1961), Sec. 6.521.
81   Part of this section appeared in my essay 'Dialogue, Dialectic and Conversation' which appeared in the collection *The Gadamerian Mind*, ed. T. George and G.-J. van Heiden (London: Bloomsbury, 2021.)

to be said because of the ambiguity and incompleteness in what has been said. Wittgenstein argues that when we ask after the meaning of a word, we feel that it ought to point to something.[82] Gadamer describes this as the logical instinct of language, its unerring tendency towards a goal, to rendering a subject matter whole.[83] The uneasy relationship between word and concept is sustained by their formal incommensurability: no determinate instance of a word can capture the indeterminacy of its related concept and no concept can be rendered fully determinate by the words that strive to articulate it. This asymmetry also holds between words and images. Despite this, word and concept are mutually dependent: a concept cannot be determined as a concept without the usage of the word[84] and though concepts can be objects of pure reflection their purchase upon the experienced world requires that 'they . . . be converted (back) into the valid or appropriate words'.[85] Furthermore, no concept or image can be brought into reflection without the word. Within language-being, the mutually sustaining antagonism between both word and concept, word and image places them in continuous dialectical motion.

As modes of *Dasein*, there is no point where we come into language. Becoming aware of ourselves entails a becoming aware of already being a linguistic creature immersed in the continuous interplay of word and concept, an interplay which oscillates between confusion, abstraction and application. Whilst the abstract possibilities generated by conceptual thinking offer an escape from the context-bound limitations and perplexities of a word's meaning, the concrete determinations of meaning associated with a word enable concepts to achieve specific applications within actuality. In everyday experience, the uneasy synthesis of word and concept is overlooked. Knowing 'how to go on' within ordinary language entails a forgetfulness of the possibility that a word can always mean otherwise and that a concept is always susceptible to new determinations of meaning. The ever-present possibility of such fracture is revealed when customary usage is challenged or when the circumstances in which a specific subject matter is conventionally applied change: established meaning and sense bifurcate. This echoes the division of sense and meaning which underpins Gadamer's critique of aesthetic alienation. However, in response to this bifurcation, Gadamer

---

82 Wittgenstein, *Blue and Brown Books*, 1.
83 Hans-Georg Gadamer, *Hegel's Dialectic, Five Hermeneutical Studies* (New Haven: Yale University Press, 1976), 91 and 92. Gadamer comments further, 'But as much as logic and grammar might correspond to each other in that both are what they are in concrete use, the natural logic lying in the grammar of every language is by no means exhausted in the function in being pre-figuration of philosophical logic' (ibid., 92).
84 Ibid., 93.
85 Ibid., 99.

suggests that it is the 'natural logic of language' that endeavours to consider possibilities for healing a subject matter's fragmented meaning. Thought turns to exploring the unstated speculative meanings held within a received term in an effort to discover a new synthesis of word and concept. Reflective thought in its movement towards the whole, rearticulates language's own impetus towards completeness. This reaffirms the nature of Gadamer's language ontology: in seeking other possible determinations of meaning for a subject matter, 'thought can turn for its own instruction to this stock (of possibilities) that language has built up: the logical advance work that language has done for it'.[86]

The idea of a language world continually revealing and hiding its own possibilities emphasizes that Heidegger's conception of language as the house of being is fundamental to Gadamer's thinking. In seeking to discover further determinations of meaning for a problematized subject matter, thought turns to the stock of possibilities already held within the 'collective mind' of language-being. The 'speech-created' world is the storehouse of such possibilities. However, this is not to say that it is to any other logically possible meaning that thought turns. The question for hermeneutically orientated reflection is to discern which abstract possibility promises a new concrete application of concept to experience. Hermeneutic reflection is not an exercise of pure reason. No matter how abstract its thinking, hermeneutic reflection is always already primed in its hermeneutic receptiveness. *What makes one new determination of meaning applicable rather than another involves the question of hermeneutic fit.* Propositional and factual meanings are always underpinned by those contextual structures and involvements which render factual assertions meaningful in the first place. The negative turn away from the everyday word in a practice towards reflection reveals how the *entente* between factual or propositional terms and their significant background has been broken. A newly discovered conceptual implication within a subject matter might render the conventional circumstances of its application questionable just as a change within the context of its application might question its sense. In either case, the rupture of the 'living word' forces a practice into reflection in search of new determinations of meaning able to restore the 'hermeneutic fit' between a problematized concept and the circumstances of its use. Gadamer insists that the 'natural logic of language' impels us to find a new synthesis of concept and contextual application capable of returning us to the everyday cohesiveness of the 'living word'. Exposure to the realms of the speculatively possible 'challenges thought to stir

---

86 TM 429.

itself' and search out completer accounts of a problematized meaning. It is here that the formalized techniques of dialectical thought within a hermeneutical practice come into their own. Gadamer insists that 'theoretical knowledge is originally not opposed to practical activity but is its highest intensification and perfection'.[87] The key role of theory within negative hermeneutics is to uncover the possibilities inherent within practices and liberate them towards futures already latent within them.[88] The task of theory is 'to grasp what' within our practices 'has taken hold of us' and to understand its limits and its possibilities 'with a heightened clarity'.[89] 'So theory itself is a practice'.[90] This emphasizes that hermeneutical reflection is essentially *praxis* though it requires engagement in the *techné* of a practice to emerge. Hermeneutics has the task of translating thought's formal logics into the language of application. It is language's quest for the concretion of meaning that brings the abstractness of thought 'back to earth'. As an exercise in metaphysical contemplation, dialectical analysis can expand the formal range of possibilities *ad infinitum* but the question remains: which possibility achieves the 'hermeneutical fit' required to return the abstract concept to the vitality of the living word? Which possibility achieves a new summative understanding within a practice?

Hermeneutical reflection is always already primed in its receptiveness. Prejudices constitute the initial directedness of our ability to experience something *as* something.[91] Such reflection never takes place *in abstracto*. It is always sensitized by horizons of unresolved problems, open conceptual ambiguities and unresolved oppositions. The genius of language is that a chance remark, an unexpected use of words or a sudden discovery of an unfamiliar linguistic perspective enables the emergence of a fresh orientation towards

---

87 Hans-Georg Gadamer, 'On The Primordiality of Science', in *On Education, Poetry , and History* (Albany: State University Press of New York, 1992), 19.
88 The argument that theory is the highest intensification of a practice (i.e. of a practice in a reflective mode) constitutes Gadamer's strongest argument against the empty abstractions of metaphysics. The speculative element with philosophical hermeneutics concerns nothing other than the application of philosophical reasoning by a mode of *Dasein* to clarify and draw out what is entailed in its mode of being. Gadamer clearly states that his aim is to avoid the abstractness of metaphysics 'and to present and defend a mode of rationality belonging to practical reason against the perfection of a logical self-understanding specific to the sciences'. 'This,' he states, 'seems to me to be the true and authentic task of philosophy today.' See Gadamer, 'Autobiographical Reflections', 61.
89 Gadamer, 'Classical and Philosophic Hermeneutics', 61. D. S. Wright argues in this context that 'Reflective thinking seeks to make a practice explicit, self-conscious and subject to criticism and revision'; see *Philosophical Meditations on Zen Buddhism* (Cambridge: Cambridge University Press, 2000), 204.
90 Hans-Georg Gadamer, 'Hermeneutics as Practical Philosophy', in *The Gadamer Reader*, ed. R. Palmer (Evanston: Northwestern University Press, 2007), 230.
91 See Gadamer, 'The Universality of the Hermeneutical Problem', 82.

a problematized subject matter. The concept achieves a new hermeneutic fit between it and the circumstances of its use.

Though dialectical analysis can expand the potential range of a subject matter's possible meanings *ad infinitum*, the practical question remains: which 'theoretical' possibility offers the best 'hermeneutical fit' with the problematized subject matter within a living practice? This question cannot be answered by 'proof and demonstration alone'. It is language itself that discloses the answer. An insight suddenly comes to mind as if by its own accord. We recognize that from the many other logically possible contenders, 'it' speaks to us and it does so because it shows itself as having the hermeneutic fit we seek. The newly won insight does not arrive *ex nihilo*. To the contrary, its intuitively apprehended hermeneutical fit demonstrates that it is a perfectly reasonable and plausible response to the question that generated the need for an insightful answer in the first place. It makes sense of something in experience which when we initially experienced it, did not. To discern the hermeneutic fit of the insight is to see that it has *already* transformed our understanding of the problem that called for a response.

The achievement of a new hermeneutic fit between a concept and the circumstances of its application may allow a 'return to the living word' but such a return will always be limited. Any new synthesis of a concept and the circumstances of its application remains vulnerable to a twofold disruption. Such a synthesis is finite and subject to historical change: changes in a concept's meaning may disrupt the customary circumstances of its deployment just as changes in cultural behaviour may empty a social concept of any applicative relevance. However, driven by language's inherent tendency to completion, reflection will once again seek out a further synthesis of meaning and application. Does this mean that the dialectic of word and concept amounts to nothing more than the episodic replacement of one mode of insight by another? The notion of non-identical repetition suggests otherwise.

On one level, the answer to this question is straightforward. We have argued that the notion of non-identical repetition is fundamental to the idea of hermeneutical reflection. The history of practice does not consist of endless repetitions of failure. From the point of view of hermeneutical reflection, it is a question of what is different about each failure and what those differences indicate with regard to shifts within a practice's narrative. This draws us to a more substantial point. If the being of hermeneutical reflection is a being-in-motion, hermeneutical reflection and the insights it affords depend on being kept in motion or, to put it another way, hermeneutical reflection has in effect no beginning and no end, it is always 'underway'. This is a point of some consequence.

If the beginning was with the word (*logos*) and if it can also be said of language-being that 'it is now and ever shall be', word 'without end', one arrives at the unsolvable problem of a starting point. Yet as Gadamer well knew, for language-being there can be no beginning since it is and always was already. 'Hermeneutic reflection neither starts at a zero point nor ends in infinity.'[92] Whoever has language has the world and as that world has neither beginning nor end, there is no end to the narratives which shape and give sense to our existence and yet without narrative structures human life seems senseless. As Wolfgang Iser remarks, 'the ground from which human beings have sprung' seems 'unfathomable, human beings have become unavailable to themselves: we are but do not know what it is to be'. The fluid ontological character of our language-being can never be reconciled with language's anticipation of meaning and completion. The infinite nature of language-being formally prohibits any closure of meaning and disallows the possibility of any final word. And yet, language rests on the assumption of completable meaning. However, this does not mean that a complex experience only becomes meaningful on the arrival of its final meaning. To the contrary, it is the projected expectation of a final meaning that provides the criteria for bringing ongoing manifolds of experience into intelligible wholes. Gadamer sometimes refers to this as 'transformation into structure'.[93] Clusters of experience become meaningful in that they point to or intend a possible outcome. The antinomy between language-being's denial of a final word and the constitution expectation of completion within linguistic consciousness is the ground of a notable dialectical turn.

It is precisely because we have no hope of a-final-all-revealing-word that we strain in conversation to listen out for words that offer some clue to ongoing experiences and what they may possibly point to. Our linguistic horizons are made up of streams of unresolved difficulties and problems. These horizons are distinctly plural, linked by placeholder words and concepts which allow sets of local meanings to interpenetrate and transform each other. Hence, hearing words used in a strange context or coming across an unexpected alignment of poetic images can suddenly make surprising sense of ambiguities, unresolved tensions or conflicts within our immediate horizon. Because placeholders function across and between language horizons, concepts from a foreign text can suddenly

---

92 Gadamer, 'Autobiographical Reflections', 28.
93 TM 110.

change our attitude towards ambiguities within our more familiar horizon. An overheard remark, an unexpected meeting or the arrival of new words and concepts can miraculously overcome the fractures between word and concept that hinder the flow of understanding within a practice. The achievement of a new summative alignment may return us to the 'living word' but this does not achieve any final completeness. Though there is no final word, the integrative powers of the *living word* anticipate what completeness might entail.

The constant fascination with the play of experience in word, image and thought potentially directs us ever deeper into our practical involvements. As finite language-beings, we always want to hear more. We wait for those moments of sense that language anticipates but which we cannot directly see coming. However, when they emerge what prevents them from remaining purely episodic moments of insight? We have seen that Gadamer's language ontology is completely at odds with grasping ourselves as fixed essences. We can, however, conceive of ourselves as ever-unfolding patterns of relations which are entirely the product of our existence as practice beings in the speech-created world. Engaging with the subject matters of that world is to engage with tradition both as understood and as expressed ever anew. On one level, this gives rise to the paradox of all traditionary material, that is, of being one and the same and yet different. Clearly, reflection returning to a subject matter that is already underway in language-being is a return to the same. But with the ever-changing nature of our personal and social circumstances, each return is different and can be differentiated from previous returns. The principle of non-identical return within hermeneutics means that the return to a traditionary text or issue 'is no mere reproduction or repetition' but a turn to a new creation of understanding. Recursiveness is no mere repetition. It establishes those points of non-identical repetition which add to the ongoing story of a concept's becoming. Nietzsche was only partially right when he argued that linguistic means of expression are useless for expressing becoming. He should have noted that as language-beings in flux we only begin to discern ourselves in those emergent narrative patterns that participation in language-being enables. There is, of course, no conclusion to the process, only a provisional summing up, a moment of being brought to see ourselves differently.

In summary, this part of our study has argued that when practices fail, they do so because language's formal epistemological anticipation of completion is incommensurable with the ontological possibility of achieving completion within language-being. The protean paradox at the heart of practical being, as conceived by negative hermeneutics, is that whatever a given practice projects as its summative goal, that goal can be dissolved either by the contingencies of circumstance or by the excess that is language-being. And yet, the unrealizable quest for formative completion within language-being creates the conditions whereby moments of summative completion become possible. At this point, the dialectical core of negative hermeneutics shows itself. Despite its negativity, the assumption of the possibility of regulative completion drives practices towards summative reconfiguration and renewal. The constant dialectical tension between the regulative and the summative within language-being sustains understanding's movement. What drives the antinomic play between regulative and summative completion in hermeneutical reasoning is the logical instinct towards completeness within language itself. This play is no mere oscillation between language's deconstructive and constructive tendencies. In the 'floating world' of language-being, the non-identical repetitions produced by the recursive play between the summative and the regulative generate a consequentialism of unintended effects. These prompt the emergence of those ever-changing narratives through which we become discernible to ourselves. Within language-being, we are the ongoing effect of the provocative powers of our own practices. The speculative entailments within language-being allow negative hermeneutics not only to overcome metaphysical nihilism but also to confirm language-being as the ontogenetic ground of our being. In so doing, it can build trust and confidence in that which has sustained our existence. Negative hermeneutics is antithetical to those epistemologies of understanding that regard 'knowing' as a method of fixing and controlling rather than as a process of interaction and participation. If hermeneutical *praxis* is to be considered as 'way' of knowing in the broader speculative sense, the notion of 'way' must be divorced from any suggestion of a definitive method or technique. If negative hermeneutics points to a 'way of knowing' it does so because that 'way' both arises from and is a consequence of its practical involvements. The 'way of knowing' that is hermeneutical does not guide interpretation but reveals itself in the practice of interpretation.

17. Hermeneutical openness as *praxis*

There are plentiful philosophical resources within negative hermeneutics that question the epistemological credibility of *any* wisdom tradition. By definition, the systematic articulation of a given form of practice will be historically finite and subject to the conceptual limitations of its time. Furthermore, no conceptualization of a practice will be adequate to its ontological complexity. A practice will always be in excess of how it is described. Considered as a 'way of knowing', every practice presupposes and is defined by the whole that it anticipates. Though a practice may anticipate its final and ideal completion, such anticipations are far from final but are subject to constant change.

Within Gadamer's language ontology, no wisdom tradition is subject to definitive articulation. This is an unavoidable consequence of the dialectical interplay of regulative and summative completion within language-being. The more language and thought pursue regulative completion, the more they disrupt the final understanding they seek. And yet, because language-being is always in excess of any projected whole, the pursuit of regulative completion within the *Sprachswelt* also creates the conditions whereby new and unexpected forms of summative completion can emerge. Given the irresolvable tension between the regulative and the summative within the dialectic of the word, any postulation of a wisdom system is folly. D. S. Wright argues accordingly, 'Enlightenment is empty . . . no thought or experience of enlightenment is final or absolute.'[94] This invokes the prospect of nihilism but only if practices are taken to anticipate fixed, final or 'static' conceptions of enlightenment. However, from the premise that *no thought or experience of enlightenment is final or absolute, it cannot be concluded without contradiction that no form of enlightenment is possible*. The only appropriate conclusion is that whatever meaning is projected, it remains permanently open to question. Attempts at closure whether those of absolute affirmation or absolute denial always 'unwisely resist (or are blind to) the change that is always underway'.[95]

Hans Waldenfells brings Gadamer's hermeneutical orientation close to the Buddhist doctrine of 'the open-hand'.[96] Waldenfells cites a seminal passage in *Truth and Method*:

> Experience is initially always experience of negation: something is not what we supposed it to be. [. . .] The dialectic of experience has its own fulfilment not in definitive knowledge but in that openness to experience that is encouraged by experience itself.[97]

Gadamer's position does not imply an indifferent neutralism. One has to be immersed within practices and their traditions to generate the informed

---

94 Wright, *Philosophical Meditations on Zen Buddhism*, 204.
95 Ibid.
96 See Hans Waldenfels, *Absolute Nothingness, Foundations for a Buddhist-Christian Dialogue* (New York: Paulist Press, 1980), 124.
97 TM 354–5.

questioning able to open their guiding assumptions. Whatever the practice whether artistic or medical, it always remains open to the questions: 'What is it?, Why should it be pursued? and To what end?' Within open-handed practice, everything remains under review, each reformation giving rise to another conception of what that practice is and how its goods might be achieved. For such a practice there is no single way. What can be inferred from the constant reworkings of a practice is not that (static) enlightenment is impossible but rather than enlightenment is ongoing.[98] Reflective or hermeneutical practice entails a continuous awakening, a continual being reminded of the limitations of one's presuppositions. There can be no single path since the notion of what that path is or was changes with every evaluation. Whatever the path is reveals itself in the pattern of those non-identical repetitions that its constant pursuit makes apparent. This links the concept of a 'way' with *Bildung*. Neither involves a determinate set of precepts but a hermeneutical disposition or way of being. The notion of an *accomplished practitioner* develops the argument further.[99]

18. Seeing understandingly

The 'way' of hermeneutical understanding is 'to see understandingly'. This is the principal virtue which arises from the pursuit of hermeneutical practice. This practice cannot be taught as a philosophical doctrine but only acquired through reflection on the negativities of experience.[100] Negative hermeneutics emphasizes the need to articulate a mode of knowingly disposing oneself optimistically towards the inevitable negativities of practical engagement. This mode of knowing cannot be easily transposed into traditional epistemological categories which divide knowing between 'knowing that' (facts) and 'knowing how' (*techné*).

'Seeing understandingly' implies an intuitive mode of knowing which Goethe and Blake would have recognized as the ability to see both the universal in the particular and the particular in the universal. Matthiessen insists that for the Zen practitioner it is necessary to coinhabit the realms of the universal

---

98 Mark McIntosh, *Mystical Theology* (London: Blackwell, 2006), 140.
99 The reference here is in part derived from Nietzsche's notion of an accomplished nihilist: a thinker who is consciously aware of metaphysical nihilism and how to take creative advantage of it. The accomplished or affirmative nihilist has the creative strength to create meaning in spite of the fact that the world appears meaningless (see WP 585A and 585B).
100 Friedrich Nietzsche, *Beyond Good and Evil*, trans. R. Hollingdale (London: Penguin, 1973), Sec. 20.

and the particular so as to see each through the perspective of the other.[101] For negative hermeneutics it is the movement between perspectives that is primary. Understanding and experience involve constant exchange between the particular circumstances of experience and the reflective realm of concepts and subject matters which give shape and sense to how particulars are experienced. The question is how to articulate this relationship and how to demonstrate the formative importance of seeing understandingly within the humanities. The key ontological relation underpinning central to grasping the movement of particular and universal is that between linguistic being and the language-being. It is this ontological relationship which establishes the possibility of seeing understandingly and discloses how 'seeing understandingly' involves a transcendent relationship. This does not involve transcending practice but engaging with the transcendent element within practice. Gadamer insinuates this when he argues that as linguistic agents with distinct world views, we 'always come from afar and stretch into the distance. In language, the reality beyond every individual consciousness becomes visible'.[102] The objective correlative here is not an empirical world of things but language-being itself, that is, that totality of past, actual and logically possible meanings contained in language-being which transcends every individual language speaker though not speakers as a whole. Each language practitioner is connected through the language of his or her practice to the transcendent, that is, to both past configurations of meaning which inform their practice and to future unrealized configurations of meaning inherent within what their current practice anticipates.

'Seeing understandingly' (which entails the reflective subjectivity of hermeneutical consciousness) only arises when the practice from which it emerges is problematized by the negativity of experience. However, the negativity of experience is not the *non plus ultra* of negative hermeneutics. The negativity of experience is dependent on the prior application of the 'anticipation of completion' as a form of thought which seeks to render the shifting manifolds of experience intelligible. Within language-being, the *Vorgriff* establishes the phenomenological framework which conditions the formal possibility of the negativity of experience. Gadamer speaks of the negativity of experience in which 'all fore-sight is proved limited', 'where the expectation and planning of finite beings is itself shown to be all too "finite and limited," and where what is anticipated fails to comply with what is experienced'.[103] The negativity of

---

101 Peter Matthiessen, *Nine-Headed Dragon River, Zen Journals* (Boston: Shambhala, 1998).
102 TM 449.
103 TM 356, 357.

experience is evidently dependent upon the operation of the *Vorgiff* acting as the enabling form of intelligible experience, giving it shape and direction. The negativity of experience can only challenge previous projections of meaning on the basis of a prior anticipation of their possible completeness.

In the context of negative hermeneutics, the pursuit of completeness renders a practitioner's confrontation with negativity inevitable. It reveals their practice to be limited and finite but in revealing those limitations as limitations it also reveals them to be portals opening towards an infinity of other possibilities for meaning with language-being. The possibilities inherent in x+ only become apparent through the negation of those anticipated by x. This is not a theoretical insight but articulates an understanding won by negative experience. It is only through the thwarting of one's own anticipations and expectations that the possibility of other ways of thinking and being becomes a tangible rather than a theoretical option. The fact that the negativity of experience cannot be taught but only undergone emphasizes, once again, that prior participation in language-being is all important. The negativity of experience is a phenomenological demonstration of the axiom that with regard to consciousness (*Bewusstein*), language-being is always more than the anticipations and expectations of one's immediate knowing. The negativity of experience brings to light the naive limitations of practical consciousness and turns that consciousness towards what transcends it. Yet there is something more fundamental in this.

The *Vorgriff* inherent in linguistic consciousness is not just a formal precondition of the negativity of experience but also of the possibility of 'the inner historicality of experience' itself.[104] The phrase appears as an aside in the context of Gadamer's discussion of *pathos mathei*, yet it is explosive in its understated implications: it makes visible the ontogenetic capacities of negativity.[105] By providing a temporal framework for intelligible experience, the *Vorgriff* renders practices and their traditions thinkable as processes moving towards self-specifying and ever-revisable ends. This framework of temporality sets the conditions by means of which a practitioner's own sense of historicality emerges. Within language-being, the *Vorgriff* provides the phenomenological framework for a historical structuring of experiences. By projecting into existence the *wozu* and *woher* of a practice, the *Vorgiff* institutes a measure against which a practice can be perceived as unfolding, extending or deviating

---

104 TM 356.
105 Ibid.

from. By structuring experience within the temporal trajectory of a project's 'away-from-which' and 'towards-which', the *Vorgriff* establishes an a priori framework for historical knowledge and critique. Accordingly, the *Vorgriff* temporalizes understanding and provides the negativity of experience with its constitutional significance within hermeneutics. By temporalizing experience, the *Vorgriff* establishes the framework whereby negative challenges to a practice allow a practitioner's characterology to emerge. As the *pathei mathos* argument demonstrates, the negativity of experience does not just reveal a catalogue of misjudgements but also discloses the unseen dispositions underlying them. Negativity both provokes and individuates hermeneutical consciousness. It establishes the reflective space from within which 'seeing understandingly' in relation to a specific practice can emerge. Within language-being, each instance of the negativity of experience reiterates the *same* phenomenological form, that is, that sense of disorientation and frustration when projections of completion breakdown. However, each instance of negativity remains distinct arising from the particularities and circumstances of a given practice. Whereas the incommensurability in language-being between regulative and summative completion guarantees that the form of negative experience endlessly repeats itself, the occasion of each realization of negativity is always individual and infinitely variable. These variations are, however, productive. The perpetual return of failure and disappointment within a practice discloses patterns of non-identical repetition. On the emergent differences between each non-identical repetition of the same, an expanding history of a practitioner's engagement can be built. The weaknesses, wrong turns and revisions provoked by the negativity of experience not just facilitate the inner historiography of experience but also contribute to the ongoing and ever-changing formation of a practice and its tradition. When fused with the negativity of experience, Gadamer's language ontology has profoundly provocative ontogenetic consequences for unfolding the mode of being (*Dasein*) that we are. The argument supports the claim that within becoming, the *Vorgriff* establishes the experiential structures which allow for the emergence of reflective knowledge.

Before we continue to develop the notions of the 'accomplished practitioner' and 'seeing understandingly', several informative qualifications are pertinent.

1. Though its hermeneutical lessons are extensive, the negativity of experience cannot itself be taught. Its emergence presupposes prior immersion in a practice.

2. Whereas it is possible to follow a practice by dull rote and to execute its tenets unthinkingly, the 'way' of hermeneutical practice demands reflective involvement. Hermeneutical practice without the supposition of subject awareness is inconceivable: the problematization of practice challenges the learning, skill and composure of its practitioner.
3. The emergence of hermeneutical consciousness is not an isolated event but expressive of that dialectic of experience which sees the assumptions and aspirations of practices constantly challenged. The ongoing dialectic suggests that there is no continuous, no direct route to understanding and enlightenment. The notion of what 'the way' is changes and is amended with each disruption of practice. This in turn forces a difference in the way a practice's past and its anticipated future come to be grasped. The accomplished practitioner comes to discover that there is no singular 'way' of understanding to be arrived at, promoted or taught.
4. Seeing understandingly presupposes an ontology of the artwork as a continuing never-ending conversation. The accomplished practitioner has learned that the work before them is not finished but ongoing. Seeing understandingly entails perceiving a work as a living response to a set of historically perceived parameters and as an opening towards the unrealized possibilities it entails. Seeing understandingly entails perceiving a work as a continuous conversation with the received problematics of its tradition and as an anticipating of the possibilities that its tradition makes available.

An irony of the dialectic of experience is that whereas its repetitions destabilize the received *woher* and *wozu* of a practice, it consolidates the 'selfication' or style of a practitioner. Pursuing a practice entails a lot more than adopting a body of techniques or methods. It demands that the practitioner confronts their style, character and dispositions as they emerge from the recursive negativities of practical experience. Put another way, a practitioner only finds their 'way' having subjected themselves to the discipline of their chosen practice. What becomes of the practitioner only the practice will tell. There is nothing definitive in such an emergent narrative other than the growing confidence and trust of the practitioner in the lessons their practice endows. It is clear that one cannot speak of a fixed 'way'. How that practice is grasped will change as the fields of experience which form it change. Nevertheless, from an ontological point of view, continuous engagement in the vicissitudes of a practice remains ontogenetically productive. The effects of such participation reveal to the practitioner in an ongoing and ever-revisable manner the emergent character of their practical being. It is precisely the reiterations of the non-identical within the repetitions of practice which provoke the emergence of formative knowledge *within* becoming. The power of practice creates worlds which allow humans to 'step out of the river of life and take residence on the shore'.[106] Human existence (*Dasein*) is a matter of being practised. Let us now return to the related themes of the accomplished practitioner and the 'seeing understandingly'.

Whereas the naive or unreflective practitioner is subject to the singular disruptions and distresses of negative experience, the accomplished practitioner knows such negativity to be far from singular but an integral part of the processes of change and continuity that sustain a practice. The accomplished practitioner has come to know that no matter how exemplary, a work is neither final nor complete but always points to something beyond itself. 'Seeing understandingly' senses how a work is both marked by its limitations and yet by pointing to what lies beyond them transcends those limitations. This indicates that the hermeneutical axiom x is always equivalent to x+ reveals something of the nature of hermeneutical consciousness itself.

For the accomplished practitioner engaging with a subject matter is to perceive it not as something-in-itself but as a placeholder for the centripetal and centrifugal movements of understanding. Such an 'awakened' mode of seeing is a form of discernment able to see in a subject matter the simultaneity of its being as an instantiation of a particular body of concerns and an opening towards the unrealized potentials of those concerns. The accomplished practitioner has a *hermeneutical interest* in the direct expansion of the subject matters shaping their practice: they have come to know that there is always more to be known. So as not to be distracted by the individual details of a work or to be overwhelmed by its aesthetic force, the accomplished practitioner assumes a reflective way of seeing. Through experience the practitioner has come to know that what a work presents in the here and now is not all that is there to see. The accomplished practitioner always strives to see beyond the immediacy of a given work and to discern in it both what has informed it and to discern in it hints for what it has yet to reveal. 'Seeing understandingly' is not a way or method of seeing but an experientially evolved openness to the speculative dimensions of a practice which though they reach beyond the given are nevertheless always anchored in it. Seeing understandingly grasps a work both in terms of the possibilities to which it is responding and the possibilities which it opens up.

---

106 Sloterdijk, *You Must Change Your Life*, 217.

Being conversant with the subject matters of practice is always to be conversant with how they are both concretized in the singularities of experience and yet also reflect their speculative content. The accomplished practitioner has to be orientated 'to both universal and particular – to inhabit both perspectives and not be dominated by either'.[107] They are not overwhelmed by the everyday particularities of practice, striving to see beyond them though never to fully withdraw from them, intensely engaged in a practice but never subsumed by it.[108] 'Seeing understandingly' is an acquired practical virtue of hermeneutical engagement enabling the practitioner to see the ever-shifting life of the subject matters that inform their practice.

Concepts and images have abstract connotations reaching beyond everyday experience but unless such abstract elements can be embodied by a practice in a set of particular instantiations, they will fail to infuse the everyday world with sense and meaning. This renders the space of hermeneutical distanciation a space of articulation in which new possibilities for understanding arise. The accomplished practitioner is able to see the artwork as pointing to more than itself although always remaining itself. In this connection, subject matters have an infinite capacity to give sense and meaning to sensible particulars. However, unless subject matters are actualized in specific works they remain abstract and cannot be received into a practical environment. It is not just that subject matters have to be concretized in practices in order to render practical experiences intelligible but also that without such points of embodiment, practitioners lose access to the transcendent possibilities for meaning that lie beyond within these points. The accomplished practitioner sees in every given work not just a requiem for all that a tradition has brought to fruition but a portal opening out onto epiphanies of meaning yet to come. In conclusion, it might be said that the 'way of hermeneutics' approaches the transcendent through the immediacy of a practice and considers the immediacies of practice as the outcome of possibilities within the transcendent. Understanding their codependence, the accomplished practitioner inhabits both perspectives simultaneously.

Tempered by the negativity of experience and mindful of its inevitable return, the accomplished practitioner comes to recognize the positivity within the negative. The capacity of negative experience to disclose the operative presence of hidden prejudices or the suppression of alternative modes of understanding is made possible by the excess of our being which practice explores. Despite the

---

107 Matthiessen, *Nine-Headed Dragon River, Zen Journals*, 190.
108 Wright, *Philosophical Meditations on Zen Buddhism*, 194.

vicissitudes of experience, the accomplished practitioner knows that a specific line of interpretation or engagement within a practice can always be challenged. The principle of hermeneutic excess guarantees that (within language-being) things can always be otherwise. The negation of a particular interpretation does not formally negate other possible interpretations of a subject matter within language-being. That such possibilities cannot be grasped in advance does not speak against them. The 'negativity of the word' reiterates its own positivity: things can always mean more. Negativity within hermeneutical philosophy can never be absolute: there are always other possibilities. Within language-being, negative hermeneutics reveals that nihilism, as a linguistic act, always stands on an ecstatic ground, always pointing beyond itself to other possible alignments of meaning. In effect, the language ontology upon which negative hermeneutics depends dissolves the ground upon which any universal proclamation of nihilism can be made. Negative hermeneutics engenders the expectation that there is always more that can be understood.

If, logically speaking, no claim to meaning can be absolute, a new interpretation or paradigm of understanding cannot claim completeness. Despite any compelling novelty, a fresh paradigm of practice will invariably overlook some dimension of its subject matter. The language ontology of hermeneutics accordingly exhibits a dialectics of excess and lack: whilst the dialectic always anticipates more to be said, it also denies that what is said is all that can be said. Within the framework of language-being, negative hermeneutics suggests that affirmation and denial are not binary opposites but differing aspects of the same ontological relation: the act of denial anticipates more to be said whilst the act of affirmation discloses the fact that it is always limited by what has not as yet been said. In the immediate tensions of practice, the accomplished practitioner discerns the constant coming-to-be and the passing away of its past and future determinations of meaning. The immediacy of practice and what mediates it are not ontological opposites. In being committed to actual practice and in seeking to fulfil its demands, the accomplished practitioner is also committed to what transcends that practice and can make it 'more'. Yet, this commitment to transcendence is not a negation of practice. To the contrary, the transcendence of a practice's immediate concerns does not negate them but expands them. The accomplished practitioner strains to see in the visible what is not yet visible and to discern in what is said the coming to voice of what has not yet been heard.

19. Hermeneutical *praxis*

Within negative hermeneutics, hermeneutical praxis involves a deepening participation in the subject matters that guide its reflections. The negativity of experience is an experience of opening, a becoming conscious that there is more to the experience than initially supposed. Such negativity reminds the practitioner that irrespective of its performative power, a work of art always remains, hermeneutically speaking, incomplete. As an ongoing involvement with its subject matter, a work can only ever realize certain of its expressive or communicative options. Incompleteness does not necessarily imply omission or absence. Rarely do musical 'variations on a theme' exhaust their possibilities. Yet, only because of the performed variations can the presence of other unrealized possibilities be disclosed. This underscores two Gadamerian themes. First, to understand a work is not to appreciate its given truth-claim or its technical competence alone but is to see where it is going, that is, to see what its particular form of compositional reasoning opens up. To understand a work is to think with it, to sense the direction of its travel and to grasp what remains possible within it. Second, other possibilities for understanding are never just theoretical. They arise from and, indeed, are limited by the concrete circumstances of a practice and the assumptions of its enabling tradition. Both these points emphasize that the negativity of experience is dialectical. The realization that work x is incomplete entails a growing awareness that it is limited or, in other terms, x can only be grasped as x when it's seen to be superseded by x+. In such instances, x is no longer seen as an aesthetic particular but as a site of disclosure in which the movements of x+ can be discerned. *Being weathered by the negativity of experience teaches the practitioner how to see the incompleteness of a work as a gateway to seeing it more completely.* The lived experience of negation brings to the accomplished practitioner the poise of seeing understandingly. Hermeneutic *praxis* of the accomplished practitioner always looks more deeply into the immediate in order to see in it the simultaneous interplay of past and future possibilities. Hermeneutical practice embraces the paradox of detached involvement and involved detachment.

We come to the next section of our argument. The suggestion that the 'way' of hermeneutical *praxis* cannot be taught as a *techné* gives rise to questions about the complex relations between hermeneutical practice and education. Exploring these will both illuminate the nature of practical judgement within hermeneutics and emphasize the paradigmatic role of aesthetic experience as an exemplar of hermeneutical reasoning. In this respect, let us turn to the question of practical confidence and faith in practice.

For the practitioner, the negativity of experience takes many forms: becoming aware of frustrated expectancies or of being guilty of inexplicable oversights. Such negativity can prompt a crisis of confidence within a practice with a loss of certainty about what is to be done next. Solitary experiences of negativity force the practitioner into reflective mode aware of how their presuppositions have been problematized. Nietzsche shows how in the extreme case the quest for truth bites its own tail and renders itself a lie.[109] However, Nietzsche's argument does not permit a universal proclamation of nihilism which renders all practical involvement meaningless. The negativity of experience is arguably a limit experience: it reveals that a particular way of interpreting the world is untenable, not that the world itself is meaningless. Within a language ontology there are always alternatives to discredited interpretations: negation is never be absolute. Gadamer proposes that language's formal propensity towards completeness always strives to articulate new alignments of meaning that will allow a practice to 'go on' albeit differently. Though disappointed by such moments of breakdown, the accomplished practitioner knows that new modes of their practice will arise. This does not detract from the difficulties experienced in moments of crisis. The task of hermeneutical reflection remains practical: how to escape the paralysis of doubt and uncertainty and find the next steps within a challenged practice? Although hermeneutical reflection (*theoria*) is allotted this responsibility, theory cannot itself meet it. About this, Gadamer is clear. No pre-established method can guide the practitioner away from the initial bewilderment of negative experience. This brings us to an important junction in our argument. What connects the question practical judgement with hermeneutical praxis? How does a practitioner escape from the paralysis of doubt and uncertainty when their practice enters a limit situation? As we shall shortly see, answering this question will bring to culmination the pivotal issue of why overcoming nihilism is so critical to the future of hermeneutics and the humanities.

Gadamer argues that 'practical philosophy requires that we give direction to action called for by concrete situations in which we are required to chose the thing to be done: – no learning or mastered technique can spare us deliberation

---

109 Nietzsche speaks of the catastrophe slumbering in theoretical culture when it is realized that the presuppositions of science are illogical: 'a culture built on the principle of science must perish when it begins to become illogical, i.e. to turn and flee from its own consequences' (*The Birth of Tragedy* (Cambridge: Cambridge University Press, 2019), 88, Sec. 18.

and decision'.¹¹⁰ 'Practical thinking', he suggests, 'is neither a theoretical science in the style of mathematics nor an expert-know how in the sense of a knowledgable mastery of operational procedures.'¹¹¹ Are there no guidelines to assist the practitioner in finding a creative response to negativity?

When there is so much that is teachable within hermeneutics, it is almost counter-intuitive to argue that there are no guidelines to practical judgement. Established philological techniques can determine the provenance of disputed texts whilst recognized procedures can dictate the protocols of legal disputation. Such skills rest on the public transmission of established modes of expertise (*techné*). Yet the fundamental paradox of practical judgement remains: it is one thing to know techniques of interpretation in theory but quite another to know how and when to apply them. Such circumstances truly individuate a practitioner: 'we are required to choose the thing to be done; and no learned and mastered technique can spare us the task of deliberation and decision.'¹¹² The analogy between hermeneutical reasoning and aesthetic reasoning emerges once again. Though the intelligibility of artworks is dependent upon shared rule-like conventions, there are no rules governing what an artist must do when confronted with radical challenges to their practice. Just when and where to apply a technique in medical, military or artistic practice requires delicacy, discernment and judgement. Coming to such judgement is necessarily difficult, lonely, singular and singularizing. Accomplishment in practice can be defined precisely by the ability to work in a rule-like manner without guideline or rule. Acquiring the ability to act alone with confidence is a criterion of becoming an accomplished practitioner. Plainly, practical reasoning is not universalizable: its judgements always appertain only to a specific practice, its context and goals. This emphasizes the paradox of practical judgement in hermeneutics: whilst the form of its practical reasoning is universal, its judgements cannot be anything other than individual. Whereas the form of the question, 'What steps can be taken that allow a troubled practice to go on?' is universal, the answer cannot but be both individual and without precept. Given the negativity of experience, practical reasoning concerns judging what actions will allow the practitioner to proceed. However, the rhetoric of the phrase 'knowing what to do' should not confuse us.

The foregoing discussion of practical judgement suggests a misleading opposition between 'knowing' and 'not knowing' what to do, between having

---

110 Gadamer, 'Hermeneutics as Practical Philosophy', 231.
111 Ibid.
112 Ibid.

guidance for action and having none. This is a conceptual cul-de-sac for two reasons. First, in the context of negative hermeneutics, metaphysical nihilism does not culminate in annihilation. The hermeneutical ontological principle of x always equals x+ is pertinent. Within a language ontology, nihilism is always a false negative. Though an established world interpretation underpinning a practice may be rejected as illusory or false, within language-being there are always others which are plausible. Negative hermeneutics entails the expectation that there is always more to the understood than the understood. Within language-being, a practitioner caught within a limit situation can be reassured of being's promissory note: there is always more to be understood. Nihilism is in this context a false negative. Second, although, epistemologically speaking, there may be no explicit guidelines to assist in the creative transformation of negative experience, ontologically speaking, the practitioner is always guided by the unspoken entailments of tradition and its conventions. Though a practice may be critically challenged by nihilism, within language-being it never operates *ex nihilo*. Language-being grounds a practice in numerous possibilities for thinking about itself differently. Though such possibilities are often 'in plain view', custom and prejudice can obscure their presence. The emergence of a limit situation may disarm the practitioner in such a way that they may 'not know' what to do next but the hermeneutic axiom that consciousness is more being than knowing implies that in their linguistic being the practitioner is already speculatively linked to frameworks of thinking able to evaluate their practice differently. There is always more to a practitioner's knowing than their knowing is initially aware of. The question for the practitioner is twofold: how to retain faith in language-being as holding more possibilities for meaningfulness than we can presently imagine and how to solicit from language-being this excess of hidden knowing? The role of practical judgement is key.

Hermeneutic reflection never commences *ex nihilo* but arises from practical engagement in a discipline and the specific challenges it may pose. For Gadamer, 'hermeneutic reflection neither starts at a zero point and (nor) ends in infinity' (GR 28): it is ongoing. Furthermore, as a form of practical reasoning hermeneutical reflection is neither abstract nor 'theoretical' but it needs practical examples to exemplify its concerns. The pressure need for practical judgement is always contextual: it is a call for active intervention in specific non-generalizable circumstances where rule and method afford no obvious guidance. That we are rooted ontologically in the conceptual stock of language-being means that hermeneutic reflection can neither commence *ex nihilo* nor be reduced to nothing by nihilist critique. On the grounds of the principle of excess that characterizes language-being, Gadamer holds that in seeking to discover further determinations of meaning for a problematized practice, hermeneutical reflection can always return to the implicit stock of possibilities held within it. The 'speech-created' world houses such possibilities: 'thought can turn for its own instruction to this stock (of possibilities) that language has built up: [it can attend to] the logical advance work that language has done for it'.[113] All language users have access to language's conceptual and ontological endowment though none can capture it in totality. The endowment is manifest not just in individual reflection but also in the concrete objectifications of the written record and the visual image. However, this stock of possibilities lies not in the objects of cultural inheritance per se but in the unrealized possibilities (for action) they suggest. Once again, the profound importance of the humanities as the transmitter of rejuvenated possibilities of meaningfulness cannot be more strongly emphasized.

Negative hermeneutics recognizes that the facticity of human existence means that for every individual, the challenge of negativity is inescapable whether it takes the form of a natural calamity, a limit situation or an economic crisis. Negativity is constitutive of *Dasein*'s mode of being. The humanities preserve and transmit not prescriptive rules as to how to deal with the inevitable recurrence of negativity but a canonic repertoire of individual responses to the facticity and the dialectics of experience. Clearly, though, examples of survival against impossible odds on the battlefield or acts of unspeakable generosity in situations of real emergency are not universalizable. They do not provide rules of how to act in the direst of circumstances. What such responses universalize is not a precept for action but a reminder of the ever-present possibility of such action. No matter how constraining negative circumstances may seem, the inspired serendipitous intervention exemplifies how other ways of thinking and responding are always available even if initially unseen. Within language-being negativity is never annihilation. As a linguistic act within language-being, nihilism always implies the other speculative side of the meaning limit it strives to impose.[114] The creative responses of the humanities to limit situations emphasize this fundamental precept of hermeneutical thinking: even though the finitude of our understanding may initially blind us to grasping how it is always possible to think of a crisis differently, indeed, as an opening on to the unexpected.[115] Practice in both the humanities and hermeneutics exemplifies a faith in the

---

113 TM 429.
114 Wittgenstein, *Tractatus Logico-Philosophicus*, 3, Preface.
115 The Chinese term *Weijei* does not literally imply crisis and opportunity as is often claimed but it does suggest an opening on to something confidentially seen.

redemptive power of creative intervention. The ontological prioritization of possibility over the constraints of actuality and the immediate is once again emphasized. Odo Marquard picks this point up when he argues that the 'human sciences' are the main bulwark against the constraints of a single way of looking at or managing the world.

> They (the humanities) help us to emigrate from a world that is only objectified or whose story is only the story of progress and because they do this, the human sciences have to do with education – because education ensures one's capacity to emigrate.[116]

The transcendence that hermeneutics offers does not seek escape from difficult predicaments but, rather, for ways of seeing through them to possibilities they hold. Jürgen Moltmann implies that the accomplished practitioner knows that *praxis* is always in 'practical opposition to things as they are' precisely because they endeavour a creative reshaping of them.[117] Waldenfells offers a similar remark: 'to recognise what is does not mean to recognise what is just there at this moment, but to have insight into the limitations within expectation and planning'.[118]

None of these points absolves the practitioner from the necessity of coming to their own solitary judgements about next steps in limit situations. Though the humanities hold hugely instructive 'stocks' of recorded and fictional responses to human disaster and tragedy, they do not instruct by providing rule, method or case book. This is the telling paradox at the heart of all humanities education. Precisely because their emergence is unexpected and context dependent, creative responses to negativity are individual and particular. This defines their exemplary nature: they are not reducible to repeatable *techné*. Their very 'ingeniousness' discloses their unrepeatable singularity.

The nouns 'ingenuity' and 'genius' are linked by the Latin root *gignere*, to beget, to present from an innate ability. What makes this connection conceptually revealing is that the products of genius or ingenious practice are rule-like in nature but do not themselves offer any transcribable rule.[119] Paradoxically, though the

---

116 Marquard, *In Defense of the Accidental*, 102.
117 Jürgen Moltmann, *Theology of Hope* (London: SCM Press, 2002), 314.
118 Waldenfels, *Absolute Nothingness, Foundations for a Buddhist-Christian Dialogue*, 125.
119 Kant suggests, 'Fine art is the art of genius. . . . The concept of fine art, however, does not permit of the judgement upon the beauty of its product being derived from any rule that has a concept for its determining ground and that depends, consequently, on a concept of the way in which the product is possible. Consequently, fine art cannot of its own self excogitate the rule according to which it is to raise its product.' See Immanuel Kant, *Critique of Judgement* (Oxford: Oxford University Press, 2007), 137.

humanities cannot instruct by providing repeatable *techné*, they remain from an existential perspective profoundly instructive: they demonstrate that responses to crisis and negativity are indeed possible. Education in the humanities (and indeed in the history of science which holds numerous examples of ingenious responses to initial failure) is key to upholding the horizon of the possible against the constraints of the actual. However, the central question remains: how to pass from what is instructive to action itself. It is only through the risking of creative intervention that the as yet unrevealed possibilities for meaningfulness held with language-being can be induced to disclose themselves. To induce language-being to disclose its as yet unrevealed stock of possibilities demands that practices do not succumb to the challenges of negativity. If they do, the movement which is fundamental to the life of coming to understand differently is threatened. And yet, what turns the focus of hermeneutic reflection on a limit situation into a hermeneutical intervention?

One meaning of the Greek term crisis (*krisis*) implies a situation of intense difficulty in which the need for decision and intervention has become vital. And yet, as Kant well knew from the instances of moral and aesthetic reasoning, practical judgement is formal without rule or certainty. There are no fixed guidelines for action and no guarantees of a positive outcome. From the point of view of hermeneutics, however, this does not render practical judgement blind: it is always framed by the guidance of tradition. The nihilistic insistence that because practical engagement has no certainty of outcome it is meaninglessness misses the point. Practice and tradition can never offer certainty but only the likely, the well-tried and the probable. To question practical judgement for its lack of certainty undermines faith in the meaningfulness of practical action and thereby diminishes its capacity to disclose further aspects of language-being. To inhibit such disclosures is to undermine the unfolding of life's possibilities. The dialectical relation between language-being and linguistic consciousness is once again emphasized. Whereas, on the one hand, the unforeseen and the unpredictable (within language-being) can disrupt the expectations of a practice (linguistic consciousness), on the other hand, they can suddenly disclose unseen ways thinking and doing within language-being. Negation within language-being always has the capacity to provoke new meanings: negation *sive* affirmation.[120] Hermeneutical faith in the *logos* (spirit) of the word expresses a predilection of the possible over the immediate.[121]

---

120 Waldenfels, *Absolute Nothingness, Foundations for a Buddhist-Christian Dialogue*, 125.
121 Paul S. Fides, *The Promised End, Eschatology in Theology and Literature* (Oxford: Blackwells, 2000), 73.

Acting without method or rule might suggest that, epistemologically speaking, practical judgement is unknowing and unable to elucidate the reasonable ground for its action. Yet from an ontological perspective, such action is never unknowing but guided by the horizons of language-being. Given ontological priority of language-being over linguistic consciousness, confronting the demands of practical judgement implies that the practitioner already implicitly knows (can intuit) what to do. In a critical situation, the demand for the justifications of rule and method can appear as an obfuscation. For a practitioner to be guided by tradition implies a trust and confidence in the stock of 'knowledge' transmitted through that practice. This suggests that in limit situations it is language itself that guides us towards completeness and the rendering of a practice 'whole' once again. Here 'whole' does not mean achieving completion in the sense of arriving at a final outcome but a return to a practice functioning as a whole, that is, to acting with confidence and critical decisiveness so as to provoke the unfolding of further possibilities from within its being.

Gadamer is rightly sensitive to the etymological connections between being-whole, well-being, health and *holon* which in Greek implies that which is intact, undamaged, entire and complete.[122] The parallel between the ontological characterizations of illness and a disrupted practice hobbled by uncertainty and loss of confidence is striking. Illness disrupts the 'right functioning' of the organism. Becoming well or becoming whole once more 'means meeting the challenge of finding a way back from a condition of disruption to being able to take up one's work' again.[123] Making whole does not mean returning to a stable state but returning to risk, action and movement, or to knowing in Wittgenstein's phrase 'how to go on' with confidence and without rule or precedent. Wholeness in the context of a hermeneutics of practice implies a fluidity of integrated action, a functioning as a whole. For the disrupted practice the key question remains: how to return to such right and proper functioning in the light of the negativity of experience?

The question emphasizes once more the importance of maintaining the stock of knowledge that is 'the humanities' not because it embodies conservative canons of excellence but because it contains invaluable literary, historical and philosophical exemplars of practical responses to finitude and negativity. The humanities demonstrate that creative responses to dire circumstances are always possible. They exemplify the productivity not of rule or method but of

---

[122] Hans-Georg Gadamer, *The Enigma of Health* (Cambridge: Cambridge Universe Press, 1996), 88.
[123] Ibid., 40.

the unexpected, the serendipitous and the spontaneous. The argument here is won in the negative. Without this stock of knowledge, it would not be possible to see beyond immediate: an experience of negativity would be overwhelming. Consequently, any diminution of such knowledge limits the practitioner's scope in responding to the challenges of negativity. In times of crisis, the humanities embody an ever-present and critical reminder that possibility not only precedes actuality but is also capable of transforming it. Humanities practices do not instruct the practitioner but offer exemplars of how previous practitioners have wrestled with the negativity of experience. Such exemplars demonstrate how creative action always remains a possibility even in the most trying of circumstances. There is an obvious loneliness to practical judgement. The circumstances of its demands are unavoidably individual. We cannot make practical judgements for one another. All practitioners share the bond of having to act decisively without being certain about how to do so. As we have argued, in times of uncertainty acquiring the confidence to act 'unknowingly' without rule or method is crucial. Why is belief in the possibility of creative action and intervention so critical to our central argument?

That the question of action or, in Wittgenstein's phrase, 'knowing how to carry on' should become important in any debate about hermeneutical *praxis* is only to be expected. As we have seen, movement is the life of understanding. Action unfolds the possibilities for being within our *Sprachswelt*. Action enhances the becoming which is *Dasein*. Within the speech-created world, creative action provokes the disclosure of other ways of thinking capable of transforming and overcoming the negativity of experience. The question of action is related to that of nihilism in that any commitment to creative action in the absence of rule or method requires belief in the worthwhileness of what is wagered. Nihilism not only undermines the confidence necessary to risk oneself in creative action but by inhibiting such action, it undermines the very possibility of furthering hermeneutical understanding and engagement by drawing out the speculative endowments of language-being. Maintaining confidence in the worthwhileness of creative action is central to transcending the negativity of nihilism. Indeed, reflecting upon the ontological importance of action within language-being discloses the transcendental condition of hermeneutical understanding itself. This affirms, once again, the importance of the *Vorgriff der Vollendung* within our debate.

20. The transcendental conditions of hermeneutical praxis

This section contends that action (praxis) makes manifest the transcendental conditions of hermeneutical practice! Defending this contention draws us towards the culminating arguments of this chapter. It will demonstrate how the interrelated questions of understanding's movement, the nature of creative action and the organizational capacities of the *Vorgriff der Vollendung* are fundamental to any consideration of practice. To answer the question of why action is of seminal importance for any hermeneutics of action it is necessary to distinguish between those actions which stimulate and enhance the possibilities within our mode of being as a *Dasein* and those actions which disclose the transcendental conditions of hermeneutical action and understanding itself.

What we might describe as level one actions are those which stimulate and extend the movements that sustain the unfolding of understanding, namely those actions which bring us to think differently about a practice such that we are 'moved on' in our appreciation of what is in play within it. Such actions entail practical judgements stemming from creative insights which arise independently of rule and method. This demonstrates why the issue of practical confidence is so important. *Without the ability to make insightful interventions where rule and method do not apply, the continued movements of understanding would come to a halt.* Level two actions sustain the ontological structures which enable practical action in the first place. In so doing, level two actions sustain the ontological structures which allow a meaningful existence to arise. This emphasizes why overcoming the question of nihilism with its ability to dissipate the confidence to act without any formal grounds is so crucial to the possibility of creative practice as defended by negative hermeneutics. Though second-tier actions precondition the possibility of first-tier actions, crucially, first-tier actions also sustain the being of second-tier action. Any undermining of the confidence to participate in level one actions atrophies the ontological structures of level two actions which condition the very possibility of hermeneutic understanding. Since the organizational capacity of the *Vorgriff* is only triggered by its particular case applications, by undermining confidence in the meaningfulness of level one actions, nihilism corrodes the application of language's anticipatory powers of structuring on which hermeneutical experience depends. By inhibiting action, nihilism jeopardizes the fundamental ontogenetic capacities of language. Consider the following.

1. In bringing a world into being, language also brings a *way* of being into existence. Such a way of being is maintained by the actions (the creative interventions, the interpretations, projections and expectations) that keep it in motion.
2. To speak about a way of being is to speak of the practices which form a way of life. This is by default to have placed that way of being within the anticipatory structures of language which articulate its intelligible form.
3. In speaking of the *woher* and *wozu* of a practice, language announces the anticipatory forms which prestructure our grasp of a practice as hermeneutical spaces of provocation, loss and achievement. Accordingly, as events in the language world, practical judgements, creative actions and hermeneutical interventions instantiate the *Vorgriff der Vollendung* as fundamental to the possibility of hermeneutical understanding.

The anticipation of completeness establishes a 'transformational structure' rendering activities intelligible by bringing them into a space of temporal distanciation in which the pattern of their 'away from which' and 'towards which' becomes discernible. Analogous to Kant's categories of judgement, the organizational capacity of the *Vorgriff* is triggered only in and through its particular case applications. To reiterate Cassirer's point, 'we perceive the universal only within the actuality of the particular, (and) only in it can the cultural universal achieve its actualisation, its realisation as a cultural universal.'[124] It is through its application in linguistic activity and other forms of practical engagement that the form structures the complexities of experience. Practical activity is central to sustaining the capacities of this organizational form. In so doing, the *Vorgriff* instantiates what Chiurazzi calls the 'transcendental relation', a relation for which there is never an actual representation since it is only given in reference to that which it makes possible, that is, relations between representations themselves.[125] In Heideggerian terms, the *Vorgriff* temporalizes existence, allowing a *Dasein* to come to itself through the existential structures of *woher* and *wozu* that articulate its practice. The closing pages of Heidegger's *Introduction to Metaphysics* suggest that 'tasks' (practices) only unfold within

---

124 Cassirer, *The Logic of the Humanities*, 25. Insert added.
125 Gaetano Chiurazzi, *Dynamis Ontologia Dell' Incommensurable* (Milano: Edizioni Angelo Guerini, 2017), 17.

the processes of temporalization that characterize their ontological structure. It is within the constant movement between its 'no-longer-now' and its 'not-yet-now' that a practice unfolds its effective and consequential being.[126] Negative hermeneutics extends Heidegger's insight suggesting that the relation between the 'no longer' and the 'not yet' is indicative of an ontological structure rooted not so much in existence per se but in language's own ontology.[127] 'Here,' as Gadamer remarks, 'we are getting to the foundations.'[128] The *Vorgriff* that comes to being in and through language is not pregiven before language but presents itself from within language-being and cannot be thought apart from it. By creating the space of the in-between, the *Vorgriff* establishes the transcendental conditions which allow the movement of understanding to become discernible. When language emerges into being, the *Vollzug* comes forth as part of its being. The two are codependent presupposing a distinction that in actuality is 'really no distinction at all'.[129] Language and its forms come forth in a presentational act: as foundational, they show themselves. The 'word' that is 'in the beginning' (so to speak) is a performative act: it brings a form of life into being. Cassirer comments, 'the underlying forms of language *appear* and are: there is nothing more to be explained'.[130] Language and its forms announce themselves: there is no getting beyond or behind language-being to explain it. The *Vollzug* temporalizes a mode of 'being in the world' and in so doing establishes the ontological structures within which hermeneutical experience become possible. In so far as it annunciates itself through practical action, the *Vollzug* projects the foundational temporal structure within which the possibility of hermeneutical experience can arise. The ontological dependence of hermeneutical experience upon the *Vollzug* can be briefly summarized. The emergence of the *Vollzug* has the following enabling consequences:

1. *The emergence of differential space.* The act of speaking about an activity as a practice instantiates the temporal form which renders the practice intelligible as a practice, that is, it establishes its *wozu* and *woher*. This opens the differential space within which a practice can intelligibly unfold. It is in such differential distances that we live.[131]

---

126 Martin Heidegger, *Introduction to Metaphysics* (New Haven: Yale University Press, 2014), 229.
127 TM 474.
128 TM 475.
129 Ibid.
130 Cassirer, *The Logic of the Humanities*, 176.
131 Gadamer, *The Enigma of Health*, 58.

2. *Tradition and critique.* 'The anticipation of completeness' expedites a 'transformation into structure'. It renders activities intelligible by placing them in spaces of temporal distance allowing the patterns of their 'away from which' and 'towards which' to become discernible. This establishes the temporal spans within which repetition and recursion can occur. This confirms the *Vollzug* as the transcendent ground of tradition and *praxis*. Through the provocations and non-identical repetitions of negative experience, a practice evolves its sense of narrative identity. This produces a critical and revisable conception of itself. Through *praxis* and its non-identical repetitions, a pattern-seeking creature comes to discern the character and style of its engagements. The differential space between the 'where from' and the 'where to' sets the ground for normative comparison, critique and learning between practices. How does a practitioner face up to the inevitable challenges that will disrupt their ambition? What makes a particular practical life instructive is the extent to which it illuminates a response to limit situations. Without the *Vorgriff*'s projective framework, the possibility of normative comparisons between practices and traditions disappears.
3. *Meaningfulness.* The differential space established by the *Vollzug* opens a space of expectancy in which the possibility of meaningfulness can unfold. Moltmann argues, 'Meaningful action is always possible only within a horizon of expectation, otherwise all decisions and actions would be desperate thrusts into a void and would hang unintelligibly and meaninglessly in the air'.[132] Lötz makes a similar point: without the 'toward *which*' and the '*from to*' directionality of meaning constitution, a work will remain a mere collection of facts without internal coherence: 'successful seeing and successful understanding is only possible ... if we have an idea of that towards which the process would lead'.[133] 'Meaning here is both the ongoing result of (anticipatory) seeing as well as its presupposition.'[134]
4. *Action.* Though the differential space of *Vollzug* establishes the possibility of meaningfulness, it remains a space of unease since the meaning anticipated can never be fully achieved. In consequence, the horizons of meaning which arise within a tradition and its practices remain open, unresolved and ambiguous. Gadamer insists that in cases of ambiguity,

---

132 Moltmann, *Theology of Hope*, 310.
133 Lötz, *The Art of Gerhard Richter*, 44.
134 Ibid.

it is language's own drive towards the universal and the general that pushes the unquiet practitioner towards a completer grasp of the meanings underpinning her practice. In spaces of hermeneutical unease, a practitioner must risk what they already know in order to know it more completely. It is language's propensity towards the universal that draws the practitioner towards that 'something anticipated' which keeps the dialectics of experience in play. Language's formal anticipation of completion establishes the projective space in which the mode of being that we are can unfold its possibilities. Moltman observes tellingly in this respect, that meaningfulness in 'human life must be risked if it would be won'.[135] Creative action, practical involvement, self-expenditure all require horizons of anticipation which render the potential risks of such action meaningful. It is practical action that unfolds the meaningfulness that a practice entails for its practitioners. Indeed, such practical action is self-justifying. What validates it is not its correspondence to any external norm but, rather, the extent to which it achieves a new integration of insight within its grounding practice. Recursions, non-identical repetitions, the continuance of practical traditions and the narrative movement of individual and collective identities all depend on the 'fundamental' form of language's anticipatory structure.

Within language-being, the ontological consequentiality of the *Vollzug* and its differential spaces is plainly of foundational importance for negative hermeneutics. The transcendental efficacy of this form is demonstrated appropriately enough by arguments in the negative. Consider what would be lost were it not for the enabling capacities of the *Vollzug*.

1. Without its grammar of expectancy it would impossible to think of the directional nature of a practice, its where-from and its where-to.
2. Lacking such differential spaces suggests that repetition, recurrence, non-identical repetition, tradition and its critique as well as the unfolding structures of *Bildung* would not be conceivable.
3. Furthermore, without the *Vollzug*'s differential spaces, the impetus to completion that unfolds a *Dasein*'s possibilities and brings it into productive collision with other hermeneutic vectors is inconceivable.

---

135 Moltmann, *Theology of Hope*, 321.

The ontogenetic capacities of the *Vollzug* clearly sustain the ontological structures upon which action and creative intervention depend. These transcendent structures establish the preconditions for negative hermeneutics and its philosophy of openness. However, as we have argued, only through creative action can the structures which sustain such a hermeneutical ontology be upheld. Without creative interventions into the possibilities for meaning that language-being holds, hermeneutic movement and the unfolding of meaningfulness it enables are compromised. This returns us to the problem of nihilism as the main inhibitor of practical activity and its capacity to further unfolding hermeneutical understanding. To determine why nihilism and uncertainty threaten practical action we need a more precise grasp of the vulnerability of practical action to nihilism's dissipating hyperbolic doubt. At issue here is the confidence required of the practitioner to initiate creative interventions and judgements. This interlocks the questions of nihilism, uncertainty, confidence and action. In a clear but unexpected way Kant's conception of aesthetic objects as exhibiting rule-like structures without rule helps to unravel this issue.

Creative judgements and interpretations are modes of action within an artistic or hermeneutic practice. They transform our understanding of a subject matter so that we come to see it profoundly differently. Such judgements are rule-like in that they establish both how everything we once knew of a subject matter should now be grasped and how future approaches to that transformed subject matter might now be initiated. However, creative judgements in an artistic and or hermeneutic practice remain *without* rule in the sense that they can only ever be singular in their application. They are not repeatable technical judgements which can be relied on to produce the same predictable results.[136] Creative judgements and new interpretive projections are anything but predictable. They generate different, unexpected, unpredictable and unrepeatable insights. Such judgements are not made according to rule but emerge spontaneously from within the 'conversation' that constitutes them. In other words, they arise from *participation* within a practice.

Though a new reading of a subject matter may seem a clear development of the anterior logical possibilities held within the generating practice, it is impossible to predict when a new perspective will arise. Though its *post-factum* emergence may seem rule-like it remains without rule. In so far as such spontaneous irruptions establish new ways of thinking about a practice, it becomes clear why soliciting them through practical action is a principal theme in negative

---

136 cf. Kant, *Critique of Judgement*, 139.

hermeneutics. Confidence of action is vital to hermeneutical thinking. Without the confidence to act, neither will the fresh perspectives necessary for the rejuvenation of a practice be drawn out nor will the grammars of expectancy which ground the possibility of creative action become operative. Should the latter fail, both the temporal spaces requisite for the development of a practice's becoming and the emergence of narrative directions and sense-giving patterns within a practice atrophy. *In short, lack of confidence in action erodes a way of life whose sense and form are only sustained by action. Practical action upholds and perpetuates the conceptual spaces upon which its capacity to create meaningfulness depends.* As nihilism's hyperbolic doubt casts doubt on the possibility of all meaning it inhibits any willingness to face the uncertainties of action for the sake of an uncertain result. Why does nihilism undermine confidence in those ways of life which have always contributed to rendering existence meaningful?

Gadamer follows Nietzsche and Heidegger in suspecting that it is the Cartesian heritage within science that demands strict certainty for knowledge claims which erodes confidence in practical action.

> The objectifying procedures of natural science . . . attempt to become certain about entities by methodically organising its knowledge of the world. Consequently it condemns as heresy all knowledge that does not allow this kind of certainty and there cannot serve the growing domination (of the scientific outlook).[137]

The valorization of the scientific method promotes nihilism by suspending the question of meaning. Moltmann comments tersely, 'to raise the question of meaning is either to have taken a wrong turning, or else to express consciously or unconsciously a need for something other than the existing institutions.'[138] By demanding rigorous epistemological credentials for all claims to truth the traditional stocks of knowledge, established cultural practices, mythic tales and epic sagas all of which that lend colour and sense to existence are paralysed. The issue is not whether such stocks of traditional knowledge can be externally validated but whether we can have confidence in their 'truthfulness', that is, in their capacity to integrate experience as meaningful. Gadamer remarks with unusual terseness, given that language itself has always sustained our being in the world, why does that which 'has always supported us need to be grounded?'[139] This suggests that nihilism confuses two forms of certainty: 'the certainty of science

---

137 TM 476.
138 Moltmann, *Theology of Hope*, 306.
139 TM xxxvii.

is very different from the certainty acquired in life . . . Life is full of uncertainty and unpredictability but this can be surpassed with confidence won from life itself'.[140] The contrast is between a formal demand for epistemological certainty and the acceptance of life's productive uncertainties. In a formal sense, there is no determinable meaning or certainty to life and yet within that uncertainty everything we have learned to value has evolved. Everything meaningful has sustained us within that uncertainty. It is uncertainty and language's drive for completeness that opens us to the concealed possibilities of the future whereas the demand for certainty prior to any practical action stifles spontaneity, creative risk and adventure. The claims of history, tradition and art are indeed distinct from those of the sciences: they have something evidently meaningful to them (*einleuchtend*): they let something shine in.

> This concept of evidentness belongs to the tradition of rhetoric. The *eikos*, the verisimilar, the probable ('*wahrscheinliche*' 'true shining'), the 'evident', belong in a series of things that defend their rightness against the certainty of what is proved and known. [. . .] The idea (here) is always that what is evident has not been proved and is not absolutely certain, but it asserts itself by reason of its own merit within the realm of the possible and the probable.[141]

The demand for strict methodological certainty is nihilistic in that it refuses the claims of the possible and the probable within practical knowledge. The demand inhibits practical action by questioning the meaning and worth of creative intervention, discredits the stocks of traditional knowledge and practice upon which life has always depended and frustrates a practice's capacity to generate new alignments of meaning from within itself. Embarking upon creative action in the absence of rule or method requires belief and confidence in the worthwhileness of the outcome wagered. By demanding that traditional practices verify their claims to meaning as certain and verifiable truths, conventional epistemological methodologies both undermine the confidence necessary to risk oneself in creative action and question the worthwhileness of such engagement. The discrediting of traditional practices, folk tales and literatures as void of serious epistemological truth content devalues their inestimable worth as a stocks of knowledge concerning how to act in the face of the uncertainties of existence without rule or knowledge. Such literatures archive numerous examples of acting in a rule-like manner but without rule. Their ontological significance is that they both record and exemplify the

---

140 TM 238/9.
141 TM 485.

possibility of such action. Furthermore, tradition's stock of knowledge provides devices for us to rethink and respond to experiences of practical crisis in new and unexpected ways. Finding new ways 'to go on' allows the practitioner to place the doubts of metaphysical nihilism to one side and through renewed practical action restore the hermeneutical movements that both ground and excite understanding. Gadamer and Moltmann sense that a solution to the crisis of nihilism does not arise *ex nihilo* but only from a revaluation of the stocks of knowledge within tradition and language-being. This is not to return to the past but to use their images and concepts to think about present challenges differently. Maintaining that stock of knowledge against the hyperbolic doubts of nihilism is crucial to the renewal and unfolding of hermeneutical practices. However, whilst understanding the nihilistic effects of the demands of scientific methods upon the possibility of practical action is one thing, knowing how to avoid it is another. By questioning either the worthwhileness or the formal verifiability of a practice's knowledge claims, the nihilistic consequence of the demand for epistemological certainty hinders the forward motion of a practice's momentum towards its projected expectations. By hindering the unfolding of its possibilities and diminishing its chances of producing new alignments of meaningfulness, hyperbolic doubt stifles a practice's momentum towards completion.

How is the detrimental influence of nihilism upon practical reasoning in the arts and hermeneutics to be displaced? Why does theory in the form of nihilism continue to hold us in its thrall? A plausible answer lies in Gadamer's response to the question of why it is that everything that has sustained us (tradition and its practices) needs to be formally grounded? Why cannot we derive practical confidence from the fact that the ungrounded (language-being) has grounded our practices and given them momentum? Why cannot we 'trust' and have confidence in those ways of life which despite their lack of formal grounding have always contributed to rendering existence meaningful? The question returns us to a number of themes at play within our argument: summative completeness, certainty and the transition of experience's complexities into transformative structures.

Philosophical hermeneutics is marked by the idealist conviction that aesthetic judgements and insights speak to us more because of our practical involvements than because of the preferences of subjective consciousness. They emerge spontaneously from within the 'conversation' between the interactive elements of practice, its conventions, its materials and its practitioners. An emergent aesthetic response to a work may be one of many possible interpretations. With hindsight it may be seen to be a clear development of anterior logical possibilities held within a work yet it remains the case that it is impossible to predict the occasion of its emergence. As Nietzsche argues, thoughts and judgements arise when they will[142] and in Kantian terms such emergences are indeed without rule. Yet, they remain rule-like, that is, they do not arise *ex nihilo*. They emerge within a specific practice and reveal themselves to be consistent with the context they transform. Like Heidegger's notion of *Lichtung*, they throw light on the situations from which they emerge[143] and yet though without rule they show themselves to be both 'possible' and 'probable'. Yet if such insights are not a consequence of rational demonstration, in what does their possibility and probability lie? This returns us to the question of summative completeness.

A *leitmotif* of this study has been how everyday life is lived out against a background of unresolved and contradictory experiences. The very notion of the 'anticipation of completeness' as a regulative idea implies that everyday experience is open-ended and inconclusive. Yet, as our previous arguments have suggested, the power of the vital image in painting and the living word in poetry resides in their ability to reveal the possibilities for meaningful coherence laying unseen in the half-remembered and fragmentary complexes of everyday experience. This is the high point of Gadamer's reconstruction of aesthetic *mimesis*. The image is not a reconstruction of an empirically given object but a representation (a showing or a realization) of the meaningfulness that coheres as a possibility within the flux of experience. The ability of images and words to transform the fragmentary into an intelligible structure constitutes their summative power. Such images make evident the possibilities residing in incoherent experience offering a vision of the broken and fragmented rendered whole. The mimetic quality of such summative images is anticipatory: they offer a vision of what experience suggests is yet to come. The persuasive 'certainty' of such images is not subject to demonstration but is annunciated in the appearance of the images themselves. Such images render the complexities of experience thinkable. 'They introduce new relations, new reflections and a new form of the world itself by mediating the sensual presence with rationality in the universality of an image.'[144] The image shines back into experience and reveals across significant passages of time, unnoticed patterns and relations. By raising passages of experience to their

---

142   Friedrich Nietzsche, *Beyond Good and Evil* (Cambridge: Cambridge University Press, 2010), Part 1, Sec. 17.
143   Heidegger, *Being and Time*, 171.
144   Lotz, *The Art of Gerhard Richter*, 29.

summative completeness they show us in Wittgenstein's phrase, 'how to go on' within the world they reveal.

The undeniable certitude that accompanies the address of the painted image or the poetic figure reflects the fact that they address us interrogatively. The phenomenological certitude of their address indicates that *hermeneutical experience is never in the third person*. As Gadamer insists, though the content of such experiences cannot be formally proved, their evident certainty is demonstrated by reason of what they let shine in (*einleuchtend*).[145] As Keller remarks hermeneutical truth always contains an element of self-implication, a suggestion which the claim that the truth of hermeneutical experience lies in its integrative power confirms. The phenomenological certitude of such experiences reaffirms that hermeneutical insights cannot be taught: they arise in and through practical engagement with the disciplines that generate them. Such insights are applied truths: we grasp them when we grasp that they apply to us.

What endangers the hermeneutical certitude of experiences is the demand for formal verification. To question the certainty of art's address is not just to question an interpretation of the world but to stifle a whole way of 'going on'. It is to call into doubt the worthwhileness of the practices that generate the images that so forcefully address us. To question the worthwhileness of such practices and inhibit their exercise is to lead the structures that sustain those practices into atrophy. In consequence, the continuance of a way of life is jeopardized as are the conditions for achieving new modalities of its understanding. Losing the ability to act with confidence diminishes the hermeneutical interactions from which new possibilities for a way of life might arise. The most serious consequence of the negative effects of hyperbolic doubt is that the *Vollzug der Vollendung*, which temporalizes practices and generates their sense of purpose and meaningfulness, is put into abeyance. The ongoing processes of becoming, of learning and transformation which constitute the 'humanities' are jeopardized. The demand for formal certainty introduces a doubt which corrodes confidence in the worthwhileness of maintaining the forward momentum of those actions which by default renew the forms which sustain, give direction and meaning to the becoming which has emerged as a 'way of life'.

Though everything that such images render clear could logically be otherwise, it remains the case that in a contingent universe things have developed as they have. Even if existence lacks an essential meaning, by rendering the difficulties of existence meaningful, the languages of word and image have de facto sustained

---

145 TM 485.

our mode of existence without any formal grounding. To abandon that sustenance on the grounds that it lacks demonstrable epistemological certainty would disrupt the world-making capacities of such images, deprive our existence of its future possibilities and condemn our mode of being to nothingness. Negative hermeneutics substantiates Nietzsche's suspicion that the extent to which one can endure to live in a meaningless world depends on whether one can organize a small portion of it oneself.[146] If one's creative confidence is such that one can risk creative action in an uncertain world, the hyperbolic doubt of nihilism can be overcome. This underscores Keat's notion of negative capability, that is, that ability to reside within uncertainty, and doubt, accepting it but 'without (recourse to) any irritable reaching after fact and reason'.[147] To put it another way, the uncertainty with which the demand for certainty corrodes practice is displaced by the confidence of creative action. To act hermeneutically is to have confidence in the transcendent enablement of language-being, the practical traditions it enables and in the possibility of unravelling more of their inherent possibilities.

21. A post-metaphysical philosophy of practice

The solution to the problem of hyperbolic doubt lies not in refuting it but in bypassing it. The claims of practical understanding can never be vindicated by an intelligible reality beyond the grasp of our finite comprehension. We simply cannot know such an unconditional. When Gadamer claims that 'Being is language', he implies that that language-being is both 'self-presentation' and '-attestation'. Its being resides in its performative nature: it is an *Urphänomen*, it 'appears and is'. It is an 'irreducible fact', an 'absolute limit',[148] 'enclosed by nothingness'.[149] This suggests that language-being is to be conceived of as continuous becoming and withdrawing without qualification or diminishment by anything beyond it. Language-being simply exists. It is, to use Nietzsche's phrasing, 'not something that becomes, not something that passes away. Or rather: it becomes, it passes away, but it has never begun to become and never

---

146 WP 585A.
147 John Keats, *Letter to George and Tom Keats, 21(?) 27 December 1817.* cf. https://www.poetryfoundation.org/articles/69384/selections-from-keatss-letters.
148 Cassirer, *The Logic of the Humanities*, 176.
149 Friedrich Nietzsche, *The Will to Power* (London: Weidenfeld and Nicolson, 1968), Sec. 1067.

ceased from passing away'.[150] Language-being can be conceived of as a process of infinite renewal.

Language-being considered as a continuous beginning sets the foundations for negative hermeneutics as an infinite process of unfolding. First, the notion of an absolute beginning circumscribed by nothingness renders redundant any philosophical speculation about an unconditional reality. Reasoning becomes earth-bound once again, limited to exploring the nature of finite being and its endless possibilities for meaningfulness. Considered as a totality of possible meaningfulness, language-being renews its being in every moment in which one finite determination of meaning displaces another. In short, the notion of language-being as an ever-self-renewing totality of relations of meaningfulness circumscribed by nothingness delimits the worldly range and scope of negative hermeneutics. Language-being and the transcendental structure of the *Vollzug der Vollendung* are co-originates and codependents. With the word, come the beginnings concomitant with its emergence.

1. *The opening of differential space.* By bringing a world into being, language announces a way of being within in that world. Within language-being, the *Vollzug* temporalizes a mode of 'being in the world' (*Dasein*) and establishes the ontological structures within which hermeneutical experience becomes possible. The act of speaking about an activity as a practice instantiates the temporal form, which renders that practice intelligible by presupposing its *wozu* and *woher*.
2. *The beginning of the in-between.* The differential spaces in language which Gadamer refers to as the spaces of the in-between are those in which tasks, projects and narratives can unfold. The announcement of such differential space brings the space of a practice's becoming into being. The space of the in-between frames the temporality which allows a practice to develop and which conditions the possibility of all journeying and adventure within hermeneutics.
3. *Repetitious beginnings and recurrences.* The temporal span initiated by the directionality of the *Vollzug* creates the space within which repetition and recursion become possible. Through the provocations and non-identical repetitions of negative experience, a practice forges a sense of its narrative identity allowing it to establish both critical and revisable conceptions of itself. The differential space between the 'where from' and the 'where

---

150 Ibid., Sec. 1066.

to' of a practice opens the hermeneutical space allowing actions and interventions to establish their narrative character. This establishes grounds for normative comparison and learning between practices. What makes a particular practical life instructive is the extent to which it illuminates a response to limit situations. Without *Vorgriff*'s projective framework the possibility of normative comparisons between practices disappears.

4. The possibility of meaningfulness. The *Vollzug* opens a space of expectancy in which the possibility of meaningfulness can unfold within a practice. Meaningful action is enabled by a horizon of expectation which gives it both cohesive sense and direction. Lötz argues that without the 'away-from-which' and 'towards-which' of expectation, meaning constitutions would remain a mere collection of facts lacking any internal coherence: 'successful seeing and successful understanding is only possible . . . if we have an idea of that towards which the process would lead'.[151] 'Meaning [. . .] is both the ongoing result of (anticipatory) seeing as well as its presupposition.'[152]

5. *The possibility of action.* Though the differential space of the *Vollzug* establishes the possibility of meaningfulness, it remains a space of uneasiness: the regulative meanings anticipated can never be fully achieved. It is language's propensity towards the general and the universal that pushes the unquiet practitioner towards a completer grasp of their practice. Creative action, practical involvement and self-expenditure all require a horizon of anticipation within which the risks of action become meaningful and worthwhile.

Within language-being, the ontological consequentiality of the *Vollzug* is of foundational importance for negative hermeneutics. Without its grammar of expectancy, it would be impossible to think of the directional nature of a practice. The impetus to completion that unfolds *Dasein*'s possibilities and brings them into productive collision with other hermeneutic vectors would be inconceivable. *The implication is, then, that the ontogenetic capacities of the Vollzug and its grammar of expectation sustain the ontological structures upon which action and creative intervention depend.* In conclusion, it is the transcendental structure of the *Vollzug* which announces the possibility of hermeneutical life.

---

151 Lötz, *The Art of Gerhard Richter*, 44.
152 Ibid.

What have these arguments concerning the provocation of practice achieved? We have established the primacy of language-being within negative hermeneutics. Language-being emerges as a totality of meaning relations bounded by nothingness. Any attempt by reason to probe beyond the determinate nature of existence is rendered redundant. Such an amputation of the metaphysical foundations of language re-earths philosophy in actuality by insisting that it can only meaningfully engage with the infinite play of possibilities within language-being. This does not mean that negative hermeneutics becomes a hermeneutics of loss. To the contrary, as it circumscribes us within a philosophical framework which prioritizes possibility over being, negative hermeneutics assumes a posture of a perpetual openness towards the future possibilities within language-being. The ontology of excess characteristic of language-being allows negative hermeneutics to become a hermeneutics of infinite increase. From the perspective of finite linguistic consciousness, it might be argued that the *Vollzug* only leads procedurally to an eternal recurrence of the same, that is, the repeated failure of practices to complete and realize their formal expectancies. As the impetus to regulative completion, the *Vollzug* is always self-postponing. It can never complete itself. Yet the eternal recurrence of hermeneutical failure neither renders our existence meaningless nor does it render us completely unavailable to ourselves.

A meaningful existence has never depended upon securing a indubitable ground for its claims to meaning and identity. Even if there were such 'absolute ground' we could not know it as all our knowing is relational. As all knowing is finite, a meaningful existence has always depended on ever-shifting and revisable platforms of contingent meaning. It is the transience of these platforms that renders them useful. They can both be amended according to the demands of existential circumstance and expand the perspectives through which we view ourselves. Narrative frameworks are always subject to disruption by unexpected collisions between different hermeneutic vectors. Yet these collisions also enable the emergence of new and unexpected alignments of meaningfulness. Any unchanging essence would be beyond the grasp of our finite understanding whereas existing amongst a multiplication of contingent fields of meaning renders us more discernible to ourselves. Precisely because we are forever moving between such fields, the serendipitous and aleatoric initiation of chance beginnings gives our existence unexpected shape and direction. For beings whose knowing is finite and relational, the serendipitous and the aleatoric have a much underrated status. Both are capable of disclosing what is at play within language-being. A practice's ability to map and stabilize disruptions and differences within new alignments of meaningfulness establishes self-referential continuities with former renditions of itself. The power of practice to create such platforms allows humans to 'step out of the river of life and take residence on the shore'[153] establishing an existence beyond the momentary. Creative responses to the negativity of experience are instrumental to the formation, continuance and transformation of the 'form of life' (*Bildung*) that we are. Whoever has language 'has' the world and if that world has neither beginning nor end, there is no end to the narratives which shape and give sense to our existence. Through conversation and practical exchange, we encounter the mystery that we are. This implies that when we engage in conversation and are inclined to listen acutely to its twists and turns not to discern what we could never hear (the final word) but to catch a sound of 'the living word', that is, that phrase or remark which quite spontaneously lights up and makes summative sense of some of the concerns shaping the narrative of our existence. This shines some light on Wittgenstein's remark in the *Tractatus* that 'there are those for whom after a long period of doubt the sense of life became clear to them (and) have then been unable to say what constituted that sense'.[154] The 'living word' is not a final word in which all difficulties are resolved. It is not a statement or proposition but a poetic word or image which gives sense and shape to experience's many contradictions. It is a 'living word' precisely because it gives a recognizable sense to the intricacies of our practical and experiential engagements. The living word is a moment of summative understanding which discloses itself to us. This brings us to the creative paradox at the heart of negative hermeneutics.

At the heart of negative hermeneutics is the insight that what language-being takes away (the possibility of a final word), the eternal play of language gives back but in the form of the summative or living word. Though finite and precarious, such summative moments form patterns of relations which are entirely the product of our being in the speech-created world. The episodic revelations of summative meaning enabled by the 'living word' lose their randomness when over time they establish a discernible pattern or narrative. As language-beings in flux, we only start to discern ourselves in the emergent narrative patterns that our participation in the practices of language-being provokes. There is, of course, no conclusion, only a provisional summing up, a moment in the continuing conversation that brings us to see ourselves differently. Because of language-being, words tell and promise more than we can ever say of ourselves. Perhaps, this is why are so easily drawn into conversation. We sense in its

---

153 Sloterdijk, *You Must Change Your Life*, 217.
154 Wittgenstein, *Tractatus Logico-Philosophicus*, Sec. 6.521.

converse the approach of a future self capable of addressing us and revealing to us what we are presently becoming. What we are and have yet to become are both the achievement and provocation of practice. The maintenance and extension of our life form, the perpetuation of its movement and the unfolding of its future possibilities are entirely dependent upon embracing the risks and uncertainties of hermeneutical action. But why is maintaining belief in the possibility of creative action so critical?

By demanding formal certainty where none can be given and by questioning the worthwhileness of any creative intervention, nihilism threatens a cessation of action within language-being. This undermines the projected anticipations of the *Vollzug* which give shape and purpose to any action. As a consequence, life begins to lose its sense of futurity and elected purpose. Once again, the pivotal importance of retaining confidence in the possibility of creative activity despite the challenges of negativity is emphasized. Life's enervating sense of being open to future possibilities is dependent upon the anticipations of completeness inherent in the *Vollzug*'s structuring of experience. Given the ontological codependence of both action and *Vollzug*, any diminishment of action will weaken a practitioner's sense of futurity. By undermining confidence in the worthwhileness of creative action, nihilism undermines the conditions upon which life's sense of a meaningful future depends.

Ontologically speaking, creative action sustains hermeneutical being. Not only does it galvanize a practice in pursuing its projections but those pursuits generate serendipitous collisions of meaning prompting further unexpected realignments of meaning. Within language-being, the ability to act 'without rule' requires confidence in the likely worthwhileness of the action. Even though one might not know the current direction of one's practice, continued risk and experiment can be justified by the excess of meaning in language-being. The need to maintain a sense of future worthwhileness makes evident why rebutting nihilism's corrosive power is critical to sustaining the possibility of creative insight. By inducing doubt over the meaningfulness of *any* creative action, language-being is itself diminished and life's possibilities impoverished. The conditions sustaining the continued growth and expansion of hermeneutical being are jeopardized.

It is easy to challenge nihilism's metaphysical claim about the absence of universal meaning but more difficult to overcome the sense of uncertainty and lack of confidence that it plays on. A finite mind cannot stand outside language-being in order to determine whether the practices it enables are ultimately worthwhile. In this respect, negative hermeneutics shares with nihilism a profoundly anti-metaphysical stance: both descry belief in intelligible essences beyond the horizons of the finite. However, whereas nihilism regards the negation of intelligible essences as an epistemological loss depriving life of its supposed intelligible ground, negative hermeneutics values such negation as life-affirming. For negative hermeneutics, the grounds of meaningfulness lie not in any 'beyond' but in the cumulative non-identical repetitions of changing experience. Within language-being, negation can never be absolute. Language's surplus of meaning always implies that within a practice there is always more to be understood. Negation always offers an invitation to become open to other modes interpretation. That there is no certainty of outcome for a creative intervention does not imply that it should not be embarked upon. For negative hermeneutics, all those things which have added colour, sense and direction to existence (tradition, language and cultural practice) can and never will be rendered epistemologically certain. Despite their lack of a formal ground, to erode practical confidence in their creative capacity is to undermine sources of potential meaningfulness and to weaken the movement of hermeneutical life itself. However, once nihilism's theoretical underpinning is undone, there is no longer any reason not to wager a creative intervention. It is only through such action that the excess of meanings within language-being can be provoked and determine a response to the negativities of experience.

What makes existence compelling for finite beings is not certainty but the confidence to extend the continuous movement of meaningfulness within language-being. The challenge for hermeneutical practices is to maintain that movement despite the negativity of experience. Yet although the surplus of unrealized alignments of meaning within language-being suggests that creative experimentation has every chance of success, there can be no formal certainty of outcome. Indeed, uncertainty of outcome is generic to creativity: it demands the confidence to act unaided in the face of uncertainty.

The uncertainty of the creative act or interpretive wager is emphasized by the Kantian argument that the production of a transformative artwork is not governed by the following of rules. The creative judgement is not a matter of *techné*: it does not adopt established procedures to achieve pre-envisioned and repeatable outcomes. Negative hermeneutics adapts Kant's claim that creativity is rule-like but fundamentally without rule. If the generation of an artwork were simply a matter of obeying pre-established rules, creative practice would forfeit its creativity and entail endless repetitions of sameness. From a hermeneutic perspective, what makes an artwork truly singular is not an essential aesthetic property but the fact that its disruptive emergence within a practical tradition forces us to see that tradition in profoundly different ways. The vitality of a practical tradition does not rest on any repetition of sameness but upon continuities of creative disruption. The ontological relation between an artwork and its enabling tradition is clearly dialectical.

Of course, no artwork emerges independently of its enabling conditions. Insofar as it reflects the *conventions* of its sustaining tradition, it is 'rule-like'. And yet, no practical tradition can be sustained unless the work it enables functions independently. Paradoxically, then, for a work to bring rejuvenating differences to its grounding tradition, it also has to operate 'without rule'. A creative work has to have the capacity to transform its enabling conditions in such a way that those conditions can no longer be seen in the same way. The future being of a tradition is paradoxically dependent upon continuities of disruption that are 'without rule'. Yet these disruptions are possible only if the practitioner has the confidence to operate without clear rules or instructions.

What sustains such confidence in the face of uncertainty? First, the principle of excess within language-being suggests that no matter how demoralizing the challenges of negativity, there are always logical alternatives to interpretations though they may not be easily discerned. Second, previous experiences of overcoming of practical crises give plausible reason to be optimistic about the arrival of new insights. Third, the experienced practitioner knows how continued willingness to face up to negativity creates the circumstances in which new insight might arise. Given the excess of meaning within language-being, it is not at all unreasonable to wager on the possibility of arriving at new aspects of a practice. Should creative confidence be stifled, however, no creative wager will be made and a possibility for transforming hermeneutical understanding will be lost. Nihilism will have succeeded. How, then, in the face of negativity, unknowingness and uncertainty can the practitioner remain disposed to creative efforts to rejuvenate their practice?

It is a question of trusting both the transcendent possibilities inherent in one's practice and that continued activity in that practice will induce their disclosure. The transformative insight emerges from within the auto-poetic spaces of the tradition in which the practitioner participates. Participation maintains the ontogenetic capabilities of a practice to summon such disclosures. This emphasizes the consequentiality of Gadamer's ontologization of the dialogical.

Negative hermeneutics does not limit its treatment of the dialogical solely to matters of conversational exchange. It is not the 'exchange' of meanings per se that matters here but what comes to mind as an unplanned and unexpected consequence of already participating in such exchanges. What is at issue is what arises from the complex ontological interactions between language-being, tradition and practice that the dialogical facilitates. All three elements are ontologically codependent. Language-being maintains its being through the multiple linguistic and cultural traditions it sustains whilst communicative practices are dependent on the traditions housed within language-being itself. As has been argued, the precepts, vocabularies and terminologies of practice and tradition are speculative in that they reach out to frameworks of meaning which transcend their operating assumptions. However, precisely because these precepts are language based, their meaning is porous and vulnerable to being disrupted by practices which accord those same terms with a different sense. This insures that the relations between language-being, tradition and practice are held within a dialectical reciprocity allowing a change of meanings in one practice to alter the understanding of that term in another. The dialogical facilitates hermeneutical events that extend far beyond questions of meaning exchange. This emphasizes the importance of maintaining the conceptual and linguistic endowments of the humanities.

It is not a matter of conserving these disciplines per se but of preserving the future potentialities for transformative understanding they hold. This confirms that dialogical activity is a principal ontological catalyst for inducing unexpected alignments of meaningfulness to emerge. The genius of the dialogical whether verbal or visual is that a chance remark or the sudden discovery of an unfamiliar cultural perspective can provoke the emergence of a fresh orientation towards a problematized subject matter. Such words and images address us because in their 'transformation into structure' we recognize an illuminating alignment of meaningfulness, which our anticipations of completeness have vaguely sensed but not concretized. Though we are, in effect, already primed to recognize such transformations the emergent 'image' or 'word' does not add to a pre-existent body of knowledge but, rather, transforms how the practice which generated it is understood. Though there is no certainty of outcome, the reinvention of a practice's possibilities and the sustaining of its 'becoming' depends on practitioners maintaining their confidence to act.

The foregoing arguments betray a certain Nietzschean inflection. Maintaining the confidence to act creatively in a metaphysically meaningless world requires renouncing formal belief in truth and certainty for it is this belief which devalues contingent hermeneutical practices though they have given existence its sense of futurity.¹⁵⁵ If, however, it is the finite and contingent outlooks of practice which have given structure to our being, the question of the existence or non-existence of truth and certainty becomes irrelevant. This reflects Nietzsche's call to 'remain true to the earth'¹⁵⁶ and reinvokes Keat's notion of negative capability, that ability to reside within uncertainty, mystery and doubt, accepting it 'without (recourse to) any irritable reaching after fact and reason'.¹⁵⁷

Though negative hermeneutics does not offer an analysis of how epiphanic insights assert their presence in dialogue, it provides clear and compelling phenomenological descriptions of their ability to transform complexities of negative experience into intelligible structures allowing a practice to continue in its unfolding. Reticence about providing anything more than a phenomenological description is philosophically tactful. Attempting more would entail transcending language-being in the vain hope of gaining an overview of its activities. Yet, as Wilhelm Humboldt well understood, stepping outside language-being would only mean stepping into another of its circles.¹⁵⁸ This implies that the only way to understand a discursive system is to understand it from the inside, that is, to understand how it achieves the transformative effects that address us so directly. It is evident that images and words do 'speak' directly to us and that continued participation in language-being facilitates such events.

We argued in Chapter 4 that it is possible to understand the poetics of such emergent truths and to show that their hermeneutical justification is far from arbitrary. Their 'truth' is made evident by their work of integration, by unfolding a practice's possibilities in unexpected but coherent ways. All this is the achievement of language. Epistemologically speaking, there is nothing more to be said: this is simply what language does. Yet, insofar as such insights occur within language-being there is always more to be said. Negative hermeneutics is constrained and sustained by the negative. Though there can be no exhaustive understanding of the workings of negative hermeneutics, such negativity remains dialectically sustaining. For a finite mind a more exhaustive (though never complete) understanding of the ways of negative hermeneutics is always possible. Yet, that possibility can be kept open only so long as practices remains creatively active. For this to be possible, theory's demand for strict certainty has

---

155 Friedrich Nietzsche, 'Do not believe those who speak of superterrestrial hopes. They are poisoners whether they know it or nor', *Thus Spake Zarathustra* (London: Penguin Books, 1969), Part 1, Sec. 3.
156 Ibid.
157 Keats, *Letter to George and Tom Keats, 21(?) 27 December 1817.*
158 See William Outhwaite – '*Cherche pas à Comprendre:* Cosmopolitan Hermeneutics in Difficult Times', an essay in the as yet unpublished volume L'ubomir Dunaj and Kurt C. M. Mertel, eds, *Hans-Herbert Kögler's Critical Hermeneutics* (London: Bloomsbury, 2021), 348–80.

to be renounced as both unwarranted and detrimental to life. It is as Nietzsche, Rosenzweig and Wittgenstein suspected, the metaphysical demand for certainty and truth which needlessly denigrates the contingent cultural practices that have sustained our mode of life. The possibility of transformative insight remains so long as the confidence to act within the practices that generate it can be upheld. If that confidence can be sustained the continued movement of hermeneutical understanding and the unfolding of its attendant existential possibilities can be affirmed and in consequence the gnawing doubts of nihilism displaced. With the insight that uncertainty in the form of tradition has sustained every practice, any reason to distrust such uncertainty simply dissolves.

Negative capability is inherent within language-being itself. Indeed, language-being is sustained by its inherent negative capabilities. Language-being has an infinite capacity for new alignments of meaning and it is negativity that draws these possibilities out. Given that language-being is a vast network of shifting linguistic alignments each structured by the anticipations of their *Vollzug*, both negation and displacement and the restructuring they inspire are a constant feature of its being. The search for completion will necessarily destabilize a practice but, at the same, time stimulate the conditions of its renewal. This suggests that the negative capabilities of language and the unsettling provocative languages of practice sustain language-being itself.

22. Summative thoughts

As we draw our reflections on hermeneutics, practice and negativity to a close, what can be concluded? Here we face another paradox. If our arguments are to remain consistent with the *Sprachsontologie* that circumscribes their operation, there is no final conclusion to be arrived at; there is no objective co-relative beyond language-being that can validate any conclusions arrived at within it. Rather, what we encounter in this paradox is a decisive fissure between different modes of philosophical analysis, between those which look to external metaphysical notions of truth and certainty to justify their claims and those which are content to ground their claims in the criteria of justification established by the practices that generate them. Though it seems paradoxical to conclude that no final conclusion is possible for our reflections, such a claim is consistent with the mode of hermeneutical reasoning that encompasses this chapter. This chapter must remain open to a scrupulous rethinking of what can only be its provisional outcomes. Only then can such outcomes become 'hermeneutical' in as far as exposing their limitations allows them to 'become more'. In the context of the all-enveloping horizon of language-being, hermeneutical inconclusiveness is not a weakness but an opening to further insight and learning. Neither is such inconclusiveness an excuse for hermeneutical indecisiveness regarding the precarious nature of creative intervention within a practice. The issue is not just that any final conclusion would halt the movement of thought upon which the unfolding of understanding depends but also that it would incapacitate the fundamental *woher* and *wozu* of any hermeneutical judgement. Hermeneutical reflection is not only dependent upon these temporal projections entailed in its judgements but it is also subject to them. Firstly, on the *woher* of philosophical hermeneutics.

The pivotal ontological notion of language-being in philosophical hermeneutics is anchored in a doctrine of concerning the radical finitude of all understanding, an orientation of thinking that derives primarily from Rosenzweig and Heidegger. It is this doctrine that formally debars philosophical hermeneutics from achieving any final position. In this respect, philosophical hermeneutics extends the amputation of metaphysical doctrines of Being, truth and essence carried out by Nietzsche. Once these notions are exposed as the philosophical errors they are, access to the metaphysical certainties of idealist and rationalist thought is closed. In consequence language-being is affirmed as the only all-circumscribing and unbreachable horizon of understanding. Any passage to intelligible worlds beyond language is cut off. In consequence, philosophy assumes for Rosenzweig a primarily narrative structure, unfolding what is *already* contained within our language horizon. Heidegger likewise argues that philosophy becomes a 'hermeneutic' opening (interpretation) of what is already given in our ontic understanding (*Verstehen*) of *Dasein*. For Wittgenstein too philosophy entails a radical abandonment of metaphysics in favour of a deep meditation upon the limits of those language games that circumscribe existence. The dialogical conception of *Sprachlichkeit* which dominates the *wozu* of Gadamer's language ontology gives clear expression to the radical finitude of all existence within which it is said. As creatures of language we are irrevocably circumscribed by its being: there is simply no getting beyond or behind it. *All doctrines of metaphysical transcendence are negated and are to be abandoned as nihilistic and world alienating.* As was argued in the introduction of this chapter, negative hermeneutics entails an affirmative *Ja-sagen,* a 'saying-yes' to the complexities of experience and the opportunities for growth they offer. If every aspect of our being is circumscribed by language, there is no possibility of transcending its horizon to comprehend language-being as a whole. No definitive conclusion is possible. This implies as suggested that the deconstructive critique of hermeneutics is flawed in its view that such inconclusiveness is indicative of a failure. To the contrary, negative hermeneutics affirms that hermeneutical reasoning has an infinite capacity to extend our perspectival knowledge of subject matters. *Being within a practice means that there can be no final judgements, only better ones.* This emphatically confirms the importance of maintaining the stock of knowledge that is the humanities. Though it is impossible to exhaust the perspectives they explicitly and implicitly contain, they remain an inexhaustible resource for extending the possibilities for understanding. The movement of hermeneutical reflection is key to unfolding their potential for new perspectives of understanding. Here, within the all-encompassing character of language-being, Iris Murdoch's remark that 'one seeks clarification by moving concepts around' gains a certain poignancy.[159] One comes to understand more of language-being and what it contains not by transcending it but by achieving new summative perspectives *within* it. Murdoch suggests that philosophical progress is often made when different descriptions of a problem are attempted. Though philosophical hermeneutics eschews the possibility of transcendence beyond language-being, it affirms its possibility *within* language-being. This is not a matter of a new perspective displacing an established one but, rather, one in which, as Gadamer puts it, 'the new object' (perspective) is 'seen to contain the truth about the old one'.[160] Negative hermeneutics articulates this point poignantly. It affirms the infinite number of finite permutations of meaningfulness within language-being and rejects any idea that such understandings are limited because of being in juxtaposition to a fictional infinity beyond its grasp. In pointing beyond itself, linguistic meaningfulness does not point to something outside language but to other alignments of significance within language-being. Negative hermeneutics involves an affirmation, a saying yes to existence and its possibilities. Grounded in the transcendent movements within language-being, every development of an expressive form changes the parameters of what we think is possible within it. Possibilities extend as the form extends. What we think of as possible opens further unimagined possibilities. Negative hermeneutics implies that we have seriously misunderstood the requirement for certainty in hermeneutic practices: there is no underlying foundation or objective correlative that can legitimate their claims. Here the *woher* of philosophical hermeneutics – its grounding in the radical finitude of understanding – begins to anticipate its philosophical

---

159 Iris Murdoch, *Metaphysics as a Guide to Morals* (London: Penguin, 1992), 332.
160 TM 354.

wozu, namely a way of life that is positively embraced as synonymous with an affirmation of the infinite possibilities for summative understanding within finite being.

What the ontological structure of philosophical hermeneutics anticipates is a negative hermeneutics that eschews any appeal to metaphysical forms, intelligible truths or unchanging essences. For negative hermeneutics hermeneutical truth concerns above all matters of experiential integration within a practice. Such truths are not legitimized by the alleged certainties of rational method which stand outside the practices that generate them. Negative hermeneutics emphatically affirms the contingent and finite since it is in the infinite extent of their movements that understanding continually extends and renews itself. Negative hermeneutics anticipates a 'way of life' yet to come that has sufficient confidence in the transformative capacities of its creative practices that it can to renounce any need to seek external epistemological justification for their insights.

Philosophical hermeneutics, however, is clearly marked by traditional discourses about methodological legitimations and certainty. In this respect, it continues to be marked by a metaphysics of uncertainty. In contrast, negative hermeneutics articulates a conviction that though implied by the language ontology of philosophical hermeneutics Gadamer never articulates fully, namely that it in relation to their insistence upon formal certainty, the dogmatic demands of both religious metaphysics and rationalist method have historically much to answer for. Like philosophical hermeneutics, negative hermeneutics grasps that because of the radical finitude of our understanding, the demand for indubitable truth in religion and science is unrealizable. Both hermeneutical positions reject the metaphysical suppositions inherent in nihilism's denial of truth and meaning. The two positions imply that the impossible demand for epistemological certainty and nihilism's denial of attainable meaning are strange bed fellows: both render us uncertain about the legitimacy and worthwhileness of our practical actions. Such uncertainty is dehabilitating as it inhibits the practical involvement upon which the transformation of understanding depends. However, negative hermeneutics surpasses philosophical hermeneutics in its full embrace of an anti-metaphysical language ontology that renders both the demand for epistemological certainty beyond our practices and nihilism's scepticism about meaning meaningless. There simply is no reason to heed their demands. Once their claims are set aside, the illusory demand for certainty in science and religion which is responsible for alienating us from the contingencies of actuality can be renounced. With that renunciation, there is no longer any reason not to trust the uncertain and the finite since in the form of tradition they have always enabled, served and sustained our practices. Put another way, negative hermeneutics draws a strong distinction between formal epistemological certainty and practical certitude and insists that the two should not be confused. Epistemological certainty within *Sprachlichkeit* is an unattainable fiction. On the other hand, certitude in practice although metaphysically foundationless is grounded on the summative insights, expanding skills and wisdom of continuous practical engagement. Certitude in practice is key. Of course, certitude in practice lacks the certainty of being grounded in formal epistemological foundations. Yet, here, lies a fateful misunderstanding. Certainty and certitude are not to be confused. That the contingencies of practical certitude lack the formal grounding of epistemological certainty is no reason to undermine the meaningfulness and worthwhile nature of practical engagement. The demands of epistemological certainty and the scepticism of nihilism both dissipate confidence in practical action. We can neither transcend the language world to test the claims to truth made within it nor can we believe in the worthwhileness of our practices action if we adhere to the nihilist tenet that existence has no intelligible meaning. And yet, both the hermeneutical truth and the meaningfulness of our actions have never depended upon their being legitimized by authorities external to the practices that give rise to them. Against this negative hermeneutics anticipates a way of life confident enough to set to one side the demand made upon the claims to truth made by our practices for verifiable certainty and confirmable meaning. Such a way of life grasps that there is no longer any reason for confidence in our practical actions to be blighted by the metaphysics of uncertainty which arises as a consequence of disillusion with the formal criteria for certainty and truth laid down by scientific methodology and religious conviction. Negative hermeneutics postulates a way of life that no longer feels that the claims to hermeneutical truth made by its practices are missing something because they cannot be confirmed by universal criteria of epistemological certainty. Negative hermeneutics is emphatically a life-affirming outlook which celebrates the infinite possibilities for meaningfulness within the finitudes of existence. It grasps that the demands for formal certainty corrode the personal certitudes of practice and that such demands are nihilistic in that they question the worthwhileness and meaningfulness of finite understanding. Tradition is built upon such formal uncertainty. The claim for certainty is nihilistic in that it universally corrodes confidence in the certitudes of practice which have shaped our localized sense of a meaningful and worthwhile existence. Abandoning the formal demand for certainty in hermeneutical and creative practices frees them from the metaphysics of uncertainty which has for so long undermined the certitudes of practice and their particular claims to truth. There is no definitive conclusion here, only a shift of perspective effected by a change of understanding. The metaphysics of uncertainty which has for so long haunted hermeneutical and humanities practices can only be displaced by maintaining trust in the evolving certitudes of practice and their ability to transform our understanding of existence. Such certitudes, their worthwhileness and their meaningfulness are upheld by continuous creative and practical action whose transformative historical effects are often incalculable. In summary, negative hermeneutics anticipates a way of life that is no longer haunted by the supposed metaphysical certainties that lead us to doubt the certitude of our hermeneutical practices. It senses a way of life that no longer experiences the death of God, of truth and the disappearance of foundations as a loss. The passing of such illusions enables us to able celebrate finitude, limit and negation as the condition of endless learning and the continuous transformation of understanding within our practices. Embracing such 'negative capability' affirms negative hermeneutics as a continuous dialectic of experience whose non-identical repetitions establish the cognitive content of our unsettled practices.

Bibliography

Primary Sources

German

Gadamer, Hans-George, *Gedicht und Gespräche*, Hamburg: Insel Verlag, 1990.

Gadamer, Hans-George, *Gesammelte Werke*, Tübingen: Mohr Siebeck, Uni-Taschenbücher, 1987.

Gadamer, Hans-Georg, *Hermeneutik-Asthetik-Praktische Philosophie: Hans-Georg Gadamer im Gespräche*, Heidelberg: C. Wiener Universitäts Verlag, 1993, rev. 1994.

Gadamer, Hans-Georg, *Hermeneutische Entwürfe, Vorträge und Aufsätze*, Tübingen: Mohr Siebeck, 2000.

Gadamer, Hans-Georg, *Kunst als Aussage, Gesammelte Werke*, Band 8, Tübingen: Mohr Siebeck, 1993.

Gadamer, Hans-Georg, *Wahrheit und Methode*, Tübingen: J. C. B. Mohr, 1960.

English

Gadamer, Hans-Georg, *Literature and Philosophy in Dialogue: Essays in German Literary Theory*, translated by R. H. Paslick, Albany, NY: State University of New York Press, 1994.

Gadamer, Hans-Georg, *On Education, Poetry and History: Applied Hermeneutics*, edited by D. Misgeld and G. Nicholson, Albany, NY: State University of New York Press, 1992.

Gadamer, Hans-Georg, *Philosophical Hermeneutics*, translated by David E. Linge, Berkeley, CA: University of California Press, 1976.

Gadamer, Hans-Georg, *The Gadamer Reader*, edited by R. E. Palmer, Evanston, IL: Northwestern University Press, 2007.

Gadamer, Hans-Georg, *The Relevance of the Beautiful*, London: Cambridge University Press, 1986.

Gadamer, Hans-Georg, *Truth and Method*, edited and translated by Joel Weinsheimer, London: Sheed and Ward, 1989.

Secondary Sources

Adorno, Theodor, *Aesthetic Theory*, London: Routledge and Kegan Paul, 1984.
Adorno, Theodor, *Hegel: Three Studies*, Cambridge, MA: MIT Press, 1993.
Andrews, Ian, *Chance, Phenomenology and Aesthetics, Heidegger, Derrida and Contingency in Twentieth-Century Art*, London: Bloomsbury, 2021.
Aristotle, *Ethics*, edited by J. A. K. Thomson, London: Penguin, 1975.
Arthos, John, *The Inner Word in Gadamer's Hermeneutics*, Notre Dame, IN: University of Indiana Press, 2009.
Bauman, Zygmund and Rein Raud, *Practices of Selfhood*, London: Polity, 2015.
Bloch, Ernst, *The Principle of Hope*, Vol. 1, translated by N. Plaice, Oxford: Blackwell, 1986.
Bloch, Ernst, *The Spirit of Utopia*, Stanford, CA: Stanford University Press, 2000.
Brown, Nahum, *Contemporary Debates in Negative Theology*, London: Palgrave/Macmillan, 2017.
Bruns, Gerald, 'The Hermeneutical Anarchist: Phronesis, Rhetoric and the Experience of Art', in *Gadamer's Century: Essays in Honor of Hans-Georg Gadamer*, edited by Jeff Malpas, Ulrich Arnswald, and Jens Kertscher, 45–76. Cambridge, MA: MIT Press, 2002.
Caputo, John, *Hermeneutics, Facts and Interpretation in the Age of Information*, London: Pelican, 2018.
Caputo, John, ed., *The Religious*, London: Blackwell, 2002.
Caputo, John, *Truth, The Search for Wisdom in the Postmodern Age*, London: Penguin-Random House, 2016.
Carman, Taylor, *Heidegger's Analytic, Interpretation, Discourse and Authenticity in Being and Time*, Cambridge: Cambridge University Press, 2007.
Cassirer, Ernst, *The Logic of the Humanities*, Clinton, CT: Yale University Press, 1974.
Chiurazzi, Gaetano, *The Experience of Truth*, Albany: State University of New York Press, 2014.
Clark, Timothy, *The Poetics of Singularity*, Edinburgh: Edinburgh University Press, 2005.
Collingwood, R. J., *The Idea of History*, London: Oxford University Press, 1970.
Collini, Stefan, *Speaking of Universities*, London: Long Verso, 2017.
Collini, Stefan, *What Are Universities For?* London: Penguin, 2012.
Danto, A. C., *The Transformation of the Commonplace*, Cambridge MA: Harvard University Press, 1981.
Davey, Nicholas, 'Displacing Hermeneutics with the Hermeneutical', *Duesquesne Journal of Phenomenology* 1, no. 1 (2020): 17, Article 6.
Davey, Nicholas, 'Experience, Its Edges and Beyond', *Open Philosophy* 2, no. 1 (2020): 229–331.
Davey, Nicholas, 'Gadamer's Aesthetics', in *The Stanford Encyclopedia of Philosophy*, (2007). http://plato.stanford.edu./entries/gadamer-aesthetics/.

Davey, Nicholas, 'Lest We Forget: The Question of Being in Philosophical Hermeneutics', *The Journal of the British Society for Phenomenology* 40, no. 3 (October 2009): 234–8.

Davey, Nicholas, 'Philosophical Hermeneutics: An Education for All Seasons', in *Education, Dialogue and Hermeneutics*, edited by Paul Fairfield, 39–60, London: Continuum, 2011.

Davey, Nicholas, 'Philosophical Hermeneutics, Art and the Language of Art', *Aesthetic Pathways* 1, no. 1 (December 2010): 4–29.

Davey, Nicholas, 'Sitting Uncomfortably: A Hermeneutic Reflection on Portraiture', *The Journal of the British Society for Phenomenology* 34, no. 3 (October 2003): 231–46.

Davey, Nicholas, 'The Hermeneutics of Seeing', in *Interpreting Visual Culture: Explorations in the Hermeneutics of the Visual*, edited by Ian Heywood and Barry Sandywell, 3–30, London: Routledge, 1999.

Davey, Nicholas, 'Truth, Method and Transcendence', in *Consequences of Hermeneutics: Fifty Years After Gadamer's Truth and Method*, edited by J. Malpas and S. Zabala, 25–54, Evanston, IL: Northwestern University Press, 2010.

Davey, Nicholas, *Unquiet Understanding*, Albany, NY: State University of New York Press, 2006.

Davies, Oliver and Denys Turner, *Silence and the Word, Negative Theology and Incarnation*, Cambridge: Cambridge University Press, 2002.

Dickinson, Colby, *Theology and Contemporary Continental Philosophy, The Central Centrality of Negative Dialectic*, New York: Rowman & Littlefield, 2019.

Dilthey, Wilhelm, *Selected Writings*, edited by H. P. Rickman, London: Cambridge University Press, 1976.

Dostal, Robert, *The Cambridge Companion to Gadamer*, Cambridge: Cambridge University Press, 2002.

Ellis, Fiona, 'Religious Understanding, Naturalism, and Desire', in *New Models of Religious Understanding*, edited by Ruth Ellis, 42–58. Oxford: Oxford University Press, 2017.

Estrada, Paola Cesar Duque, *Gadamer's Rehabilitation of Practical Philosophy*, an unpublished manuscript with Edinburgh University Press, 2017.

Faye, Jay, *After Postmodernism, A Naturalistic Reconstruction of the Humanities*, Basingstoke: Palgrave and Macmillan, 2012.

Fiddes, Paul S., *The Promised End: Eschatology in Theology and Literature*, Oxford: Blackwell, 2000.

Fiumari, Gemma Corradi, *The Other Side of Language: A Philosophy of Listening*, London: Routledge and Kegan Paul, 1990.

Foster, Matthew, *Gadamer and Practical Philosophy, The Hermeneutics of Moral Confidence*, Atlanta: Scholars Press, The American Academy of Religion, 1991, No. 64.

Gander, Hans-Helmuth, *Self-Understanding and Life-world: Basic Traits of a Phenomenological Hermeneutics*, Bloomington: Indiana University Press, 2001.

Gjesdal, Kristin, *Gadamer and the Legacy of German Idealism*, Cambridge: Cambridge University Press, 2009.

Goethe, Johann, *Maximen und Reflexionen*, München: Deutscher Taschenbuch Verlag, 1968.

Gordon, Peter Eli, *Rosenzweig and Heidegger: Between Judaism and German Philosophy*, Berkeley: University of California Press, 2005.

Grondin, J., *Introduction to Philosophical Hermeneutics*, Albany, NY: State University of New York Press, 1994.

Habermas, Jürgen, *Knowledge and Human Interests*, London: Heinemann, 1972.

Habermas, Jürgen, *Postmetaphysical Thinking*, London: Polity, 1995.

Habermas, Jürgen, *The Liberating Power of Symbols: Philosophical Essays*, London: Polity, 2001.

Hampshire, Stuart, *Thought and Action*, London: Chatto & Windus, 1959.

Heidegger, Martin, *Being and Time*, translated by John Macquarrie, London: Blackwell, 1960.

Heidegger, Martin, *Introduction to Metaphysics*, New Haven, CT: Yale University Press, 2014, 92.

Heidegger, Martin, *Poetry, Language and Thought*, translated by Albert Hofstadter, New York: Harper, 1971.

Heisig, James W, *Philosophers of Nothingness, An Essay on the Kyoto School*, Honolulu: University of Hawai'i Press, 2001.

Iser, Wolfgang, *The Range of Interpretation*, New York: Columbia University Press, 2000.

Kant, Immanuel, *Critique of Pure Reason*, translated by Norman Kemp Smith, London: Macmillan, 1970.

Kant, Immanuel, *Kritik der reinen Vernunft*, Hamburg: Felix Meiner, 1956.

Kant, Immanuel, *The Critique of Judgement*, translated by J. C. Meredith, Oxford: Oxford University Press, 1978.

Kearney, Richard and Jens Zimmermann, eds, *Reimagining the Sacred*, New York: Columbia University Press, 2015.

Keller, Catherine, *Cloud of the Impossible; Negative Theology and Planetary Entanglement*, New York: Columbia University Press, 2015.

Kertscher, Jens, 'We Understand Differently, If we Understand at All: Gadamer's Ontology of Language Reconsidered', in *Gadamer's Century, Essays in Honour of Hans-Georg Gadamer*, edited by Jeff Malpas, Urlich Arnswald, and Jens Kertscher, Cambridge, MA: The MIT Press, 2002, 135–56.

Kögler, Hans Herbert, *The Power of Dialogue*, Cambridge, MA: MIT Press, 1996.

Krajewski, Bruce, *Gadamer's Repercussions*, Berkeley, CA: University of California Press, 2004.

Kramer, Lawrence, *Interpreting Music*, Berkeley, CA: University of California, Press, 2011.

Kramer, Lawrence, *Music as Cultural Practice, 1800–1900*, Berkeley, CA: University of California Press, 1990.

Lang, Christian Lang, *Hermeneutik, Ideologiekritik, Ästhetik*, Hanstein: Forum Academicum, 1981.
Lawn, Christopher, *Gadamer: A Guide for the Perplexed*, London and New York: Continuum, 2006.
Lotz, Christian, *The Art of Gerhard Richter*, London: Bloomsbury, 2017.
Louth, Andrew, *Discerning the Mystery, An Essay on the Nature of Theology*, Oxford: Clarendon, 1989.
MacGregor, Neil, *A History of the World in 100 Objects*, London: Allen Lane, Penguin, 2010.
MacIntyre, Alasdair, *After Virtue*, London: Duckworth, 1982.
MacIntyre, Alasdair, *Whose Justice? Which Rationality?* London: Duckworth, 1988.
Makkreel, Rudolf A., *Imagination and Interpretation in Kant: The Hermeneutical Import of the Critique of Judgement*, London: University of Chicago Press, 1990.
Margolis, Joseph, *The Arts and the Definition of the Human: Towards a Philosophical Anthropology*, Stanford, CA: Stanford University Press, 2009.
Marquard, Odo, *In Defense of the Accidental*, Oxford: Oxford University Press, 1999.
Marquard, Odo, *In Defense of the Accidental, Philosophical Studies*, London: Oxford University Press, 1991.
Matthiessen, Peter, *Nine-Headed Dragon River*, Boston: Shambhala, 1998.
McIntosh, Mark, *Mystical Theology*, Oxford: Blackwell, 2006.
Michel, Johann, *Homo Interpretans, Towards a Transformation of Hermeneutics*, London: Rowman and Littlefield, 2019.
Midgley, Mary, *Science and Poetry*, London: Routledge, 2001.
Milbank, John, *The Word Made Strange: Theology, Language, Culture*, Oxford: Blackwell, 1998.
Moules, Nancy (with Grahan McCaffrey, James C. Field, Catherine M. Laing), *Conducting Hermeneutic Research, From Philosophy to Practice*, New York: Peter Lang, 2015.
Mueller-Vollmer, Kurt, ed., *The Hermeneutics Reader*, London: Blackwell, 1985.
Murdoch, Iris, *Existentialists and Mystics*, London: Chatto & Windus, 1997.
Nelson, Eric S., *Chinese and Buddhist Philosophy in Early-Twentieth-Century German Thought*, London: Bloomsbury Academic, 2019.
Nietzsche, Friedrich, *Human, All Too Human*, translated by R. J. Hollingdale, Cambridge: Cambridge University Press, 1986.
Nietzsche, Friedrich, *The Gay Science*, translated by Walter Kaufmann, New York: Vintage, 1974.
Nietzsche, Friedrich, *The Will to Power*, translated by Walter Kaufman and Roger Hollingdale, London: Weidenfeld and Nicolson, 1968.
Nightingale, Andrea Wilson, *Spectacles of Truth in Classical Greek Philosophy: Theoria in its Cultural Context*, Cambridge: Cambridge University Press, 2005.
Nussbaum, Martha C. *Not for Profit: Why Democracy Needs the Humanities*, Princeton: Princeton University Press, 2010.

O'Connor, Brian, *Adorno's Negative Dialectic, Philosophy and the Possibility of Critical Philosophy*, Cambridge, MA: The MIT Press, 2004.
Orange, Donna M., *The Suffering Stranger, Hermeneutics for Everyday Clinical Practice*, London: Routledge, 2011.
Pannenberg, Wolfhart, *Theology and the Philosophy of Science*, London: Darton, Londman and Todd, 1976.
Pippin, Robert B., *The Persistence of Subjectivity: On the Kantian Aftermath*, Cambridge: Cambridge University Press, 2005.
Pollock, Benjamin, 'Franz Rosenzweig'. http://plato.stanford.edu/entries/rosenzweig
Polyani, Michael, *The Tacit Dimension*, Chicago: Chicago University Press, 2009.
Redding, Paul, *Hegel's Hermeneutics*, Ithaca, NY: Cornell University Press, 1996.
Ricoeur, Paul, *Hermeneutics*, translated by David Pellauer, London: Polity, 2013.
Ricoeur, Paul, *Hermeneutics and the Human Sciences*, translated by John Thompson, London: Cambridge University Press, 1981.
Risser, James, *Hermeneutics and the Voice of the Other: Re-reading Gadamer's Philosophical Hermeneutics*, Albany, NY: State University of New York Press, 1997.
Risser, James, *The Life of Understanding: A Contemporary Hermeneutics*, Bloomington, IN: Indiana University Press, 2012.
Rorty, Richard, *Philosophy and Social Hope*, London: Penguin Books, 1999.
Rosenzweig, Franz, *Understanding the Sick and the Healthy: A View of World, Man and God*, Cambridge, MA: Harvard University Press, 1999.
Rothwell, Nicolas, *Belomor*, Melbourne, Text Publishing, 2013.
Sandel, Adam, *The Place of Prejudice*, Cambridge, MA: Harvard University Press, 2014.
Scheiffele, Eberhard, 'Questioning One's 'Own' from the Perspective of the Foreign', in *Nietzsche and Asian Thought*, edited by Graham Parkes, 31–50, Chicago: University of Chicago Press, 1991.
Schleiermacher, Friedrich, *Schleiermacher: Hermeneutics and Criticism and Other Writings*, edited by A. Bowie, Cambridge: Cambridge University Press, 1998.
Schmidt, Dennis J., *Between Word and Image: Heidegger, Klee, and Gadamer on Gesture and Genesis*, Bloomington, IN: Indiana University Press, 2013.
Schmidt, Lawrence, 'Back to Basics: The Forgotten Fore-Conception of Completeness', *Duquesne Studies in Phenomenology* 1, no. 1 (2020): 1–12.
Sennett, Richard, *The Craftsman*, London: Penguin, 2008.
Sloterdijk, Peter, *After God*, London: Polity, 2020.
Sloterdijk, Peter, *The Art of Philosophy*, New York: Columbia University Press, 2012.
Sloterdijk, Peter, *You Must Change Life*, London: Polity, 2013.
Small, Helen, *The Value of the Humanities*, Oxford: Oxford University Press, 2013.
Smith, Christopher, 'Plato as Impulse and Obstacle in Gadamer's Development of a Hermeneutical Theory', in *Gadamer and Hermeneutics*, edited by Hugh Silverman, 23–41, London: Routledge, 1991.
Steiner, George, *Real Presences*, London: Faber & Faber, 1989.
Strawson, Galen, 'Against Narrativity', *Ratio* 17, no. 4 (December 2004): 428–52.

Tate, Dan, 'Transforming Mimesis: Gadamer's Retrieval of Aristotle's Poetics', *Epoché* 13, no. 1 (2008): 185–208.
Taylor, Charles, *Modern Social Imaginaries*, Durham, NC: Duke University Press, 2004.
Taylor, Charles, *The Language Animal, The Full Shape of the Human Linguistic Capacity*, Cambridge, MA: The Belknap Press of Harvard University, 2016.
The Cloud of Unknowing, translated by A. C. Spearman, London: Penguin, 2001.
Vattimo, Gianni, *Art's Claim to Truth*, New York: Columbia University Press, 2008.
Vattimo, Gianni, *Of Reality, The Purposes of Philosophy*, New York: Columbia University Press, 2016.
Waldenfels, Hans, *Absolute Nothingness, Foundations for a Buddhist-Christian Dialogue*, New York: Paulist Press, 1980.
Wargo, Robert J. J. *The Logic of Nothingness*, Honolulu: University of Hawai'i Press, 2005.
Warnock, Mary, *Imagination*, London: Faber & Faber, 1976.
Weinsheimer, Joel, *Gadamer's Hermeneutics: A Reading of Truth and Method*, New Haven, CT: Yale University Press, 1985.
Weinsheimer, Joel, *Philosophical Hermeneutics and Literary Theory*, New Haven, CT: Yale University Press, 1991.
Williams, Rowan, *Being Human*, London: SPCK, 2018.
Williams, Rowan, *Faith in the Public Square*, London: Bloomsbury, 2012, 72.
Williams, Rowan, *Grace and Necessity, Reflections on Art and Love*, London: Morehouse, 2005, 28–31.
Williams, Rowan, *On Christian Theology*, Oxford: Blackwell, 2000.
Williams, Rowan, *The Edge of Words*, London: Bloomsbury, 2014.
Williams, Rowan, *The Tragic Imagination*, Oxford: Oxford University Press, 2016.
Wittgenstein, Ludwig, *Philosophical Investigations*, London: Blackwell, 1953.
Wittgenstein, Ludwig, *Tractatus Logico Philosophicus*, London: Routledge and Kegan Paul, 1961.
Wright, Dale S., *Philosophical Mediations on Zen Buddhism*, London: Cambridge University Press, 1998.

Index

accomplished practitioner 61, 92, 208–10, 214, 241, 244–51
action 56, 107, 131, 140, 154, 157, 179, 186, 191, 250, 252, 253, 256, 258, 261–2, 266, 271, 275
  creative 257, 258, 262–5, 269, 271, 274, 284
  hermeneutics of 258, 274
  liberation of 129
  ontological importance of 257
  possibility of 271
  practical 41, 53, 55, 103, 197, 255, 258, 260–4, 266, 283, 284
actuality 22, 29, 30, 34, 35, 44, 45, 50, 51, 53, 55, 57, 64, 74, 94, 95, 103, 104, 140, 157, 161, 192, 197, 201, 233, 254, 257, 259, 260, 282
  being of 52
  conception of 217
  differential spaces 25
  engagement with 47, 48
  experiences of 225
  as finite and uncertain 48, 49
  ontological 135, 215
  phenomenological experience of 83
  philosophy in 272
Adorno, Theodor 69, 69, 83, 83, 125, 125, 225
Aeschylus 74, 205
aesthetic alienation 29–32
aesthetic attentiveness as practice 18
aesthetic categories 50
aesthetic completeness 22–4, 79, 102, 103, 110, 120, 224–32
aesthetic completion 102
aesthetic consciousness 28
aesthetic disinterestedness 32
aesthetic estrangement 29
aesthetic object 30, 85
aesthetic phenomena 30
aesthetics 21, 49, 50, 91, 94, 95, 97, 99, 105, 123 n.11, 168, 230, 231, 251, 266
aesthetic theories 97

After Virtue (MacIntyre) 138
agency 41–4, 53, 93, 95, 100, 101, 113, 114, 117, 118, 120, 132, 134, 135, 172, 207–9, 211, 212
aletheic operations 169, 170
alienation 28–35, 37, 47, 75, 161–3, 233
Ancient Chinese Philosophy 122
anthropologies of practice 144–55
anticipation of completion/completeness (*Vorgriff der Vollkommenheit*) 22, 65, 68, 77–81, 84–95, 97–100, 170, 174, 181, 191, 192, 196–8, 201, 208, 216, 218, 219, 226–9, 238, 242, 259, 261, 262, 267, 274
anticipation of formative completeness 89
anticipatory (*wozu*) moment 109
anticipatory movement 6, 78, 175, 229
anticipatory powers 174, 258
anticipatory processes 100, 173–4
anticipatory structures 56, 110, 259, 262
anti-essentialism 40, 41
anti-metaphysical posture 10, 13
aphorism 83
apophantic denial of God 169
apophantic language 29, 30, 33, 61, 69, 159, 168, 169
apophantic speech 60
apophatic entanglements 212, 214
apophatic language 30, 60, 61, 69
apophatic relationality 213
apophatic speech 60
apotheosis 13
appearances 46, 81, 85, 87, 95, 110, 111, 161, 162, 200, 267, 284
application 12, 124, 126, 130, 156, 191, 194, 195, 197, 208, 219, 227, 233–6, 242, 258, 259, 263
  dialogical 32
  personal 37
  theoretical 63
applied truths 268
Aristotle 125, 176

Art of Gerhardt Richter, Hermeneutics, Images and Meaning, The (Lotz) 96, 151
Art of Philosophy, The (Sloterdijk) 144
arts 5, 9, 12, 26–30, 27, 28, 33, 40, 64, 82, 86, 96, 97, 101–4, 107, 109, 110, 123, 129, 134, 150, 153–5, 173, 174, 176, 177, 188, 218, 219, 225, 227–32, 249, 265, 266
art's address 32, 268
 truth of the artwork 105, 275
artworks 29, 30, 32, 82, 83, 87, 88, 96, 97, 104–8, 110, 111, 132, 153, 172, 196, 245, 251, 275, 276
auto-activity (*Selbsttätigkeit*) 129
auto-poeisis 76, 81, 129, 143, 150, 156, 195, 276

bad infinity 66, 67
Bauman, Zygmund 32
Baumgarten, A. 88
becoming (*Werden*) 3, 40, 42, 46, 47, 59, 65, 70, 75, 89, 90, 93, 95, 114, 117, 120, 121, 126, 129, 131, 139, 152, 162, 177, 196–8, 206–8, 223, 224, 233, 238, 244, 246, 249–51, 256, 257, 264, 268–71, 277
becoming more 92, 110, 148, 196, 212, 215
Being and Time (Heidegger) 33, 159
being as actualisation of the possible 64, 259
Being/being 13, 17, 19, 25, 29, 36, 43, 52, 56, 113, 117, 121, 145, 162–4, 166, 180, 195, 280
being-in-language 100, 123–4
being-in-motion (*Bewegtheit*) 216
being-in-the-world 65, 88, 129, 133, 156, 166, 260, 264, 270
Belomor (Rothwell) 72–3
Berg, Alban 83
Berio, Luigi 165
Bewegtheit 216
Bewusstein (consciousness) 50, 153, 189, 243
Bildung 3, 15, 38, 55, 57, 75, 93, 118–20, 146, 149, 185, 203, 204, 225, 226, 241, 262, 273
Bildungsformat 93
Bildungsphilosophie 148

Bildungsprozess 213
bios 131
Blue and Brown Books (Wittgenstein) 222
Boland, Eavan 230
bringing-into-question 17, 19
bringing-new-modes-of-understanding 17, 19

campos confusionis 88
Cassim, Barbara 125–131
Cassirer, Ernst 64, 87, 104, 140, 142, 180, 181, 259
centripetal and centrifugal motion 175, 177, 217, 246
certainty 10, 11, 27, 28, 38, 40, 45, 54, 60, 120, 154, 201–3, 265, 267–9, 274, 277–9, 282, 283
characterology 93, 118, 244
Chiurazzi, Gaetano 259
Christian metaphysics 59
Cixous, Helene 77
classical metaphysics 156, 161
classical philosophical theory 157, 158
cognition 11, 40, 134
cognitive content 2, 5, 7, 12, 103, 105, 115
cognitive truth 66, 68
commodification 18, 29
concept 8 n.2, 11, 13, 25, 40, 42, 48, 52, 54, 57, 58, 79, 94, 95, 100, 101, 128, 158, 163, 164, 173, 177, 178, 182, 183, 189–91, 211, 223, 231–9, 242, 247, 266
'The Concept and Tragedy of Culture' (Simmel) 180
conceptual language 113
confidence 202–6, 258, 264, 274, 279
confidence of action 264
consequentialism of effects 154, 176, 230, 239
constitutive completeness 197, 201
contemporary hermeneutics 27
conversation 37, 40, 144, 231, 237, 245, 263, 266, 273, 276
Cooper, David 122, 123 n.11
copy 50, 95, 174
corrosive scepticism 10
creative disruption, continuities of 276

creative response repetoire 5, 7, 9, 28, 251, 253, 254, 256, 273
creativity 3, 4, 18, 140, 142, 275
crisis (*krisis*) 203, 224, 250, 253, 255, 257, 266
Culler, Jonathan 170
cultural alienation 35
cultural disaster 46
cultural monadisms 36
cultural nihilism 35, 36
cultural pluralism 36
cultural practices 8, 21, 132, 136, 146, 147, 153, 163, 180, 181, 264, 279
cultural relativism 36
cultural tradition 128, 163, 277
cumulative learning 86, 149

Daoism 134
Darstellung 49–51, 97
Dasein 29, 31, 33–5, 42, 46, 49, 79, 79 n.42, 96, 120, 135–6, 139, 143, 145, 150, 153–5, 157, 159, 160, 166, 205, 215, 216, 218, 219, 233, 235 n.88, 244, 246, 253, 257–9, 262, 270, 271, 280
deconstruction 4, 10, 20, 21, 32, 63, 65–8, 91, 114, 157, 158, 160, 230
Deconstruktion 129
Denken 159, 160
Derrida Jacques 20
dialectical consequentiality 180
dialectic of loss and hope 88
dialectic of word and concept 232–9
dialectics 4, 6, 15, 21, 42, 70, 75, 77–9, 86, 90, 99, 104, 111, 113, 114, 120, 121, 132–4, 146, 154, 164, 167, 173, 176, 180, 181, 186, 187, 194, 197, 203, 205, 208, 211, 219, 220, 225–8, 232–9, 245, 253, 255, 284
dialogue 10, 39, 119, 144, 278
differential space 5, 6, 15, 24–6, 44, 53, 54, 57, 58, 65, 77, 79, 88, 93, 104, 106, 109, 110, 118, 122, 123, 125, 147–51, 154, 156, 161–70, 174, 180, 198, 260–2, 270, 271
Dilthey, Wilhelm 18, 39, 128
disclosure 20, 29, 71, 78, 92, 110, 111, 163, 169, 174, 206, 210, 219, 249, 255, 257, 276
disinterestedness 32

distance 161–3
distanciation 28–35, 52, 75, 146, 161–4, 247, 259
dual axiom 182, 183
dualist ontology 52

education 106, 142, 152, 172, 222, 249, 254, 255
educational practices 178
Ein Mädchen oder ein Weibschen (Mozart) 137
Eliot, T. S. 173
emergence, emergency 3, 7, 23, 24, 68, 73, 74, 82, 96, 102, 106, 113, 118–21, 125, 127, 142, 143, 150, 171, 174, 176, 179, 184, 187, 188, 197, 204–6, 208–10, 221, 224–6, 230, 235, 239, 244–6, 252–4, 260, 263, 264, 267, 270, 272, 275, 277
'The End of Philosophy' (Heidegger) 159, 160
energeia 131
Enigma of Health, The (Gadamer) 41, 157
Enlightenment 128, 141, 240, 241
enviromentality 34
epiphanic 29, 72, 96, 142, 146, 226, 278
episteme 126, 129
epistemological awareness 8
epistemological bias 24
epistemological deficit 49–51
epistemological negativity 45
epistemological perspective 25, 49
epistemological prejudice 24, 47, 49, 55
epistemological scepticism 157
epistemological violence 10
epistemology, participatory 9, 10, 13, 31, 32, 36–9, 51, 53, 55, 120, 121, 130, 152, 155, 156, 160, 171, 176, 201, 208
Erfahrung 24 n.16, 38, 106, 183
essence 10, 11, 13, 41, 74, 120–2, 132, 158, 159, 201, 208, 232, 238, 272, 275, 280
essentialism 41, 42, 120
ethical disaster 46
etymology 86, 135
event 37, 49, 83, 89, 118, 121, 122, 125, 131, 162–4, 189, 196, 226, 245, 259, 277, 278

everyday experience 82–3, 89, 153, 225, 226, 231, 233, 247, 267
everyday practices 47, 158, 160
evidentness 265
excess 6, 14, 40, 52, 60, 92, 100, 117, 124, 148, 168, 179, 186, 187, 209, 210, 217, 227, 239, 240, 247, 248, 252–3, 272, 274–6
existence 11, 15, 19, 22, 29, 35, 39, 45–9, 51, 53–6, 58, 61, 83, 130, 133, 137, 145, 150, 154, 155, 160, 161, 175, 181, 192, 194, 195, 197–200, 202, 203, 208, 213, 215, 216, 218, 221, 227, 232, 237–9, 243, 246, 253, 258–60, 264–6, 268, 269, 272, 273, 275, 277, 278, 280–4
  human 4, 36, 150, 246, 253
existential orientation 34, 35
ex nihilo 44, 59, 121, 127, 184, 216, 217, 219, 236, 252, 266, 267
expectations of completion 21–4, 151, 180, 197
experience. *See specific entries of experience*
experience of negativity 65, 73, 74, 93, 169, 204, 206, 211–13, 214, 215, 257
experiential objects 89, 90
experiential process 105, 108, 115
experimentalism 49, 54
expression 5, 8 n.1, 18 n.4, 22, 42, 45, 48, 57, 66, 77, 78, 82, 83, 99, 102, 116, 120, 137, 139, 145, 146, 154, 158, 189, 190, 203, 238, 280

factical existence 46, 47, 51, 54–6
failure 9, 26, 35, 56, 61, 64, 77, 80, 86, 111, 114, 154, 179, 180, 181, 192, 196, 197, 236, 244, 255, 272, 281
'Feldweg' 171
Feyerabend, Paul 2
finite being 13, 57, 242, 270, 275, 282
finitude 1, 18, 25, 26, 45, 47, 48, 50, 54–6, 58, 59, 61, 63, 71, 72, 74, 84, 92, 98, 108, 154, 191, 205, 211, 232, 253, 256, 280–2, 284
flux of existence 192
fore-conception of completeness. *See* anticipation of completion/completeness (*Vorgriff der Vollkommenheit*)

formal completeness 81–5, 102
formative experience 3, 82, 175
form of life 11, 42, 45, 49, 54, 69, 120, 132, 136, 143, 145, 159, 198, 215, 260, 273, 274
Foster, M. 10 n.3, 122
Foster, Matthew 122, 123
fragmented transcendence 83
'The Future of Hermeneutics' (Vattimo) 44, 114

Gadamer, H.G. 1, 2, 5, 11, 12, 14, 17, 19, 21, 22, 27–35, 37, 38, 41–3, 49, 50, 52, 54, 56–8, 60, 65, 68–72, 74, 75, 78–89, 93–101, 104, 109, 115–17, 120, 122, 123, 123 n.11, 125–8, 130–6, 138, 140, 142, 143, 147, 150–3, 155, 157, 160–3, 165–8, 170, 175–7, 183, 186, 188, 190, 191, 197, 200–5, 211–13, 215–18, 220–5, 228, 229, 231–5, 235 n.88, 237, 238, 240, 242–4, 250, 253, 256, 260, 261, 264, 267–70, 276, 280, 281, 282
Gebilde 100
Geist 183
Geisteswissenschaft 2, 71, 128, 186 n.10
Geworfenheit 136
Gödel, Kurt 2
God/gods 147, 162, 163, 168, 169, 284
Goethe, Johann 241
Goodman, Nelson 40

Habermas, J. 116 n.4
Hadot, Pierre 123, 129, 144–55
Hegel, G. W. F. 64, 66, 72, 96, 162, 166, 183, 189, 204
Hegel's Practical Philosophy (Pippin) 122
Heidegger, Martin 11, 20, 29–31, 33, 34, 45, 52, 56, 59, 60, 69, 78, 79, 97, 110, 114, 115, 117, 121, 122, 129, 135–9, 142, 143, 145, 153, 154, 157, 159, 160, 164, 168, 171, 191, 200, 201, 207, 218, 234, 259, 260, 264, 267, 280
Henrich, Dieter 39
hermeneutical aesthetics 18
hermeneutical awareness 203–5
hermeneutical consciousness 15, 89, 130, 204, 206, 223, 244–6
hermeneutical defenestration 206, 209

hermeneutical differentiation 194, 194
hermeneutical engagement 1, 8, 21, 44, 92, 165, 205, 247, 257
hermeneutical experience 1, 2, 4, 41, 44, 57, 63, 65, 73, 77, 78, 85, 92–5, 101, 102, 102, 107, 107, 109, 109–11, 118, 121, 122, 146, 151–3, 155, 156, 164, 165, 167–72, 184, 192–4, 205, 219, 258, 260, 268, 270
hermeneutical mapping 194, 195
hermeneutical movement 105, 108, 171, 220, 226, 266
hermeneutical object 85–90, 92, 105–8, 193, 198, 201, 229, 230
hermeneutical ontology 43, 57, 120, 263
hermeneutical openness 86, 239–41
hermeneutical philosophy 248
hermeneutical poetics 114, 115, 163, 173, 177, 178, 180
hermeneutical practice 179, 180, 182, 183, 192, 193, 199, 209–11, 221, 235, 241, 245, 249, 258, 263, 266, 277, 281, 284
hermeneutical *praxis* 117, 128, 130, 131, 134, 239, 249–57
  transcendental conditions of 258–69
hermeneutical reasoning 63, 80, 239, 250, 251
hermeneutical reflection 18, 20, 39, 72, 79, 80, 90, 115, 116, 236, 237, 250, 281
hermeneutical self 207, 212, 213
hermeneutical thought/thinking 5, 7, 24, 58, 77, 90, 102, 103, 123, 128, 160, 161, 164, 189, 205, 217, 253, 264
hermeneutical truth 65–8, 76, 90, 109, 118, 119, 158, 196, 268, 282, 283
hermeneutical understanding 23, 61, 63, 101, 106, 108, 109, 122, 151, 156, 164, 173, 192, 206, 212, 217, 228, 230, 231, 241, 257–9, 263, 276, 279
hermeneutical vectors 56, 114, 129, 136, 166, 171, 172, 184, 192, 219–21, 262, 271, 272
hermeneutic application 12
hermeneutic community 31, 66, 129, 143, 163, 167
hermeneutic displacement 193–6
hermeneutic excess 209, 248
hermeneutic fit 234–6

hermeneutic intelligibility 23, 56, 74, 87, 140, 153, 251
hermeneutic orientation 224, 240
hermeneutic participation 101
hermeneutic perspectivism 58, 68, 92, 185, 275
hermeneutic philosophy 21, 38, 91, 92, 248
hermeneutic porosity 170, 171, 177, 184, 188, 222, 223
hermeneutic practitioner 187, 188
hermeneutic reflection 3, 7, 9, 15, 77, 106, 115, 118, 151–3, 179, 206, 234, 235, 237, 252, 253, 255
hermeneutics as creative retrieval 11
hermeneutics as *via negativa* 3, 8 n.1, 13, 36, 61
hermeneutics of negativity 1–4, 9–15, 19, 21, 26, 45, 49, 54, 61, 63–5, 68, 79, 86–9, 93, 94, 96, 102, 103, 110, 138, 169–70, 179, 194, 197, 199, 210, 248, 253
hermeneutics of practice 1, 3–5, 9, 11, 15, 19–21, 23, 35, 41, 42, 44, 46–9, 54, 55, 63, 76, 77, 94, 100, 101, 104, 113–15, 117, 119, 122, 123, 125, 129, 130, 151, 160, 195, 256
hermeneutics of suspicion 66
hermeneutic sublime 22
hermeneutic surplus 5, 64, 92
hermeneutic theory 20, 172
hermeneutic therapy 2, 49, 54, 145
hermeneutic windows 172, 206
higher education 18, 29
historical event 37, 89
homo repetition 148
horizons, of meaning 56, 72, 76, 109, 124, 125, 171, 182–4, 186, 199, 219, 223, 261
human beings 39–41, 146–7, 154, 237
  vs. animal 131, 147, 148
humanism 39, 41
humanities 1, 2, 4–5, 7, 8, 10–13, 17, 18, 19, 21, 24, 26–9, 31, 32, 34–61, 77, 86, 92, 102, 105, 114, 115, 118–21, 128, 132, 135, 138, 155, 166, 170, 200, 216, 225, 250, 253, 255–7, 268, 277
humanities, epistemological and ontological basis of humanities 5, 8, 60

human sciences   59, 186, 216, 254
Humboldt, Wilhelm   278
Hume, David   97

identity   10, 42, 75, 79, 81, 84, 97, 120, 141, 168, 208, 215, 224, 261, 270, 272
image   22, 23, 50, 51, 79, 94–104, 106, 107, 109, 110, 151–3, 163, 164, 173–8, 182–4, 228, 230, 231–3, 247, 266–8
  as emergence   102, 174, 176
  making   99
  revealing image   231, 232
imagination (*Phantasie*)   56, 80, 90, 97, 174, 175, 215–17
imagination, hermeneutic imagination   90, 174, 175, 217
imitatio/imitation   49–51, 97, 127
immeasurable   217–21
in-between   25, 80, 81, 148, 161, 173, 260, 270
inchoate experiences   99
incommensurability   5, 6, 14, 15, 22, 51–4, 57, 58, 60, 110, 116, 151, 186, 192, 194, 199, 225, 233, 244
indefinables   11, 40
infinity   22, 53, 57, 66, 67, 78, 84, 87, 94, 113, 189, 191, 213, 227, 237, 243, 252, 281
instabilities of understanding   182–4
integration   109, 194, 196–9
intelligence   134, 149, 151, 157, 177
interpretation   8, 14, 18, 23–5, 30, 31, 33, 37, 39, 40, 41, 44, 46, 54, 58, 59, 63, 66–8, 72, 76–7, 84, 88, 89, 94, 100, 105, 108, 115, 119, 128, 130, 131, 137, 143, 152, 153, 172, 179, 180, 193–5, 197, 201, 204, 206, 209, 210, 226–8, 239, 248, 251, 263, 268, 275, 276, 280
inter-relational epistemologies   50
Introduction to Metaphysics (Heidegger)   259
intuition   9, 12, 32, 37, 83, 87, 177, 181–3, 191
intuitive pulsion   168
irresponsible hermeneutics   20
Iser, Wolfgang   12, 40, 76, 84, 106, 129, 194–7, 237

Janacek, Leos   165
Ja-sagen   4, 280
Judt, Tony   32

Kant, Immanuel   13, 32, 41, 85–8, 122, 125, 127, 132, 182, 183, 191, 255, 259, 263, 267, 275
  aesthetics   32, 86, 263
Kantianism   87
Keats, John   215, 278
Keller, Catherine   13, 212, 268
Kramer, Lawrence   172

language   56, 57, 61, 80, 85, 87, 91, 96–7, 100, 102, 105, 108, 109, 119, 122, 124, 128, 134, 140, 147, 150, 159, 160, 165, 166, 173, 174, 189, 213, 232–4, 260, 262
  limits of   213, 214, 280
  and transcendence   3, 14, 281
language-being   3–6, 14, 20, 22, 25, 30, 31, 57, 58, 60, 61, 64, 78, 86, 89, 94, 96, 102, 108–11, 113–15, 123, 128, 134–5, 150, 163–72, 180, 183–5, 188–90, 192, 193, 195, 197, 201, 208–10, 212–21, 223–4, 228, 233, 234, 237–40, 242, 244, 248, 252, 253, 255–7, 260, 262, 266, 269, 270–2, 274–81
language consciousness   114, 170
language games   171, 214, 222, 280
language horizon   166, 167, 171, 184, 223, 224, 237, 280
language ontology   5, 41, 57, 86, 92, 108, 110, 111, 165, 191, 210, 211, 223, 224, 230, 232, 234, 238, 240, 244, 248, 250, 252, 280, 282
language worlds   33, 56, 57, 60, 85, 100, 108, 109, 113, 135, 158, 170–2, 193, 202, 218, 234
Lao-Tzu   133, 135
Lebensform   127
legal hermeneutics   18
legitimacy   5, 7, 13, 19, 20, 29, 35, 36, 43, 46, 47, 66, 67, 120, 282
lexicography   124
Lichtung   267
Liebrucks, B.   128
life span   56, 192, 198

life-world 1, 28, 30–4, 38, 56, 66, 119, 120
likelihood 27, 54, 81
likeness 174
liminal spaces 40, 75–7, 87, 88, 118, 192, 193, 194, 195
limit situations 250, 252–6, 261, 271
linguisticality 65, 86–8, 93, 133
linguistic-being 113, 124, 135, 169
linguistic consciousness 30, 31, 115, 124, 134, 135, 164, 167, 169, 180, 189, 193, 210, 212–15, 220, 222, 223, 237, 243, 255, 256, 272
linguistic experience 88
linguistic intelligibility 22
linguistic perspectivism 65
linguistic practice 21, 47, 86, 132, 134, 171
linguistic relations 9, 20, 25, 69
literature 12, 36, 37, 40, 107, 109, 153, 218, 222, 224, 227, 228, 231
lived experience 32, 96
living word 21, 226, 231, 232, 234, 236, 238, 267, 273
logical commensurability 84
logical completeness 65, 102, 110
Logic of the Humanities, The (Cassirer) 64
logos 237, 255
Lotz, Christian 96–8, 100, 109, 151–3, 171, 173–7, 183, 231, 261, 271

McIntosh, M. 241 n.98
MacIntyre, Alasdair 136–44
Maritain, Jacques 168
Marquard, Odo 216, 254
Matthiessen, Peter 241
meaning 10, 11, 15, 18–20, 22, 26, 35, 36, 47, 61, 78–81, 88, 90, 92, 101, 103, 111, 113, 119, 124, 129, 151, 152, 157–9, 166, 167, 169, 177, 184, 188–91, 193, 203, 218, 219, 222, 282
 core and peripheral 193, 222, 223
 and emergence 125, 171
 ideality of 182, 184, 199
 porosity of 188, 222, 223
meaningfulness 21, 31, 35, 36, 47, 65, 81, 82, 85, 86, 88, 90, 100, 101, 105, 107, 109, 119, 124, 152, 166, 170, 184, 190, 227, 230, 252, 253, 255, 258, 261–3, 266, 267, 270–2, 274, 275, 277, 281, 283
meaninglessness 58, 255
medical hermeneutics 18
Medieta, Eduardo 146
metaphor 222
metaphysical beliefs 49, 201
metaphysical nihilism 11, 36, 108, 119, 202, 239, 252, 266
metaphysical sickness 55, 58, 158, 160
metaphysical truths 11
metaphysics 34, 57, 156, 158–60, 282–4
method 4, 5, 8 n.1, 13, 20, 24, 27, 32, 38, 45, 46, 50, 54, 55, 63, 72, 95, 128, 131, 134, 138, 145, 156, 161, 179, 186, 209, 231, 239, 245, 246, 250, 252, 254, 256–8, 264–6, 282, 283
methodological starting points 20
mimesis 41, 49–51, 267
mimetic art 97
mimetic image 50
misunderstanding 1–4, 7, 19, 21, 28, 31, 45
Moltmann, Jürgen 254, 261, 262, 266
momentous, and the momentary 162, 231, 273
monistic ontology 52, 57
moral philosophy 122
Muir, John 30
Murdoch, Iris 281
musical experience 165
musicality 116
musical language 164, 168
musical performance 82, 190
musical practice 117, 149
Music as Cultural Practice (Kramer) 172

narrative 40, 42, 56, 72, 74, 75, 86, 94, 98, 118, 120, 136, 152, 159, 160, 176, 185, 186, 198, 201, 218, 222, 224, 236–9, 245, 261, 262, 270, 272
Naturwissenschaft 2
necromantic acrobatics 157
negation 7, 11, 13, 14, 60–1, 63–9, 94, 105, 169, 211, 212, 214, 222, 243, 248–50, 275, 279, 284
negative capacity 13–15, 44–6, 93, 94, 110, 115, 187, 207, 211, 212, 215, 222, 269, 278, 279, 284
negative dialectics 1, 3, 22, 71, 111, 167

negative hermeneutics   22, 24–6, 35–9, 55–61, 63, 68, 82, 86, 90, 94, 96, 100, 104, 108, 110, 111, 128, 134, 137, 142, 144, 151, 157, 159–61, 169, 170, 173, 179–81, 182, 196–8, 200–3, 211–17, 221, 225–6, 228–30, 232, 235, 238, 239, 241–3, 248, 249, 252, 253, 258, 260, 262–4, 269–76, 278, 281–4
negative hermeneutics as enabling posture   25
negative moments   8, 69, 71, 75, 94, 182–4, 199, 207
negative poetics   180, 182
negative receptions   26–8, 63
negativity of experience   2–5, 61, 65, 69–75, 93, 94, 118, 151, 170, 187, 199, 204, 206, 209, 211, 212, 215, 241–5, 247, 249–51, 256, 257, 273, 275
negativity of provocative expectations   190–3
negativity redemption   211–17
negentropic   14, 94, 192
nemein (to manage)   121
neo-Kantian philosophical language   41
Nietzsche, Friedrich   2, 11, 11 n.4, 19, 27, 34–6, 39, 41, 43, 45–8, 52–4, 57, 66, 77, 96, 107, 113, 131, 145–50, 152, 154, 157–60, 168, 169, 173, 191, 197, 208, 223–5, 229, 238, 250, 264, 267, 269, 277–80
nihilism   10–15, 19, 24, 35–9, 46, 47, 53, 55, 105, 107, 108, 110, 119, 179, 180, 196, 197, 201, 202, 230, 232, 240, 248, 250, 252, 257–9, 263–6, 269, 274–6, 279, 282
nihilism, impact on practical reasoning   266
nihilistic scepticism   11
non-identical repetition   15, 77, 101, 126, 146, 149, 207–9, 223, 224, 236, 238, 239, 244, 261, 262, 270, 275, 284
normative ethics   123
nothingness   13, 22, 213, 269, 270, 272

Oakeshott, Michael   40
objectivity   154
oikonomia (economy)   121
oikos (house)   121

ontic consciousness   29
ontogenetic processes   142, 144, 148–9, 171, 180, 203, 212, 239, 243, 259, 263
ontological dependence   127, 260
ontological difference   153
ontological dualism   57
ontological engagement   8, 203
ontological enquiry   29
ontological placement   139, 180, 188, 191
ontological priority   31, 52, 53, 115, 135, 137–40, 145, 153, 163, 169, 193, 212, 215, 220, 254, 256
ontological reading   42, 120
ontological surplus   49–51
ontology   131–5. *See also specific entries of ontology/ontological*
ontology of becoming   208
opening possibility   66
openness   9, 14, 17, 19, 26, 29, 65, 70, 106, 121, 135, 144, 183, 184, 192, 220, 224
Oriental aesthetics   36
original   50, 51, 95, 97, 98, 123, 129, 167, 169, 174, 207

Pannenberg, Wolfhart   128, 129, 141
paradox   21, 23, 27, 63, 84, 89, 92, 95, 102, 111, 127, 153, 162, 215, 230, 238, 249, 251, 254, 273, 276, 279
part and whole   6, 84, 121, 146, 165, 167, 176, 190, 191, 219
participation   3, 5, 8–10, 12, 21, 25, 38, 84, 90, 93, 96, 99, 101, 103, 107, 118–20, 124, 130, 146, 161
participatory epistemology   9, 10, 13, 31, 32, 36–9, 51, 53, 55, 120, 121, 130, 152, 155, 156, 160, 171, 176, 201, 208
participatory hermeneutics   13
participatory ontology   53, 86, 220
participatory practice   100, 121
passive nihilism   35, 36
pathei mathos   74, 172, 205, 221, 243, 244
pathos of distances   146–8
performance   38, 40, 78, 80, 82–5, 116, 150, 151, 155, 157, 165, 186, 190, 198, 201
perspectival multiplication   25–6

philological hermeneutics 168
philology 11, 128, 135, 251
philosophical anthropology 43, 120
philosophical practice as immunology 146
philosophical theory 54, 102, 160, 203
Philosophy as a Way of Life (Hadot) 144
philosophy of religion 169
photographic image 28
Pickstock, Catherine 207
Pippin, Robert B. 73, 122
placeholders 23, 99 105, 116, 166, 167, 175, 176, 183, 214, 222, 227, 237, 246
Plato 50, 52
Platonic/Platonism 53, 105, 126, 127, 156–61
play 5, 8, 9, 20–2, 24, 31, 34, 35, 38, 43, 44, 56, 57, 59, 65, 66, 68, 73, 77, 80, 83, 85, 86, 92, 94, 95, 99, 100, 103, 107, 115, 117–22, 124, 125, 129, 130, 131, 133, 135, 136, 138, 142, 145, 155, 157, 160, 163, 167–9, 171, 173, 174, 182, 189, 198, 216–18, 221, 223, 224, 229–32, 238, 239, 258, 262, 266, 272, 273
Plessner, Helmuth 39
poetic image 28
poetics 8, 50, 114, 121, 122, 125, 156, 161, 169, 170, 176, 180, 278
poetics of hermeneutic practice 113, 115, 122, 170–8, 180, 217
poetics of practice 113–78, 180
poetry 27, 32, 37, 60, 71, 86, 107, 133, 153, 168, 185, 267
poiesis 126, 129
Popper, Karl 2
portraiture 98, 143, 175
positivity 1, 26, 61, 68, 69, 71, 75, 79, 94, 247
positivity of negative outcomes 199–202
post-Gadamerian hermeneutics 118
post-metaphysical philosophy of practice 269–79
postmodern thought 24
post-structuralism 4, 10, 32, 76
practical application 12
practical confidence 38, 119, 120, 203, 250, 258, 266, 275

practical judgement 126, 154, 249–52, 255–9
practical philosophy 122, 123
practical reasoning 128, 142, 251, 252, 266
practice 162, 167, 218, 277
  confidence of 202–6
  and instabilities of understanding 182–4
  as onto-genetic process 180, 203
  provocative 217–18
  and repetition 184–8
  and speculative movement 188–90
  and theory 155–6, 160–1
practice-*praxis* relation 133–44
practicing existence 145
practitioner, accomplished 61, 92, 208–10, 214, 241, 244–51
praxis 44, 66, 68, 115, 117, 118, 125–35, 156, 164, 172, 235, 239–41, 261
prejudice 1, 3, 12, 24, 25, 27, 28, 47–9, 52, 54, 55, 60, 73, 93, 105, 141, 142, 172, 194, 235, 247, 252
prelude 164, 165
present at hand 33
presentation 49, 61, 84, 85, 97, 99, 127, 188, 215
probability 27
problem 10, 24, 28, 46–9, 67, 74, 107, 161, 194, 200
process ontology 98
prohairesis 131
propositional analysis 37
propositional language 30
provocations of practice 179–284
provocative capacity 180, 181, 222
provoked self 206–9

questioning, practice of 43, 44
question of practice 114–17, 123

Range of Interpretation, The (Iser) 194
ready to hand 29, 33
reality 34, 35, 50, 51, 67, 81–3, 98, 105, 116, 158–62, 169, 189, 223, 231, 242, 269, 270
recurrence 145, 146, 180, 253, 262, 270, 272
recursion 8, 195, 222–4, 262, 270

recursive looping 9, 77, 106, 118, 194, 195, 223
redemption 75
're-earthing' theory 155–6
reflective distanciation 163
regional ontology 55
regulative anticipation of completeness 89
regulative axioms 218
regulative completeness 193–9, 201, 206, 226–8, 228, 230, 239, 240, 244, 272
regulative ideal 196, 199
regulative principle 87, 92, 225–7, 232
relationality 212, 221
relational ontology 9–11, 53, 171, 176, 208, 213, 220
relativism 65, 93, 128
religious practices 163, 185
Renaissance aesthetics 36
repetition 8, 9, 15, 145–6, 148–50, 152, 184–8, 222–4, 262, 270–1
representation 49, 67, 69, 94–5, 96, 97, 99, 102, 103, 105, 110, 259, 267
response repertoires 5, 7
responsible hermeneutics 20
rhetoric 35, 64, 68, 82, 84, 251, 265
Richter, Gerhard 97
Ricoeur, Paul 19, 52
Rosenzweig, Stefan 37, 40, 52, 150, 200, 218, 279, 280
Rothwell, Nicholas 72, 73, 98

Sache (subject-matter) 7, 9, 11–19, 23, 25, 26, 39, 43, 45, 50–3, 58–61, 64, 67–9, 75–7, 84, 88, 90, 92, 93, 98, 100, 101, 103, 104, 106, 108, 110, 114, 118, 126, 129, 134, 135, 138, 150, 154, 163, 164, 170–2, 176, 179, 180, 183, 186, 190, 191, 193, 194, 199–201, 209, 210, 212, 217, 219, 220, 225–8, 230, 233, 234, 236, 238, 242, 246, 247, 249, 263
Sandel, Adam 163
scepsis 38, 68, 90, 119, 120
scepticism 38, 186, 210, 282
Schleiermacher, Friedrich 1
Schopenhauer, Arthur 76
science 9, 27, 28, 32–4, 71, 134
scientific method 35, 264, 266, 283

scientific thinking 33
seeing understandingly 241–9
Sein 50, 189
self-forming practices 41
selfication 150, 203, 207, 245
self-understanding 12, 73, 93, 118, 119, 172, 176, 204, 208, 235 n.88
Sennet, Richard 116, 134, 137, 146, 185
sense-making practices 28, 82, 119
sensuous content 177, 183, 184
sensuous materiality 177
sickness 44–6, 49, 55, 58, 158–60
signs 22, 22, 67, 98, 188
Simmel, Georg 180
Sloterdijk, Peter 21, 40, 41, 144–55, 157, 184, 207
Socratic questioning 43
speculative completeness 22
speculative language 30, 37
speculative movement 188–90
speculative totality 22, 23, 26, 64, 107, 219
speech created world 34, 159, 234, 253, 257, 273
spirit, the spiritual 5, 122, 132, 145, 146, 148, 168, 177, 185, 255
spontaneity 140, 142, 207, 265
Sprachlichkeit 22, 102, 133, 171, 177, 181, 218, 280, 283
Sprachgeschaffene Welt 150
Sprachsontologie 108, 182, 201, 279
Sprachsphilosophie 117
Sprachswelt 172, 173, 180, 182–6, 188, 190, 191, 197, 199, 202, 225, 240, 257
statements 13, 20, 30, 69, 78, 84, 115, 124, 133, 145, 167, 169, 273
Steiner, George 18, 32
story 92, 198, 216, 238, 254
strategic differentiations 29
subject agent 208, 224
subject-centred epistemologies 27, 55
subjectivity 12, 37–9, 41, 135, 139, 150–3, 155, 179, 204, 205, 242
subject-object epistemologies 32–3
substance 168, 204, 215
substantive truth 19
summative completeness 21, 65, 226–31, 266–8

supersensible 22
symbol 67, 188

tai chi 185
Tao Te Ching (Lao-Tzu) 133
techné 143, 235, 241, 249, 251, 255
technology 27, 33, 34, 185, 186
temporality 79, 83, 98, 106, 136, 243, 270
text 36–8, 78, 79, 81, 84, 101, 143, 151, 156, 158, 170, 185, 196, 206, 222, 224, 229
theme and variation 137, 167, 249
theological hermeneutics 18
theoretical scepticism 19
theoria 120, 130, 142, 145, 161–4, 250
thing-in-itself 81, 85
thinking-with 103, 167
thought and language 15, 96, 220, 240
Tractatus (Wittgenstein) 273
tradition 136–44, 194, 202, 203, 219, 240, 261, 262, 266, 269, 275–7, 279, 283
   as continuities of conflict 141
   and practice 255
   and reason 141–2
traditional metaphysics 42, 200
transcendence 3, 4, 9, 13–15, 23, 31, 36, 52–3, 60, 88, 103, 105, 108, 124, 135, 138, 144, 242, 248, 254, 258, 263, 280, 281
transformation into structure 101, 237, 261, 277
transformative questions 43–59
translation 123–5, 194
truth 13, 15, 34–7, 45, 47, 51, 60, 65, 66, 68, 70, 82, 91, 92, 106, 108, 109, 118, 119, 141, 158, 164, 187, 199–203, 212, 217, 225, 232, 277–80, 282, 284
Truth and Method (Gadamer) 28, 78, 82, 85, 100, 101, 123 n.11, 189, 216, 240
   'Transformation into Structure' section 82
truth-claim (*Wahrheitsanspruch*) 28, 29, 36, 46, 65, 66–8, 76, 90–1, 106, 109, 157, 158, 249
truthfulness 85–95
Tugendhat, Ernst 115
Twilight of the Idols (Nietzsche) 168

uncertainty 11, 18, 19, 26, 27, 28, 34, 35, 38, 39, 47, 48, 54, 55–8, 61, 191, 200–2, 215, 219, 256, 263–5, 269, 274, 276, 279, 282–4
understanding 1–7, 9, 18, 21–6, 30, 33, 34, 40, 45–7, 50, 54, 55, 58, 60, 61, 63, 65, 76, 88, 89, 92, 94, 95, 101, 103, 106, 108–10, 115, 117, 118, 120–2, 128, 130, 131, 138, 151, 152, 155, 156, 164, 170, 172, 173, 177, 180, 182–4, 189, 190, 192, 198, 199, 203, 210, 211, 215, 218, 220, 225, 242, 247, 281
   as movement 6, 15, 19, 40, 46, 54, 61, 101, 111, 113, 115, 122, 185, 260
   as undergoing 106
universal truth 10, 36, 119, 157
unknowing 129, 134, 214, 256, 257, 276
unspoken horizons of meaning 56
Urphänomen 269

'Variations on the St. Anthony Chorale' (Brahms) 137
Vattimo, Gianni 18 n.4, 26, 46, 114–15, 164
vectors, hermeneutical 56, 114, 129, 136, 166, 171, 172, 184, 192, 219–21, 262, 271, 272
Verstehen 115, 280
via negativa 3, 8 n.1, 13, 36, 61
Videeen, Hana 135
virtue, hermeneutical 74
visual image 95
Vollzug 22, 260–3, 270–2, 274, 279
Vollzug der Vollendung 268, 270
von Cieszkowski, August 129
von Webern, Anton 83
Vorgriff 77–80, 85, 87–95, 97–9, 101–11, 174, 182, 184, 190, 191, 194, 196, 198, 199, 208, 225, 228, 242–4, 259, 260, 261, 271
Vorgriff der Vollendung 56, 88, 98, 100–11, 147, 150, 171, 172, 174, 175, 179, 182, 184, 190, 193, 199, 207, 225, 257–9
Vorstellung 49, 97

Wahrheitsanspruch 84, 109, 110
Waldenfells, Hans 240, 254
Warnock, M. 178 n.135

way of knowing   17, 211, 239, 240
way of travel, practice as   219
way of understanding   117, 131–5
ways of life   2, 20, 29, 47, 48, 51, 52, 56, 59, 117, 131, 132, 145, 200, 259, 264, 266, 268, 282–4
Weltanschauung   8 n.1, 140
Werdensphilosophie   127, 128
whole, wholeness   6, 9, 13, 26, 28, 61, 65, 68, 69, 82–4, 87, 93, 98, 101, 103, 104, 107, 109, 121, 132, 145, 146, 157, 165, 167, 176, 189–91, 215, 219, 225–7, 229, 231–4, 237, 240, 242, 256, 267, 268, 280
Williams, Rowan   37, 56, 146, 154, 168
Wissen   50, 189
withheld   39, 167, 198, 207, 221
Wittgenstein, L.   2, 23, 24, 29, 35, 43–55, 57, 66–8, 84, 107, 122, 125, 152, 158, 159, 184, 193, 200, 203, 212–14, 222, 223, 227, 232, 233, 256, 257, 268, 273, 279, 280

woher und wozu   106, 109, 136, 142, 171, 191, 192, 198, 208, 229, 245, 259, 260, 280–2
word, the living word   21, 226, 231, 232, 234–6, 238, 267, 273
words   48, 50, 54, 56, 57, 59, 85, 91, 100, 128, 129, 134, 135, 138, 158, 182, 189, 190, 218–20, 222, 223, 228–30, 232–9, 240, 248, 260, 267, 268
world   25, 73, 96, 101–3, 113, 130, 135, 150, 153, 160, 164, 199, 200, 204, 212, 213, 215, 225, 237, 268
worldly estrangement   156–61
world orientation   52
Wright, D. S.   235 n.89, 240
writing, practice of   77

You Must Change Your Life (Sloterdijk)   144

Zeitgeist   186
Zen philosophy   134

www.ingramcontent.com/pod-product-compliance
Lightning Source LLC
Chambersburg PA
CBHW071803300426
44116CB00009B/1185